SQL Server 2022 Revealed

A Hybrid Data Platform Powered by Security, Performance, and Availability

Bob Ward

Foreword by Rohan Kumar

Apress®

SQL Server 2022 Revealed: A Hybrid Data Platform Powered by Security, Performance, and Availability

Bob Ward
North Richland Hills, TX, USA

ISBN-13 (pbk): 978-1-4842-8893-1

ISBN-13 (electronic): 978-1-4842-8894-8

https://doi.org/10.1007/978-1-4842-8894-8

Managing Director, Apress Media LLC: Welmoed Spahr
Acquisitions Editor: Jonathan Gennick
Development Editor: Laura Berendson
Coordinating Editor: Jill Balzano

Cover image designed by Freepik (www.freepik.com)

Distributed to the book trade worldwide by Springer Science+Business Media LLC, 1 New York Plaza, Suite 4600, New York, NY 10004. Phone 1-800-SPRINGER, fax (201) 348-4505, e-mail orders-ny@springer-sbm.com, or visit www.springeronline.com. Apress Media, LLC is a California LLC and the sole member (owner) is Springer Science + Business Media Finance Inc (SSBM Finance Inc). SSBM Finance Inc is a **Delaware** corporation.

For information on translations, please e-mail booktranslations@springernature.com; for reprint, paperback, or audio rights, please e-mail bookpermissions@springernature.com.

Apress titles may be purchased in bulk for academic, corporate, or promotional use. eBook versions and licenses are also available for most titles. For more information, reference our Print and eBook Bulk Sales web page at http://www.apress.com/bulk-sales.

Any source code or other supplementary material referenced by the author in this book is available to readers on GitHub (https://github.com/Apress). For more detailed information, please visit http://www.apress.com/source-code.

Printed on acid-free paper

*I've said this before, but it is worth repeating because it matters.
This book is dedicated to the #sqlfamily, the most dedicated and
passionate and largest technical community I know of
in the world. Without you we would not have a product.*

Table of Contents

About the Author

Bob Ward is a principal architect for the Microsoft Azure Data team, which owns the development for all of SQL and Azure SQL. Bob has worked for Microsoft for 29 years on every version of SQL Server shipped from OS/2 1.1 to SQL Server 2022, including Azure SQL and Azure Arc. He is a well-known speaker on SQL Server and Azure SQL, often presenting talks on new releases, internals, and specialized topics at events such as the PASS Summit, SQLBits, Azure Data Conference, VSLive, Microsoft Build, Microsoft Inspire, Microsoft Ignite, and many other events. You can follow him on Twitter at @bobwardms or LinkedIn at https://linkedin.com/in/bobwardms. Bob is the author of Apress books *Pro SQL Server on Linux*, *SQL Server 2019 Revealed*, and *Azure SQL Revealed*.

About the Technical Reviewer

Erin Stellato is a senior program manager on the SQL Experiences team, helping advance tools that customers use daily with Azure SQL. She is passionate about data and chocolate, not always in that order. She previously worked as a consultant and was a Data Platform MVP and has been an active member of the SQL Server community as both a volunteer and speaker. Her areas of interest within the engine include Query Store, Extended Events, statistics, and performance tuning, and she also enjoys helping accidental/ involuntary DBAs figure out how SQL Server works.

Acknowledgments

I want to first thank God for sending his one and only son, Jesus, for the forgiveness of my sins, the immersion of the Holy Spirit, and the promise of everlasting life. Without my faith, I am nothing.

I want to thank my wife, Ginger, so much for her love and dedication to me for all of our years together but especially during the writing of this book. You patiently allowed me to work crazy hours and situations even on some of our vacation time to bring this book to life. I also want to thank my sons Troy and Ryan, and Ryan's wife Blair, my daughter-in-law. You all give me hope for the future as I see you all grow and exhibit grace and truth in everything you do.

This is my fourth book with Apress, and I want to personally thank Jonathan Gennick from Apress. Jonathan gave me my first chance at authoring when many publication companies turned me down. Thank you, Jonathan, for always supporting me and letting me "write my way." I also want to thank Jill Balzano from Apress whom I've never met in person but who always is so kind and professional despite all the crazy deadlines we try to meet.

I asked Erin Stellato to be my technical reviewer because she is one of the deepest experts on SQL and just an incredible person. Turns out it was a blessing when she joined Microsoft during the writing of the book as we could discuss confidential information. Erin, thank you for your thoroughness and great attitude as we all put immense pressure on you to review so many chapters late in the cycle.

There were so many people at Microsoft who supported my work on this book. But, first, I want to thank Joe Sack, Pedro Lopes, and James Rowland-Jones who no longer work at Microsoft but were a huge part of helping me craft the story of SQL Server 2022, which you see in this book.

At Microsoft I want to thank my leaders who support all of my efforts including Rohan Kumar, Peter Carlin, Asad Khan, and Sanjay Mishra. The true heroes of this book are all the people at Microsoft in the engineering team who helped me with all my questions and the review of complex topics and for giving me some great quotes. This list is long, but I have to call out everyone who helped because each of them helped in a way that made the entire book and the product worth the effort. Thank you, Ajay Jagannathan, David Pless, Kevin Farlee, Derek Wilson, Kate Smith, Kendal Van Dyke, Sasha Nosov, Travis Wright, Hanuma Kodavalla, Naveen Prakash, Joachim Hammer, Chuck Heinzelman, Mine Tokus, Hugo Queiroz, Tim Chen, Dani Ljepava, Mladen Andzic, Andreas Wolter, Srdan Bozovic, Vlad Rodriguez, Mirek Sztajno, Dylan Gray, Devin Rider, Robert Dorr, Peter Byrne, Jack Li, Mike Ray, Van To, Lee Woods, Sarah Kaufman, Conor Cunningham, Tejas Shah, Amit Khandelwal, Pam Lahoud, Purvi Shah, Aditya Badramraju, Taryn Pratt, Lani O'Brien, Nancy McGrory, Ebru Ersan, Umachandar Jayachandran (UC), Nicholas Simmons, Sharanya Bhat, Dilan Galindo Reyna, Ryan Stonecipher, Ravinder Vuppula, Thierry Fevrier, Aashna Bafna, Panagiotis Antonopoulos, Pieter Vanhove, Ankit Mahajan, Swaroop Moida, Fang Hou, Balmukund Lakhani, Parag Paul, Jakub Szymaszek, Yuqing Li, Perry Skountrianos, Pratim Dasgupta, Milos Vucic, Nikolas Ogg, David Liao, Chandrashekhar Kadiam, and Brian Carrig.

I also want to thank some of my colleagues on the engineering team who worked tirelessly to help me with workshops and events. Thank you, Marisa Mathews and Rie Merritt. You all work so hard behind the scenes that no one understands the effort you put in. And a special thank-you to my colleague Buck Woody. You are a dear friend and one of the most talented people I know. You always make traveling on the road a fun adventure.

Thank you also to the Microsoft Mechanics team for helping us highlight the amazing technology of SQL. Thank you, Jeremy Chapman and Celine Allee. Being on your show is always a privilege and fun experience.

I also want to thank members of our marketing team who were great partners during the launch and release of SQL Server 2022 including Matthew Burrows, Miwa Monji, Eric Hudson, Sonya Waitman, Guy Schoonmaker (thank you for your deck wizardry), and Emilija Dufresne.

Thank you, everyone, even for the smallest email response that helped make this book possible.

Foreword

Today's modern business landscape is dynamic and fast moving – with data playing a fundamental role. Organizations need to quickly gain insights from data to inform customer experiences and empower their employees. Currently, many companies operate in a hybrid environment, with data in the cloud and on-premise. That's why we are so excited about the upcoming release of SQL Server 2022, a key part of our evolving data and intelligence strategy. At Microsoft, we have made significant investments in SQL, creating the most connected SQL database ever with this newly launched product – and it's incorporated into a Microsoft data ecosystem that gives organizations a seamless way to connect across their databases, analytics, and governance platforms.

I can think of no person more qualified to take you through a deep dive into SQL Server 2022 than our principal architect, and 29-year Microsoft veteran, Bob Ward. Bob's depth of knowledge is second only to his enthusiasm and passion for the SQL community.

In his informational book, Bob delivers a closer look at new solutions that enable you to do more with your data and guide you to take advantage of new capabilities. Bob will introduce Azure Synapse Link for SQL Server 2022, which gets you from data to insights faster and easier than ever.

Bob will cover database engine innovations including built-in query intelligence, Ledger for SQL Server and Contained Availability Groups, as well as Azure Synapse Link for SQL, which combines data from on-prem and cloud data. This enables near-real-time analytics over your most important operational data, all without the need to build and manage complex packages and pipelines – or the need to write a single line of code for ETL movement. You'll learn about SQL Managed Instance for managed disaster recovery and use the power of built-in Distributed Availability Groups (DAGs) to seed and link databases to Azure.

Additionally, Bob shares easy-to-consume information on Microsoft Purview, which you can use to create a policy for access rights and then publish across many SQL Servers, allowing you to have a central governance hub.

We hope you enjoy reading about, exploring, and deploying SQL Server 2022 as much as we enjoyed developing it. We want to extend our sincere thanks to our incredibly engaged SQL community. Your feedback over the years has helped us make a powerful platform that will reduce complexity, accelerate innovation, and deliver insights to inform business decisions. Thank you for giving us an opportunity to support your efforts and innovations!

Rohan Kumar
Microsoft Corporate Vice President, Azure Data

Introduction

Like *SQL Server 2019 Revealed*, the manuscript for this book saw plenty of mileage. I was back on the road again in late 2021 and in 2022, and many of the chapters were written or polished in places like Las Vegas (multiple times); Orlando; London (including the London Underground); Charleston, South Carolina (where my son Troy lives); Greenville, South Carolina; Dallas (where my son Ryan lives); Poolville, Texas (where my wife's family lives); Austin; Genesee, Colorado (where Ginger and I have a small mountain retreat); Siesta Key, Florida (thank you, Tom and Janet Grubish); Redmond, Washington (multiple times); Chicago; and Atlanta. This includes a number of times writing pages in hotels, airplanes, trains, and even the front seat on a road trip while Ginger drove. But I was always most effective finishing off a chapter or making edits in the confines of my home in North Richland Hills, Texas.

This book is a complete knowledge transfer from me to you on everything I learned, absorbed, tested, and exhaustively poured my brain into about SQL Server 2022 from its inception as project Dallas right up to the General Availability release of the product. And it is my honor and pleasure to do that. All those late nights and weekends of study, testing, looking at source code, talking to program managers and developers, and thinking of scenarios based on my 29 years of experience are all in this book. I tried to bring both the high-level "what and why" with deep "how it works" so you can learn SQL Server 2022 from all angles. The number of pages alone in the book is a testament toward that goal. I've also tried to provide a deep set of examples in almost every chapter. I want you to not only read about why SQL Server 2022 is special but try it out for yourself to see it in action. I think you will also love in almost every chapter quotes from our engineering team on their perspective on why they believe SQL Server 2022 is a great release.

If you like knowing the history and "behind the scenes" of SQL Server 2022, start with Chapter 1 where you will also get an insight into the overall story of SQL Server 2022. If you want to understand differences in installing SQL Server 2022 from previous releases including what has been removed and new Azure connectivity options, take a look at Chapter 2.

All of the other chapters can be read in succession or on their own as separate topics. If you want an immersion into how SQL Server is connected to Azure, Chapter 3 is a complete resource. There are plenty of screenshots in this chapter to show you the entire Azure experience. Even if you don't have an Azure subscription, check out how we are connecting to Azure for disaster recovery (DR), analytics, and security.

Perhaps you want to dive right into the engine. Built-in query intelligence is so vast I needed two chapters to cover it all. Chapters 4 and 5 include very interesting exercises you can try yourself all on your own laptop with Evaluation or Developer Edition.

Chapter 6 is "all engine," and I believe you will like the 25+ major features we have introduced in SQL Server 2022 including Ledger for SQL Server, "hands-free" tempdb, and Contained Availability Groups.

If you have heard of S3 object storage but are not sure how to use it, you will like Chapter 7. I'll show you how to access parquet files and delta tables from SQL Server using our Polybase technology. Or perhaps you are looking for a new place to host your backups, so I'll show you how to back up and restore native SQL backups to and from any S3-compatible storage provider.

I think many believe we have forgotten about the Transact-SQL (T-SQL) language. You might be surprised to see the new T-SQL functions and language enhancements we have poured into SQL Server 2022 in Chapter 8.

There are not many new features in SQL Server 2022 specific to Linux, but I want to make sure you know the fundamentals. In Chapter 9 I'll show the basics of deploying and using SQL Server on Linux, containers, and Kubernetes.

I believe Azure is the best cloud for SQL Server, so Chapter 10 is a journey for you to learn how to deploy, optimize, and manage SQL Server 2022 on an Azure Virtual Machine.

And finally I wanted a way to close out the book with how SQL Server has become a force everywhere you need it. So Chapter 11 is how SQL Server exists "edge to cloud" in ways you have never dreamed with a story of consistency and flexibility.

If you have liked reading my books before or maybe this is for the first time, I hope you enjoy the book in all its aspects. I write in a very conversational style, which many have told me helps them "visualize me speaking to them" as they have seen me present in various events both in person and online. I also want you to have resources, so you will see plenty of online references throughout the book for you to dive in deeper.

Anytime your write a book like this, you want readers to have the latest information. So keep up to date with the latest examples and errata for the book at `https://aka.ms/sql2022bookexamples`. Or check out my free workshop materials at `https://aka.ms/sql2022workshop`.

I love to hear from readers, so you can either give the book a rating on Amazon or email me directly at `bobward@microsoft.com`. I always want to know how you feel about the book or if you want to learn more about SQL Server 2022.

Bob Ward
North Richland Hills, TX
September 2022

CHAPTER 1

Project Dallas Becomes SQL Server 2022

SQL Server 2022 was already in the making before SQL Server 2019 was released. In this chapter of the book, I will walk you through the history of SQL Server 2022, as it began with a project that turned into one of the most successful releases in SQL Server history.

I'll also give an introduction into why you want to consider using SQL Server 2022 as a data platform that is cloud connected, intelligent, and industry proven.

My goal is that you will read this chapter, get excited, and be hungry to delve into the following chapters of the book to learn all the details you need to know about SQL Server 2022.

Project Dallas

In December of 2019, I found myself celebrating the release of SQL Server 2019 and catching up with all my colleagues on the SQL Server team in building 43 on the Microsoft campus in Redmond. It was a heady time for SQL Server and me. I had just traveled some 50,000 miles over the last calendar year getting the message out on SQL Server 2019. I had launched my second book, *SQL Server 2019 Revealed* (`https://aka.ms/sql2019book`), telling the entire story of our latest SQL Server release. I felt proud of the release and was able to tell all the great customer feedback and stories to many in the engineering team. On that trip I spoke to a large crowd of all the engineers who worked on the release in an internal meeting organized by the famous Slava Oks, Distinguished Engineer at Microsoft and Lead Development Manager for the SQL Server 2019 release.

I spent some of my time in Redmond catching up with my longtime friend from CSS, Robert Dorr, who now worked for Slava. I spent time at lunch telling Bob all the tales from my travels and my experiences launching the product and authoring the book. SQL Server 2019 was tagged project Seattle by Slava, Travis Wright, and Tobias Ternstrom.

1

© Bob Ward 2022
B. Ward, *SQL Server 2022 Revealed*, https://doi.org/10.1007/978-1-4842-8894-8_1

I told Bob at lunch, "Hey, I think you and I should come up with the project name for the next version of SQL Server." Bob started a year after me, so together we represented 55+ years of experience with SQL Server. That day Bob (as he often does) was sporting a Dallas Cowboys jersey. I proposed the project name should be called Dallas. After lunch I stopped by Slava's desk and pitched the idea. He told me, "It makes sense. This new version should be a tribute to the two 'Bobs' who have worked so hard for SQL Server over the years." Slava sent out an email the next day to our teams, and thus the project name Dallas was born. Sometimes that is how project names are created at Microsoft.

Even though we had just shipped SQL Server 2019, discussions had already begun about what type of new functionality could be part of project Dallas. For me, my focus would change drastically. On this same trip, I had meetings with my manager, Asad Khan, Vice President of Program Management (PM) across all of Azure SQL and SQL Server, which would lead me to start working on Azure SQL. But I still had my ear to the ground on project Dallas.

Already in late December of 2019, my colleague Amit Banerjee was putting together a proposal for the project. As we turned the corner to start 2020, little did I or anyone know all of us would have to adapt to a worldwide pandemic. In all honesty, the pandemic accelerated work for our teams in the cloud, which led to a slowdown in planning for project Dallas. The good news is that based on our engineering systems, much of the work we design and build in the cloud just naturally applies to SQL Server; Intelligent Query Processing (IQP) and SQL Ledger are great examples.

The focus on the cloud worked out very well for me personally, as I was already on the path to work on Azure SQL. I didn't realize that the pandemic would speed up that work in the form of a partnership with Anna Hoffman for the Azure SQL Workshop (`https://aka.ms/azuresqlworkshop`), which then led to the popular Azure SQL Fundamentals learning path (`https://aka.ms/azuresqlfundamentals`) and a huge series of videos called Azure SQL for Beginners (`https://aka.ms/azuresql4beginners`). And since we had moved to all digital for our content, why not a third book? Thus was born *Azure SQL Revealed* (`https://aka.ms/azuresqlbook`), which launched in the fall of 2020.

But what about project Dallas?

Throughout calendar year 2020, project Dallas work had started under the leadership of Slava on the development side and Amit for program management. One example is degree of parallelism (DOP) feedback under a project called Gaia. Gaia had big ambitions and is an endeavor we are still working on, but the DOP feedback concept was born out of it, and you will hear more about this in Chapter 5 of the book. Other capabilities like Parameter-Sensitive Plan (PSP) optimization, cross-platform backups, buffer pool scan, Query Store hints, multi-write replication, SQL Ledger, T-SQL language improvements, and more were all under way. We were actively working through improvements for project Dallas but had not really landed on the full plan for a release. Again, the cool thing about how we do things now is that many of these features were designed for Azure SQL, but we knew because of our engine compatibility they could be fit into Dallas at any time.

As we moved further along calendar year 2020, it became clear to me that project Dallas would not make it into an actual release until calendar year 2022 at the earliest. I had meetings with Slava, Amit, Asad, and Travis Wright late in 2020 to discuss the plan. All of us agreed, along with our Vice President of Azure Data, Rohan Kumar, that we needed a new major version of SQL Server sooner rather than later. But we also agreed that trying to do anything sooner than 2022 would not result in a great release. In late calendar year 2020, I would hear for the first time the words *SQL Server 2022*.

Becoming SQL Server 2022

When this book is released, I will have been at Microsoft 29 years, all working on SQL. Throughout these years I've seen many changes, reorganizations, and transitions, more than I can even remember. But two changes happened early in calendar year 2021 that surprised me and gave me concern for project Dallas. Slava Oks left the SQL team to work in Azure (note: Slava would eventually leave Microsoft in the fall of 2021), and Amit Banerjee left Microsoft. In addition, Travis Wright pivoted from a role in the program management leadership team to work as a development manager for Azure Arc. Losing someone like Slava was pretty hard for me personally. I have worked with Slava in SQL for 20 years. All the journeys we had together (Slava is the one who taught me debugging in case anyone ever wanted to know that small fact; I thought I knew what debugging was until I met Slava) from SQL Server 2005 to SQL Server on Linux and of course SQL Server 2019. I also would deeply miss Amit. I actually mentored Amit when he first joined Microsoft and then enjoyed all those years as colleagues in engineering. I was really looking forward to partnering with Amit to release Dallas. But I knew the opportunity he was moving to was important for him and his family. I was happy and excited for these folks, but as you can imagine, I quickly was in a few meetings with Asad Khan on how to handle the situation and ensure Dallas moved forward.

For other teams or other companies, losing leaders like this would rock them to the core and greatly affect the ability to release a product. But not SQL Server. Asad was still our PM leader. Peter Carlin, the longtime SQL Server and Azure SQL engineering leader, would become our vice president over all of Azure SQL and SQL Server (and even more today). Rohan Kumar was still our Vice President of Azure Data. Hanuma Kodavalla, Technical Fellow at Microsoft and longtime SQL veteran, would be our engineering leader for all the developers to make Dallas a reality. Asad would promote the famous Joe Sack to run the program managers for all of SQL Server. And in a huge move, we promoted Pedro Lopes to be the technical lead PM for Dallas. Pedro is not only an incredibly talented, well-respected technical leader but someone I personally call a friend. And well, I guess we still had me. SQL Server is in my blood, so of course I needed to stay the course and see project Dallas to the end no matter what challenges came up. In the spring of 2021 with these organizational announcements, we also tentatively agreed on some key aspects to Dallas:

- Project Dallas would be called SQL Server 2022.

- We would announce this release as a Private Preview in the fall of 2021.

- We would announce a Public Preview in late spring of 2022.

- We would target the General Availability of SQL Server 2022 in the fall of 2022.

With a goal for a Private Preview in the fall of 2021 (we made the decision to announce this at the Microsoft Ignite virtual event, which we knew at this time was in early November 2021), we had to get more organized than ever and start cranking out some builds. Joe assigned Pedro to be our de facto release program manager holding the reins to ensure everyone was meeting release criteria and getting features lined up for an announcement.

Our marketing team assigned Matthew Burrows to be the lead marketing manager for SQL Server 2022. Matt quickly started building weekly virtual team meetings to talk about SQL vNext (we always call a version vNext until we 100% agree on the exact name) including myself, Joe Sack, Pedro Lopes, James Rowland-Jones, and Sonya Waitman (Sonya works with Matt in marketing and was so valuable throughout the entire release). We would soon add another party to this band, Kendal Van Dyke. Joe hired Kendal to run our Early Adoption Program (EAP) since our first announcement would be a Private Preview program, which required customers to register with Microsoft to test and try out early builds. Kendal was a longtime veteran of Microsoft as a customer engineer and a well-respected person in the community and within Microsoft. I quickly met with Pedro and Joe and asked how I could best help us march toward Private Preview. They both responded very quickly, "Build us a deck!"

So in the late spring of 2021, I started "doing my thing" to build an "NDA" (for anyone with a nondisclosure agreement with Microsoft) deck we could use. The very first attempt for an overview of SQL Server vNext looked like the following Figure 1-1.

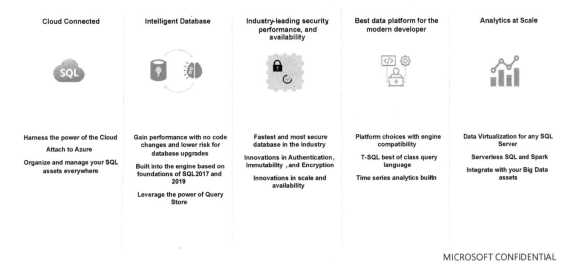

Figure 1-1. *The first SQL Server vNext slide*

You can see in Figure 1-1 there are not really any specific features listed, just themes. Plus, you will notice at the time we were still debating the future of Big Data Clusters (BDC). Project Austin, named by James Rowland-Jones, was an early proposal to reinvent BDC with serverless SQL and Spark.

Note   You may have read that in February of 2022 we announced the retirement of SQL Server Big Data Clusters, which explains why it was not a part of the SQL Server 2022 release. You can read more at `https://cloudblogs.microsoft.com/sqlserver/2022/02/25/the-path-forward-for-sql-server-analytics`.

I knew all the planned features for Dallas, but at this time I didn't have a 100% commitment that we could talk about all of them yet. One thing I knew is that these "pillars" represented the major categories for features in the release.

To build a foundation for a true public deck on SQL Server vNext, we first needed acknowledgment on the name. We got that from Matthew Burrows about 1 month out from Ignite. SQL Server 2022 would be the name. We also got a much clearer picture of all the features we knew would make the release, so I built this first version of an all-up SQL Server 2022 slide with major features with some rebranding for categories which you can see in the following Figure 1-2.

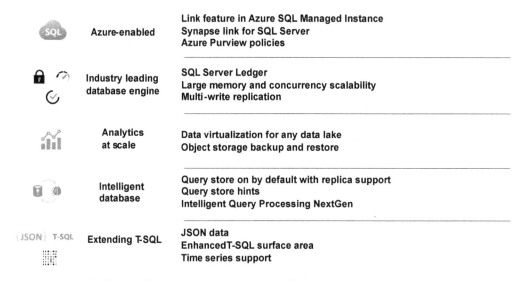

Figure 1-2. *The first all-up SQL Server 2022 slide*

With this in mind, we all decided to keep the announcement for SQL Server 2022 very close to the chest. I was still presenting virtually and even in person (yes, it is true I started presenting at in-person events such as the SQL Server and Azure SQL Conference as early as June 2021). And I would always get asked the question, "When is the next version of SQL Server coming out?" or even better "Will there be a new version of SQL Server?" Both fair questions since we were very quiet on this subject, and by the summer of 2021, it would have been almost 2 years since we released SQL Server or even talked about it.

I then built out more slides talking about each of these areas, including all the features we knew would be in the release. I consulted with Pedro regularly on exactly what we could commit would be in the release, even if it were not immediately in Private Preview builds.

Announcing SQL Server 2022

Preparing for an announcement of this magnitude is no simple task, and our entire team worked tirelessly in October and right up to the announcement for Ignite to have everything in order.

Asad Khan and Anna Hoffman recorded their Ignite presentation announcing SQL Server 2022 (you can see their original session at `https://learn.microsoft.com/en-us/events/ignite-nov-2021/azure/breakouts/brk225/`).

Joe, Pedro, and Kendal worked to make sure everything was lined up to have the Private Preview build and EAP registration setup.

Matthew and Sonya worked to get our main website (`https://aka.ms/sqlserver2022`) up and running and build a blog, which would be authored by our Corporate Vice President of Azure Data SQL Engineering, Peter Carlin (my manager, Asad Khan, works for Peter, and Peter works for Rohan Kumar) at `https://cloudblogs.microsoft.com/sqlserver/2021/11/02/announcing-sql-server-2022-preview-azure-enabled-with-continued-performance-and-security-innovation`.

As we prepared for the big launch announcement, the famous Microsoft Mechanics team (led by Jeremy Chapman) reached out to me about recording a Mechanics video on SQL Server 2022. Microsoft Mechanics (`https://aka.ms/microsoftmechanics`) is just a cool team. The preparation that goes into the demos, the script, and the animations is a pure marvel. I recorded the session weeks before the announcement in my home in North Richland Hills, Texas, in one take! The result was a very popular video at `https://aka.ms/sqlmechanics22`. It was the #1 watched video produced for Microsoft Ignite. These types of videos are also a forcing function to get demos working even with early builds. I was able to collaborate with the Managed Instance team to get the link feature for Managed Instance working (along with Anna who demonstrated this in Asad's session) with very early builds of both SQL Server 2022 and SSMS (SQL Server Management Studio). I worked with our team to get Synapse Link working and was able to craft up a fun demo (with a big thanks to Anna for building a machine learning model in Spark) with a bit of a Texas twist! And then a demo for what you will probably find out as you read this book is my favorite feature: Parameter-Sensitive Plan (PSP) optimization. PSP is "all engine," so I spun up an Azure Virtual Machine with "pre-CTP" bits and was able to modify a demo that Pedro Lopes and my good friend from development Jack Li gave me.

In the weeks leading up to the announcement, Joe Sack asked me to do a few NDA presentations on SQL Server 2022 to some of our key partners to prepare them for our launch. It was pretty fun to do these as it was the first time I had actually told anyone about SQL Server 2022 outside of Microsoft.

One last piece of promotion for the SQL Server 2022 Private Preview launch was a partnership with Intel for an article in *WIRED* magazine. The resulting article at `https://www.wired.com/sponsored/story/data-is-driving-the-future-of-business` was wildly popular and received a lot of views at launch and for months afterward.

One other interesting twist for me was a trip to Redmond the week before Ignite in late October 2021. Due to the pandemic, I had not traveled to Redmond since February of 2020. I went to Redmond for a few reasons. First, I needed to record a webinar in our Microsoft studios on SQL Server 2022 with Matt Burrows and Anna Hoffman. You can see that webinar on-demand at `https://aka.ms/sqlserver2022webinar`. The second reason was to record a demo for the PASS Summit keynote with Rohan and Peter Carlin. It was fun to record this because I recorded the demo using the PSP demo I did for Microsoft Mechanics, but the twist was having Conor Cunningham interrupt me during my recording. We kind of planned this out, but funny enough we captured it in the first take. It was fun to do since both of us were used to being on stage live with Rohan for the PASS keynote, which couldn't happen in 2021. You can watch the recording of that keynote at `https://youtu.be/Ydlg1KpmrKU?list=PLoGAcXKPcRvYWLmrDZJ9XTdSJAd uAefm7`. The third reason I traveled to Redmond was to meet some of my colleagues in person for the first time in almost 2 years. It was great to see folks in person again. While I was up there, Rie Merrit, who runs our MVP program, asked if I would do a preview announcement of SQL Server 2022 for the MVPs since we were making our big announcement the next week. It was really fun to do that session because it was the first time I had told a fairly large audience about SQL Server 2022. I'm used to keeping this type of confidential information, but it is still hard. For example, we had reserved slots for the PASS Summit the week after Ignite for SQL Server 2022 sessions but couldn't even tell the PASS event organizers the details of our sessions. In addition, Thomas LaRock had invited me and others to come speak at their SQL Live event in Orlando in November (`https://sqllive360.com/ECG/live360events/Events/Orlando-2021/SQL.aspx`), and I had reserved a session called "Microsoft SQL Engineering Session Under Wraps." The organizers were asking me, "Can't you tell us anymore about this?" and my answer was "Not really." At the MVP session, I could hear Thomas in his head going, "Ah, that is why Bob couldn't tell us." I had the same issue with sessions I was doing at the SQL Server and Azure SQL Conference (formerly SQLIntersection) in December in Las Vegas.

It was a whirlwind week, which also marked my 28th work anniversary at Microsoft. From SQL OS/2 to now, I would have never dreamed I would be still working on SQL Server.

Finally, on November 2nd at Microsoft Ignite, Scott Guthrie announced SQL Server 2022. We launched all of our other assets along with Asad's session as well at Ignite. I also feel that LinkedIn can be a powerful method to make announcements, so I crafted a LinkedIn article the day of launch at `www.linkedin.com/posts/bobwardms_activity-68613220823887664896-mBzK`.

I felt the reception of SQL Server 2022 Private Preview was very positive. I think many in the industry and community quite frankly wondered whether we would ever build another major version of SQL Server. I personally saw reviews and comments of surprise that we not only were building another version but also we were including some very fairly major enhancements including all the Azure-connected features, built-in query intelligence, SQL Ledger, and data virtualization. It was a little awkward to make this announcement because we started with Private Preview, which is not how we announced SQL Server 2019. There was a precedence for this with SQL Server 2017, but I realized the frustration this caused for some who were anxious to download the bits and see what was inside.

Right after Ignite was the famous PASS Summit, which was now being organized and run by Redgate, and for 2021 it was all virtual. Microsoft was the primary sponsor, so I lined up four sessions that we at Microsoft would present on SQL Server 2022:

>**Introduction to SQL Server 2022** – This was an "all-up" session for everything in SQL Server 2022 that we were announcing for the product.

>**SQL Server 2022: The hybrid data platform** – I also did this session as a deeper dive into all of the Azure-connected features of SQL Server 2022.

>**SQL Server 2022 storage engine capabilities** – I asked David Pless to do a deep drive into the core engine areas of SQL Server 2022: security, performance, and availability.

>**Azure SQL and SQL Server 2022: Intelligent database futures** – I asked Pedro to do a deep drive into the new built-in query intelligence features of SQL Server 2022.

Our sessions were very well attended, and I thought the survey results showed folks were excited. This is because during the virtual Microsoft Ignite, we didn't really get to go into many details about all the features of SQL Server 2022. PASS was our first chance to do this for the community in a public fashion. If you registered for that event (the general sessions were free), you can watch the recordings of our talks. But you can also see the original decks we used at `https://aka.ms/sqlserver2022decks` (use the Private Preview folder to see our original decks). If you look closely at the first slide for these decks which you can see below in Figure 1-3, you will notice an image of downtown Dallas, Texas, paying tribute to project Dallas. The backstory there is that for the webinar filmed in October 2021, our production team built a cool intro slide and it had a downtown city on it but it was Chicago (just to show a cool downtown image – they didn't know the project name). I asked the team to change to an image for downtown Dallas. Kind of my "Easter egg" in the original decks paying tribute to our project name.

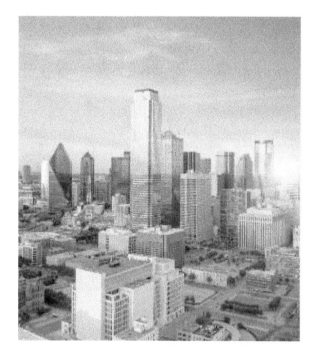

Figure 1-3. *The intro SQL Server 2022 deck with the city of downtown Dallas*

As we were moving toward the end of calendar year 2021, someone told me that our PASS Summit sessions were only available for free to those who signed up for the event. So I asked Rie Merrit if she knew anyone who would host me for a free virtual presentation on SQL Server 2022. Rie quickly found the Virtual DBA Fundamentals group, so I did an overall SQL Server 2022 presentation for them, which you can see at `https://youtu.be/M1h4kSZYdu4`. Shortly after this I found out that PASS had posted all of our SQL Server 2022 sessions on PASStv at `https://www.youtube.com/user/SQLPASSTV/videos`.

All was going well into December of 2021, and we were riding high and ready to crank it up in 2022. And then one day Joe Sack called me to tell me he was leaving Microsoft. As much as I was happy for Joe to pursue new opportunities, privately I was crushed because not only is Joe a friend but I really felt he would be vital to make SQL Server 2022 a success. But SQL Server is more than one person. It is the legacy and tradition of one of the most successful products in the history of Microsoft. I knew we still had all the right people to bring it home for a successful release in 2022.

Private to Public Preview

After the announcement of Joe Sack leaving, I received another call from my longtime friend at Microsoft, Ajay Jagannathan. Ajay told me that he would be taking over from Joe to manage all the program management for SQL Server (as well as Azure Arc data). We have a deep bench at Microsoft, so knowing that Ajay and Pedro would be leading our efforts to release SQL Server 2022 buoyed my spirits.

Early in the year, we faced some challenges (which also caused some challenges for me for this book) and encountered some surprises. The biggest challenge was that several features we had announced for SQL Server 2022 were not available yet in CTP builds. CTP 1.0 was the first build to come out in November in 2021 followed by CTP 1.1 in December 2021 and CTP 1.2 in January 2022. You can see my SSMS connected to the very first official CTP build here in Figure 1-4.

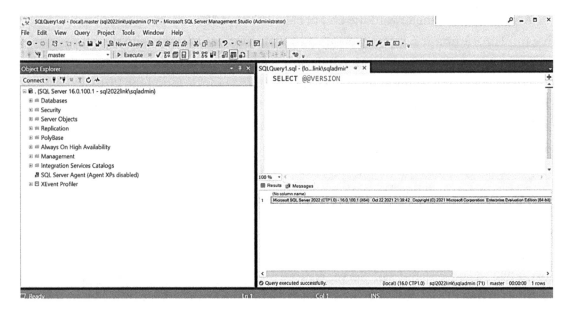

Figure 1-4. *The first CTP build of SQL Server 2022*

Unfortunately, not all features were fully baked at this point, and some were not even in these early CTP builds. The good news is that our PM team had started to document existing features in a GitHub repo created by Kendal Van Dyke. Here is a look at the GitHub repo we used during Private Preview in the following Figure 1-5.

📁 demos	Update readme.md	10 days ago
📁 docs	Update README.md	2 days ago
📁 media	JRJ new page for media sample data	2 months ago
📄 .gitattributes	lfs setup	2 months ago
📄 .gitignore	JRJ new page for media sample data	2 months ago
📄 LICENSE	Initial commit	5 months ago
📄 README.md	JRJ final draft of object storage integration docs	2 months ago

☰ README.md   ✎

▓ Microsoft

SQL Server Early Adoption Program Repository

This GitHub repository contains code samples and documentation that demonstrate how to use Microsoft SQL Server 2022 new features and scenarios. Each sample includes a README file that explains how to run and use the sample.

🔗 Releases in this repository

To see the complete list of resources in this repository, navigate to Releases

Working in GitHub

To work in GitHub, go to https://github.com/microsoft/sqleap and fork the repository. Work in your own fork and when you are ready to submit to make a change or publish your sample for the first time, submit a pull request into the master branch of sqleap. One of the approvers will review your request and accept or reject the pull request.

Each sample should be in its own folder with a README.md file that follows the template. Generated files (e.g., .exe or .bacpac) and user configuration settings (e.g., .user) should not be committed to GitHub.

Figure 1-5. *The Private Preview GitHub repo*

With these challenges also came some great momentum. I found many internal Microsoft customer teams and sales groups wanting me to present to them SQL Server 2022. The word had spread fast about the new capabilities of SQL Server 2022, especially the cloud-connected features. Folks at Microsoft wanted to learn this quickly so they could start educating their accounts.

Then I found out that I would hit the road again at more events than I could have imagined. SQLBits was back in person in London in March 2022. The SQL Server and Azure SQL Conference was held in Las Vegas in April 2022. And Dell Technologies World was back in person in Las Vegas in early May of 2022. At each of these events, I gave the message of SQL Server 2022 and all its rich capabilities (with the amazing assistance of so many of my colleagues to make it all happen).

Then as we prepared to launch the first Public Preview (CTP 2.0) of SQL Server 2022, my friend Pedro Lopes announced he was leaving Microsoft in May of 2022. Could our team take these losses of key experts and leaders for SQL Server and still deliver? As much as I was saddened to see Pedro leave, I realized something as I saw other people on our team step up. We all have a great passion to do what is right to build and deliver a great product. One that matters. One that has value.

The Path to General Availability

We moved forward and announced the first Public Preview at the Microsoft Build virtual conference in late May of 2022. You can see myself and others present at Build at `https://aka.ms/sqlserver2022build`. The summer moved fast. I presented SQL Server 2022 both internally and externally at events like HPE Discover, Microsoft Inspire, the Data Platform Summit, and various other user group and Data Saturday events. Along the way we updated our CTP build to 2.1, and then came the first Release Candidate build in August of 2022. When a Release Candidate build comes out, you know the General Availability is imminent. As I make my final updates to this chapter the General Availability is very close. I'm excited to know we will "make the name".

For me it was an interesting challenge for the book because I wanted to squeeze every possible update to our features that came in preview builds right up to the product launch. I believe I was able to accomplish that, but you will find a few "at the time of the writing of this book" moments in some of the chapters.

Introducing SQL Server 2022

Now that you know the history and "behind the scenes" of how we made it to the release of SQL Server 2022, let's step through an overview of what is in SQL Server 2022 to set the stage for the rest of the book.

Built on a Foundation

One of the lessons I learned as I toured the world in 2018 and 2019 presenting SQL Server 2019 at big events and directly to customers was that I forgot to talk about previous releases and the foundation of SQL Server 2019.

The next step for SQL Server

SQL Server 2016
Query Store
Polybase
Always Encrypted
Row Level Security
It just runs faster
Std Edition surface area

SQL Server 2017
SQL Server on Linux
Containers
Adaptive Query Processing
Automatic Tuning
Graph database
Machine Learning Services

SQL Server 2019
Data virtualization
Intelligent Query Processing
Accelerated Database Recovery
Data classification

Figure 1-6. *Major capabilities of previous SQL Server releases*

Customers I would talk to were not even on SQL Server 2016 and were not aware of features like Query Store, Polybase, Always Encrypted, or Intelligent Query Processing. This wasn't their fault but mine for not getting the word out more about SQL Server 2016 and 2017. SQL Server releases are cumulative, so everything you learn about in this book for SQL Server 2022 comes with features as you see in Figure 1-6. *SQL Server 2019 Revealed* can give you deep insights into what was in SQL Server 2019 that you also get when you upgrade to SQL Server 2022. More importantly, we built new features in SQL Server 2022 as *enhancements* to these capabilities or used them in new and innovative ways. With this context in mind, let's look at the major *new* enhancements for SQL Server 2022.

Wheel of Power

In 2019, I built a slide for my presentations on SQL Server 2019 with "quadrants" to show the major capabilities of the release. (You can see this slide in the first chapter of *SQL Server 2019 Revealed*.) After presenting SQL Server 2019 several times, I started to call this my "camera slide." That is because anytime I would display it at an event, everyone took photos of it (which is pretty humbling). But the concept is the same. Create a single slide that captures the major capabilities of the release.

For SQL Server 2022, I did something similar with a different twist. Figure 1-7 represents what I call the "Wheel of Power."

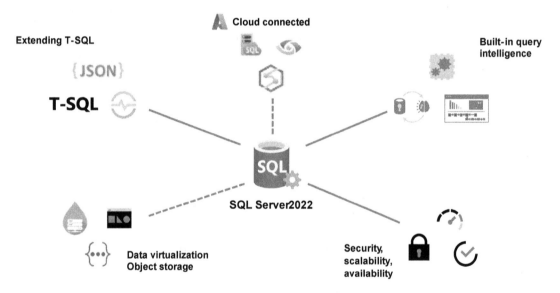

Figure 1-7. The SQL Server 2022 "Wheel of Power"

The "dash" lines represent areas where SQL Server can connect to sources outside of the server or VM. Not every area has the same investment, but this provides a nice categorization of our features. And as you read the rest of the book, you can see several chapters are organized around the spokes of the wheel.

Cloud Connected

Cloud connected represents a set of features to connect SQL Server to Azure in new and exciting ways never seen before. These cloud-connected features give SQL Server 2022 a unique place in *hybrid computing*. You will learn all the details of these features in Chapter 3 of the book. Here are the highlights:

Link feature for Azure SQL Managed Instance

Using the power of built-in Distributed Availability Groups, you can now use Azure SQL Managed Instance for disaster recovery. Azure SQL Managed Instance is a managed SQL instance in the form of Platform as a Service (PaaS). You will be able to fail over back and forth between SQL Server 2022 and Azure SQL Managed Instance. The first iteration of this capability uses an offline approach (backup and restore) with a complete online failover to come in the future.

Synapse Link for SQL Server 2022

Use your SQL Server 2022 instance to feed operational database changes to Synapse Analytics for near-real-time analytics. This is a great solution to reduce the need for ETL applications and use the power of Synapse to combine your SQL Server data with other data sources to support analytics.

Microsoft Purview policy management

Managing authentication and access to SQL Server resources at scale can be painful and error-prone. Microsoft Purview will allow you to publish *policies* from a central location to manage access to SQL Server or any Azure SQL virtual machine, instance, or database. Microsoft Purview is dependent on Azure Active Directory (AAD) authentication, which is also now available for SQL Server 2022.

Built-In Query Intelligence

In SQL Server 2016, we introduced Query Store to capture in the database key performance information. In SQL Server 2017, we enhanced the query processor (QP) in the engine to help you get faster performance with no code changes. In SQL Server 2019, we stepped up the game by adding more query processor scenarios and branded this Intelligent Query Processing (IQP).

In SQL Server 2022, we have enabled Query Store by default, added support for read replicas, and introduced hints to shape query plans. We built a new set of enhancements for the *next generation* of Intelligent Query Processing including some features that work together with Query Store.

This is one of the most exciting areas of investments for SQL Server 2022, and you will learn all about this in Chapters 4 and 5 of the book.

Industry-Proven Database Engine

We don't have a product if we don't have an industry-proven database engine. And we don't have an engine if we don't invest in security, scalability, and availability in every release. I call this the "meat and potatoes" of SQL Server. You will read about many of these features in Chapter 6 of the book, but here a few highlights:

Ledger for SQL Server

Blockchain technology can provide tamper-evident "ledgers" of changes but has traditionally been implemented in distributed systems. SQL Server 2022 includes the ability to declare database tables as "ledger tables" to provide a built-in, tamper-evident record of changes.

System page latch concurrency

System page latch concurrency has been a significant pain point for workloads using tempdb since SQL Server has been a product. We have chipped away at this problem by guiding users how to create multiple files for tempdb and introducing features like tempdb metadata optimization in SQL Server 2019 and concurrent PFS updates. In SQL Server 2022, we have further improved concurrency for operations that require access to other system pages. I personally believe we might have achieved a "hands-free" management of tempdb, but you need to see it for yourself.

Contained Availability Groups

An often asked feature from our customers is now a reality. You can now create a Contained Availability Group, and we will replicate instance-level objects like SQL Agent jobs, linked servers, and logins to secondary replicas.

Data Virtualization and Object Storage

In SQL 2016 we introduced the concept called *Polybase*. The original idea was to use T-SQL to access non-relational file formats in Hadoop systems without having to move the data. We expanded this concept in SQL Server 2019 to support data sources such as Oracle, Teradata, MongoDB, and SQL using ODBC drivers. SQL Server now could become a *data hub* for data virtualization.

In SQL Server 2022, we have introduced a new method to access other data using the same T-SQL constructs but under the covers using REST APIs to access connectors like **S3**, Azure Data Lake, and Azure Blob Storage. In addition, we've added support to recognize common file formats natively including parquet and delta tables.

Related to this capability, but not dependent on it, is the ability to execute **native backup and restore** of a database to *object storage* systems that are **S3 compatible**. This now opens up more options to store SQL backups than just disk or Azure Blob Storage via URL. I think you will be interested in how I use this feature to perform a migration from AWS RDS to SQL Server.

You will learn more details about data virtualization and object storage in Chapter 7 of this book.

Enhancing T-SQL for Developers

SQL Server still provides some of the best interfaces and features for developers. The T-SQL language is very rich for just about any type of scenario to access or manipulate data. We have a tradition of using the T-SQL language to access any new feature we build.

In SQL Server 2022, we continue this tradition by enhancing T-SQL functions to process **JSON**-formatted data, adding new and enhanced **T-SQL functions** based on developer feedback and ANSI compatibility, and bringing T-SQL functions to process **time series** data from Azure SQL Edge into the SQL Server 2022 engine.

You will see examples of all of these T-SQL enhancements in Chapter 8 of this book.

Getting Started with SQL Server 2022

You now have read an overview of what is possible with SQL Server 2022 and know that the following chapters of the book help you learn details of each of these areas of the Wheel of Power. You may be asking, "How can I get it and just start using it?"

How to Get SQL Server 2022

Besides obtaining SQL Server through your normal license channels, you can download the Developer or Evaluation Edition of SQL Server 2022 from `https://aka.ms/getsqlserver2022`.

Chapter 9 of this book shows you how to download SQL Server container images or SQL Server Linux distributions.

An alternative to obtain SQL Server 2022 is to use the marketplace for an Azure Virtual Machine. Chapter 10 of this book covers all the details to get and deploy SQL Server 2022 in Azure.

Installing SQL Server 2022

The setup and installation process for SQL Server 2022 is the same as it has been in past releases with just a few changes. To learn how to install and deploy SQL Server 2022, go to `https://aka.ms/deploysqlserver2022`. Chapter 2 of this book provides more details on how to install and upgrade to SQL Server 2022 on Windows. Chapter 9 of this book covers details of how to install SQL Server 2022 using a container image, on Linux distributions, and on Kubernetes clusters. Chapter 10 of this book covers details on how to install SQL Server on Azure Virtual Machines.

Learn All the Features and Editions

While this book is a comprehensive look at SQL Server 2022, you may also want to consult our documentation to look at the new features and examples. In addition, our documentation always lists the exact set of features that are enabled per SQL Server edition such as Enterprise or Standard. Use the link `https://aka.ms/sqlserver2022docs` to see the latest version of the documentation for SQL Server 2022.

Learn About Pricing and Licensing

I sometimes get questions about licensing for SQL Server, and I'm sure SQL Server 2022 will be no different. However, instead of trying to explain all the nuances of licensing, the best reference is our documentation on pricing and licensing at `https://aka.ms/sqlserver2022licensing`.

Get Training on SQL Server 2022

As with SQL Server 2019 and Azure SQL, you can learn more about SQL Server 2022 with our workshops. Use our main workshop site at `https://aka.ms/sqlworkshops` or go directly to the SQL Server 2022 workshop at `https://aka.ms/sql2022workshop`. We also have in the plans a Microsoft learning path at `https://aka.ms/learnsqlserver2022`.

I also call myself an open source presenter, so you can find all the decks I and others have built at `https://aka.ms/sqlserver2022decks`.

Go Deeper with Our Blog Series

Go deeper on each SQL Server 2022 feature with a blog series from our program managers at Microsoft at `https://aka.ms/sqlserver2022blogs`.

Download Book Code and Samples

You can download the code and scripts for all samples from this book from the GitHub repo listed in the introduction of this book. And as with other books I've written, you also find the code, scripts, and any errata about this book at `https://aka.ms/sql2022bookexamples`.

A Cloud-Connected, Intelligent, and Industry-Proven Data Platform

I often called SQL Server 2019 a modern data platform because that release can be used for so much more than just what a database engine provides. SQL Server 2019 provides capabilities needed for a data platform including data virtualization, a robust engine, and machine learning services

SQL Server 2022 takes a hybrid data platform to the next level. SQL Server 2022 is connected to the cloud on your terms in new and innovative ways never seen before. SQL Server 2022 comes with built-in query intelligence, solving some of the most common and expensive query tuning problems you and developers face today. And SQL Server 2022 comes with an industry-proven database engine with innovations in security, scalability, availability, and data virtualization and enhancements to the most popular database language in the world: T-SQL.

Ajay Jagannathan, our Principal Group Program Manager over SQL Server, gave me his perspective:

> *This is a special release of SQL Server. During planning for every major version of SQL Server, we spend considerable cycles to look at several key themes that will define the release. This includes industry leading innovations, cloud born as well as mission-critical features and most importantly customer and community feedback. This has helped us in shaping SQL Server as the most popular commercial relational database on the planet. For SQL Server 2022, it was critical for this release to be an integral part of the Microsoft Intelligent Data Platform by bringing some of the latest innovations such as Link feature for MI, near real-time analytics with Azure Synapse Link and governance with Microsoft Purview. It doesn't stop there, our customers will also get to leverage advancements to SQL Server's industry leading mission critical capabilities spanning much desired themes around T-SQL language, intelligent query processing, performance, security, availability, and scalability to name a few. And by becoming the first Azure Arc integrated release out of the box our customers can leverage Azure benefits anywhere, in their environment of choice through hybrid and multi-cloud deployments. Not only am I proud of the work done by the entire SQL Server product team to bring this release to our customers, partners and community, my dear friend and colleague Bob Ward does a phenomenal job in this book to help deep dive into several areas of the product*

and simplify it for the audience. Reading this book will give passionate SQL Server users a clear understanding of the features and the ability to maximize these capabilities in their environments. I can't wait for our customers to get started with SQL Server 2022 and hear all the cool scenarios where they are leveraging the features to solve their business problems.

If you want to learn more about the installation and upgrade experience of SQL Server 2022, Chapter 2 can be used to start your journey.

Note   For those who are veterans to install SQL Server, not much has changed for setup, so if you want to install the Developer Edition for Windows and just dive into Chapter 3 to start learning, fire away! There is one aspect to installation that enables some cloud-connected features, so you may want to read more about those in Chapter 2 first. Remember that deployment guides to install SQL Server with container images, Linux, and Kubernetes are in Chapter 9 and details on how to deploy with an Azure Virtual Machine are in Chapter 10.

CHAPTER 2

Install and Upgrade

One of the first things you will want to do is to install SQL Server 2022 so you can explore all the goodness it has to offer. The great news for anyone familiar with SQL Server is that the installation experience for SQL Server 2022 is fairly identical to previous releases with a few minor changes.

If you are an experienced SQL Server user, in this chapter you can review the highlights of what is different for SQL Server 2022. If you are someone new to SQL Server, don't worry. First, the installation process is amazingly simple, and our user experiences walk you through all of it. Second, if you need a "step-by-step" process, go straight to our documentation at `https://aka.ms/deploysqlserver2022`.

How to Install SQL Server 2022

You may be used to getting started with SQL Server by installing the Developer or Evaluation free edition of SQL Server and evaluating the product. SQL Server 2022 supports both of these editions, so if you just want to jump in, go to `https://aka.ms/getsqlserver2022` and start testing!

I know that some people want to know more about the installation of SQL Server before they go "straight for the bits." In this section of the chapter, I'll review the prerequisites to install SQL Server and discuss the differences from previous versions and deployment options.

This section of the chapter focuses on installation of SQL Server on Windows. The section titled "**Deploying on Other Platforms**" later in this chapter discusses installation on Linux, containers, Kubernetes, and Azure. The details for deploying on these platforms can be found in Chapters 9 and 10 of the book.

25

© Bob Ward 2022
B. Ward, *SQL Server 2022 Revealed*, https://doi.org/10.1007/978-1-4842-8894-8_2

Prerequisites

The prerequisites, including resources required, to install SQL Server 2022 on Windows have not changed from previous major versions of SQL Server, except the specific Windows operating system versions or Linux distributions we support. As in the past, we will support versions of Windows Server and Windows (client) that are "officially" supported, including any specific updates of Windows required to be supported. Consult the SQL Server 2022 release notes for any possible changes to prerequisites for SQL Server 2022 at `https://docs.microsoft.com/sql/sql-server/sql-server-2022-release-notes`.

One difference for prerequisites from previous versions of SQL Server is the requirement to be connected to Azure to support some of the new *cloud-connected* scenarios. The most important requirement is that if you choose to set up Azure-connected scenarios during installation, you will need an Azure subscription and a service principal.

Note   Some cloud-connected scenarios like Managed Instance and Synapse Link do not require any special steps during setup. New capabilities like Azure Active Directory (AAD) and Microsoft Purview integration do require this configuration.

I'll describe the exact steps for this requirement later in this chapter in the section titled "**Setting Up the Azure Extension for SQL Server**." I'll also go more into the specifics of how SQL Server is connected to Azure in Chapter 3 of the book.

To find all the exact resource requirements you need to install SQL Server 2022 on Windows, review the documentation at `https://aka.ms/deploysqlserver2022`.

What Is Different for SQL Server 2022?

Installing SQL Server 2022 on Windows using the "wizard" is remarkably similar to installing SQL Server from previous releases. Therefore, I won't show you a "screen-by-screen" experience. See the complete set of steps at `https://aka.ms/deploysqlserver2022`.

> **Note**   I will make the boastful claim that I have probably installed and uninstalled SQL Server 2022 more than anyone in the world. I honestly lost count from November 2021 to November 2022 how many times I've installed and uninstalled SQL Server 2022. Maybe only beat by our automation tests at Microsoft!

Rather, I'll discuss differences from previous releases. Let's look at each of these differences from a perspective of running a SQL Server setup.

Azure Extension for SQL Server

The first option you will be presented with before choosing features is the Azure extension for SQL Server. The Azure extension for SQL Server feature represents software running on the computer or VM where SQL Server is installed to connect it to Azure. The capability for this extension is not new as it is found through **Azure Arc–enabled SQL Server** (you can read more at `https://docs.microsoft.com/sql/sql-server/azure-arc/overview`). You can still use the method in the documentation to connect SQL Server 2022 to Azure. We are just providing a method to do this as an integrated part of SQL Server setup.

This is a big topic to cover, so to learn more about the prerequisites and how to fill out the information for this feature, see the section later in this chapter titled "**Setting Up the Azure Extension for SQL Server.**"

Feature Differences

There are several differences when choosing features during installation, mostly around features that are removed. You can see these differences by looking at the SQL Server 2019 setup feature selection in Figure 2-1 and the features I've highlighted that are now removed.

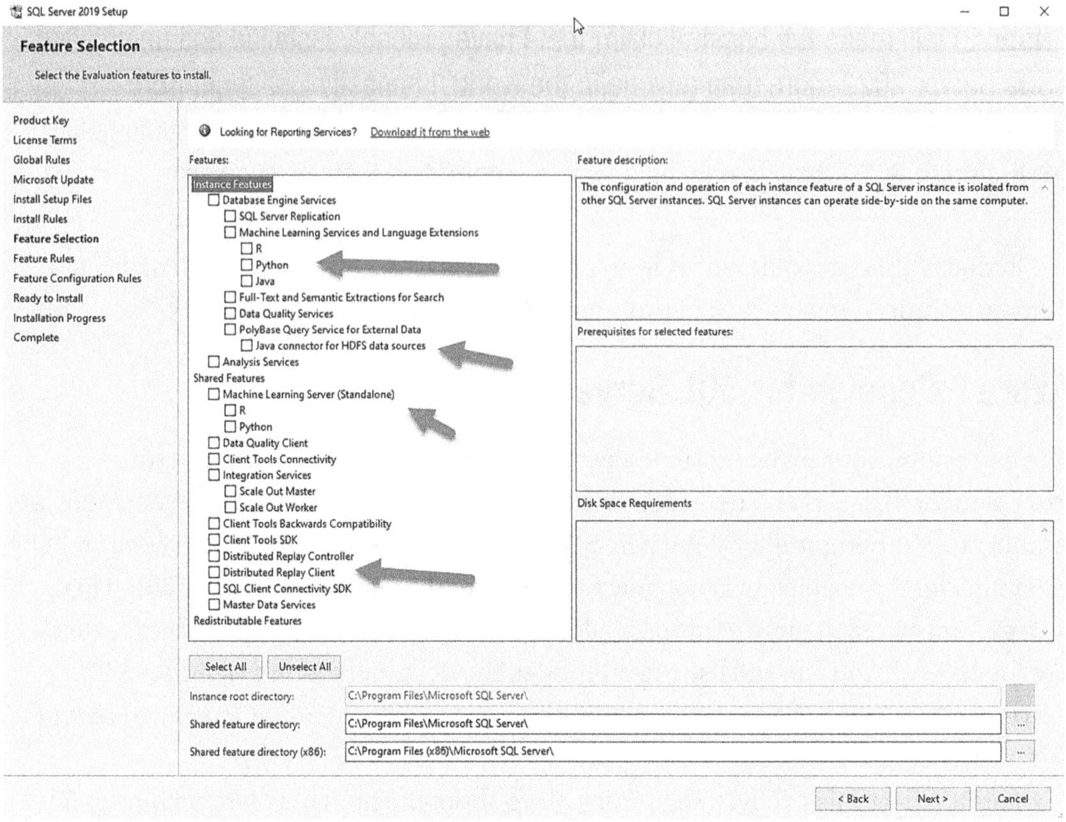

Figure 2-1. *SQL Server 2019 setup features with features removed highlighted*

Figure 2-2 shows a shorter list of features now available during setup.

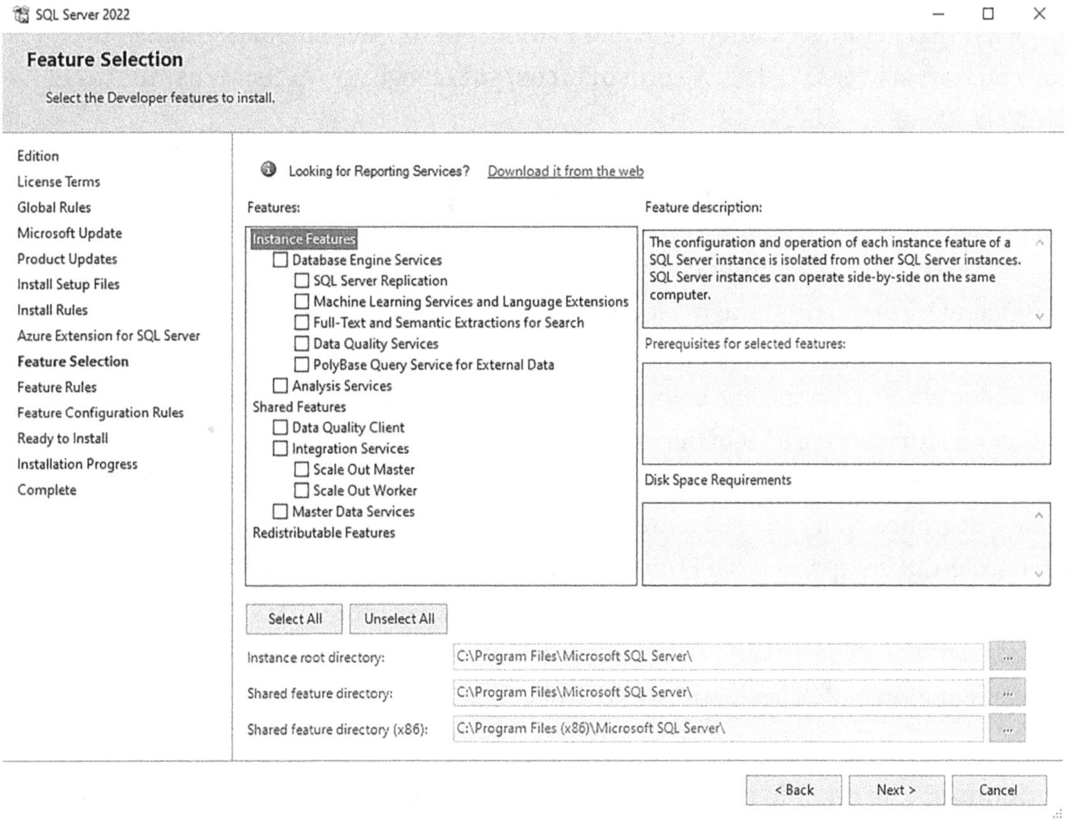

Figure 2-2. *The SQL Server 2022 feature selection*

Let's look further at the features removed from SQL Server 2022.

Removal of R, Python, and Java

In SQL Server 2016, 2017, and 2019, we included options to install open source runtime packages for R, Python, and Java as part of machine learning services and the language extension feature. While this was convenient for many, we found a lot of our customers using this feature wanted to use their own runtime package. We also had to figure out how to update the open source packages we installed. Because of this, we felt it didn't make sense to continue to install these packages as part of setup. In SQL Server 2022, we no longer offer these packages as an option during setup. If you want to use machine learning services or language extensions, you still must choose this feature during setup.

Instead you can install your own packages. See the documentation at `https://docs.microsoft.com/sql/machine-learning/install/sql-machine-learning-services-windows-install` to get started for R and Python. For the Java language extension, you can start at `https://docs.microsoft.com/sql/language-extensions/install/windows-java`.

Removal of Polybase Hadoop Connectivity with Java

In SQL Server 2016, we introduced the concept of Polybase, the ability to query data in different formats and storage "where they live" using T-SQL. The original design translated T-SQL statements into Java code to query files in Hadoop systems. It was revolutionary, but the specific connection to Hadoop systems never really took off as a popular feature among a lot of our customers.

In SQL Server 2022, we have discontinued providing this feature along with Polybase scale-out groups. You can read more about the retirement of Polybase to Hadoop with Java, scale-out groups, and Big Data Clusters at `https://cloudblogs.microsoft.com/sqlserver/2022/02/25/the-path-forward-for-sql-server-analytics/`. However, the concept of Polybase is still alive and well. You will see in this book in Chapter 7 a new implementation of Polybase using REST APIs.

Important   In order to use Polybase REST APIs, you need to select the Polybase Query Service for External Data feature. This will install the Polybase services. The Polybase REST APIs do not use these services but are baked directly into the engine. However, for now you must select this feature to enable configuration options to support Polybase REST APIs. Polybase services for ODBC drivers also require you to select this feature and do use Polybase services.

Removal of Machine Learning Server

In the summer of 2022, we announced the retirement of Machine Learning Server and stated it would no longer be a feature in the next version of SQL Server. Therefore, it is not a feature option in SQL Server 2022 setup. You can read more about this retirement statement at `https://docs.microsoft.com/lifecycle/announcements/microsoft-machine-learning-server-retiring`.

Removal of Distributed Replay

Distributed replay is a tool to replay SQL Profiler traces and has been in the product for many years. We have decided to unbundle this feature from SQL Server installation and will make it available in a separable download package. I will be transparent with the readers of this book that we have not enhanced this capability for quite some time.

Memory Recommendations

In the past we introduced in setup the ability to configure "max server memory" for the instance of SQL Server, which includes *recommended* values. The recommend value for "max server memory" comes from our documentation at `https://docs.microsoft.com/sql/database-engine/configure-windows/server-memory-server-configuration-options`.

We have determined that we didn't quite calculate this correctly, and we've updated the method in SQL Server 2022 setup. Be aware that this recommendation is very conservative in my opinion, so I would be careful about using it. The calculation for "max server memory" is ~75% of *available* free memory at the time setup is run. We built this to apply it across many different workloads and configurations. It is also important to note that this recommendation doesn't consider other SQL instances, so if you run multiple SQL instances on the same server, you need to carefully consider the value for "max server memory" for each instance.

Other Installation Methods

SQL Server setup for Windows still supports options without a user interface through the command line. You can find examples of how to do this and see all the options at `https://docs.microsoft.com/sql/database-engine/install-windows/install-sql-server-from-the-command-prompt`. The only differences for SQL Server 2022 are the removal of options for discontinued features as described earlier in this chapter and the addition of new parameters to support the Azure extension for SQL Server.

If you are new to setting up SQL Server, you should know that the SQL Server Evaluation and Developer Editions come with an "easy setup" mode with an installer that installs just the defaults without going through any screens. If you choose this method, the Azure extension for SQL Server feature is not selected. If you want the full setup experience with the Evaluation or Developer Edition, choose the Custom option from the initial setup screen.

Setting Up the Azure Extension for SQL Server

In 2020, we announced a new hybrid capability for SQL Server called Azure Arc–enabled SQL Server. The concept is to take an existing installation of SQL Server and connect to Azure to provide new capabilities such as viewing instance details in the Azure portal, Microsoft Defender, and best practices assessments. The process of setting up SQL Server with Azure Arc is done from the Azure portal or through scripts. SQL Server 2022 provides an integrated method to install this in the SQL Server setup process, through a setup feature called the **Azure extension for SQL Server**.

The Azure extension for SQL Server provides the following capabilities for SQL Server 2022:

- Microsoft Defender for SQL

- SQL Assessment (which you can read more about at `https://docs.microsoft.com/sql/sql-server/azure-arc/assess`)

- View of a connected SQL Server in the Azure portal along with other Azure SQL resources

- Azure Active Directory (AAD) authentication

- Access policies in Microsoft Purview (Purview integration requires AAD, which also requires the Azure extension for SQL Server)

You will learn more about these features in Chapter 3 of the book. I will describe more about the role of Azure Arc–enabled SQL Server in Chapter 11 of the book. Just connecting SQL Server to Azure does not cost you anything. It is only when you select certain services such as Microsoft Defender or Purview that you incur subscription costs.

Note   The Azure extension for SQL Server is not supported when running SQL Server on an Azure Virtual Machine. SQL Server uses the Infrastructure-as-a-Service (IaaS) Agent Extension to provide capabilities like Defender, assessments, and AAD authentication. You can read more about the IaaS Agent Extension at `https://docs.microsoft.com/azure/azure-sql/virtual-machines/windows/sql-server-iaas-agent-extension-automate-management`.

Figure 2-3 shows the information needed to set up the Azure extension for SQL Server.

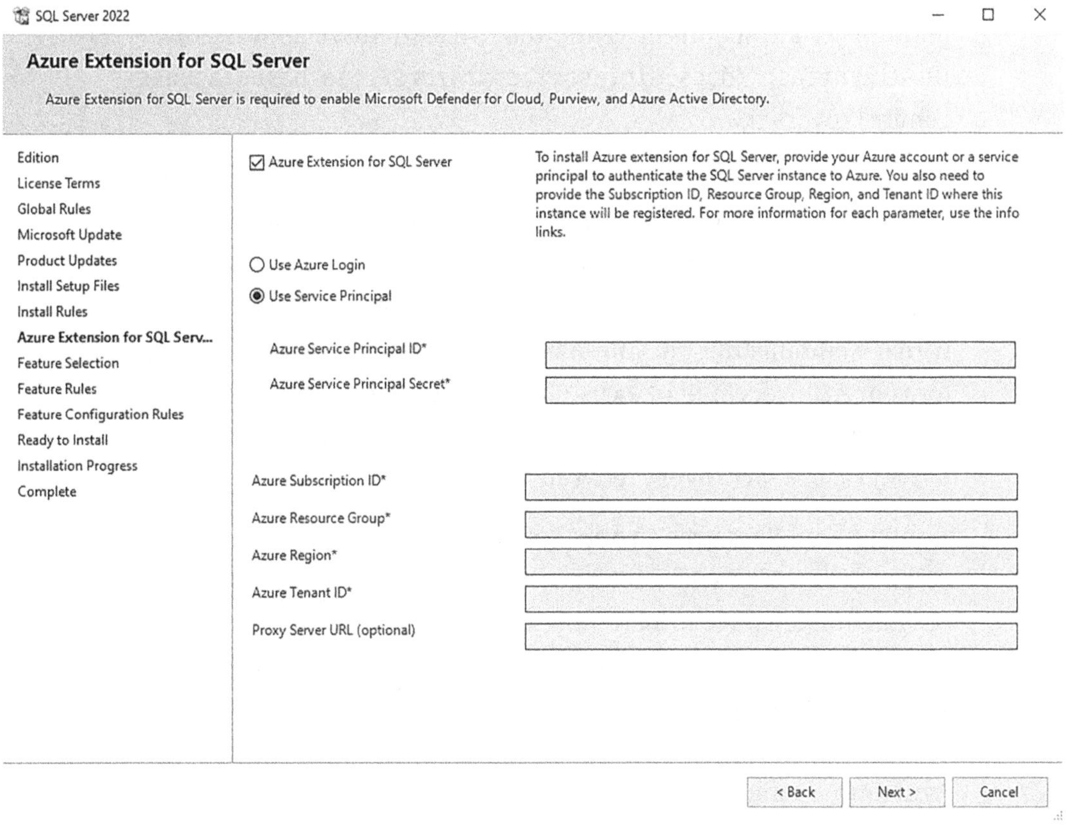

Figure 2-3. *Setting up the Azure extension for SQL Server*

I'll describe how to fill out these fields with information for Azure. I have some example files that can help you in this chapter in the **ch2_install** folder for the samples that come with the book.

What You Should Know First

Let me stop here before you read on to give you some guidance on Azure topics that I will discuss as part of filling out these fields:

- The following information assumes you have an **Azure subscription and your SQL Server is connected to the Internet directly or will be through a proxy**. If you don't have an Azure subscription, check with your organization. Or you can get started at `https://azure.microsoft.com/get-started/`.

- Read up on the concept of **Azure Role-Based Access Control (RBAC).** RBAC is a permission system in Azure to give you rights to perform certain actions in Azure. You can learn more about Azure RBAC at `https://docs.microsoft.com/azure/role-based-access-control/overview`.

- You need to check your permissions within your Azure subscription to ensure you can create a resource group and custom permissions for Azure Arc or the ability to create a custom role and a service principal. If these examples fail due to lack of permissions, check with the administrator of your Azure subscription. The permissions for your Azure account or a custom role to be used with a service principal can be found at `https://docs.microsoft.com/sql/sql-server/azure-arc/overview#required-permissions`.

- A valid **Azure Resource Group**. You may have one already you want to use, or you can create a new one. You can use this documentation page to learn how to create a new resource group: `https://docs.microsoft.com/azure/azure-resource-manager/management/manage-resource-groups-portal`. When you create the resource group, choose an **Azure region** that is supported for Azure Arc–enabled servers, which is documented at `https://docs.microsoft.com/sql/sql-server/azure-arc/overview#supported-azure-regions`.

- I recommend you install the az command line interface (CLI) from `https://docs.microsoft.com/cli/azure/` or use the Azure Cloud Shell (which you can learn more about at `https://docs.microsoft.com/azure/cloud-shell/overview`).

- If you decide to use a service principal, you will need to create a **custom role** in Azure that includes the following permissions: `https://docs.microsoft.com/sql/sql-server/azure-arc/overview#required-permissions`. To learn how to create a custom role, go to `https://docs.microsoft.com/azure/active-directory/roles/custom-create`.

Note   For my tenant at Microsoft, I didn't have permission to create a custom role in the Azure portal. However, I was able to create one using the az CLI as documented at `https://docs.microsoft.com/azure/role-based-access-control/custom-roles-cli`. You can see my example JSON file from the samples for this chapter called **sqlazureext.json**. The script to create the role using this JSON file is in the sample file **createcustomrole.ps1**.

- If you decide to use a **service principal**, you can do this with the az command line interface (CLI) to create one for your subscription and resource group: `https://docs.microsoft.com/cli/azure/create-an-azure-service-principal-azure-cli`.

You will assign the service principal to the custom role and resource group you created. You can see an example of how to do this with the script **sqlazureextsp.ps1**.

When you create a service principal with the CLI, you will get a JSON result that will contain values for fields you will need for this screen. ***Be sure to save this result, especially the password.*** I'll show you how each field from the output lines up with the fields on the feature screen for SQL Server setup.

The resulting JSON should look like this:

```
{
  "appId": "<appid GUID>",
  "displayName": "<service principal name>",
  "password": "<password>",
  "tenant": "<tenantID GUID>"
}
```

Note   Don't include the quotation marks when using these values on the feature setup screen.

Service principals are highly privileged accounts in Azure. I created my service principal at the resource group scope, but the permissions assigned with the custom role are highly privileged. If you decide to disconnect and remove your SQL Server from Azure, make sure to remove the service principal.

Providing Values for the Feature Setup

With these resources created, you can fill out the fields from Figure 2-3 (all of these fields except Proxy Server URL are *required*).

Checking the Azure Extension for SQL Server

If you don't want to install the Azure extension for SQL Server, you can uncheck this box. Leave it checked to install the extension. Remember that you don't incur any costs just to set up the extension.

Login or Service Principal

You have a choice to use an Azure login from your subscription or a service principal. If you select **Use Azure Login**, you will be presented with a screen to log in with your credentials per your company requirements (Microsoft requires MFA). Once you sign in, we validate your account has the right permissions to set up the extension. Then we will auto-populate the following fields:

Azure Tenant ID

This is an ID for your Azure Active Directory associated with your account.

Azure Subscription ID

This is the default subscription ID for your Azure account. We will register your SQL Server under this subscription. You can choose a different subscription from a drop-down list.

Azure Resource Group

We will choose a resource group under your subscription, which we will use to register your SQL Server. You can choose from a drop-down list a different resource group.

Azure Region

We will choose the Azure region from the resource group, but you can choose a different region from a drop-down list.

Proxy Server URL

You can optionally put in a proxy URL if your SQL Server cannot directly connect to the Internet. By default, the agents installed with the extension on the server will use outbound TCP port 443 to connect to Azure services over the Internet. You can set up a proxy server. If you use a proxy server, put in the URL of the proxy in this field. You can read more about this at `https://docs.microsoft.com/azure/azure-arc/servers/manage-agent#update-or-remove-proxy-settings`. **Leave this field blank** if you are not using a proxy.

If you decide to use a service principal, you will need to fill in information that you collected when you created the service principal using a custom role:

Azure Service Principal ID

This is the value of **appId** from the JSON result of creating the service principal.

Azure Service Principal Secret

This is the value of **password** from the JSON result.

Azure Subscription ID

This is the subscription ID value you used as part of the –scopes parameter when you created the service principal.

Azure Resource Group

This is the name of the resource group you created as a prerequisite and used in the –scopes parameter to create the service principal.

Azure Region

The name of the Azure region where you created the resource group. The name of the region here should not contain spaces and should be lowercase. My region was East US, so the value should be eastus.

Azure Tenant ID

This is the value of the **tenant** from the JSON result when you created the service principal.

Proxy Server URL can also be used in this scenario.

What happens now?

When you hit the Next button, there will be a delay of several minutes before you can proceed. This is to do some validation to connect to Azure. During the installation, the Azure Arc Agent and the Azure extension for SQL Server will be installed to connect and register with Azure. You can see these agents by looking at installed programs after setup has successfully completed as seen in Figure 2-4.

Name	Publisher	Installed On	Size	Version
Microsoft Edge	Microsoft Corporation			105.0.1343.33
Azure Connected Machine Agent	Microsoft Corporation		195 MB	1.21.02043.412
Microsoft SQL Server 2022 RC0 Setup (English)	Microsoft Corporation		40.7 MB	16.0.900.6
Browser for SQL Server 2022 RC0	Microsoft Corporation		11.6 MB	16.0.900.6
Microsoft SQL Server 2012 Native Client	Microsoft Corporation		9.71 MB	11.4.7462.6
Microsoft OLE DB Driver for SQL Server	Microsoft Corporation		8.28 MB	18.5.0.0
Microsoft ODBC Driver 17 for SQL Server	Microsoft Corporation		7.01 MB	17.7.2.1
Microsoft SQL Server Extension	Microsoft Corporation		113 MB	1.1.2046.65
Microsoft VSS Writer for SQL Server 2022 RC0	Microsoft Corporation		2.34 MB	16.0.900.6
Microsoft Visual Studio Tools for Applications 2019	Microsoft Corporation		14.2 MB	16.0.31110
Microsoft SQL Server Management Studio - 19.0 Prev...	Microsoft Corporation		2.63 GB	16.0.19061.0
Microsoft Visual C++ 2013 Redistributable (x86) - 12....	Microsoft Corporation		17.1 MB	12.0.40664.0
Microsoft Visual C++ 2015-2019 Redistributable (x86)...	Microsoft Corporation		17.9 MB	14.29.30139.0
Microsoft Visual C++ 2015-2019 Redistributable (x64)...	Microsoft Corporation		20.1 MB	14.29.30139.0
Microsoft Help Viewer 2.3	Microsoft Corporation		12.1 MB	2.3.28307
Azure Data Studio	Microsoft Corporation		570 MB	1.38.0
Microsoft SQL Server 2022 RC0 (64-bit)	Microsoft Corporation			

Figure 2-4. *Azure Arc Agent and Azure extension for SQL Server*

In addition, the **Azure Connected SQL Server Onboarding role** will be assigned automatically to the service principal. This role is required to connect SQL Server to Azure.

The setup logs show the details of what happens with a PowerShell script that setup executes (this is in the **details.txt** file from the SQL Server setup logs):

```
SQLArcOnboard: --SqlArcOnboardPrivate: --------------------------------
---------
SQLArcOnboard: Getting setting AZURESERVICEPRINCIPAL: source = UI, type =
Microsoft.SqlServer.Configuration.ArcOnboard.SqlArcServicePrincipal.
```

SQLArcOnboard: Getting setting AZURESERVICEPRINCIPALSECRET:
source = UI, type = Microsoft.SqlServer.Configuration.ArcOnboard.
SqlArcServicePrincipalSecret.
SQLArcOnboard: Getting setting AZURESUBSCRIPTIONID: source = UI, type =
Microsoft.SqlServer.Configuration.ArcOnboard.SqlArcSubscriptionId.
SQLArcOnboard: Getting setting AZURETENANTID: source = UI, type =
Microsoft.SqlServer.Configuration.ArcOnboard.SqlArcTenantId.
SQLArcOnboard: Getting setting AZUREREGION: source = UI, type = Microsoft.
SqlServer.Configuration.ArcOnboard.SqlArcRegion.
SQLArcOnboard: Getting setting AZURERESOURCEGROUP: source = UI, type =
Microsoft.SqlServer.Configuration.ArcOnboard.SqlArcResourceGroupName.
SQLArcOnboard: Getting setting AZUREARCPROXYSERVER: source = UI, type =
Microsoft.SqlServer.Configuration.ArcOnboard.SqlArcProxy.
SQLArcOnboard: Powershell results Installed Powershell version
5.1.20348.643
SQLArcOnboard: Powershell results Az already installed. Skipping
installation.
SQLArcOnboard: Powershell results Az.ConnectedMachine already installed.
Skipping installation.
SQLArcOnboard: Powershell results Az.Resources already installed. Skipping
installation.
SQLArcOnboard: Powershell results Arc for Servers resource not found.
Registering the current machine now.
SQLArcOnboard: Powershell results Microsoft.Azure.PowerShell.Cmdlets.
ConnectedMachine.Models.Api20210520.Machine
SQLArcOnboard: Powershell results Getting managed Identity ID of
BW-SQL2022.
SQLArcOnboard: Powershell results Arc machine managed Identity does not
have Azure Connected SQL Server Onboarding role. Assigning it now.
SQLArcOnboard: Powershell results Installing SQL Server - Azure Arc
extension in the background.
SQLArcOnboard: Powershell results Microsoft.Azure.PowerShell.Cmdlets.
ConnectedMachine.Runtime.PowerShell.AsyncOperationResponse
SQLArcOnboard: Powershell results Completed Onboarding process.

Within the Azure portal (portal.azure.com), you can search for the resource group you created and will see two resources as seen in Figure 2-5.

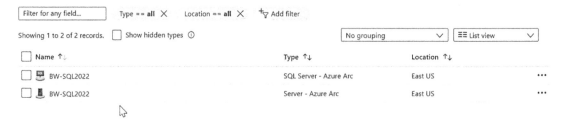

Figure 2-5. *Azure Arc–enabled SQL Server in the portal*

If you select SQL Server – Azure Arc, you will see interesting information on the main portal page as seen in Figure 2-6.

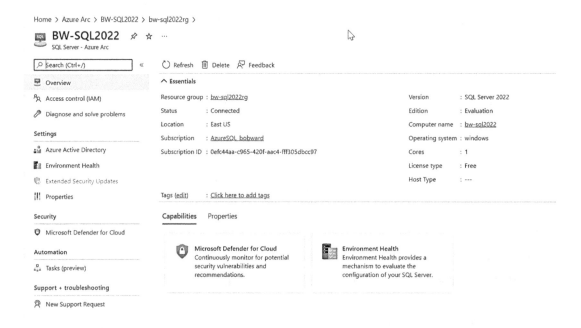

Figure 2-6. *Azure Arc–enabled SQL Server main portal page*

Connect to Azure After Setup

If you decide not to select the Azure extension for SQL Server feature during SQL Server 2022 setup, you can connect your SQL Server 2022 instance with Azure at a later time following the steps at `https://docs.microsoft.com/sql/sql-server/`

CHAPTER 2   INSTALL AND UPGRADE

azure-arc/connect. Or you can go back and "add a feature" to the existing SQL Server 2022 instance, which provides you with the same screens as with the original setup. You can also connect many SQL instances at scale using steps found at https://docs.microsoft.com/sql/sql-server/azure-arc/connect-at-scale.

Removing the Azure Extension for SQL Server

You can disconnect your SQL Server 2022 instance at any time from Azure using the steps documented at https://learn.microsoft.com/en-us/sql/sql-server/azure-arc/connect#delete-your-arc-enabled-sql-server-resource. If you decide to completely remove the connection to Azure, I recommend you also remove the Azure extension for SQL Server using SQL Server setup.

Deploying on Other Platforms

This chapter has focused more on the experience of installing SQL Server on Windows. SQL Server is supported on other platforms including Linux, containers, and Kubernetes. Chapter 9 of this book will cover those experiences, but if you want to jump right in, you can use these resources:

SQL Server on Linux – https://aka.ms/sqllinux

SQL Server on containers – https://aka.ms/sqlcontainers

SQL Server on Kubernetes – https://aka.ms/sqlk8s

Note   This page contains instructions on deploying a SQL container on Azure Kubernetes Service (AKS). Consult your Kubernetes platform documentation on the proper method to deploy pods and containers.

Be sure to consult the latest release notes for SQL Server 2022 on Linux and containers at https://docs.microsoft.com/sql/linux/sql-server-linux-release-notes-2022.

In addition, SQL Server 2022 can be deployed on Azure Virtual Machines. Chapter 10 of this book will go through more details on this experience. To get more information on SQL Server on Azure Virtual Machines, consult our documentation at https://aka.ms/sqlazurevm.

Side-by-Side and Multi-instance Installations

Like previous releases of SQL Server, SQL Server 2022 supports side-by-side installations on the same computer with different versions (supported versions) and multiple instances (aka named instances). There are no differences in support for both side-by-side and multi-instance installations from previous SQL Server releases. For more information, consult our documentation at `https://docs.microsoft.com/sql/sql-server/install/work-with-multiple-versions-and-instances-of-sql-server`. SQL Server on Linux supports multiple instances by using containers.

How to Upgrade to SQL Server 2022

SQL Server 2022 supports upgrades from previous releases of SQL Server with the same methods as in previous versions. You can read more at `https://docs.microsoft.com/sql/database-engine/install-windows/upgrade-sql-server` for all the details.

At the time of the writing of this book, the plan was to support an "in-place" upgrade from SQL Server 2012 Service Pack 4 or any higher version and database restore upgrades from SQL Server 2008/2008R2 and higher.

The Importance of dbcompat

Over my career at Microsoft, it has become apparent that one of the reasons customers do not upgrade to a new major version of SQL Server is because the latest version is not compatible with their application.

For the past several SQL Server versions, we have been trying to convince customers and developers to test for compatibility with the database compatibility level (dbcompat) of user databases. If you upgrade a SQL Server database to a new version, we maintain the previous dbcompat. You can read more on why this could be a new strategy for compatibility for you at `https://aka.ms/dbcompat`. Note that using an older dbcompat gives you more time to explore and test the latest dbcompat levels, which enable new capabilities like Intelligent Query Processing (IQP), which is discussed more in Chapters 4 and 5 of this book.

Configuration

Although this chapter is specifically designed to give you guidance on installation and upgrades, the configuration of SQL Server post installation is also an important topic. However, there are very few changes to SQL Server instance configuration in SQL Server 2022:

- There are a few new server-level **sp_configure** options. They will be discussed throughout this book as they relate to new features for SQL Server 2022.

- The SQL Server Configuration Manager has been enhanced to allow you to control the services (start and stop) for the Azure extension for SQL Server feature.

Other than that, there are no new instance-level configuration changes.

You will learn about new database-level configuration options as you explore new features throughout the book.

Easy to Install and Upgrade

SQL Server has been known for some time as a simple install-and-upgrade experience, and none of that changes in SQL Server 2022. As part of that experience, we have provided an integrated setup to get connected to Azure if that is part of your hybrid strategy.

If you read over all the details of this chapter, you are pretty much ready to dive in and learn about features. So let's roll! The next chapter is about connecting SQL Server to the cloud in ways never before seen in the industry, which brings together SQL Server and Azure to provide disaster recovery, analytics, and security.

CHAPTER 3

Connect Your Database to the Cloud

SQL Server runs on any platform you need, edge to cloud. Regardless of where you run SQL Server, we have seen a trend in the industry and for our customers to *connect* SQL Server to the cloud. *Connect* is a pretty broad term, so in this chapter you will learn the details of exactly how SQL Server 2022 can be connected to the cloud.

First, I'll give you my perspective on what *hybrid* means and how SQL Server has been a hybrid platform over the years. Then I'll go into each of the main areas where SQL Server 2022 is now Azure enabled in ways never seen before. This includes managed disaster recovery, near-real-time analytics, and new security capabilities. As part of this story, I'll describe how Azure Arc is used to enable some of these technologies.

In this chapter there are examples for you to go through to learn how these features work. For any of these features, you will need an Azure subscription and the ability to connect your SQL Server to Azure, either directly connected to the Internet or through a proxy. Your company or organization may already have an Azure account for you to use or a subscription. However, if you need your own, start at `https://azure.microsoft.com/get-started`. I'll describe more throughout this chapter specific access rights you may need for each scenario and any special connection configurations you may want to use like a proxy.

The Hybrid SQL Server

In this section of the book, I'll give you my perspective on what the term *hybrid* means in relation to SQL Server, a brief history of how SQL Server has had hybrid capabilities in previous releases, and an overview of what is special about SQL Server 2022.

© Bob Ward 2022
B. Ward, *SQL Server 2022 Revealed*, https://doi.org/10.1007/978-1-4842-8894-8_3

What Is *Hybrid*?

I'm sure many of you have thought about what *hybrid* means, and my research shows there are several definitions and thoughts in the industry. I like to simply define the term *hybrid* in relation to a compute or data platform as the following:

- A product or service offered both on-premises and the cloud *with consistency*

    SQL Server definitely meets this qualification given that SQL Server runs in the cloud with Azure SQL: SQL on Azure Virtual Machines, Azure SQL Managed Instance, and Azure SQL Database. Notice my emphasis at the end of the phrase: "with consistency." I say this because you might be able to find other products that exist on-premises and in the cloud, but do they have the same consistency story as SQL Server? Same core database engine, same T-SQL language, and same tools.

- A product on-premises connected to the cloud to *enhance* data capabilities

There are two keywords in this phrase: connected and enhance. *Connected* means to connect data *somehow* from an existing feature in the on-premises product. *Enhance* means there is true business value to this connection. You will see in this chapter that I believe SQL Server 2022 does both.

Let's first look at how SQL Server has been connected to Azure over the years to set some context.

SQL Server Hybrid Over the Years

The most basic feature SQL Server has included for hybrid for several releases is backup. Starting with SQL Server 2012, you are able to back up or restore databases to and from Azure Blob Storage using a syntax that includes a URL. This feature has been enhanced over the years and still exists today, which you can read about at `https://docs.microsoft.com/sql/relational-databases/backup-restore/sql-server-backup-to-url`.

There are other methods to connect SQL Server to Azure including using existing features to extend high availability, redundancy, or queries. For example, you can extend an Always On Availability Group to Azure, which you can read about at `https://docs.microsoft.com/previous-versions/azure/virtual-machines/windows/sqlclassic/virtual-machines-windows-classic-sql-onprem-availability`.

You can also set up transaction replication where the publisher is an on-premises SQL Server and a subscriber database is on an Azure Virtual Machine, Azure SQL Managed Instance, or even Azure SQL Database (you can read specific instructions on how to set this up for Azure SQL Database at `https://docs.microsoft.com/azure/azure-sql/database/replication-to-sql-database`).

And finally, any Azure SQL service can be the data source for a linked server query from SQL Server. These are fundamental methods to connect SQL Server to Azure, but SQL Server 2022 takes it to the next level.

The SQL Server 2022 Hybrid Lineup

Figure 3-1 provides a visual of all Azure-enabled capabilities with SQL Server 2022.

SQL Server 2022 Cloud connected

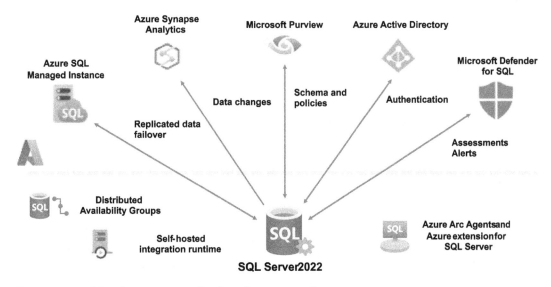

Figure 3-1. *SQL Server 2022 is cloud connected*

From left to right at the top, SQL Server 2022 has built in the ability to provide these cloud-connected features.

Azure SQL Managed Instance

The link feature for Azure SQL Managed Instance provides *managed* disaster recovery for SQL Server 2022. The built-in capability of a Distributed Availability Group (DAG) is used to bridge SQL Server and Azure SQL Managed Instance.

Azure Synapse Analytics

Azure Synapse Link for SQL Server allows SQL Server 2022 to seamlessly synchronize data in selected tables directly to Azure Synapse–dedicated SQL pools. The self-hosted integration runtime (SHIR) is used to coordinate between Synapse and SQL Server, but SQL Server also has built-in capabilities to send data to Azure.

Azure Active Directory Authentication

SQL Server 2022 can now authenticate login using an Azure Active Directory (AAD) account. This allows support for concepts like Multi-factor Authentication. You have to enable AAD with SQL Server 2022 to support Purview-integrated policy management. AAD for SQL Server 2022 requires the Azure extension for SQL Server.

Microsoft Purview

Microsoft Purview has many capabilities, but the specific new feature integrated with SQL Server 2022 is *policy management*. You can use Purview to publish a policy that will be pushed to SQL Server 2022 to support authentication and access. Purview policy management with SQL Server 2022 requires that you have configured Azure Active Directory (AAD) authentication for SQL Server because policies will be based on an AAD account. Purview policy management also requires the Azure extension for SQL Server.

Microsoft Defender for SQL

Microsoft Defender for SQL, a member of the Microsoft Defender for Cloud family, supports vulnerability assessments and advanced threat protection (ATP) for SQL Server 2022. Microsoft Defender for SQL works across many SQL technologies and supports previous versions of SQL Server. Microsoft Defender for SQL for SQL Server on-premises requires the Azure Arc Agent and an extension for monitoring. I do not cover this service in detail in the chapter. You can read more about Microsoft Defender for SQL at `https://docs.microsoft.com/azure/defender-for-cloud/defender-for-sql-usage`.

Azure Arc Agents and Azure Extension for SQL Server

The **Azure Arc Agent**, which is installed when you choose to connect to Azure in SQL Server setup or through a script method, is used to connect Microsoft Purview, enable Azure Active Directory Authentication (AAD), and support Microsoft Defender for SQL. The Azure Arc Agent supports an extension framework for specific capabilities. We have built an extension called the **Azure extension for SQL Server**. This extension communicates with Azure to store information in the registry (or mssql.conf for Linux) that the engine has enhanced to support for AAD and Purview. Microsoft Defender for SQL uses another extension called the Monitoring Agent. You can read details about the Azure Arc Agent architecture at `https://docs.microsoft.com/azure/azure-arc/servers/agent-overview`. The Azure Arc Agent and extensions are designed for SQL Server on-premises. SQL Server on an Azure Virtual Machine has a similar concept but uses a different architecture including the SQL Server IaaS Agent Extension (`https://docs.microsoft.com/azure/azure-sql/virtual-machines/windows/sql-server-iaas-agent-extension-automate-management`). At the time of the writing of this book, Microsoft Purview and Azure Active Directory authentication were not yet supported by the IaaS Agent Extension. However, it is our plan to enable this capability, and we can enhance the extension on a timeframe different than releasing a major version of SQL Server.

The rest of the chapter is devoted to a deep dive into each of these cloud-connected capabilities. You can read all sections or jump straight to a particular cloud service you want to learn about.

Managed Disaster Recovery with Azure SQL Managed Instance

You only need to worry about disaster recovery when you...well, have a disaster. But of course no one ever knows when that is, which is why having a plan for disaster recovery for your SQL Server data and installation is a key component for any production system.

How you build your disaster recovery system is typically dependent on industry terms you may know such as Recovery Time Objective (RTO) and Recovery Point Objective (RPO). Our high-availability solutions such as built-in crash recovery for SQL Server and failover clusters can help with these requirements. The reason these solutions typically don't help with disaster recovery is because a true disaster usually means your local copy of data is not available.

SQL Server provides many solutions to help including a basic database backup and restore solution where you typically store your backups in a different physical location that could be retrieved and restored should a disaster situation occur. You could even set up an Always On Availability Group with secondaries in different physical locations, but this could require a more complex cluster setup.

For SQL Server 2022, we wanted to provide a new option for disaster recovery, which I call *managed disaster recovery*.

Project Chimera and DAG

In order to understand how we built a managed disaster recovery solution, let's look at the background of this new capability.

Distributed Availability Groups

To help with disaster recovery scenarios, we built a new feature in SQL Server 2016 called **Distributed Availability Groups** (DAGs). A DAG is an availability group that spans multiple availability groups (AGs) typically across distant regions. The great thing about DAG technology is it is all built into SQL Server. In fact, AG technology is also built into SQL Server to manage data replication. Technologies like Windows Server Failover Cluster (WSFC) and Pacemaker (Linux) are used to coordinate failovers.

Figure 3-2 shows a possible DAG configuration.

SQL Server Distributed Availability Groups (DAG)

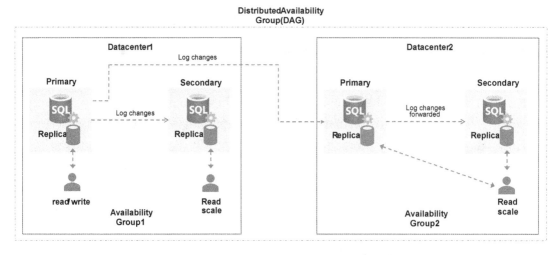

Figure 3-2. *A SQL Server Distributed Availability Group (DAG)*

You can see one interesting aspect to this design is that the primary replica in Availability Group 1 (AG1) sends transaction log changes to a secondary replica in its AG but also sends changes to the primary replica of Availability Group 2 (AG2). The primary replica of AG2 forwards log changes to its secondary replica. Users can only write changes to the primary replica of AG1. But should circumstances arise, you could fail over to AG2, and now users could write to the primary replica of AG2. All the communication and replication of data between the replicas and AGs are managed within the SQL Server engine.

The fact that both an AG and DAG were built into SQL Server gave us the idea to extend this concept as a hybrid approach. Why couldn't the second AG be in Azure? But not just in Azure, as you could definitely build a DAG between a SQL Server in your data center and the second AG on an Azure Virtual Machine. We wanted to build something new and revolutionary.

Project Chimera

Around 3 years ago, our engineering team that works on Azure SQL Managed Instance came up with an idea that led to a project called Chimera. As Dani Ljepava, Senior Program Manager with the Managed Instance team, told me, *"Chimera is a mythical beast from Greek mythology, looking like a dragon with multiple heads from different animals all in one. As we are building a hybrid capability between SQL Server and the cloud, Chimera seemed like a perfect name for the project at it* was referring to a hybrid beast – many animals in one."

The team first started out to simply build a link between a SQL Server and an Azure SQL Managed Instance (MI) so that MI could be used as a read replica and eventually a target for online migration from SQL Server. Eventually the project charter grew as we laid plans for project Dallas so that this feature could support a disaster recovery scenario for SQL Server 2022.

Dani told me, *"We were faced with solving problems* that nobody has addressed before at Microsoft and had to go through some unique challenges along the way (and still going on today as we speak). Having said that, nobody before has built an online DR between SQL Server and fully managed Azure PaaS service."

As we moved toward the Private Preview announcement of SQL Server 2022, we branded Chimera as the **link feature for Azure SQL Managed Instance**.

The Link Feature for Azure SQL Managed Instance

The link feature for Azure SQL Managed Instance allows you to connect or link an existing SQL Server database to a Managed Instance in a simple and seamless manner. We use the power of built-in availability group and Distributed Availability Group technology in the SQL Server engine along with some magic behind the scenes for Azure SQL Managed Instance.

The link feature for Azure SQL Managed Instance can be used with databases for SQL Server 2016, SQL Server 2019, or SQL Server 2022 (SQL Server 2017 support to be added later). The feature supports the ability to replicate data through AG technology to an Azure SQL Managed Instance (MI) and use the MI database for read-scale scenarios. If you eventually want to migrate from SQL Server to MI, you can then fail over to MI, and it now becomes the primary system. This is a *one-way* operation, which is why it can help you set up an online migration solution to Azure (and since we are using AG technology, it is the fastest method to migrate online to MI). This capability is sometimes referred to as *unidirectional* replication to Azure MI.

Unique to SQL Server 2022 is the ability to set up a link to Azure SQL Managed Instance where Managed Instance is declared as a disaster recovery site, failover to MI *online*, but then at some point failback *offline* to SQL Server 2022. This capability is sometimes called *bidirectional replication* to Azure MI. I'll explain in the section later in this chapter called "**Using the Link Feature for Offline Disaster Recovery**" how the failback is offline and why I call it managed disaster recovery.

How It Works

Let's take a look at how the link feature for Azure SQL Managed Instance (MI) works by seeing how to create the link and failover to MI.

Creating and Using the Link

The link feature for Azure SQL Managed Instance uses a combination of built-in T-SQL and PowerShell scripts to create an availability group on SQL Server 2022 (if one does not exist) and a Distributed Availability Group across SQL Server 2022 and Azure SQL Managed Instance (any service tier) that includes a database from your SQL Server 2022 instance. The process to create the link is also made easier through new GUI wizards in SQL Server Management Studio (SSMS) with an option in Object Explorer from a database context called **Azure SQL Managed Instance link ➤ Replicate database**.

Figure 3-3 shows the architecture and flow of creating a link to Azure SQL Managed Instance.

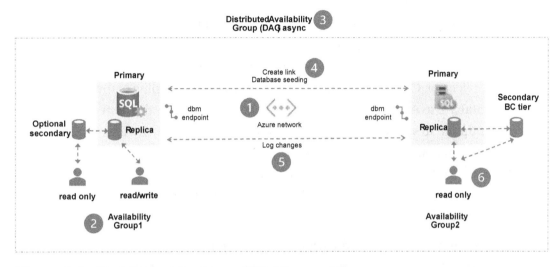

Figure 3-3. *Link feature for Azure SQL Managed Instance*

Let's break down the components of the link feature in terms of the process to create the link. SSMS automates these steps:

1. **Establish networking connectivity** between SQL Server and Azure SQL Managed Instance using Azure networking and database mirroring (dbm) endpoints.

2. **Create an availability group** (AG) on SQL Server 2022 and database mirroring (dbm) endpoint if one does not already exist. Build the AG as *clusterless* or CLUSTER_TYPE = NONE. We won't use any clustering technology for the AG because this is not an automatic failover-based solution. An existing AG could have a secondary replica already. It turns out that an interesting but not well-known feature is that if you build your own AG, *you don't have to have a secondary replica* (availability mode is not used in this case). But you must create an AG so you can create a DAG.

3. **Create a Distributed Availability Group (DAG)** including the SQL Server 2022 AG and your Managed Instance name.

4. **Create a link to Azure SQL Managed Instance** (PowerShell cmdlet). This establishes an AG for a General Purpose service tier Managed Instance or uses an existing AG from a Business Critical service tier (which already has a secondary replica). Note again that an AG doesn't have to have a secondary replica, which is why this solution can work very nicely for a General Purpose service tier. Creating the link also initiates a copy or seeding of the database to Azure SQL Managed Instance. Seeding uses the dbm endpoint to stream a copy of the database to Managed Instance. You can read more about how seeding works at `https://docs.microsoft.com/sql/database-engine/availability-groups/windows/automatically-initialize-always-on-availability-group`.

5. **Changes** now made on the primary will be transmitted automatically as log changes to Azure SQL Managed Instance.

6. Users can connect to Azure SQL Managed Instance and access the database as **read-only** and also access secondary replicas for Business Critical service tiers.

Note   When the final version of the link feature for Azure SQL Managed Instance is released, it is possible we may offer an option for you to declare your Managed Instance for disaster recovery (DR) purposes. The concept would be to make Managed Instance in this scenario license-free so you would only pay for compute and storage. If this option becomes available, you would not be able to read from the Azure SQL Managed Instance database since you are only using this for DR purposes.

Once the database is synchronized in Azure SQL Managed Instance, any changes in the transaction log are sent automatically to Azure SQL Managed Instance just like if you built your own DAG. Users can also access the database in Azure SQL Managed Instance for read purposes just like a secondary replica in a DAG.

Failing Over to Azure SQL Managed Instance

Let's say now you are ready to move your primary workload to Azure SQL Managed Instance. You can use the link feature to perform a failover. For versions of SQL Server prior to SQL Server 2022, this is a **one-way operation**.

You have two choices on the failover operation (both are manual):

Planned manual failover

If you use this option, your SQL Server instance is available, and you want to ensure there is no data loss in the failover. This will require stopping your application from making modifications to the primary replica and synchronizing the DAG.

Forced failover

With this option you are willing to accept some data loss (even though there may be no loss if the DAG is already synchronized). This option is your only choice to fail over if the SQL Server instance is not available.

When you fail over to Azure SQL Managed Instance, the database is set to read/write. We handle all the logistics for the AGs on Managed Instance. On the SQL Server side, you have the option of also dropping an AG if it was created and/or the DAG.

You will now need to change your application to connect to the Azure SQL Managed Instance server name. You also will need to migrate any instance-level objects (SQL Agent jobs, login, etc.) manually. Therefore, it is a good idea to script out all of these objects beforehand to prepare for a failover.

Using the Link Feature for Offline Disaster Recovery

So far this doesn't sound like a disaster recovery solution but a one-way migration solution, which is true. However, for SQL Server 2022, we will allow you to use Managed Instance as an offline disaster recovery site. I call this feature offline disaster recovery because even though the failover to Managed Instance is considered online, the failback is offline. The key capability we have added is the ability to restore a database from Azure SQL Managed Instance *back* to SQL Server.

Why Managed Disaster Recovery?

The title of this section of the chapter started with the words *managed disaster recovery*. I called it *managed* because with this capability your disaster recovery (DR) site uses a Platform as a Service (PaaS) SQL. SQL Server has all the capabilities for you to build a DR site, but you must manage it and make sure it is available when you need it.

Once you link your SQL Server to Managed Instance, Microsoft manages the DR site for you. Microsoft manages the entire infrastructure, availability, and backups of the SQL Server database with Managed Instance. This way you can be assured when your need your DR site, it will be available and ready to go.

SQL Server and Database Version Compatibility

You may have known for some time that we don't allow you to restore a backup of a database from a newer major version of SQL Server to an older major version. You will encounter an error on a RESTORE T-SQL statement that tells you the version of the backup is *higher* than the current version.

In reality the incompatibility is at the database level, not the instance. Each database for a major version of SQL Server has a version number. You can see this version using the T-SQL function **DATABASEPROPERTYEX**(<db>, 'Version'). You can also use the RESTORE HEADERONLY T-SQL statement to see the **DatabaseVersion** for the backup.

What happens is that when we build a major version of SQL Server, we often make changes that affect the version compatibility (not dbcompat) of the database *while* we are building the new version of the software. This includes changes like system table modifications. Since these changes rely on new version code, there is no way to access new code in older versions. There could be several *bumps* or *steps* to database versions when we build a new major version of SQL Server (turns out that each CTP build typically gets a few bumps). Once we ship the General Availability of a major version, we lock in the database version until the next major version. We never change this version in cumulative updates, which explains why they are compatible with each other. You can see the progress of these version bumps when you restore a database backup from an older version to a new version. You may see several messages in the RESTORE output like

```
Database 'WideWorldImporters' running the upgrade step from version 928 to
version 929.
```

There can be several "steps" within each major version as we build it. You can see from the version numbers we have done several of these over the years.

Since Azure SQL Managed Instance is *versionless*, it will always be *ahead* of SQL Server major versions. This is why you cannot restore a database backup from Azure SQL Managed Instance to SQL Server.

With the release of the link feature for Azure SQL Managed Instance and SQL Server 2022, we are providing a capability so an Azure SQL Managed Instance can be *compatible* with SQL Server 2022 at the database version level. This is how we can support an offline disaster recovery process. A backup of an Azure SQL Managed Instance that is marked to be compatible can be restored to a SQL Server 2022 instance because they will be using the **same database version**.

The disaster recovery concept is *offline* because your SQL Server 2022 application will be down until you have restored the database from Azure SQL Managed Instance to SQL Server 2022 and it is recovered and running.

Let's see how the link feature for Azure SQL Managed Instance could be used for offline disaster recovery with an exercise.

This exercise is based on our steps in the documentation at `https://docs.microsoft.com/azure/azure-sql/managed-instance/managed-instance-link-feature-overview#use-the-link-feature`. For this exercise we will use the steps to replicate and fail over using SSMS. You can see from this documentation page there are steps to follow the same process using T-SQL and PowerShell. This can be interesting to read to understand how replication and failover work behind the scenes.

I want to personally thank Dani Ljepava and Mladen Andzic from Microsoft. They both were instrumental in helping me create these exercises.

Prerequisites

- Deploy an Azure SQL Managed Instance with your Azure subscription. You can view a quick-start guide in our documentation at `https://docs.microsoft.com/azure/azure-sql/managed-instance/instance-create-quickstart`. When you deploy your Managed Instance, be sure to choose a collation that matches your source SQL Server collation. You can check your SQL Server collation with the T-SQL statement `SELECT SERVERPROPERTY(N'Collation')`. Also take note of the SQL Admin account you created as you need that to log in to the Managed Instance with SSMS.

- An Azure storage account with a container to store a database backup for Managed Instance. Use this documentation page for a quick-start guide to create a storage account in Azure: `https://docs.microsoft.com/azure/storage/common/storage-account-create`. Use this quick-start page to create a container in your storage account: `https://docs.microsoft.com/azure/storage/blobs/storage-quickstart-blobs-portal#create-a-container`.

- A virtual machine or computer with at least two CPUs and 8Gb RAM. The link feature is supported for both Windows and Linux. The exercises in this chapter will show you the instructions for using the link feature on Windows.

- SQL Server 2022 Evaluation Edition with the database engine feature.

- SQL Server Management Studio (SSMS). The latest 18.x build or 19.x build will work.

- You need Azure network connectivity between SQL Server and Azure. If your SQL Server is running on-premises, use a VPN link or Express route. If your SQL Server is running on an Azure VM, either deploy your VM to the same subnet as your Managed Instance or use global VNet peering to connect two separate subnets. For this exercise, I deployed an Azure Virtual Machine for SQL Server and placed it in the same subnet as Azure SQL Managed Instance. This is the fastest way to test out this feature. If you need another option, you may need to get some assistance with Azure networking. There is a complete guide to Azure networking available at `https://docs.microsoft.com/azure/networking`.

- Download the WideWorldImporters **Standard** sample backup from `https://github.com/Microsoft/sql-server-samples/releases/download/wide-world-importers-v1.0/WideWorldImporters-Standard.bak` to the machine where you will run SQL Server. The Standard backup is used because it does not contain memory-optimized tables, which would not be supported if you chose the General Purpose service tier for Managed Instance.

- A copy of the scripts from book samples from the **ch3_cloudconnected\milinkdr** folder.

Preparing the Environment

There are a few things you need to do first to prepare for creating a link to Managed Instance. The complete details can be found at `https://docs.microsoft.com/azure/azure-sql/managed-instance/managed-instance-link-preparation`. Read these carefully. These involve the following:

- Create a master key in the master database.

- Enable the availability group feature for SQL Server if not already enabled.

- As an optional but recommended step, enable startup trace flags for performance.

- Configure network connectivity between SQL Server and Azure SQL Managed Instance.

- Open up firewall and Azure Network Security Group (NSG) settings for port 5022 (dbm endpoint).

- Migrate your certificate for Transparent Data Encryption (TDE) to Managed Instance if your database is to be linked on SQL Server uses TDE.

Creating the Link to Replicate the Database

Let's now go through the steps to create the link to Managed Instance to replicate the database on SQL Server using the wizard from SSMS:

1. Restore the WideWorldImporters database to SQL Server 2022 by executing the script **restorewwi_std.sql**. You may need to edit the file path for the backup and your data and log files. This script uses the following T-SQL statements:

```
USE master;
GO
RESTORE DATABASE WideWorldImporters FROM DISK = 'c:\sql_sample_
databases\WideWorldImporters-Standard.bak' WITH
```

```
MOVE 'WWI_Primary' TO 'f:\data\WideWorldImporters.mdf',
MOVE 'WWI_UserData' TO 'f:\data\WideWorldImporters_UserData.ndf',
MOVE 'WWI_Log' TO 'g:\log\WideWorldImporters.ldf',
stats=5;
GO
```

2. We need to change the recovery model to FULL and back up the database. Execute the script **fullandbackup.sql**, which uses the following T-SQL statements. You may need to edit the file path for the backup:

```
-- Run on SQL Server
-- Set full recovery mode for all databases you want to replicate.
ALTER DATABASE WideWorldImporters SET RECOVERY FULL;
GO
-- Execute backup for all databases you want to replicate.
BACKUP DATABASE WideWorldImporters TO DISK = N'c:\sql_sample_
databases\wwi.bak';
GO
```

3. Launch SSMS and connect to SQL Server 2022. Right-click your database and select the option to replicate the database like in Figure 3-4.

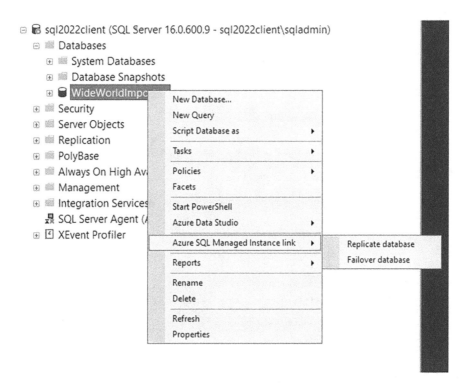

Figure 3-4. *Using SSMS to create a link to Azure SQL Managed Instance*

4. You will now go through a series of steps in the Replicate database wizard. Select Next. The first screen validates you have met the **requirements** to use the link feature.

5. Now **choose your database** to replicate and select Next.

6. Now you need to provide information for the Managed Instance you deployed. This will require you to log in to Azure and choose the subscription, resource group, and Managed Instance. You will also need to select Login to connect to the selected Managed Instance. Once this is done, your screen should look like Figure 3-5.

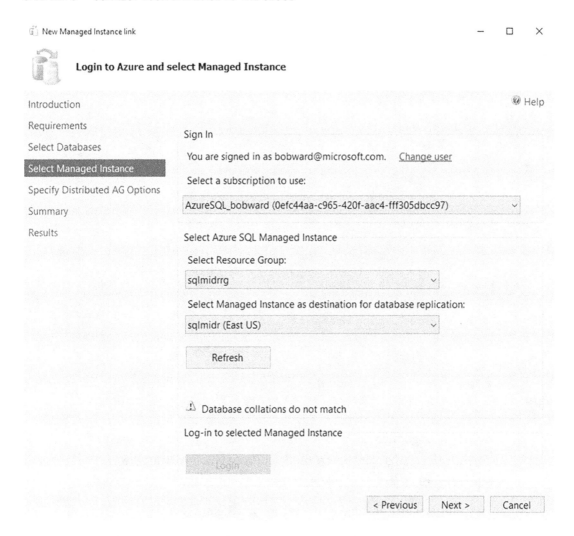

Figure 3-5. *Choosing Managed Instance to create the link*

Notice the warning for collations. I chose a different collation for my Managed Instance to show you the warning you would get if collations did not match. This may not be an issue for you if you use character data in your database that is not dependent on different collations. Select Next.

7. The next screen shows options to create the **Distributed Availability Group** (DAG). Leave these defaults and select Next.

8. The next screen is the **final step**. Select Finish. Note that the time it takes to complete the link creation depends on the size of your source database because database seeding takes place here. There is also a button to generate a script for what the wizard does. When this is finished, your screen should look like Figure 3-6.

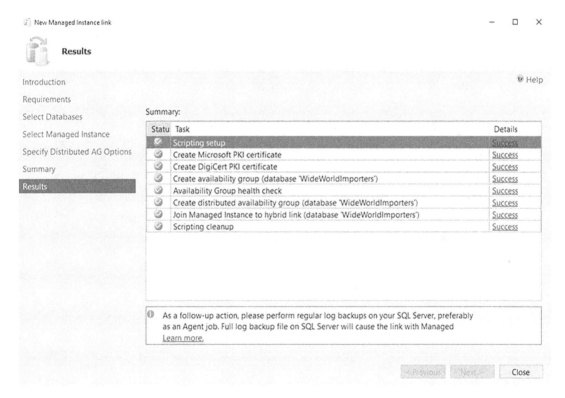

Figure 3-6. *A successful creation of a link to Azure SQL Managed Instance*

9. Navigate in the Azure portal to your Managed Instance. You
    should see your database is replicated in Azure and has a status of
    Online as seen in Figure 3-7.

Figure 3-7. *A replicated database in Managed Instance*

Note the tag at the top of this figure shows the Managed Instance
is compatible with SQL Server 2022.

10. Use Object Explorer in SSMS connected to SQL Server to see the
     status of the database as Synchronized (you will need to refresh to
     see this) and a detailed list of the AG and DAG created for the link.
     Your screen should look similar to Figure 3-8.

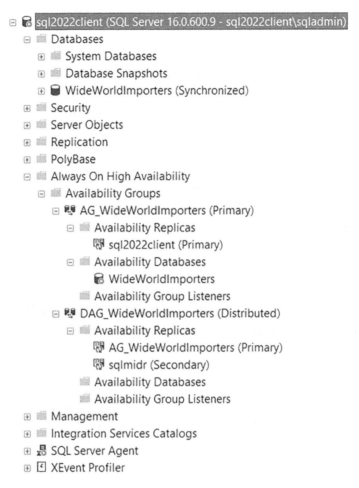

Figure 3-8. *Database, AG, and DAG status after link creation*

Since we are using the built-in capabilities of SQL Server
for an AG and DAG, you can also use a rich set of Dynamic
Management Views (DMVs) to inspect the configuration. Check
out these examples at `https://docs.microsoft.com/sql/`
`database-engine/availability-groups/windows/distributed-`
`availability-groups#monitor-health`.

11. Execute the script **checkstatus.sql** against the SQL Server 2022
instance, which uses the following T-SQL statements:

```
SELECT @@SERVERNAME;
GO
```

```
SELECT DATABASEPROPERTYEX('WideWorldImporters', 'Updateability');
GO
SELECT DATABASEPROPERTYEX('WideWorldImporters', 'Version');
GO
```

You will see the status of READ_WRITE and a database version that is the locked-in version for SQL Server 2022.

12. Connect with SSMS to the Managed Instance you have deployed. Execute the **checkstatus.sql** script. You should see the Updateability is READ_ONLY, and the database version should match SQL Server 2022.

See Changes Replicated

1. Execute the script **ddl.sql** against the SQL Server 2022 database to create two new tables. This script uses the following T-SQL statements:

```
USE [WideWorldImporters];
GO
DROP TABLE IF EXISTS [Warehouse].[Vehicles];
GO
CREATE TABLE [Warehouse].[Vehicles](
        [Vehicle_Registration] [nchar](20) NOT NULL,
        [Vehicle_Type] [nchar](20) NULL,
        [Vehicle_State] [nvarchar](100) NULL,
        [Vehicle_City] [nvarchar](100) NULL,
        [Vehicle_Status] [nvarchar](10) NULL,
PRIMARY KEY CLUSTERED
(
        [Vehicle_Registration] ASC
)WITH (PAD_INDEX = OFF, STATISTICS_NORECOMPUTE = OFF, IGNORE_DUP_
KEY = OFF, ALLOW_ROW_LOCKS = ON, ALLOW_PAGE_LOCKS = ON, OPTIMIZE_
FOR_SEQUENTIAL_KEY = OFF) ON [USERDATA]
) ON [USERDATA];
GO
```

```
DROP TABLE IF EXISTS [Warehouse].[Vehicle_StockItems];
GO
CREATE TABLE [Warehouse].[Vehicle_StockItems](
     [Vehicle_Registration] [nchar](20) NOT NULL,
     [StockItemID] [int] NOT NULL,
 CONSTRAINT [PK_Vehicle_StockItems] PRIMARY KEY CLUSTERED
(
     [Vehicle_Registration] ASC,
     [StockItemID] ASC
)WITH (PAD_INDEX = OFF, STATISTICS_NORECOMPUTE = OFF, IGNORE_DUP_
KEY = OFF, ALLOW_ROW_LOCKS = ON, ALLOW_PAGE_LOCKS = ON, OPTIMIZE_
FOR_SEQUENTIAL_KEY = OFF) ON [USERDATA]
) ON [USERDATA];
GO
```

2. Execute the script **populatedata.sql** to add data to these tables.
    Note from the script that each vehicle will get one piece of cargo.

3. Execute the script **getcargocounts.sql** against both SQL Server
    and Managed Instance in SSMS. This script uses the following
    T-SQL statements:

```
USE WideWorldImporters;
GO
SELECT v.Vehicle_Registration, v.Vehicle_City, count(*) AS cargo
FROM Warehouse.Vehicles v
JOIN Warehouse.Vehicle_StockItems vs
ON v.Vehicle_Registration = vs.Vehicle_Registration
GROUP BY v.Vehicle_Registration, v.Vehicle_City;
GO
```

You should see the same results for both SQL Server and Managed
Instance.

Failover to Managed Instance

Now let's see the process to fail over to Managed Instance.

1. Using Object Explorer in SSMS, select **Failover database** using the same option as you did to replicate the database as seen in Figure 3-9.

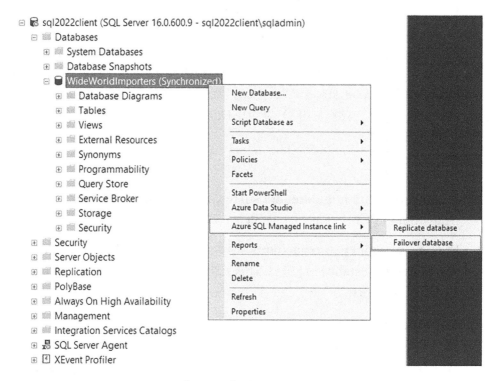

Figure 3-9. *Using SSMS to perform a failover*

2. Select Next, and you will be presented with a screen to **log in to Azure.** Choose your subscription for your Managed Instance deployment and select Next.

3. You have a choice for a ***planned or forced failover***. Select Planned manual failover and select the option you have stopped your workload (we don't have one running doing any writes). Your screen should look like Figure 3-10.

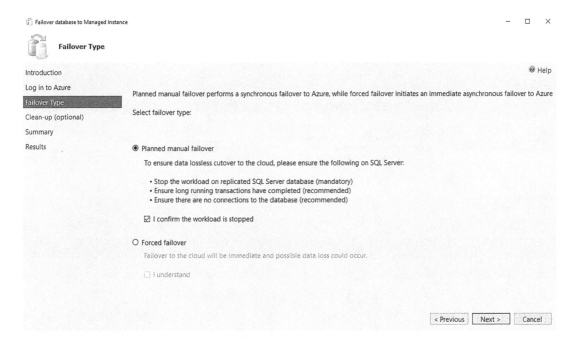

Figure 3-10. *Choosing a failover type*

Select **Next**.

4. You now have a choice to **clean up** the AG and/or DAG that was created earlier. You could choose to keep these and recreate the link later, but for purposes of this exercise, I'll check both options and select Next.

5. You are now on the final screen to complete the failover. Select Finish. This step changes the DAG to synchronize mode, checks that all log changes are synchronized by comparing LSN values on both systems, and then removes the link. When done, your screen should look like Figure 3-11.

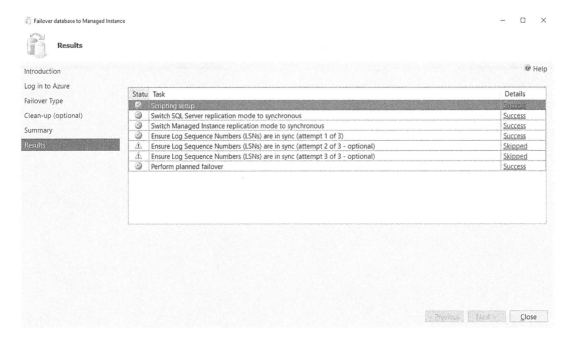

Figure 3-11. *A completed failover to Managed Instance*

6. Using SSMS execute the script **checkstatus.sql** again against Managed Instance to see the status is now READ_WRITE.

7. You can also see from SSMS on SQL Server the AG and DAG are removed.

In a real-world failover, you would now need to change your application to connect to Managed Instance and migrate any instance-level objects to Managed Instance like SQL Agent jobs, logins, etc.

Restoring a Database Back to SQL Server

As we have described in this chapter, this disaster recovery option is called offline because even though you can perform an online failover, your ability to fail back to SQL Server requires a database backup and restore. A full backup and restore could take some time, so your downtime is longer, hence offline.

The steps to restore a database from Managed Instance to SQL Server are the following:

1. Stop all writes to your workload for Azure SQL Managed Instance if you want the failback to include all changes to SQL Server.

2. Create a COPY_ONLY backup of your database from Azure SQL Managed Instance. Use the documentation to learn how to back up a database to Azure storage using SSMS connected to Managed Instance. (There are options for T-SQL as well if you want those. Start at the step `https://docs.microsoft.com/sql/relational-databases/tutorial-sql-server-backup-and-restore-to-azure-blob-storage-service#create-credential`.)

3. Restore the database from Azure storage connected to SQL Server using SSMS (there are also T-SQL options). Use the steps in the documentation starting at `https://docs.microsoft.com/sql/relational-databases/tutorial-sql-server-backup-and-restore-to-azure-blob-storage-service#restore-database`. You will need to choose a different database name on SQL Server if the original database for the link feature exists.

4. You will also need to change the application again to point to SQL Server instead of Managed Instance. In addition, you will need to migrate instance objects such as SQL Agent jobs.

5. You now have the option to recreate the link to Managed Instance to reestablish your disaster recovery site. Before you do this, you will need to drop the database linked before on Managed Instance.

Keep in Mind These Details

There are a few details to keep in mind about Azure SQL Managed Instance including the following:

-   Only one database is allowed for a created link. You can create multiple links on a SQL Server or multiple servers pointing to a single Managed Instance. Today a Managed Instance can have a maximum of 100 links. Also consider the storage required for your Managed Instance to support databases from your links.

- Any feature not supported by Azure SQL Managed Instance (e.g., filestream) is not supported with the link feature.

- In-Memory OLTP is not supported if the target Azure SQL Managed Instance uses the General Purpose service tier because this tier doesn't support In-Memory OLTP.

- Use best practices like taking regular transaction log backups, which is something you would do with any DAG setup.

- The performance impact to your workload on the primary SQL Server will be the same as if you had set up your own async-based DAG. Since we are using async, you should see a minimal impact to write performance.

- There is no listener concept for the link feature, so your application will need to be manually changed to point to Managed Instance after a failover.

- Instance-level objects such as SQL Agent jobs are not replicated. You will need to manually migrate these to Managed Instance after a failover.

For the latest updates on limits and restrictions, visit our documentation at `https://docs.microsoft.com//azure/azure-sql/managed-instance/managed-instance-link-feature-overview#limitations`.

The Future for the Link Feature for Azure SQL Managed Instance

At the time of the writing of this book, we only offered a one-way link for SQL Server 2016, SQL Server 2019, and SQL Server 2022. As you saw in this book, we also are releasing the ability to use Azure SQL Managed Instance as an offline DR site because you must manually restore a full backup to SQL Server 2022 to fail back.

There is never a guarantee for the future, but it is our intention to enhance the disaster recovery scenario with capabilities like online failback similar to how you can fail back with an availability group today with SQL Server. We would also like to explore possibilities like a synchronous DAG. I asked Dani Ljepava the vision of the team and why building the link feature to its fullest capabilities is important to Microsoft and our customers:

> *Azure SQL Managed Instance was launched as a service in November of 2018 with the aim to provide the best PAAS service that is the most compatible with SQL Server. We called the project internally at the time "cloud lifter" with the main idea that we wanted to enable customers just to lift and shift their workloads from SQL Server to a fully managed PAAS service. Since we've launched the service, our customers have asked us the following questions – I'm not yet ready to move to Azure, and I'd like to modernize in Azure, but without migrating. I want to be able to run analytics and read scale-out on Managed Instance, while still running on my SQL Server. When ready to migrate, customers asked how can I de-risk my migration to Azure? Can I easily revert back to SQL Server in case of any issues? My workload is critical, and I need the best possible minimum migration downtime. Some customers asked – I need to have a DR in the cloud between my SQL Server and Managed Instance. I'm required legally to have the ability to easily fall back to SQL Server from Azure and perform DR drills periodically. Now, if you find yourself asking one of these questions, we've built the MI link having with you in mind. The link is our extension of the "cloud lifter" promise through providing an ultimate hybrid flexibility to use Azure at your own terms, pace and time.*

Keep up with all the latest on the link feature for Azure SQL Managed Instance at `https://aka.ms/milink`.

Azure Synapse Link for SQL Server

Azure Synapse Analytics is a perfect solution for big data of all types. It is an analytics solution because it has the power and tools for applications that need to analyze data. However, the problem is: Where is the data to analyze? In many cases the data may exist in a SQL Server instance you want to analyze with Synapse. The challenge is to get the data you need from SQL Server into Synapse without having to rely on copying the data or ETL jobs. Anyone who wants to analyze data typically wants to do this in some type of *near-real timeframe.*

What Is Synapse Link for SQL Server?

Synapse Link for SQL Server is a feature of *both* SQL Server and Synapse to link data from SQL Server with Synapse in near-real time and in a seamless fashion. This involves you initially synchronizing data, and then Synapse Link will automatically capture changes in an incremental fashion allowing you to query the data in Synapse near-real time.

SQL Server has for many years included technology built into the SQL Server engine to capture changes called *change feed* including replication and change data capture (CDC). These features are built inside the SQL Server engine to *harvest* changes from the transaction log and *feed* them to another target. Transactions are not truncated from the transaction log until the target has committed the changes. Synapse Link uses some of the core capabilities of change feed to accomplish the same goal except the target will be Azure Synapse.

Azure Synapse Link is available for both SQL Server 2022 and Azure SQL Database. The Azure extension for SQL Server is not required to use this feature in SQL Server 2022. Synapse also offers link services for Cosmos DB and Dataverse. One big difference for Synapse Link for SQL is that the data is synchronized and fed into SQL pools. Keep up to date with the latest information on Synapse Link for SQL Server at `https://aka.ms/synapselinksqlserver`.

How Does Synapse Link Work?

There are several components that make Synapse Link work. Let's review Figure 3-12 to understand these components and data flow.

Azure Synapse Link for SQL Server

How it works

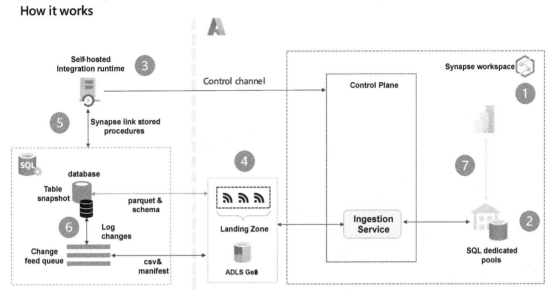

Figure 3-12. *The Synapse Link for SQL Server architecture*

Let's use the numbers in the figure to see the sequence of how components are created and data flows. Don't worry about the details of how to create these components. You will see these details in the next section with an exercise.

1. First, you will need an Azure Synapse workspace.

2. Now create a SQL dedicated pool to host the data.

3. Create a **linked service for SQL Server 2022**. This establishes a control plane within Synapse and the ability to link together SQL Server and Synapse. You will install the self-hosted integration runtime (SHIR) on the computer or network of SQL Server. This linked service is dedicated to this specific SQL Server and database. If you want to set up a link for a different database on the same SQL instance, you would need a unique linked service, which requires a different SHIR. You can only have one SHIR program running at a time on a VM or computer. But since SHIR can connect to SQL Server remotely, you could run a different

copy of the program on a different VM or computer in your network. SHIR only works on Windows, so if you use Synapse Link for SQL Server on Linux, you will need to install SHIR on a Windows VM or computer on your network that can connect to your SQL Server on Linux.

4. Create an Azure storage account called a **landing zone** and a linked service for the landing zone. This landing zone account will be dedicated to this SQL Server and database. The landing zone will store files extracted from SQL Server that Synapse understands how to ingest into SQL pool tables.

5. Create a **linked connection** based on the linked service for SQL. Choose your tables to link from the source database on SQL Server. Start the connection. SHIR executes system stored procedures in SQL Server 2022 to start the process. Snapshots of tables are captured and submitted to the landing zone via HTTPS in the form of parquet and schema files. The ingestion service in the control plane takes the landing zone files and creates tables in the SQL pools. Data is inserted into the pool tables based on the initial snapshot. Linked connections target specific tables within a database. You can have multiple linked connections for the same database, but a table can only be in one linked connection.

6. Any modifications to tables in SQL Server are recorded in the transaction log. Change feed tasks within SQL Server harvest log changes and put them in a queue, which are memory structures within SQL Server. Internal tasks publish changes from the queue to the landing zone in the form of CSV and manifest files via HTTPS. We try to keep the amount of memory required as small as possible, balanced with the need to have good throughput capturing log changes and publishing to the landing zone. SQL Server uses a pool of worker threads for the tasks to capture log changes and publish these changes to the landing zone. The worker pool is a dedicated pool for Synapse Link change feed capture and works across all databases enabled for Synapse

Link for the instance. The ingestion service in Synapse takes the landing zone files and executes modifications to affected tables in the SQL pools.

7. Optionally create a Power BI report to visualize your data directly on SQL pool tables.

Now that you understand the components and flow, let's try an exercise to see Synapse Link come alive.

Try Out Synapse Link for SQL Server

In order to complete this exercise successfully, you need to carefully follow the prerequisites, steps to set up the exercise, and each exercise step.

I want to thank Chuck Heinzelman, Mine Token, Milos Vucic, and Tim Chen for helping me understand how Synapse Link works and creating all the resources for this exercise.

Prerequisites

- A virtual machine or computer with at least two CPUs and 8Gb RAM. For my tests I used an E4ds_v5 Azure VM that comes with four vCPUs and 32Gb RAM. Your virtual machine or computer needs to be capable of connecting to Azure over the Internet or run as an Azure Virtual Machine.

- SQL Server 2022 Evaluation Edition. You only need the database engine feature for this exercise.

- An Azure subscription with permissions to create an Azure Synapse workspace and Azure Data Lake Storage Gen2 account (Synapse uses its own storage account, but you need a separate one for the landing zone).

- SQL Server Management Studio (SSMS). The latest 18.x build or 19.x build will work.

- Download the WideWorldImporters **Standard** sample backup from `https://github.com/Microsoft/sql-server-samples/releases/download/wide-world-importers-v1.0/WideWorldImporters-Standard.bak` to the machine where you will run SQL Server. The Standard backup is used because features like In-Memory OLTP are not supported with Synapse Link.

- A copy of the scripts from book samples from the **ch3_cloudconnected\synapselink** folder.

Set Up the Exercise

1. Create an Azure Synapse Analytics workspace. The following is a quick-start guide on how to create a workspace: `https://docs.microsoft.com/azure/synapse-analytics/get-started-create-workspace`.

   Here are important points to follow as you create the workspace:

   - The Data Lake Storage Gen2 account you use during the workspace is for Synapse. You will create another for the landing zone later in this exercise.

   - For network settings you must select Disable for Managed virtual network and check Allow connections from all IP addresses. If you are concerned about this requirement for security, you can set up firewall rules.

   - Although not required I like to organize my Azure resources into specific resource groups. For this exercise I created an Azure Virtual Machine running SQL Server 2022 in the same resource group as Synapse because I'll use the **Allow Azure services and resources to access this workspace** option to access Synapse instead of setting up a firewall rule.

   - For everything else I chose the defaults. Synapse Link should be supported in any region where Synapse is supported, but check `https://docs.microsoft.com/azure/synapse-analytics/synapse-link/connect-synapse-link-sql-server-2022#prerequisites` for the latest updates.

In my experience Synapse workspaces don't take longer than 5–10 minutes to deploy.

Figure 3-13 shows a portal view of my Synapse workspace after it was created.

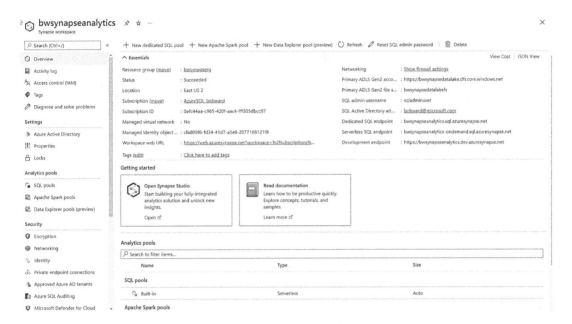

Figure 3-13. *An Azure Synapse Analytics workspace*

2. Next, we need a place to host our data, which for Synapse Link is called a **dedicated SQL pool**. Think of this as a database within Synapse to host SQL-based tables from the source SQL Server. There are a few ways to do this. One simple way is from the Azure portal. Go to the resource menu on the left side of the screen on your workspace and select **SQL pools** under Analytics pools. Select + **New**. For this exercise put in a pool name (I chose **wwisqlpool**) and leave the defaults. For a production system, you may want to choose different options here. See the section later in this chapter titled "**More Details About Synapse Link**" for more details.

3. Create a new Azure storage account to be used for Azure Data Lake Storage Gen2, which is the ***landing zone***. I used the instructions at this documentation page to create my storage account: `https://docs.microsoft.com/azure/storage/blobs/create-data-lake-storage-account`. For this exercise I used the same region and resource group as my Synapse workspace (not required), and I chose the Standard option for Performance (for production workloads, you may want Premium). For everything else I chose the defaults except on the Advanced blade, you ***MUST choose Enabled for Hierarchical namespace***. Figure 3-14 shows my storage account after creation.

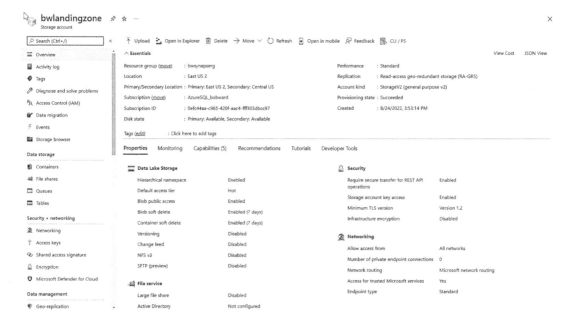

Figure 3-14. *The Azure storage landing zone account*

4. A storage account is not enough to store files from SQL Server. You need a folder or ***container***. On the resource menu for the storage account on the left-hand side of the screen under **Data storage**, select **Containers**. Then on the new screen, select **+ Container**. Type in the name of your choice (you will need it later). I called mine **wwidata**. Leave the default and select Create. This should only take seconds.

5. You now need to grant access for the Synapse workspace to the landing zone storage account. Follow steps 1 and 2 at this link in the documentation to assign the Managed Identity access to the landing zone: `https://docs.microsoft.com/azure/ synapse-analytics/synapse-link/connect-synapse-link-sql- server-2022#create-linked-service-to-connect-to-your- landing-zone-on-azure-data-lake-storage-gen2`.

My role assignment looked like Figure 3-15.

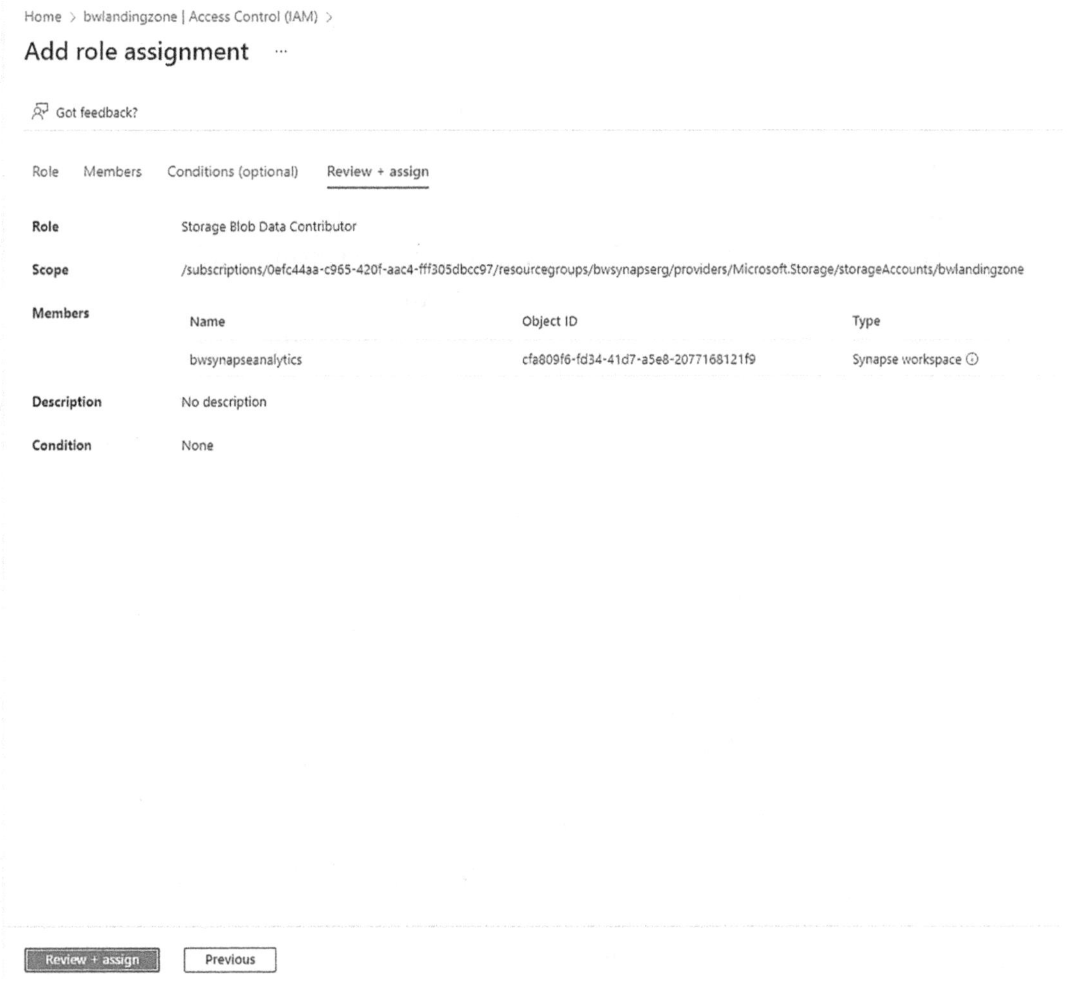

Home > bwlandingzone | Access Control (IAM) >

Add role assignment   ⋯

⟋ Got feedback?

Role   Members   Conditions (optional)   **Review + assign**

Role   Storage Blob Data Contributor

Scope   /subscriptions/0efc44aa-c965-420f-aac4-fff305dbcc97/resourcegroups/bwsynapserg/providers/Microsoft.Storage/storageAccounts/bwlandingzone

Members

Name	Object ID	Type
bwsynapseanalytics	cfa809f6-fd34-41d7-a5e8-2077168121f9	Synapse workspace ⓘ

Description   No description

Condition   None

Review + assign   Previous

Figure 3-15. *Assign the Synapse workspace access to the landing zone container*

That was a lot of steps to set things up, but take your time to make sure you are ready to work with Synapse Link.

Synchronizing Data with Synapse Link

I have provided a series of detailed steps to set up and do your initial sync of data from SQL Server to Synapse. It will seem a bit daunting as you go through all of these steps. But once you get this set up and initialized, it "just works" for changes.

1. Since we will use the WideWorldImporters backup, you need to restore this to your SQL Server instance. You can use the **restorewwi_std.sql** script logged in as a sysadmin account. You may need to edit the file path for the backup and data/log files. This script executes the following T-SQL statements:

```
USE master;
GO
RESTORE DATABASE WideWorldImporters FROM DISK = 'c:\sql_sample_
databases\WideWorldImporters-Standard.bak' WITH
MOVE 'WWI_Primary' TO 'f:\data\WideWorldImporters.mdf',
MOVE 'WWI_UserData' TO 'f:\data\WideWorldImporters_UserData.ndf',
MOVE 'WWI_Log' TO 'g:\log\WideWorldImporters.ldf',
stats=5;
GO
```

2. Let's add two new tables to the database to track vehicle cargo. Execute the script **extendwwitables.sql** against SQL Server, which executes the following T-SQL statements:

```
USE [WideWorldImporters];
GO
DROP TABLE IF EXISTS [Warehouse].[Vehicles];
GO
CREATE TABLE [Warehouse].[Vehicles](
       [Vehicle_Registration] [nchar](20) NOT NULL,
       [Vehicle_Type] [nchar](20) NULL,
       [Vehicle_State] [nvarchar](100) NULL,
       [Vehicle_City] [nvarchar](100) NULL,
       [Vehicle_Status] [nvarchar](10) NULL,
PRIMARY KEY CLUSTERED
```

```
(
        [Vehicle_Registration] ASC
));
GO

DROP TABLE IF EXISTS [Warehouse].[Vehicle_StockItems];
GO
CREATE TABLE [Warehouse].[Vehicle_StockItems](
        [Vehicle_Registration] [nchar](20) NOT NULL,
        [StockItemID] [int] NOT NULL
PRIMARY KEY CLUSTERED
(
        [Vehicle_Registration] ASC,
        [StockItemID] ASC
));
GO
```

3. Populate data into these tables by executing the script
   populatedata.sql against SQL Server.

4. The WideWorldImporters database includes some features and
   data types that are not supported by Synapse Link. Therefore,
   execute the script **alterwwi.sql** against SQL Server to remove
   some of these features (e.g., temporal tables) and columns with
   unsupported data types.

Note   It is possible that some of these data types can be supported by the time
SQL Server 2022 is released, but to be safe for the purposes of this exercise, I
removed all features or types that could cause an issue.

---

5. Both Synapse and SQL Server 2022 need a master key for encryption purposes and schemas built for Synapse.

    a. Connect to SQL Server 2022 and run the script **createmasterkey. sql**, which executes the following T-SQL statements:

    ```
    USE [WideWorldImporters];
    GO
    CREATE MASTER KEY ENCRYPTION BY PASSWORD = 'Strongpassw0rd!';
    GO
    ```

    b. The Synapse pool also needs a master key, but you don't need a password. Let's get introduced to Synapse Studio (because you will need it throughout this exercise) to do this. In the Azure portal for the Synapse workspace, in the middle of the page, click Open for the box that says **Open Synapse Studio** as in Figure 3-16.

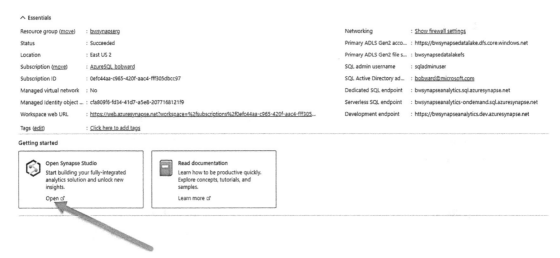

Figure 3-16. *Launching Synapse Studio*

Once you open Synapse Studio, click the icon on the left-hand menu for Data, expand the wwipool database, and select New SQL Script. Then type in CREATE MASTER KEY; and hit Run as seen in Figure 3-17.

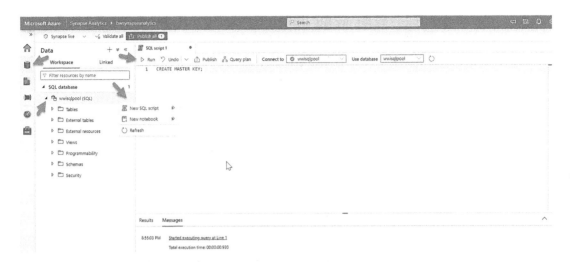

Figure 3-17. *Creating the master key in the SQL dedicated pool*

    c. Synapse Link does not automatically create schemas
when synchronizing tables from SQL Server. Since
WideWorldImporters uses schemas, we need to create these first
in Synapse. Use the same window you created the master key in
Synapse Studio to run these SQL statements after clearing out the
CREATE MASTER KEY statement:

```
CREATE SCHEMA Application;
GO
CREATE SCHEMA Purchasing;
GO
CREATE SCHEMA Sales;
GO
CREATE SCHEMA Warehouse;
GO
CREATE SCHEMA Website;
GO
```

6. We are now ready to create the **linked service to SQL Server 2022**
    from Synapse Studio. In Synapse Studio click the Manage icon
    on the left-hand menu (the last one), Linked services, and then +
    New as seen in Figure 3-18.

Figure 3-18. *Creating a new linked service for SQL Server 2022*

Type in sql in the search window and select SQL Server and hit
Continue as seen in Figure 3-19.

New linked service

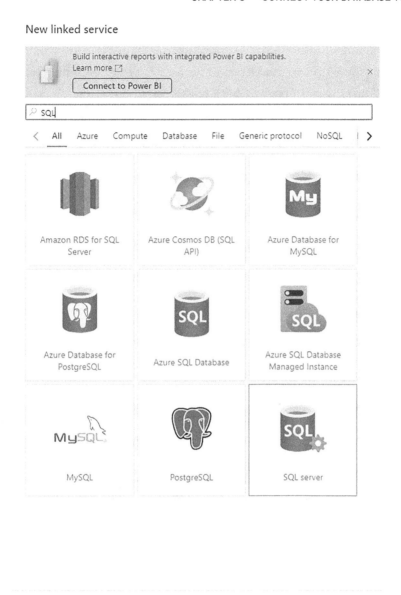

Figure 3-19. Choosing SQL Server as a linked service

You are presented with a screen to fill out several pieces of information. Stay with me on these steps because you are going to fill out some information here, move over to your machine hosting SQL Server, and then come back to this page.

Type in the name of the linked service and then in the **Connect via integration runtime** field, select the "down" arrow and then + **New** as seen in Figure 3-20.

Figure 3-20. *Selecting an integration runtime for Synapse Link for SQL*

Select **Self-Hosted** and click **Continue.**

Leave the Default name field and click Create. You will now be presented with a screen like Figure 3-21.

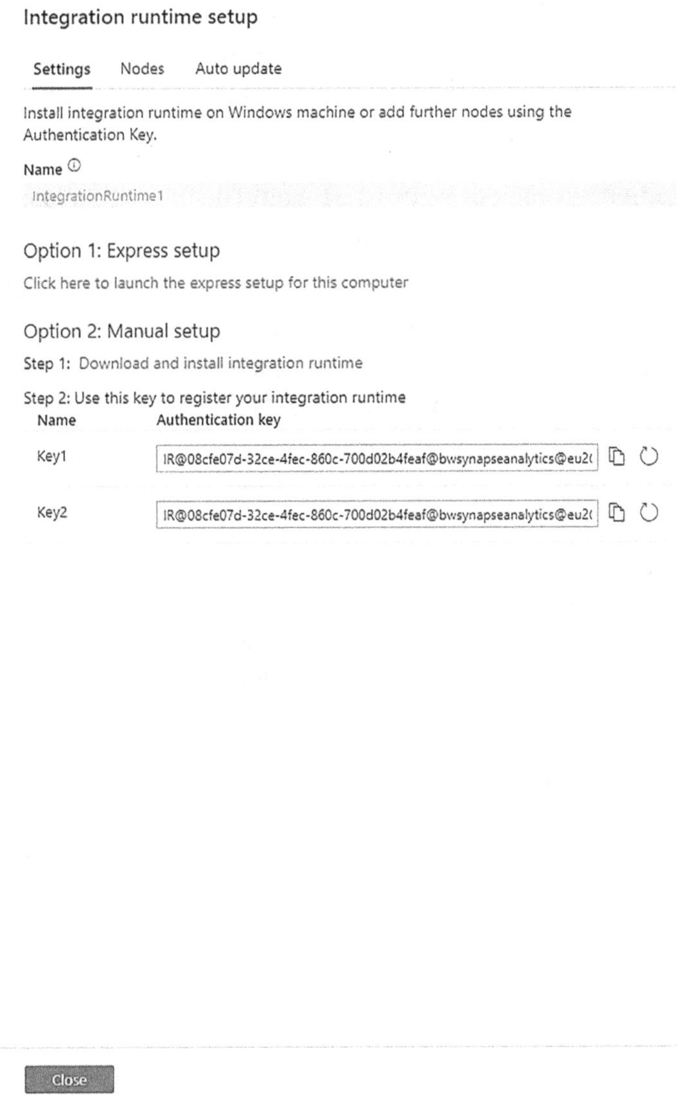

Integration runtime setup

Settings   Nodes   Auto update

Install integration runtime on Windows machine or add further nodes using the
Authentication Key.

Name ⓘ

IntegrationRuntime1

Option 1: Express setup

Click here to launch the express setup for this computer

Option 2: Manual setup

Step 1: Download and install integration runtime

Step 2: Use this key to register your integration runtime

Name	Authentication key		
Key1	IR@08cfe07d-32ce-4fec-860c-700d02b4feaf@bwsynapseanalytics@eu2(	🗐	⟳
Key2	IR@08cfe07d-32ce-4fec-860c-700d02b4feaf@bwsynapseanalytics@eu2(	🗐	⟳

Close

Figure 3-21. *Instructions to install the self-hosted integration runtime*

The integration runtime code is now installed in the control plane
for the Synapse workspace. You need to now install the self-hosted
integration runtime (SHIR) software on your machine or VM
where SQL Server is installed.

Note   SHIR can be installed anywhere on the network where it can connect to and discover SQL Server. For this exercise we will just install it locally.

Option 1 in the screen in Figure 3-21 would be the right choice if you launched Synapse Studio from the computer or VM where you planned to install SHIR. I used the portal from my own laptop when I did this exercise, so I chose Option 2 to install manually. When you click Option 2, a new browser tab will be launched to download the software. Keep the Synapse Studio browser tab open. You will need the **Authentication Key** on that screen, and when you are done installing SHIR, we need to come back to this place to finish installing the linked service.

After I clicked Download on the new web page, I chose the latest MSI version and then copied this downloaded .MSI file into my virtual machine in Azure. This file is ~1Gb in size, so it may take a few minutes to copy into your VM or machine.

While you are copying this file, launch the Standard SQL XEvent Profiler from SSMS for SQL Server (click Launch Session) as seen in Figure 3-22.

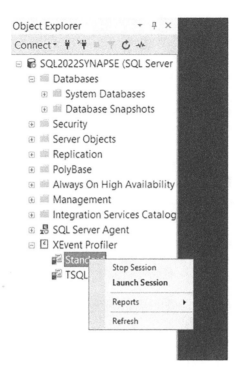

Figure 3-22. *Launching the Standard XEvent Profiler session*

This will allow you to trace all SQL traffic coming into the server. We will use this to see what type of SQL procedures SHIR sends to SQL Server 2022 later in this exercise.

Once downloaded, run the MSI file, which installs SHIR. Use all the defaults for the installation. When you finish the installation, you will be presented with a screen to enter in an Authentication Key. In Synapse Studio where you initiated the download of SHIR, copy the value for Authentication Key from either key1 or key2 and paste this into the SHIR screen, and click **Register**. Then click **Finish**. If everything was successful, your SHIR screen should look like Figure 3-23.

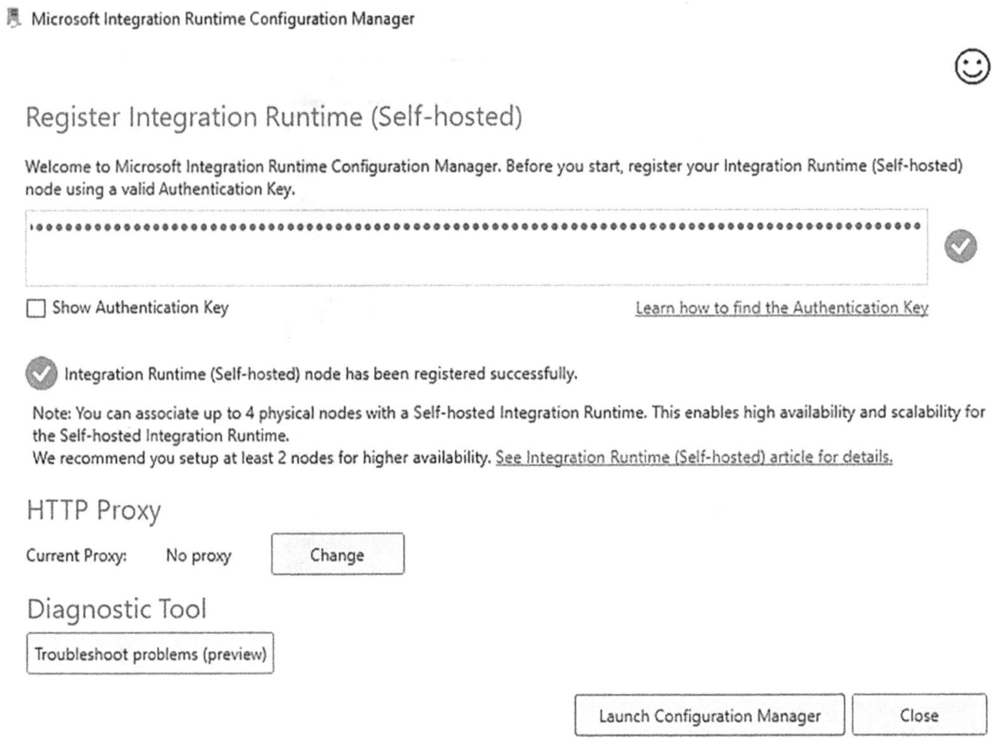

Microsoft Integration Runtime Configuration Manager

☺

Register Integration Runtime (Self-hosted)

Welcome to Microsoft Integration Runtime Configuration Manager. Before you start, register your Integration Runtime (Self-hosted) node using a valid Authentication Key.

| •• | ✔ |

☐ Show Authentication Key   Learn how to find the Authentication Key

✔ Integration Runtime (Self-hosted) node has been registered successfully.

Note: You can associate up to 4 physical nodes with a Self-hosted Integration Runtime. This enables high availability and scalability for the Self-hosted Integration Runtime.
We recommend you setup at least 2 nodes for higher availability. See Integration Runtime (Self-hosted) article for details.

HTTP Proxy

Current Proxy: No proxy | Change |

Diagnostic Tool

| Troubleshoot problems (preview) |

| Launch Configuration Manager | | Close |

Figure 3-23. *SHIR successfully registered*

Click **Close**.

On Windows Server, from the Start Menu launch the Microsoft Integration Runtime program to verify the connection to Synapse. Your screen should look like Figure 3-24.

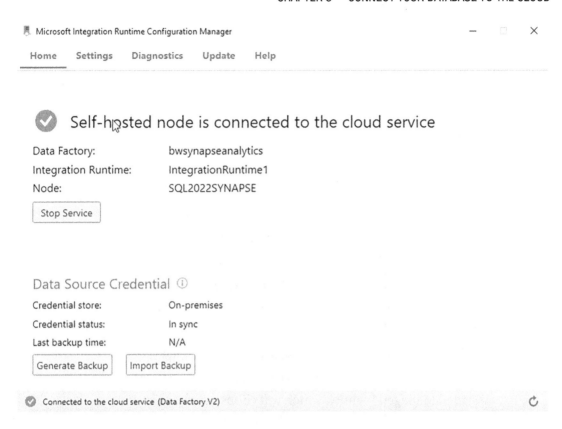

Figure 3-24. *SHIR successfully connected to Synapse*

SHIR runs as a service, so you can close out this window.

Go back to Synapse Studio and click **Close** on the integration runtime setup screen.

Don't worry about an error you might see on Connect via integration runtime. Just click the refresh icon, and all should be "green."

Now fill in the server name and database name (WideWorldImporters for this exercise). Use SQL authentication and fill in the SQL login and password you created as a sysadmin for SQL Server. First, click Test connection at the bottom right of the screen to verify the connection will work. Then if successful, click Create.

You will be presented with a screen in Synapse Studio that looks like Figure 3-25.

Figure 3-25. *A successful linked service creation for SQL Server*

7. Now we need to create another **linked service for the landing zone**. On the Linked services page, select + **New** and choose **Azure Data Lake Storage Gen2**.

Give the linked service a name. Leave Connect via integration runtime to the default. Choose Authentication type as System-Assigned Managed Identity, which will choose your Synapse workspace Managed Identity, which was automatically created when you created the workspace. This was the Managed Identity you gave access to the landing zone earlier.

Choose your Azure subscription and the storage account name for the landing zone you created. Select Test connection at the bottom of the screen. If all goes well, your screen should look like Figure 3-26.

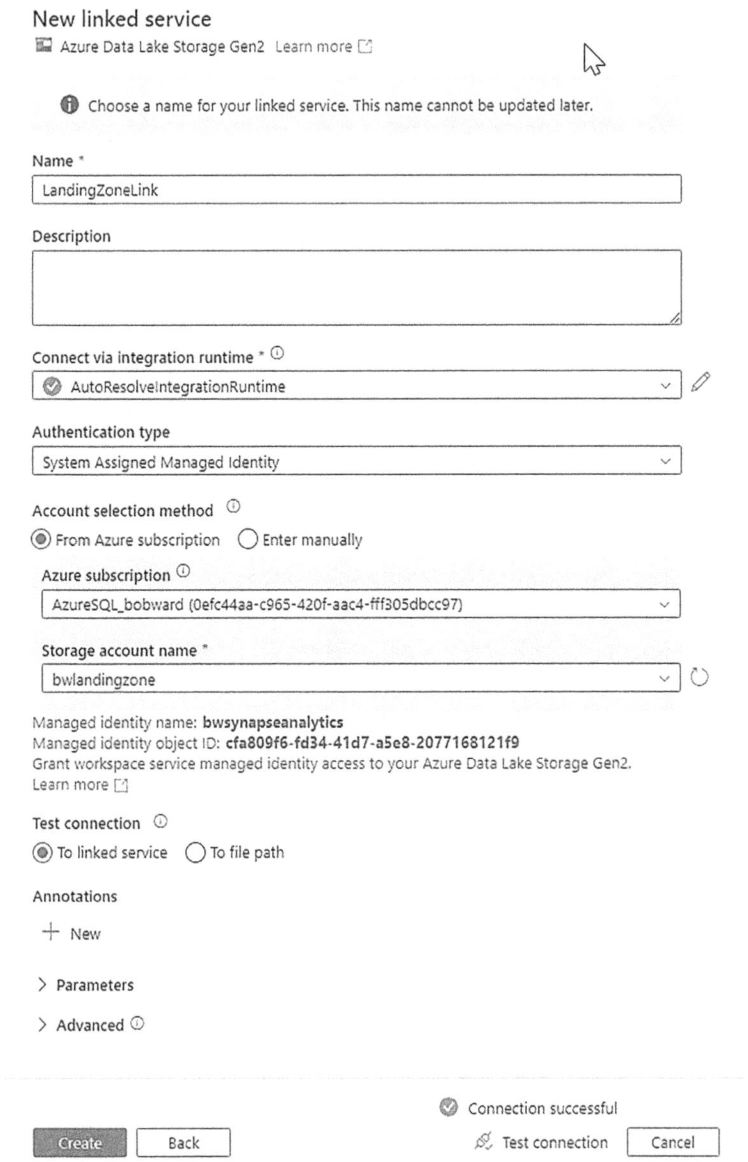

New linked service

Azure Data Lake Storage Gen2 Learn more ⬈

ⓘ Choose a name for your linked service. This name cannot be updated later.

Name *

```
LandingZoneLink
```

Description

```

```

Connect via integration runtime * ⓘ

```
✓ AutoResolveIntegrationRuntime                              ⌄
```
✎

Authentication type

```
System Assigned Managed Identity                             ⌄
```

Account selection method ⓘ

◉ From Azure subscription   ◯ Enter manually

Azure subscription ⓘ

```
AzureSQL_bobward (0efc44aa-c965-420f-aac4-fff305dbcc97)      ⌄
```

Storage account name *

```
bwlandingzone                                               ⌄
```
↻

Managed identity name: **bwsynapseanalytics**
Managed identity object ID: **cfa809f6-fd34-41d7-a5e8-2077168121f9**
Grant workspace service managed identity access to your Azure Data Lake Storage Gen2.
Learn more ⬈

Test connection ⓘ

◉ To linked service   ◯ To file path

Annotations

+ New

> Parameters

> Advanced ⓘ

✓ Connection successful

| Create | Back | ✎ Test connection | Cancel |

Figure 3-26. *Setting up the landing zone link*

Click **Create** to create the new link.

Now Click the **Publish all** option at the top of the screen like in Figure 3-27.

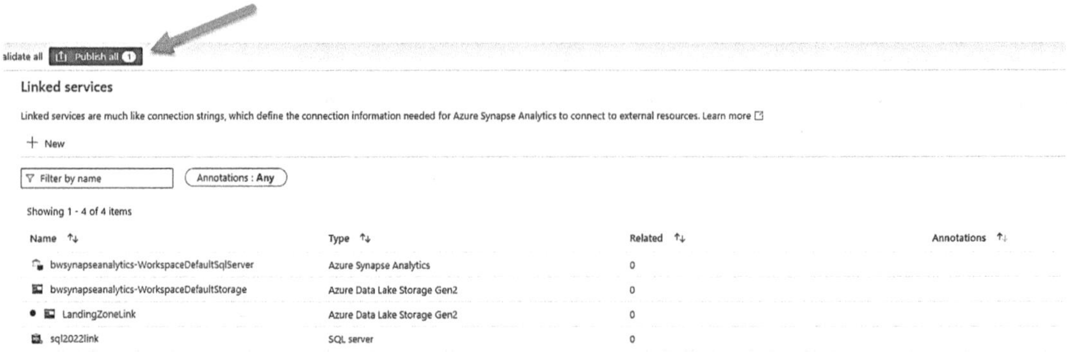

Figure 3-27. *Publishing the linked service to the landing zone*

Click **Publish**, and you will be brought back to the list of linked services. You should now see linked services for the landing zone and SQL Server (there are two other linked services that are installed by default for Synapse).

8. Now that we have linked services in place, it is time to sync data from SQL Server to Synapse by creating a **linked connection** based on linked services. Choose all the tables. In Synapse Studio click the **Integrate** icon on the left side of the screen and then click + like Figure 3-28.

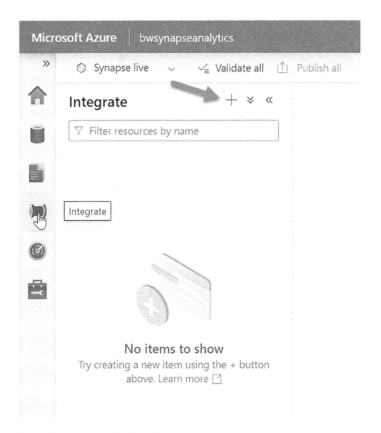

Figure 3-28. *Creating a new linked connection*

Select **Linked connection**. You will be presented with a screen to create a new linked connection. Select SQL Server as the source type and then select the linked service you created earlier for SQL Server. Your screen should refresh with a list of tables from WideWorldImporters like in Figure 3-29.

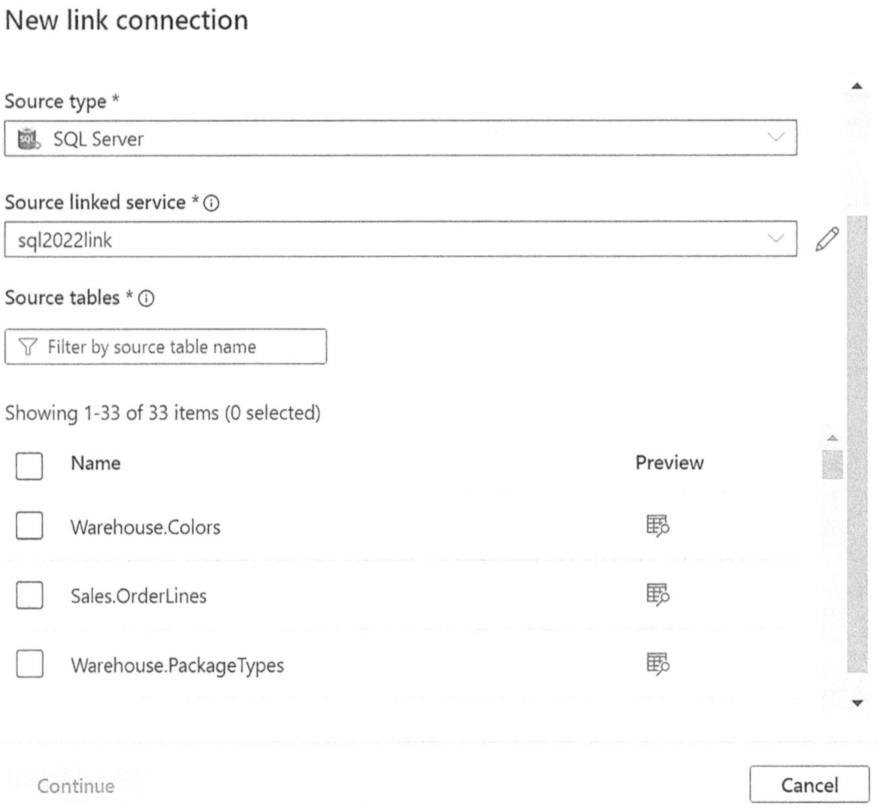

New link connection

Source type *

| 🗔 SQL Server | ⌄ |

Source linked service * ⓘ

| sql2022link | ⌄ | ✎ |

Source tables * ⓘ

| ▽ Filter by source table name |

Showing 1-33 of 33 items (0 selected)

☐	Name	Preview
☐	Warehouse.Colors	🗒
☐	Sales.OrderLines	🗒
☐	Warehouse.PackageTypes	🗒

Continue   Cancel

Figure 3-29. *Setting up a new linked connection*

You can browse a possible list of tables and even preview the
columns and data. I want all tables to be linked, so click the
checkbox next to Name (which selects all tables) and click
Continue.

For the next screen, choose the SQL dedicated pool you created
earlier. Mine was called wwisqlpool. Click **Continue**. You will now
be presented with a screen to complete the process to create the
linked connection.

Give the linked connection a name. Use the default core count
and continuous mode. You will learn more about when to make
different choices for these options in the section later in this
chapter titled "**More Details About Synapse Link**." Now select
the linked service you created for the landing zone. Type in the

container name you created earlier for the Landing zone folder path. Then select + **Generate token** (and use the defaults on the new screen). You screen should now look like Figure 3-30.

New link connection

Connection settings
Provide a name and select compute settings for the link connection.

Link connection name *

> sql2022linkconnection

Core count * ⓘ

> 2 (+ 2 Driver cores)   ∨

Mode

◉ Continuous   ◯ Batch

Landing zone linked service * ⓘ

> LandingZoneLink   ∨   ✎

Landing zone folder path * ⓘ

> wwidata   ▭

Landing zone SAS token * ⓘ

> ●●●...   👁

+ Generate token

This PREVIEW feature is licensed to you as part of your Azure subscription. By clicking "OK" you agree to the Preview Terms and Privacy Statement.

| OK | Back | | Cancel |

Figure 3-30. *Completing the linked connection*

Hit OK. You will now be on a new screen to show all the details of the linked connection. You can browse this information. For now select Publish all and then Publish. Then click **Start**. Your screen will show **Starting the link connection. This may take a few minutes**. For me a "few minutes" was about 10 minutes.

9. While this is still starting, you can go back to SSMS and view
    your XEvent Profiler session. Look for events from the **client_
    app_name** field called **AzureDataMovement**. These are queries
    from SHIR.

    In these events you will see batches that use procedures and
    T-SQL like

    • sys.sp_change_feed_enable_db. The sys.databases.is_change_
      feed_enabled column is now set to 1 for the database.

    • A database-scoped credential created for the landing zone
      storage account.

    • sys.sp_change_feed_create_table_group, which creates a *table
      group* that points to the Synapse workspace and landing zone.
      A table group is created for each linked connection for the
      database.

    • sys.sp_change_feed_enable_table. You will see an execution of
      sys.sp_change_feed_enable_table for each table in the database
      because we picked all of them in the linked connection.

    • Queries against system catalog views to get the schema of each
      table including columns and data types.

Note   At the time of the writing of this book, these procedures and T-SQL are
not documented or supported. Synapse Link must be configured through Synapse
Studio, which communicates with SHIR.

---

10. Use Synapse Studio to monitor the linked connection as seen in
    Figure 3-31.

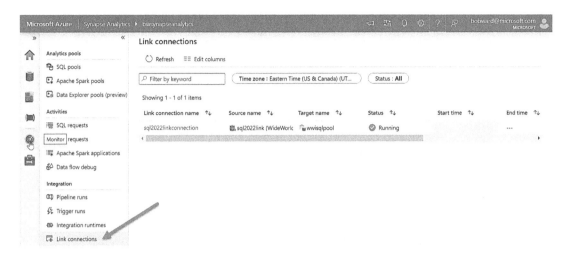

Figure 3-31. *Monitoring the linked connection for SQL Server*

Click the linked connection name to drill in for more details as seen in Figure 3-32.

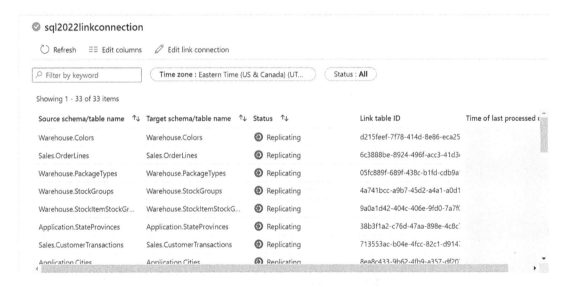

Figure 3-32. *Monitoring the status of linked tables*

The status of Replicating means the initial snapshots of the tables are synchronized to SQL pool tables.

11. Now let's see the tables in the SQL pool by using Synapse Studio like in Figure 3-33.

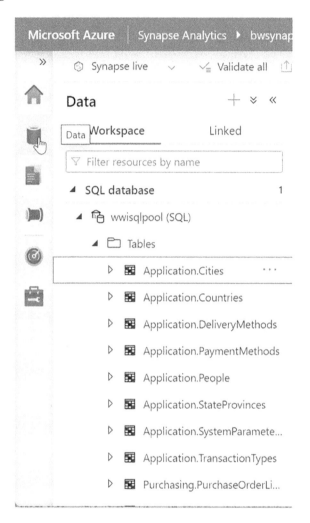

Figure 3-33. *List of tables in the SQL pool*

12. Now use Synapse Studio as you did earlier to run queries. Paste in the following T-SQL (which is found in the script **getcargocounts. sql**) to run a query to look at cargo counts:

```
SELECT v.Vehicle_Registration, v.Vehicle_City, count(*) AS cargo
FROM Warehouse.Vehicles v
JOIN Warehouse.Vehicle_StockItems vs
```

```
ON v.Vehicle_Registration = vs.Vehicle_Registration
GROUP BY v.Vehicle_Registration, v.Vehicle_City;
GO
```

The results should look like Figure 3-34, which matches the initial
population of data in these tables.

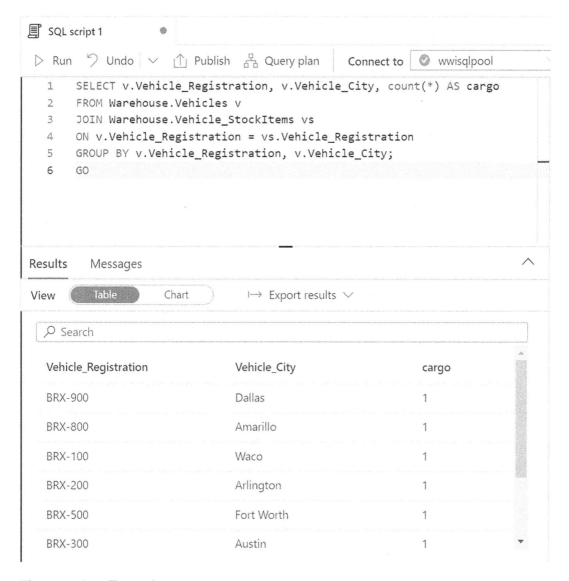

Figure 3-34. *Executing a query to get cargo counts*

13. We don't support copying or modifying files in the landing zone, but it is worth taking a look at files in the container for learning purposes. If you got to your container in the landing zone account and drill into the container, your results will look similar to Figure 3-35.

Figure 3-35. *The table group in the landing zone*

The GUID value of the folder matches the table group ID created and stored in the system table **changefeed.change_feed_table_ groups** in the WideWorldImporters database.

When you drill into this folder, you will see another folder called Tables. Drill into that, and you will see a series of more folders. Each of these represents a table. The name is the table_id stored in the **changefeed.change_feed_tables** system table stored in the WideWorldImporters database. Drill into the first folder down until you find a parquet file like in Figure 3-36.

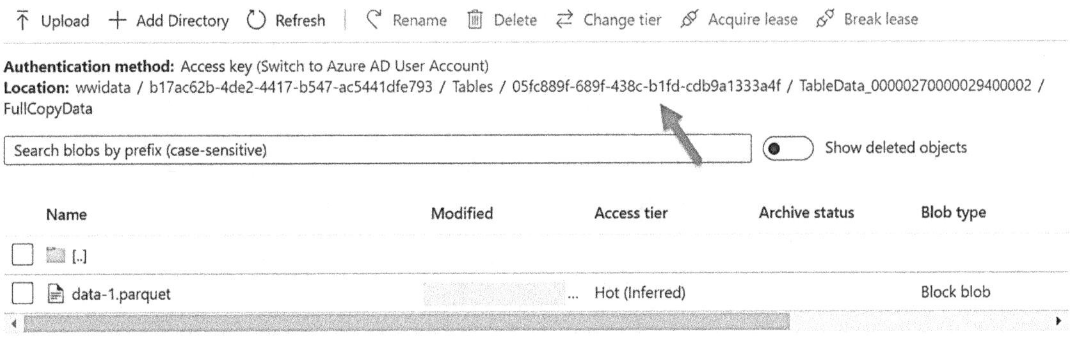

↑ Upload + Add Directory ↻ Refresh | ↰ Rename 🗑 Delete ⇄ Change tier ✐ Acquire lease ⤡ Break lease

Authentication method: Access key (Switch to Azure AD User Account)
Location: wwidata / b17ac62b-4de2-4417-b547-ac5441dfe793 / Tables / 05fc889f-689f-438c-b1fd-cdb9a1333a4f / TableData_00000270000029400002 /
FullCopyData

Search blobs by prefix (case-sensitive)				Show deleted objects

Name	Modified	Access tier	Archive status	Blob type
📁 [..]				
📄 data-1.parquet	...	Hot (Inferred)		Block blob

Figure 3-36. *Parquet file from initial seeding*

One level above the parquet file is a JSON file with schema information. You can find out which table this parquet file belongs to by using the table_id from the folder and running a query against your SQL Server 2022 database like in the script **getchangefeedtable.sql.** You will need to substitute the GUID for your table_id in the script before executing it:

```
USE [WideWorldImporters];
GO
SELECT object_name(object_id), *
FROM changefeed.change_feed_tables
WHERE table_id =  '05fc889f-689f-438c-b1fd-cdb9a1333a4f';
GO
```

changefeed.change_feed_tables also has some interesting statistics about the snapshot creation of the table.

Now that your tables have been initially synchronized into Synapse, let's see how changes are captured and automatically fed into Synapse.

Near-Real-Time Analytics with Changes from SQL Server

You have everything set up and synchronized. Now what happens? Well, the power of Synapse Link for SQL Server is that now that everything is set up, changes you make with SQL Server just show up in near-real time in Synapse.

1. Let's make changes and see them show up in Synapse. Add random amounts of cargo in SQL Server 2022 using the script **modifyvehicledata.sql** running against your SQL Server instance.

2. Look at the landing zone to see CSV files by looking at the container and drilling into the indexWorkingDir folder instead of Tables like in Figure 3-37.

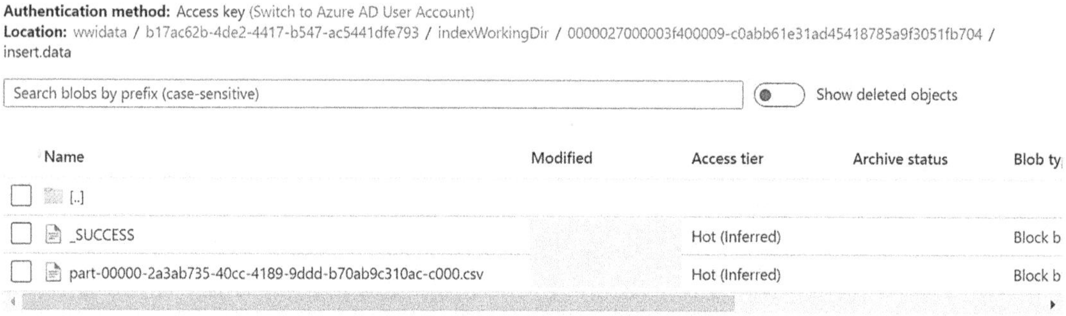

Authentication method: Access key (Switch to Azure AD User Account)
Location: wwidata / b17ac62b-4de2-4417-b547-ac5441dfe793 / indexWorkingDir / 0000027000003f400009-c0abb61e31ad45418785a9f3051fb704 /
insert.data

Search blobs by prefix (case-sensitive)				⬤ Show deleted objects

Name	Modified	Access tier	Archive status	Blob ty
☐ 📷 [..]				
☐ 📄 _SUCCESS		Hot (Inferred)		Block b
☐ 📄 part-00000-2a3ab735-40cc-4189-9ddd-b70ab9c310ac-c000.csv		Hot (Inferred)		Block b

Figure 3-37. Files in the landing zone for changes

3. Go back to Synapse Studio and run the same query from **getcargocounts.sql** to see the changes have been applied like in Figure 3-38.

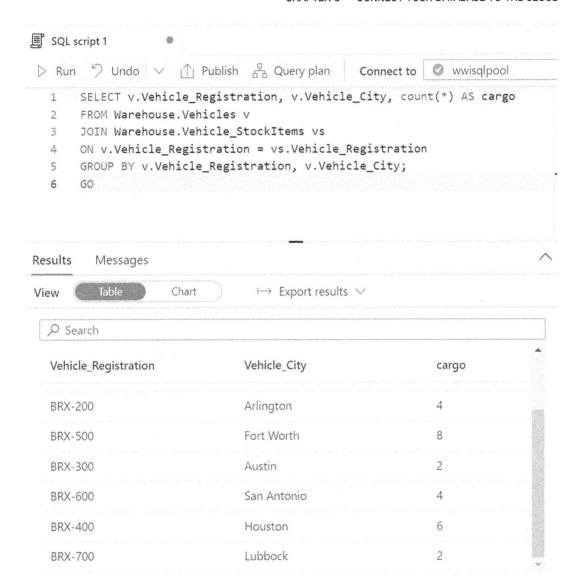

Figure 3-38. *Updated cargo counts in Synapse*

So all those steps to set up but only a few steps to see changes appear in Synapse. That is what Synapse Link provides, near-real-time changes from SQL Server automatically available in Synapse.

More Details About Synapse Link

There are a few details about Synapse Link I think you should know about. To get all the details and latest updates, be sure to consult the documentation at `https://aka.ms/ synapselinksqlserver`.

Configuration Choices

As you set Synapse Link, there are configuration choices you can make including the following:

- **SQL pool**

  When you create a SQL dedicated pool in Synapse, you can choose a performance level called a Data Warehouse Unit (DWU). We chose the default in our exercise, but for a production workload, you may want to choose another level. Your choice of DWU affects the performance of queries you run against tables in the SQL pool. But there is also a price for your performance decision. The DWU choice you make can also affect the ability to concurrently process tables for ingestion. You can change the DWU setting after you create the pool (scale up or down). You can learn more about DWU settings at `https://docs.microsoft.com/azure/synapse- analytics/sql-data-warehouse/what-is-a-data-warehouse- unit-dwu-cdwu#change-data-warehouse-units`.

- **Stopping and restarting the linked connection**

  If you stop the linked connection to SQL Server, all the Synapse Link system table data is removed, and the files in the landing zone container are deleted. All current data in SQL pool tables is not affected.

  If you start the linked connection again, we will take a new snapshot of all tables from SQL Server and place them in the landing zone. Here is an important warning. If you restart the linked connection and don't select the option Drop and recreate table on target, your linked connection will show errors because the target tables already exist. So you can either drop the tables yourself first in Synapse or use this option when starting the connection. This option can be found on the General tab under the window where you start the connection as seen in Figure 3-39.

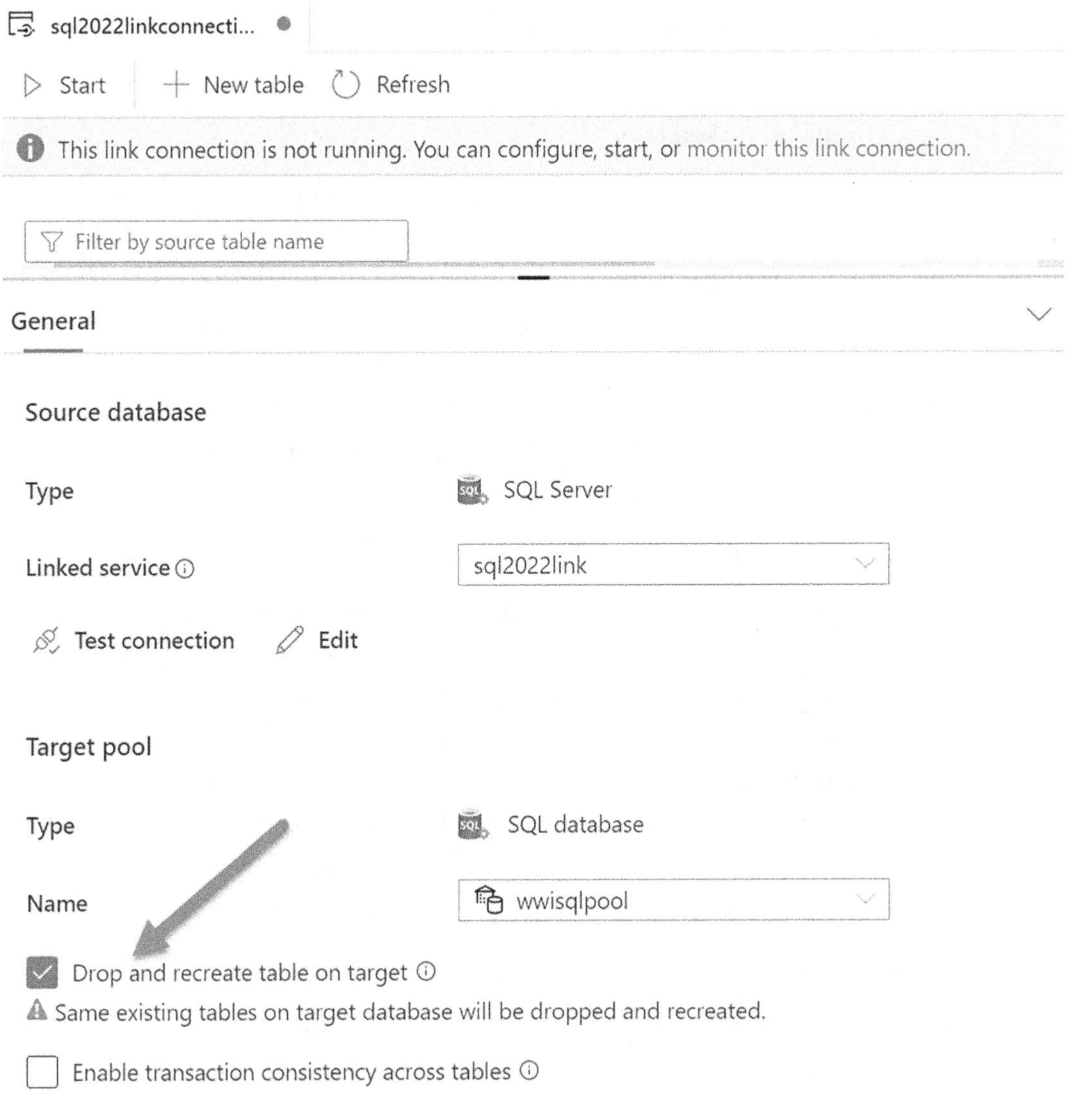

Figure 3-39. Dropping and recreating tables in Synapse pools on a linked connection start

Note   We are also looking at an enhancement to be able to pause and resume the linked connection. If the linked connection is paused, SQL Server will keep feeding data and changes into the landing zone, but these changes won't appear in Synapse until you resume the linked connection.

- **Core counts for linked connections**

    When you create the linked connection, you have a choice called core counts. These core counts are specifically designed for ingestion processing. The more cores you select, the faster your data can be ingested. But larger core counts can also affect costs. We recommend you start with smaller core counts to save costs and adjust upward. The only issue with changing core counts is you must stop and restart the linked connection, which requires a re-snapshot of all the tables (until pause and resume is available).

- **Scheduled or continuous mode**

    Another option when you create the linked connection is scheduled or continuous mode. Continuous mode means the ingestion service will always be looking for changes in the landing zone to process data. Scheduled mode allows you to schedule ingestion for certain time ranges. Scheduled mode will help you save ingestion costs but will also delay when data is available to read in SQL pool tables. Using scheduled mode will not affect any latency of transaction processing or log truncation on SQL Server 2022.

- **Adding or dropping tables to/from the linked connection**

    You can add or drop tables to/from the linked connection. A new snapshot for the new table will be created and synchronized to the new SQL pool table.

Tip   If you want to delete the Synapse workspace, you should first stop all linked connections and delete the linked service to ensure SQL Server is fully aware that Synapse Link is disabled. Otherwise, you might run into log truncation issues.

You should know that you can create multiple linked connections for the same database, but you cannot add the same source table in more than one linked connection.

- **Landing zone storage**

  The initial snapshot of tables creates a parquet file for which the size will vary based on how much data is in the SQL source table. Changes to SQL Server data result in a series of CVS and manifest files. We don't support you reading or directly changing the landing zone, so these files will remain in the landing zone until they are cleaned up. Cleanup happens in the background on a periodic basis or if the link connection is stopped (all files are removed).

- **SQL pool table index types**

  For SQL pool tables that are targets for Synapse Link, you have choices when you set up the linked connection for index types. To learn about possible index choices for your workload, read our documentation at `https://docs.microsoft.com/azure/synapse-analytics/sql-data-warehouse/sql-data-warehouse-tables-index`.

A nice deep dive by Steve Howard that talks about some of these choices and others can be found at `https://techcommunity.microsoft.com/t5/azure-synapse-analytics-blog/synapse-link-for-sql-deep-dive/ba-p/3567645`.

Transaction Consistency

Synapse Link is designed to only submit changes that are committed to the landing zone. This is a similar concept as replication and CDC technologies. For fault tolerance Synapse Link tracks Log Sequence Numbers (LSNs) to understand which transactions are committed to be fed into the landing zone.

You should expect any performance impact for Synapse Link to be similar to replication or CDC. One difference is that changes are kept in in-memory queues before being published to the landing zone, so performance to the original transactions can be less than other change feed technologies. We limit the size of what data is kept in queues and publish them to the landing zone to ensure we don't overcommit memory for these queues.

The one issue to keep track of is transaction log truncation. Like replication, we cannot truncate transactions from the log that have not been committed to the landing zone if they involve a table that is enabled for Synapse Link. So latency or issues with the landing zone can affect the ability to truncate the log.

Another option for Synapse Link is transaction consistency across tables. While this option may allow you to use small DWU options and core counts on Synapse, it affects latency of changes applied to Synapse SQL pool tables.

Monitoring Synapse Link

You have several methods to monitor Synapse Link including some that are available in Synapse Studio as you have seen in the exercises in this chapter.

You also have a series of system tables in SQL Server under the **changefeed** schema of the database you can query to see settings, table groups, and tables including some performance statistics.

There are also Dynamic Management Views (DMVs) you can use including **sys.dm_change_feed_errors** and **sys.dm_change_feed_log_scan_sessions**.

If you need to do deep debugging for Synapse Link, there are a series of Extended Events you can use. Search for names in **sys.dm_xe_objects** that start with **synapse_link**.

I've also observed a number of wait types in sys.dm_os_wait_stats that include the name synapse, so you can look at some of these waits using the following query:

```
select * from sys.dm_os_wait_stats where wait_type like '%synapse%'
```

Limits and Restrictions

There are some limits and restrictions for Synapse Link. These limits are evolving and could even be updated by the time SQL Server 2022 becomes generally available. I built the exercises in this book to ensure they would work with limits documented during the preview.

You will find in the documentation certain limits such as source data types, size of rows, the need for a primary key, and unsupported features such as replication, CDC, and In-Memory OLTP. Keep track of the detailed list at https://docs.microsoft.com/azure/synapse-analytics/synapse-link/synapse-link-for-sql-known-issues.

Synapse Link is supported when using SQL HA features like Always On Availability Groups. In an AG scenario, you need to use the name of the listener for the SQL Server name to ensure SHIR always connects to the primary.

Synapse Link Could Change Analytics for You

There are many ways to run analytic workloads in some cases directly against SQL Server. But if you are looking to separate your primary SQL Server application from analytic workloads, Synapse Link could be a great solution. The ability to have SQL Server automatically capture changes and feed them to Synapse is a compelling story.

I asked Chuck Heinzelman, Principal Program Manger over analytics for SQL Server, his thoughts about Synapse Link: "Azure Synapse Link for SQL allows customers to automatically move data from their transactional systems into an MPP-based analytical system without having to write ETL code for the data movement. In addition to the low code/no code approach, customers can benefit from near-real-time data movement as opposed to batch-based processing that comes with traditional ETL systems."

Azure Active Directory (AAD) Authentication

For as long as SQL Server has been a product, it has supported SQL authentication, the simplest but not the most secure method to log in to SQL Server. As far back as SQL Server 4.2 for Windows NT (I had to go back verify this with my old, printed manuals), SQL Server has supported a concept to log in using integrated authentication with the operating system. In SQL Server 4.2 we called this *Integrated Security*. Windows NT supported the concept of a directory server, which can be used to authenticate accounts. This technology would eventually become Active Directory (AD) for Windows Server. SQL Server has therefore supported the ability to create logins based on AD accounts and authenticate these logins using servers that support AD (domain controllers). Today we call this Windows authentication for SQL Server.

Along comes Azure Active Directory (AAD). AAD is a managed service for authentication for all types of applications and services. Think of this as a Microsoft managed set of domain controllers that you can use to create your own directory, users, groups, and authentication schemes.

Because Azure SQL Database and Azure SQL Managed Instance are PaaS services, you can't deploy your own domain controller for Active Directory. Therefore, in order to support an alternative to SQL authentication, we added support for logins and users for Azure SQL using AAD. Now you could add a login like the following to Azure SQL:

```
CREATE LOGIN [bob@contoso.com] FROM EXTERNAL PROVIDER
GO
```

The new EXTERNAL PROVIDER syntax indicates to SQL to use AAD for authentication. To use AAD with Azure SQL, consult our documentation at `https://docs.microsoft.com//azure/azure-sql/database/authentication-aad-overview`.

Now with SQL Server 2022, we have taken our implementation to support AAD and added this to SQL Server. The syntax is almost identical with Azure SQL. The engine itself already has all the code to support AAD from Azure SQL. The only difference is your SQL Server is probably not running in Azure and the virtual machine or computer is in your network.

How Does AAD Authentication Work?

In Azure SQL, we enhanced the engine to communicate directly with AAD using protocols like OAuth and OpenID. Most developers authenticate users for AAD using libraries such as `https://docs.microsoft.com/azure/active-directory/develop/reference-v2-libraries`. SQL Server as a host engine needed to do this authentication on behalf of the application. Since AAD doesn't allow direct communication to any programs, there is some setup required for SQL Server such as an *Azure app registration* and certificates. You can read more on the details about the use of these protocols with AAD at `https://docs.microsoft.com/en-us/azure/active-directory/develop/active-directory-v2-protocols`.

For SQL Server to have all the right information to communicate with AAD, it needs specific information stored somewhere. Therefore, this is where the **Azure extension for SQL Server** comes in. The extension communicates with Azure during your setup of AAD to write into the Windows registry information the engine can read and use to communicate with AAD.

> **Note**   The registry keys are internal to the product, but if you have access, you can see them at HKEY_LOCAL_MACHINE\SOFTWARE\Microsoft\Microsoft SQL Server\MSSQL15.MSSQLSERVER\MSSQLServer\FederatedAuthentication. Linux uses similar settings in the mssql.conf file.

AAD authentication for SQL Server is separate from Windows authentication. These are not integrated together. Azure SQL Managed Instance does provide a service to keep your Windows authentication accounts but integrate your authentication with AAD. You can read more at `https://docs.microsoft.com/azure/azure-sql/managed-instance/winauth-azuread-overview`.

Keep up to date with all the latest information about SQL Server and AAD at `https://aka.ms/aadsqlserver`.

Setting Up and Using AAD Authentication

Let's walk through an exercise to set up and configure AAD authentication for SQL Server 2022. These steps are based on the following tutorial at `https://docs.microsoft.com/sql/relational-databases/security/authentication-access/azure-ad-authentication-sql-server-automation-setup-tutorial`.

Prerequisites

The following are prerequisites to set up and configure AAD for SQL Server 2022. I will admit to you that there are requirements for the account you use with your Azure subscription that may take you some time to work through.

- A virtual machine or computer with at least two CPUs and 8Gb RAM. Your virtual machine or computer needs to be capable of connecting to Azure over the Internet.

- SQL Server 2022 Evaluation Edition. You will need the database engine feature, and you will also need to set up the **Azure extension for SQL Server** option during or after setup. You can use instructions that I created in Chapter 2 of the book under the section titled "**Setting Up the Azure Extension for SQL Server**" or use the instructions in the documentation at `https://docs.microsoft.com/sql/database-engine/install-windows/install-sql-server-from-the-installation-wizard-setup`. For Linux users, please check the Linux documentation at `https://docs.microsoft.com/en-us/sql/linux/sql-server-linux-configure-mssql-conf#azure-ad`.

- An Azure subscription using an Azure Active Directory (AAD) account in your organization you have deemed to be the **AAD admin** for SQL Server. This account should have the following permissions:

  - Member of the Azure Connected Machine Onboarding group or Contributor role in the resource group associated with the Azure extension for SQL Server

  - Member of the Azure Connected Machine Resource Administrator role in the resource group associated with the Azure extension for SQL Server

  - Member of the Reader role in the resource group associated with the Azure extension for SQL Server

  - Permissions to create an Azure Key Vault

Important   You will need to be able to grant **admin consent** for an Azure application. In order to grant admin consent, your AAD account must be a member of the Azure AD Global Administrator or Privilege Role Administrator. It is possible in your organization you don't have this permission, so either you will need to be granted this permission or have another AAD administrator configure this. Do not move forward until you have this permission resolved.

- SQL Server Management Studio (SSMS). The latest 18.x build or 19.x build will work.

- A copy of the scripts from book samples from the **ch3_cloudconnected\aad** folder.

Set Up AAD with SQL Server 2022

1. With your permissions properly configured, create a new **Azure Key Vault** resource. Azure Key Vault is an Azure service to store and protect keys, secrets, and certificates. Use this quick-start guide to create a new key vault at `https://docs.microsoft.com/azure/key-vault/general/quick-create-portal`. Use the same resource group and region from the SQL Server Azure Arc registration. Add your AAD admin account in the Contributor role for the key vault you created.

2. Set up access for the SQL Server 2022 instance to the Azure Key Vault. Use the Access policies option on the resource menu for the key vault. Select Add access policy. Keep 0 selected for Key permissions. Add the Get and List permissions for Secret and Certificate. Then for Select principal, use the name of the host of your SQL Server (the name of the Azure Arc SQL Server). Your screen should look like Figure 3-40.

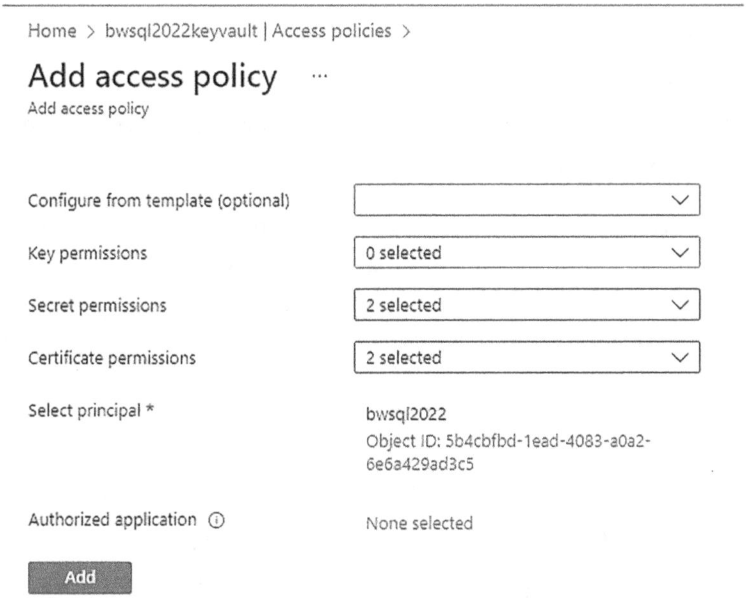

Home > bwsql2022keyvault | Access policies >

Add access policy   ...
Add access policy

Configure from template (optional)	⌄
Key permissions	0 selected ⌄
Secret permissions	2 selected ⌄
Certificate permissions	2 selected ⌄
Select principal *	bwsql2022 Object ID: 5b4cbfbd-1ead-4083-a0a2-6e6a429ad3c5
Authorized application ⓘ	None selected

Add

Figure 3-40. *Adding access policy for Azure Key Vault*

Click **Add** and then **Save**.

3. Now grant access to the Azure Key Vault to the AAD account you would like to make the AAD admin for SQL Server. This is a similar process to the preceding step except for Key permissions you need Get, List, and Create. You also need Get, List, and Set for Secret and Get, List, and Create for Certificate. It is possible you don't need this step if you used the AAD admin account to create the Azure Key Vault.

4. Now we will set up the AAD admin for SQL Server using the Azure portal.

Note   There are other options for set this including az CLI, PowerShell, and an ARM template. To learn more see the documentation at `https://docs.microsoft.com/sql/relational-databases/security/authentication-access/azure-ad-authentication-sql-server-automation-setup-tutorial#setting-up-the-azure-ad-admin-for-the-sql-server`.

Find your SQL Server Azure Arc resource in the Azure portal. You can do this by typing the word *SQL Server* in the Search field at the top of the portal and selecting **SQL Server – Azure Arc** under services. Choose your SQL Server instance.

On the resource menu for this resource under Settings, choose Azure Active Directory. Now choose Set Admin. Pick the AAD account you have selected as your AAD admin. You now will fill out information on a screen to set the admin:

- Choose Service-managed cert.

- Change your key vault to the Azure Key Vault you have created.

- Choose Service-managed app registration.

- Leave the option for Purview disabled. We will enable Purview policies in the next section of the chapter.

Your options should look similar to Figure 3-41.

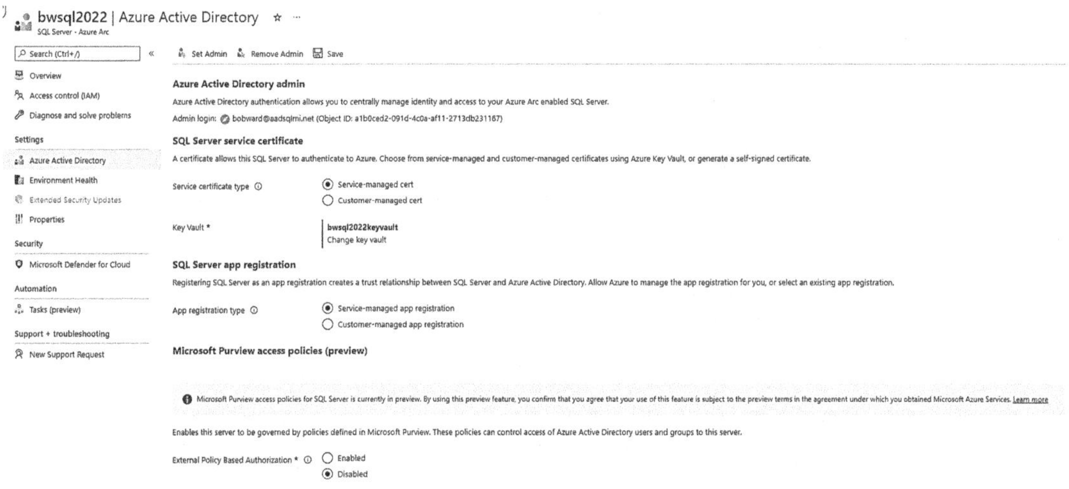

Figure 3-41. Setting the AAD admin for SQL Server

Now select **Save**. The top of the screen will show **in Progress...** Azure is now sending information to your SQL Server through the Azure extension for SQL Server. This can take a few minutes. When successful you will see a message like

Saved successfully, but admin consent may need to be granted to app 'bwsql2022-MSSQLSERVER<nnnnn>'

Note   As mentioned earlier in this chapter, you will now have information written into the Windows registry of your SQL Server (or mssql.conf file for Linux) with a path like Computer\HKEY_LOCAL_MACHINE\SOFTWARE\Microsoft\Microsoft SQL Server\MSSQL16.MSSQLSERVER\MSSQLServer\FederatedAuthentication. We don't support you modifying these registry keys, but it is interesting to see how our software connects. The SQL Server 2022 engine is enhanced to read these keys to know how to connect with Azure Active Directory to authenticate.

When this step is successful, you should see the following entry in your ERRORLOG for SQL Server:

AAD Authentication is enabled. This is an informational message only; no user action is required.

The AAD admin account is added automatically as a login in SQL
Server and placed as a member of the sysadmin role.

5. This leads right into the last step for setup. SQL Server has to use
   an Azure application as part of communicating with AAD. The app
   name you saw in the last step was created automatically for you.
   Now you must grant an *admin consent* for the Azure application.
   In the Azure portal, search for Azure Active Directory and choose
   your organization. Select **App registrations** on the left-hand
   menu. The application you want to choose was the one created in
   step 4 (mine is 'bwsql2022-MSSQLSERVER<nnnnn>). Now select
   API permissions on the left-hand menu. If you have the proper
   rights, select **Grant admin consent...**

Note   This is the step that requires you to have Global Administrator or Privileged
Role Administrator rights with your AAD. These are highly privileged rights, so you
may need someone in your organization to perform this step.

If you don't have proper permissions, this option will be grayed
out. When this step is done, your screen should like Figure 3-42.

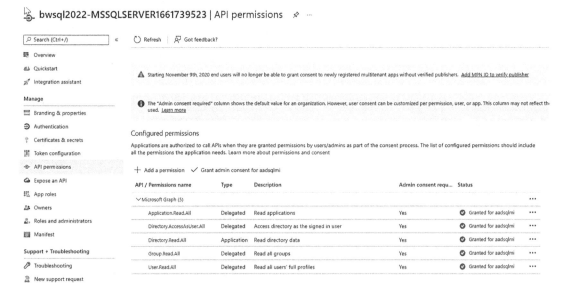

Figure 3-42. *Granting access to the Azure app for AAD authentication*

If you don't do this step, you can still use the AAD admin account already set up for SQL Server 2022. But you will not be able to add any other AAD logins or users to SQL Server. You will get an error like `Server identity does not have permissions to access MS Graph`.

Note   MS Graph stands for Microsoft Graph, which is a service in the Microsoft Identity platform used for Azure application access.

I know there are a lot of steps to set this up. But when you have it all done, using AAD authentication is very easy and powerful.

Using AAD with SQL Server

You have done all the hard work. Now it is time to try out connecting to your SQL Server 2022 instance with AAD accounts.

1. You already have an AAD-based login added from the AAD admin account you set up earlier. Let's find it. Execute the script **findaadlogin.sql** logged in as the local administrator account. This script uses the following T-SQL statements:

    ```
    USE master;
    GO
    SELECT * FROM sys.server_principals WHERE type = 'E'
    GO
    ```

    The result should be a single login with the AAD credentials you created earlier. The type = E stands for EXTERNAL_LOGIN. The only type of external logins supported today is AAD.

2. Let's try to log in with SSMS using the AAD login. From SSMS for Authentication, choose Azure Active Directory – Universal with MFA. Then type in the AAD account. Select Options and make sure Encrypt connection and Trust server certificate are checked. My login screen before I selected Connect looks like Figure 3-43.

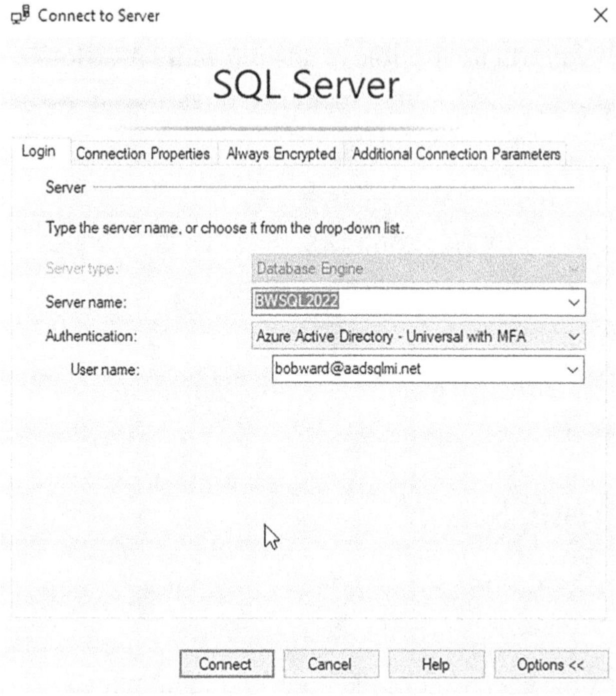

Figure 3-43. *Logging into SQL Server with AAD using MFA*

Select Connect, and you will be prompted for you Azure account information. If your AAD supports or requires MFA, you will be prompted to use whatever method has been set up (e.g., using your phone). After you have successfully signed in, you will be connected with Object Explorer in SSMS.

If you don't have other AAD logins in your group, you can just read the next set of steps, or you substitute in your own AAD accounts.

3. Let's try to add a new AAD account as a SQL login. Let's say one of my colleagues Anna Hoffman needs sysadmin access to this SQL Server but wants to use her direct AAD account instead of creating a different account. Anna's AAD account is annahoffman@ aadsqlmi.net. Now logged in as the AAD sysadmin login that was originally created and you just connected with, execute the script **createaadlogin.sql**, which uses the following T-SQL statements:

```
USE master;
GO
CREATE LOGIN [annahoffman@aadsqlmi.net] FROM EXTERNAL PROVIDER;
GO
EXEC sp_addsrvrolemember @loginame='annahoffman@aadsqlmi.net',
@rolename='sysadmin';
GO
```

Note the new syntax FROM EXTERNAL PROVIDER (which we already have supported with Azure SQL Database and Azure SQL Managed Instance).

You can now connect to SSMS with AAD with MFA or password-based authentication using this new login.

4. Now let's say another colleague Marisa Mathews needs access to a specific database as a user but doesn't really need a login or to be a member of the sysadmin role. You can do this with AAD authentication. Connected as the AAD sysadmin login, execute the script **createaaduser.sql**, which uses the following T-SQL statements:

```
DROP DATABASE IF EXISTS howaboutthemcowboys;
GO
CREATE DATABASE howboutthemcowboys;
GO
USE howboutthemcowboys;
GO
CREATE USER [marisamathews@aadsqlmi.net] FROM EXTERNAL PROVIDER;
GO
```

Now when you try to connect using SSMS with this AAD account, you need to use the **Connect to database** option under Connection Properties and specify this database. This user will only have access to the database and not the complete instance. This is very similar to the capability we provide with Azure SQL Database.

5.   One other nice option is AAD groups. Let's say Anna and Marisa were part of an AAD group called **sqlusers**. Connected as a sysadmin login, you can execute the script **createaadgrouplogin. sql**. This script uses the following T-SQL statements:

```
USE master;
GO
CREATE LOGIN [sqlusers] FROM EXTERNAL PROVIDER;
GO
```

Unfortunately procedures like xp_logininfo don't work against AAD groups, so to view membership, you will need methods to list AAD groups.

There a few other syntax options for you to create logins and users including Azure applications (passwordless accounts), which you can read more about at `https:// docs.microsoft.com/en-us/sql/relational-databases/security/authentication- access/azure-ad-authentication-sql-server-setup-tutorial#create-logins- and-users`.

We even support AAD authentication for linked servers, which you can read more at `https://docs.microsoft.com/sql/relational-databases/security/ authentication-access/azure-ad-authentication-sql-server-linked-server`.

Microsoft Purview Policy Management

To understand the power of Microsoft Purview policy management, let's take a scenario. You need to hire a consultant who has very strong skills in performance monitoring for SQL Server. You want this consultant to have access to your SQL Server but only to monitor things like Dynamic Management Views (DMVs) related to performance. You don't want to have to grant them full sysadmin rights. You will learn in Chapter 6 of the book we have new fixed server roles for just this purpose like ##MS_ ServerPerformanceStateReader##. This could meet your needs perfectly. You could even create a *guest* account in your Azure Active Directory and create a SQL Server login based on that account and assign them to the new role.

Now what if you had to do this across, say, 50 SQL Server instances? You will need to create some scripts to connect to all the instances to create the logins and assign the roles. What happens when the contract is up? It is up to you to create scripts to remove the logins you created earlier across all the instances.

What if you could use a central place to do all of this without creating and maintaining scripts or even directly creating the logins? Microsoft Purview provides a central governance hub to establish **access policies** for Azure SQL resources including SQL Server 2022 as an Azure Arc–enabled SQL Server. In addition, Microsoft has created some built-in policies to match certain scenarios such as performance monitoring, security auditing, or reading of user table data.

The following blog post at `https://cloudblogs.microsoft.com/ sqlserver/2022/08/11/microsoft-purview-access-policies-for-sql-server-2022/` by Srdan Bozovic, Lead Program Manager at Microsoft for Purview access policies for SQL, is a great glance at what is possible.

I asked Joachim Hammer, Principal Group Program Manager for security across SQL, his perspective on what Microsoft Purview provides for SQL customers. He said

> *Comprehensive, unified data governance provided by Microsoft Purview helps protect sensitive data across clouds, apps, and devices and is an important tool in the fight against the growing number of security threats. Microsoft Purview-based access policies, which are now available in SQL Server 2022, provide two advantages over the access controls that are built into today's database management systems: Access to data is efficiently managed in one place using Purview's easy-to-use policy dashboard while the enforcement happens at scale across the entire data estate. We are extremely proud to offer powerful, cloud-based data governance in the form of Purview-based access policies to our SQL Server customers, helping them govern and secure all of their SQL Server data, irrespective of where it resides, ground to cloud.*

Let's dive into the details. Let's see how Purview access policies work and then see them in action with an exercise.

How Do Purview Access Policies Work?

Like Synapse Link, you will use Purview in Azure to *author* the experience of building policies that affect SQL Server. You will learn to do this through a tool called **Purview Governance Portal** (I often call this Purview Studio).

A policy is made up of the following components:

- The **type of access** (read, performance monitoring, etc.)

- A **data source**. This will be a SQL Server instance you will register with Purview.

- A **principal** to give access. This is an Azure Active Directory account.

There are two types of policies that you can create with Purview for SQL Server:

- **Data** – This is to support the concept of a user who just needs to read data perhaps to build reports.

- **DevOps** – This is to support *admin* users for, for example, performance monitoring and security auditing.

Note   We will continue to invest here and add more types of access policies such as modification of data and self-service data access. Self-service data access allows users to request access to data through a scanned data source, and approvals can be automatically done without creating a specific policy.

Purview access policies are not just for SQL Server. Purview access policies are part of a broader concept for Purview called **Data Use Management** (DUM), which you can read more about at `https://docs.microsoft.com/azure/purview/how-to-enable-data-use-management`.

Microsoft Purview access policies rely on three capabilities you have seen already in this chapter:

- Azure Active Directory (AAD) authentication for SQL Server. This is because policies are only supported for an AAD account.

- Azure extension for SQL Server. This agent is used for AAD authentication but will also be used by Purview to provide information for the SQL Server engine to connect to Purview to extract policies.

- Enhancements built into the SQL Server engine to the security system to understand how to take policy information and allow connections and access to SQL Server based on the policy.

Figure 3-44 shows an architecture view of how Purview access policies work.

Microsoft Purview SQL Server Policy Architecture

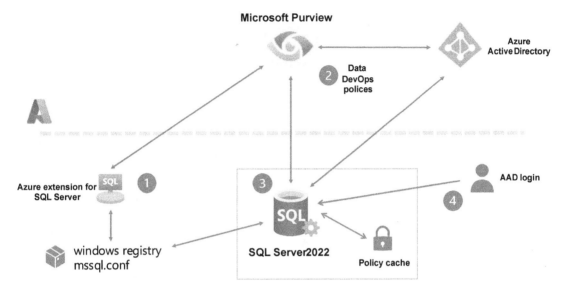

Figure 3-44. *Architecture of Purview access policies for SQL Server*

Let's look at these components further:

1. After creating a Purview account, you will use the Azure extension
   for SQL Server to **enable Purview** through the Azure Arc–enabled
   SQL Server capability (remember you already did this to get AAD
   authentication enabled, which is first required). When you enable
   Purview, the extension stores key information in the Windows
   registry or mssql.conf file (Linux) so the SQL Server engine knows
   how to communicate with Purview.

Note   For Windows, the registry key is Computer\HKEY_LOCAL_MACHINE\
SOFTWARE\Microsoft\Microsoft SQL Server\MSSQL16.MSSQLSERVER\
MSSQLServer\PurviewConfig. This is internal information, and we do not support
you reading or modifying these registry keys.

2. You will then use Purview Studio to register your Arc-enabled SQL Server instance with Purview and enable Data Use Management (DUM). You can now create policies for Data and DevOps scenarios.

3. The SQL Server engine can then pull policy information from Purview and store in a policy cache (system tables and memory structures). The engine periodically checks for updates to policies and updates the cache (or you can force a refresh).

4. The principal granted access through the policy can then log in to SQL Server and be authenticated with AAD. The engine then can use the policy cache to determine what permissions this principal has access to in SQL Server and user databases.

To make this more real to you, let's look at an exercise to see an example of a Data and DevOps policy.

Using Purview Access Policies

In this exercise I'll show you how to use two types of access policies for Purview: Data to read user data and DevOps for performance monitoring.

Prerequisites

Here are the perquisites for this exercise to use Microsoft Purview access policies with SQL Server 2022. I'd like to personally thank Vlad Rodriguez, Srdan Bozovic, and Nikolas Ogg from our Microsoft engineering teams for helping me get these exercises working:

- A virtual machine or computer with at least two CPUs and 8Gb RAM. Your virtual machine or computer needs to be capable of connecting to Azure over the Internet.

- You have fulfilled all the prerequisites earlier in this chapter for Azure Active Directory (AAD) authentication and have followed all the steps as instructed earlier in this chapter to set up AAD with SQL Server 2022.

- Permissions in your Azure subscription to create a Microsoft Purview account.

- Note that during our preview for SQL Server 2022, Purview data access policies were restricted to certain Azure regions. Please consult with this documentation for the latest updates: `https://docs.microsoft.com/azure/purview/how-to-policies-data-owner-arc-sql-server?branch=release-build-purview-sql-policy#prerequisites`.

Set Up Microsoft Purview Access Policies

1. You will first need a Microsoft Purview account. Here is a quick-start guide to create a Purview account: `https://docs.microsoft.com/azure/purview/create-catalog-portal`.

2. There are some permissions you will need to set up with Purview to allow you to create and publish policies and enable DUM. Please follow the steps in this documentation **carefully** to set up these permissions: `https://docs.microsoft.com/azure/purview/how-to-policies-data-owner-arc-sql-server#configuration`.

3. Now you need to register your Purview account with the Azure extension for SQL Server through the Azure portal. Find your SQL Server – Azure Arc resource that you created for AAD authentication in the Azure portal. Select on the left-hand menu Azure Active Directory. At the bottom of the screen that is presented, you will see a section called ***Microsoft Purview access policies.*** Click Enabled and fill out Microsoft Purview Endpoint by putting in your Purview account name like in Figure 3-45.

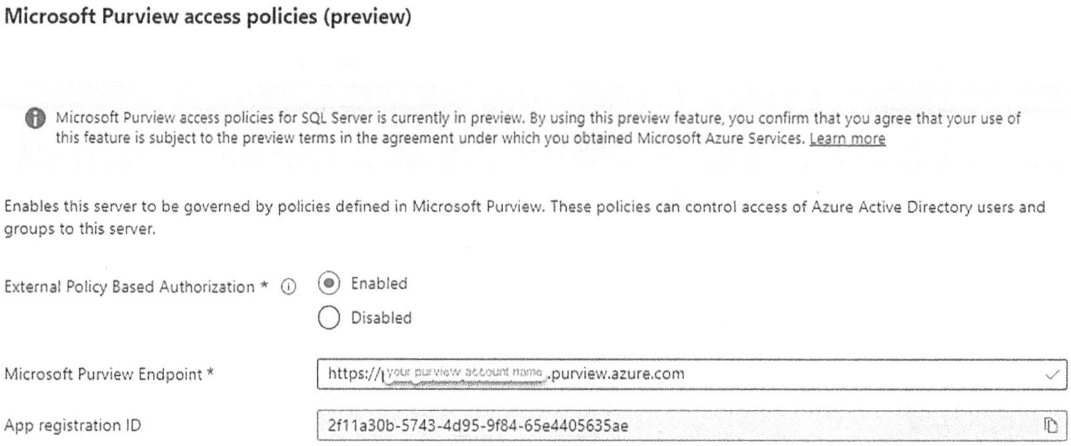

Microsoft Purview access policies (preview)

> ℹ️ Microsoft Purview access policies for SQL Server is currently in preview. By using this preview feature, you confirm that you agree that your use of this feature is subject to the preview terms in the agreement under which you obtained Microsoft Azure Services. Learn more

Enables this server to be governed by policies defined in Microsoft Purview. These policies can control access of Azure Active Directory users and groups to this server.

External Policy Based Authorization * ℹ️ ⦿ Enabled
                                        ◯ Disabled

Microsoft Purview Endpoint * | https://your purview account name.purview.azure.com   ✓ |

App registration ID | 2f11a30b-5743-4d95-9f84-65e4405635ae   ⧉ |

Figure 3-45. *Registering Purview with the Azure extension for SQL Server*

The App registration ID will be automatically filled in. This is an AAD ID associated with the Azure application that was registered when you enabled AAD authentication. Select Save at the top of this screen. The status of success or fail is a bit odd as this screen doesn't just go away when the save is successful.

When you are done, your screen should look like Figure 3-46.

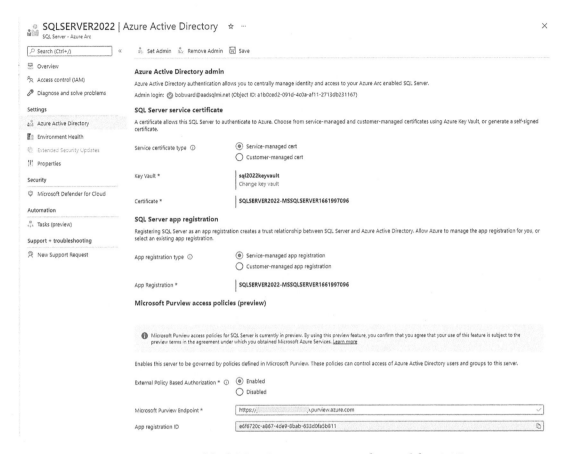

Figure 3-46. *Azure Arc–enabled SQL Server 2022 configured for AAD and Purview*

So how do you know if Purview was enabled on your SQL Server through the Azure extension? One way to see this is to view details of the SQL extension in the portal.

Search on the home page of the Azure portal for **Servers – Azure Arc**. Select Servers – Azure Arc under Services. Choose your server name at the top of this list. On the left-hand menu, choose Extensions. Now choose **WindowsAgent.SqlServer.** The Status message shows information sent to the extension on your SQL Server, which should look similar to Figure 3-47.

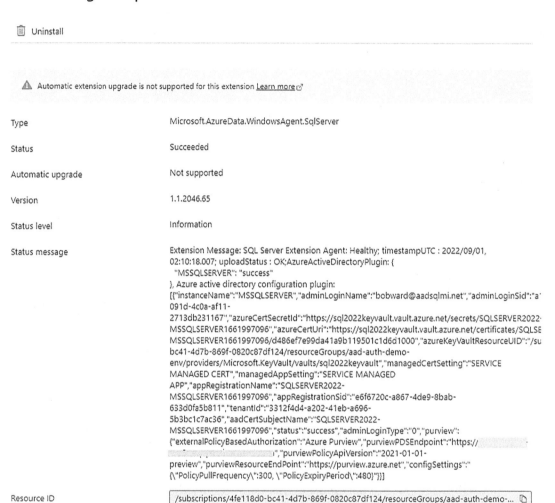

Figure 3-47. *Successful extension status for AAD and Purview*

4. You will need some AAD accounts to authorize access in
    the exercise. I will show you two scenarios for two different
    AAD accounts. For access to read data, I'll use the account
    annahoffman@aadsqlmi.net that I created in the exercise
    earlier in this chapter for AAD authentication. For the exercise
    on DevOps for performance monitoring, I'll show an example
    of a *guest* AAD account. A guest is an account that is not part
    of your AAD but you are *inviting* them to access resources in

Azure. You can read more about how to invite a guest account in AAD at `https://docs.microsoft.com/azure/active-directory/external-identities/b2b-quickstart-add-guest-users-portal`.

5. Learn the basics of how to launch Purview Studio from the Azure portal at `https://docs.microsoft.com/azure/purview/use-azure-purview-studio`. Use the AAD admin account you created earlier in this chapter for the exercises to enable AAD authentication for SQL Server 2022.

Using Microsoft Purview Access Policies

1. The first thing we need to do is **register** the SQL Server 2022 instance as a **data source**. Launch Purview Studio from the Azure portal. Choose the **Data map** icon ◈ on the left-hand menu (hover over the icons to see Data map). Your Purview account may have other data sources already registered shown in a visual tree or in a table format. Choose **Register** at the top of the screen. On the Register sources screen, type in **Arc** in the Filter by keyword field. Select SQL Server on Azure Arc–enabled servers and select **Continue**.

   You can now choose and fill out fields on the Register sources (SQL Server on Azure Arc–enabled servers) screen. Choose a name (I recommend the same name as your registered server), subscription, and server name (your registered server). Type in your registered server name in the Server endpoint field and leave the (Root) collection as the default.

   Select the Enabled option for Data Use Management, which should auto-populate the Application ID (this is the App registration ID that is listed on the Azure Active Directory screen from SQL Server – Azure Arc). Your screen should look similar to Figure 3-48.

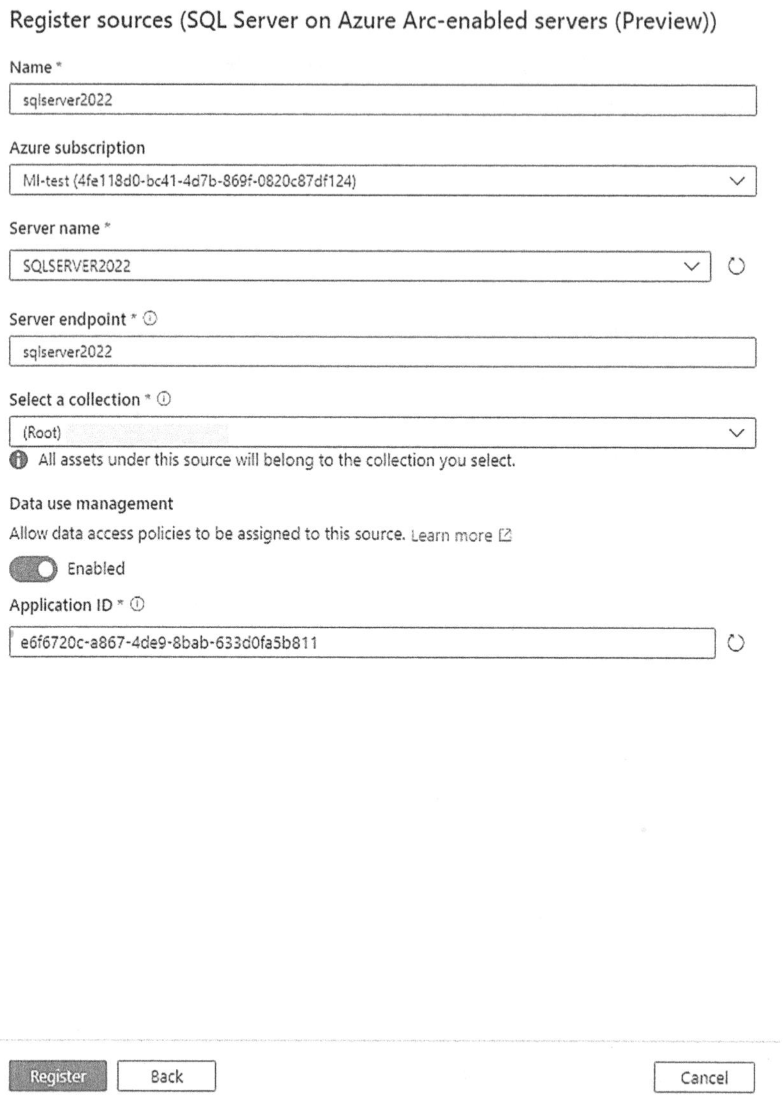
Register sources (SQL Server on Azure Arc-enabled servers (Preview))
Name *
sqlserver2022
Azure subscription
MI-test (4fe118d0-bc41-4d7b-869f-0820c87df124)
Server name *
SQLSERVER2022
Server endpoint *
sqlserver2022
Select a collection *
(Root)
All assets under this source will belong to the collection you select.
Data use management
Allow data access policies to be assigned to this source. Learn more
Enabled
Application ID *
e6f6720c-a867-4de9-8bab-633d0fa5b811
Register
Back
Cancel

***Figure 3-48.** Registering a SQL Server data source for Purview access policies*

Select **Register**. After a few seconds, you will see the list of data sources again. Select Refresh at the top of the screen to confirm your data source.

Note If you want to apply a policy against multiple SQL Server instances, you need to register each one first. You only need to register a SQL Server data source once to use with any number of policies.

---

2. Let's now create a data policy for another AAD account. I'll use annahoffman@aadsqlmi.net to be granted access to read data for our SQL Server instance. For me, since I created this account as a login in the exercises for AAD, I first deleted the login to avoid any confusion. Turns out that if a login exists for the same AAD account as a policy, we use the *union* of the permissions of the login and the policy.

Note   At the time of the writing of this book, we were looking to add more granular read access for individual objects like specific databases and/or tables in the future. This will require the SQL Server instance to be scanned using the data catalog feature of Microsoft Purview.

Using Purview Studio, select the **Data policy** icon on the left-hand menu. Select **Data policies** and then + **New policy**. Now select **Access Control** under Policy Types.

On the Access Control Policy, type in a name called **sqlreader** with the same description. Then select + **New policy statement**. Now you need to build the statement with some choices:

- For **effect** choose Allow.

- For **action** choose Read.

- For **data resources** on the new screen, choose Data source type and then choose SQL Server on Azure Arc–enabled servers. Leave Assets alone and select **Continue**. Choose your server under Data Source Name and select **Add**.

Note   If you have registered multiple SQL Server data sources, this is where you can apply a policy to one or more of them.

- For **subjects** type in the AAD account you want to give read access to in the Select subjects search window and then select **Ok**.

Your policy statement should look like Figure 3-49.

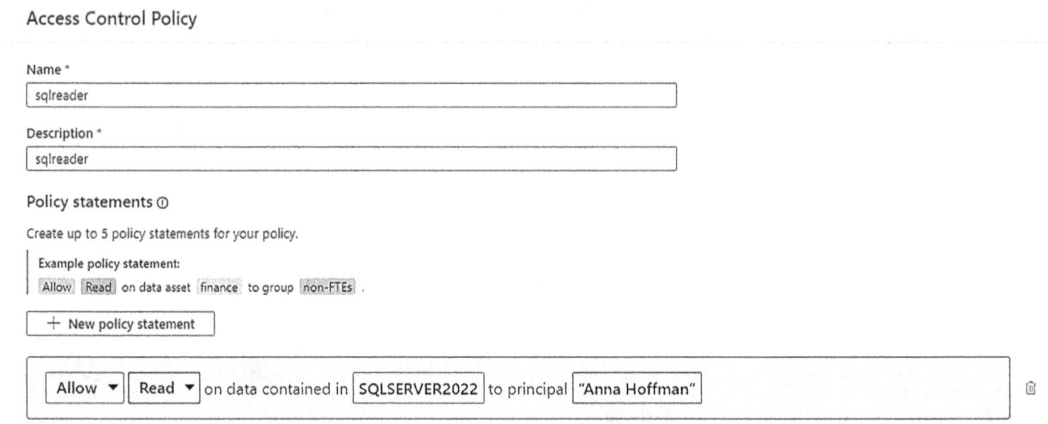

Figure 3-49. *Creating a read policy for SQL Server 2022*

Select **Save**. Now that the policy is saved, you will see your new policy on a list of policies.

3. For the policy to take affect, we need to publish it. Select your policy and select **Publish** on the right side of the screen. Choose your data source and select **Publish** at the bottom of the new screen. You should now see a Published On date and time on the screen for your policy.

4. Let's create a database and data for the new account to read. Execute the script **howboutthemcowboys.sql** against your SQL Server 2022 instance as your default sysadmin.

5. Policies are not immediately applied. SQL Server will check periodically for new policies on a polling interval. Connect to your SQL Server 2022 to immediately apply the new policy. Execute the script **policyrefresh.sql**, which uses the following T-SQL statements:

```
-- Force immediate download of latest published policies
USE master;
GO
exec sp_external_policy_refresh reload;
GO
```

Note   On a server start when SQL Server obtains information from Microsoft Purview for policies, you might see messages like the following in the ERRORLOG:

IMDS resource information. Subscription ID: 4fe118d0-bc41-4d7b-869f-0820c87df124, Resource Group: aad-auth-demo-env, Name: SQLSERVER2022.

[JSONWebTokenService::GetCertificateFromCertificateStoreBy SubjectName] [AADAuthThumbprint] Thumbprint being used for AAD authentication aRgwszCertificateThumbprint 26289598dfe 34092c141edc8a319505bdf0882b6

[CBabylonConfigSubscriber] Purview frequency setting changed. New value: 300

[CBabylonConfigSubscriber] Purview policy expiration time changed to 480 mins

[CBabylonConfigSubscriber] Received update to the config settings

[CBabylonConfigSubscriber] Purview frequency setting changed. New value: 300

[CBabylonConfigSubscriber] Purview policy expiration time changed to 480 mins

[CBabylonConfigSubscriber] Registered for setting updates successfully

Fun fact   Babylon is the original project name for Microsoft Purview.

6. Using the same technique you learned earlier in this chapter with SSMS, log into SSMS with the account you published the policy for using the MFA option (don't forget to check the Trust server certificate option). Let's check the new permissions as a reader to make sure it worked. Execute the script **querythecowboys.sql**, which executes the following T-SQL statements:

```
USE howboutthemcowboys;
GO
SELECT * FROM tothesuperbowl;
GO
```

You should get one row back (I hope this is our year<g>). The permission to read data includes system catalog views and limited Dynamic Management Views (DMVs).

7. Let's prove you only have read permissions. Execute the script **dropthecowboys.sql**, which executes the following T-SQL statements:

```
USE howboutthemcowboys;
GO
DROP TABLE tothesuperbowl;
GO
```

You should now get an error like the following:

```
Msg 3701, Level 14, State 20, Line 3
Cannot drop the table 'tothesuperbowl', because it does not exist
or you do not have permission.
```

8. Let's take a quick peek at a few new Dynamic Management Views (DMVs) to see policy information that has been pulled down from Microsoft Purview. Connect as a sysadmin to your SQL Server 2022 instance and execute the script **policydmvs.sql**, which uses the following T-SQL statements:

```
-- Lists generally supported actions
SELECT * FROM sys.dm_server_external_policy_actions;
GO
```

```
-- Lists the roles that are part of a policy published to
this server
SELECT * FROM sys.dm_server_external_policy_roles;
GO
-- Lists the links between the roles and actions, could be used to
join the two
SELECT * FROM sys.dm_server_external_policy_role_actions;
GO
```

The results of **dm_server_external_policy_actions** are all the possible types of actions a policy can be applied to. Think of these as the detailed types of permissions the Data and DevOps policies apply to. This list will expand as we provide more capabilities. The DMV **sys.dm_server_external_policy_roles** lists out the detailed roles that apply to Data and DevOps policies including reading, performance monitoring, and security auditing. You will see others in here not implemented yet and roles for Connect, which apply to all roles. This list will also expand as we add more capabilities. The DMV **dm_server_external_policy_role_actions** is a join of what actions are allowed for specific predefined roles. These DMVs will always be populated even if no policies have been created.

9. Since we have created a policy, execute the script **policyprincipals.sql**, which uses the following T-SQL statements:

```
-- Lists all Azure AD principals that were given connect
permissions
SELECT * FROM sys.dm_server_external_policy_principals;
GO
-- Lists Azure AD principals assigned to a given role on a given
resource scope
SELECT * FROM sys.dm_server_external_policy_role_members;
GO
-- Lists Azure AD principals, joined with roles, joined with their
data actions
```

```
SELECT * FROM sys.dm_server_external_policy_principal_assigned_
actions;
GO
```

Let's break down the results from these DMVs. **dm_server_ external_policy_principals** will list any AAD account you have granted access through a policy. You will only see one row for an account even if it has been granted access through more than one policy. The **aad_object_id** column maps to the unique ID in Azure Active Directory for this account. **dm_server_external_policy_ role_members** shows which roles from dm_server_external_ policy_roles the AAD account is a member of. Then finally **dm_ server_external_policy_principal_assigned_actions** shows all the permissions for an AAD account assigned through any policy.

10. Let's show an example of a DevOps policy. Let's say you hire a consultant to look at performance metrics for your SQL Server for a period of time to help tune and improve performance. You want to grant an AAD *guest* account access to your SQL Server (or many) but limit them to only access certain operations that allow them to analyze performance but make no changes or access no user data. In Purview Studio, select **Data policy** from the left-hand menu as you did in step 2. Select **DevOps policies** and **+ New policy**. For Data source type choose SQL Server on Arc-enabled servers and pick your registered SQL Server and select **Select**.

Now choose Add/remove subjects and pick the guest AAD account you created for the prerequisites. Your screen should look like Figure 3-50.

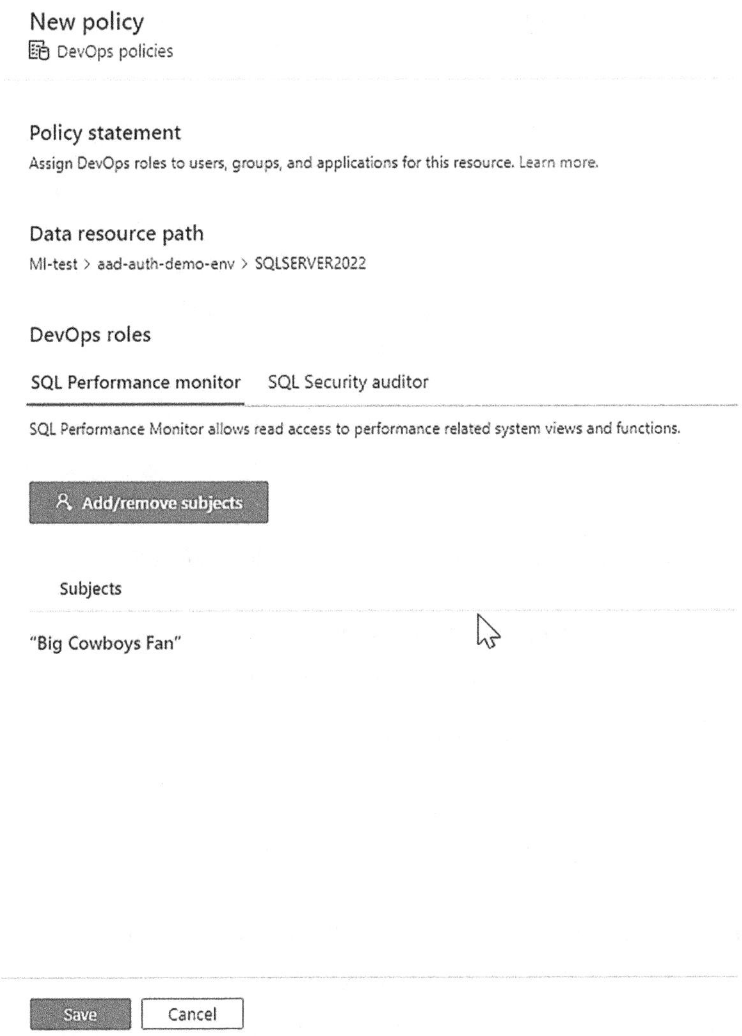

New policy

🖺 DevOps policies

Policy statement

Assign DevOps roles to users, groups, and applications for this resource. Learn more.

Data resource path

MI-test > aad-auth-demo-env > SQLSERVER2022

DevOps roles

SQL Performance monitor   SQL Security auditor

SQL Performance Monitor allows read access to performance related system views and functions.

[옷 Add/remove subjects]

Subjects

"Big Cowboys Fan"

[Save] [Cancel]

Figure 3-50. *Create a DevOps policy for SQL performance monitoring.*

Select **Save**. You don't need to publish DevOps policies.

11. On your SQL Server instance connected as a sysadmin, execute the script **policyrefresh.sql**.

12. Execute the scripts **policydmvs.sql** and **policyprincipals.sql** as a sysadmin to see the additions to the new AAD guest account and the permissions granted for performance monitoring.

13. Connect with SSMS with the guest ADD account using MFA as you have done before with other AAD accounts in this chapter.

141

As a refresher my login to SSMS looks like Figure 3-51.

Figure 3-51. *Connecting as a guest AAD account to SQL Server*

14. Execute the script **perfdmvs.sql** as the new AAD guest account.
     This scrip uses the following T-SQL statements:

```
SELECT * FROM sys.dm_exec_requests;
GO
SELECT * FROM sys.dm_os_wait_stats;
GO
```

Your results should be the same results as you see from a typical
admin who can view this type of information.

15. Execute the script **querythecowboys.sql** as the new guest AAD
     account. Notice you get the following error trying to access
     user data:

```
Msg 229, Level 14, State 5, Line 3
The SELECT permission was denied on the object 'tothesuperbowl',
database 'howboutthemcowboys', schema 'dbo'.
```

16. To ensure the account that is granted a policy to just look at
     performance data cannot make any changes, execute the script
     sp_configure.sql, which uses the following T-SQL statements:

```
EXEC sp_configure 'show advanced options', 1;
GO
```

You should receive the following error:

```
Msg 15247, Level 16, State 1, Procedure sp_configure, Line 105
[Batch Start Line 0]
User does not have permission to perform this action.
```

17. Let's say the contract for the consultant with the guest AAD account is now over. You would like to ensure the system is secure and remove access to SQL Server. Let's do this through Microsoft Purview. In Purview Studio select the **Data policy** icon from the left-hand menu. Then select **DevOps policies**. Select the checkbox next to the policy you created and select **Delete** at the top of the screen. Select Delete again.

18. Now go back to SQL Server and try to connect again with the guest AAD account. You should get a login failure error.

In this exercise you learned how to create policies with Microsoft Purview to grant access to AAD accounts to read data and execute performance monitoring analysis without having to directly create logins and assign roles in SQL Server. SQL Server has been enhanced to integrate policies from Purview into the security permission system so it naturally feels like you granted direct authentication and authorization inside SQL Server.

Tip   There is one issue you may encounter using this feature. You will need to extend how you view security information in the system. You will need to use the new DMVs in addition to other security catalog views to see who has access to your system and their permissions. Fortunately, features like SQL Server Audit and Extended Events can track any account that has access through policies.

Connecting SQL to the World

SQL Server is now not just connected to Azure. SQL Server is *integrated* with Azure to bring to you powerful solutions such as managed disaster recovery, near-real-time analytics, and centralized security and governance. Each of these solutions requires us to enhance the SQL Server engine so that the capabilities you need are seamless and work with the SQL Server ecosystem. There is no requirement to use all of these services. Pick and choose the one you want when you need it. The future for SQL Server hybrid is bright, and for Microsoft and our customers, the journey is just starting.

CHAPTER 4

Built-In Query Intelligence

For as long as I've been at Microsoft, we have attempted to put our heart and soul into one of the best query processors (QPs) in the industry. But as I saw in technical support for so many years, there were some scenarios where the QP struggled. Back in 2016, our team started a journey to make the query processor adaptable to a variety of workloads, helping users achieve consistent or improved performance with no code changes.

We first called this effort **Adaptive Query Processing (AQP)**. I first heard of this term from Joe Sack, who was the lead program manager for AQP in SQL Server 2017. AQP added the ability to respond to memory grants and support adaptive joins and introduced batch mode for analytic queries. These were all enabled by changing the database compatibility (dbcompat) level to 140 (the default for SQL Server 2017) with no code changes required. Read more about dbcompat levels at `https://aka.ms/dbcompat`. This was just the beginning.

Note Have fun and go back in time. See Conor Cunningham and me present AQP at SQLBits in 2018: `https://sqlbits.com/Sessions/Event17/Adaptive_ query_processing_in_SQL_databases?msclkid=2b8c0902c4ca11ecb 9e5158053df6fa9`.

We doubled our efforts and rebranded this concept **Intelligent Query Processing (IQP)** in SQL Server 2019. IQP included new and powerful scenarios like table variable deferred compilation and expanded memory grants and batch mode to row-based tables. You can read a detailed coverage of IQP in Chapter 2 of my book *SQL Server 2019 Revealed*, or you can dive into our documentation at `https://aka.ms/iqp`. These scenarios were all enabled with no code changes by simply changing to dbcompat level 150.

© Bob Ward 2022
B. Ward, *SQL Server 2022 Revealed*, https://doi.org/10.1007/978-1-4842-8894-8_4

Note   Approximate Query Processing did not require dbcompat 150, just an upgrade to SQL Server 2019.

As we rolled into SQL Server 2022, we decided to keep the IQP branding but also roll up the entire new set of scenarios into the term *built-in query intelligence*. This includes the *next generation (nextgen)* of IQP, new enhancements to Query Store, and these scenarios working together.

How good is built-in query intelligence in SQL Server 2022? I broke up these capabilities into two chapters. This chapter will include an introduction to all the built-in query intelligence concepts and then dive into Query Store and Intelligent Query Processing (IQP) features that don't require dbcompat 160. Chapter 5 will dive into three new IQP capabilities that are available when you enable dbcompat 160 (but again, no code changes are required).

Why so much content for just one part of SQL Server 2022? Consider these points:

- This is one of the richest areas of investment for SQL Server 2022.

- Almost every scenario in these two chapters has a story behind it. Not only do I like telling stories but I have firsthand experiences behind many of them.

- While the entire concept of built-in query intelligence is to gain performance and insights with little effort, I take time in both chapters to explain details behind each of them.

- There are many examples in both chapters for you to try out these new capabilities.

As you read these next two chapters, keep in mind the following principles our team has always used in this area:

- As much as possible, "do no harm." In other words, make sure not to break existing workloads and not make them run slower than they would if the feature were not available.

- Require no code changes to take advantage of these features (with exceptions like Query Store hints and approximate percentile).

- Allow any of these features to be individually turned off. This allows you to take advantage of ones you like and disable others that may not be the best for your workload.

Does our innovation really work? Our partner group engineering manager for the engine, Naveen Prakash, thinks so: *"Unpredictable* query performance has resulted in people unable to get in their cars or trucks failing to leave the warehouse. SQL Server 2022 *continues to raise the bar for transparent, predictable, and efficient query* processing through intelligent monitoring and adaptive execution."

So sit back and read on. Pick sections you want to read now and maybe come back later for more. Imagine yourself over the next two chapters in a past "brain melting" session I've presented.

Let's look at the overall lineup of new capabilities, dive into the *new* Query Store, and then go step-by-step to see how you can take advantage of some of the capabilities in the nextgen IQP.

Built-In Query Intelligence in SQL Server 2022

Early in the planning for SQL Server 2022, Pedro Lopes and I came up with the term *built-in query intelligence*. We did this to represent the innovation that is new in SQL Server 2022 to **gain and maintain consistent performance with no code changes**. In addition, these changes allow you to gain new insights into query performance and tune queries faster and in new ways with enhancements to Query Store. These innovations are "built in" to the engine itself and use "data" to act intelligently. That data is based on statistics or execution information from data sources like Query Store.

This collection of new capabilities includes the following:

- Query Store enhancements such as being on by default for new databases, support for queries executed against read replicas, and Query Store hints.

- New IQP scenarios including some amazing solutions to "age-old" problems for SQL Server query performance; in fact, some of the new capabilities *use Query Store.*

Figure 4-1 shows a visualization of all the new IQP features and notes which ones use Query Store.

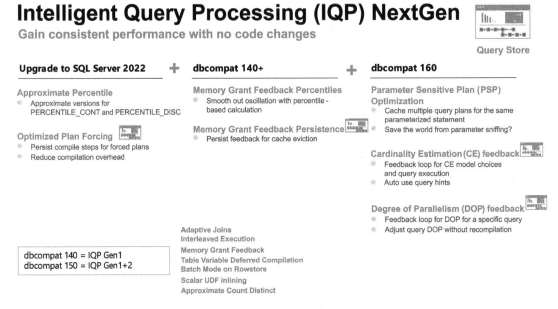

Figure 4-1. *SQL Server 2022 IQP new features*

This chapter will cover capabilities you can get without dbcompat 160 (the left two columns). Chapter 5 will dive into IQP capabilities if you enable dbcompat 160 including Parameter-Sensitive Plan (PSP) optimization, cardinality estimation (CE) model feedback, and degree of parallelism (DOP) feedback.

Note in the bottom-right corner a box describing that "IQP Gen1" is enabled with dbcompat 140. This represents the IQP capabilities we introduced in SQL Server 2017. "IQP Gen1+2" represents the IQP capabilities we introduced in SQL Server 2019 plus SQL Server 2017. It is important to know this because you might be upgrading from SQL Server 2016 or earlier to SQL Server 2022 and not realize all the previous IQP capabilities you could be using. You can always keep up with all IQP features at `https://aka.ms/iqp`.

Let's start by looking at enhancements for Query Store. There are enough new enhancements to SQL Server 2022 I call it the **new** Query Store.

The New Query Store

Query Store in my opinion is simply one of the coolest features we have ever put in the SQL Server engine. As far back as the mid-2000s, the famous Conor Cunningham approached several of us in customer support about a new way to track query performance. Up to this point, we were all "polling" Dynamic Management Views to persist query performance execution data. Conor had the idea baking into the query processor itself telemetry about query performance execution. This telemetry would be persisted in the user database in the form of system tables. He called it Query Disk Store (QDS), which is now known today as Query Store.

It took several iterations, but Conor's dream of this innovation was realized in SQL Server 2016. It was also a key piece for success of Azure SQL Database as we turned it on by default for all new databases.

I still find today many customers I talk to do not use Query Store. Some don't know exactly what it is, some have heard of it but haven't tried to turn it on, and others have used it but had issues.

By SQL Server 2019, we completed new enhancements to fix some performance issues, added wait stats information (added in SQL Server 2017), and introduced extra controls to help with query capture and better storage management of the data. All of this has set us up to move forward with a new Query Store for everyone.

If you are new to Query Store, I recommend you read over our documentation first at `https://aka.ms/querystore` before you read our SQL Server 2022 enhancements. With that in mind, there are a few fundamental principles about Query Store you need to keep in mind as you use new capabilities in SQL Server 2022:

- Query Store has an option called **capture mode**. Capture mode controls what type of queries are kept in Query Store. A value of ALL means all queries are collected (well, not exactly all since some SQL statements are never candidates for Query Store like CREATE TABLE). A value of AUTO means only meaningful queries are collected, which effectively means only queries that you care about collecting performance information are kept. A value of CUSTOM allows you to configure a more granular control of what is kept vs. ALL or AUTO. The reason this concept is important is that you may trying to use a feature that relies on Query Store but it doesn't appear to be working. It could be that the query was not eligible to be kept

in Query Store based on capture policies. You can read more about
Query Store capture mode at `https://docs.microsoft.com/sql/`
`relational-databases/performance/best-practice-with-the-`
`query-store?#set-the-optimal-query-store-capture-mode`.

- Query Store keeps all data within system tables within the context of
  a user database. This extends the storage required for the database.
  There are options (with defaults) that control what is the maximum
  size of the space used for Query Store and cleanup policies. In
  addition, there are ways to manually remove all data, or subsets
  of data, within Query Store. You can read more about Query Store
  maintenance at `https://docs.microsoft.com/sql/relational-`
  `databases/performance/monitoring-performance-by-using-the-`
  `query-store?#Scenarios`.

Armed with this knowledge, in this section I will show you why I call Query Store in
SQL Server 2022 *new* including the following:

- Query Store is now on by default for new databases.

- Query Store hints to shape query plans with no code changes.

- Query Store supports telemetry for queries against read-only replicas.

- Some new IQP features use Query Store to improve performance with
  no code changes.

On by Default

I remember vividly when we were talking about new features for project Dallas
when Pedro Lopes and Joe Sack said to me, *"Bob*, we are going to turn on Query
Store by default." My reaction was *"Hey*, we don't do that for SQL Server. We are
pretty conservative when it comes to turning things like this on by default." But their
explanation as to why we were doing this was a good one.

Here is a summary of the facts they presented:

- Query Store has been around for several releases since SQL
  Server 2016.

- We have this on by default for Azure SQL for millions of databases.
  And we have been doing this for several years.

- We changed the default on how to capture queries to a mode to ease burden on applications with ad hoc workloads (**QUERY_CAPTURE_ MODE** to AUTO).

- We added a new **CUSTOM** option in SQL Server 2019 for QUERY_ CAPTURE_MODE to give more control on what was captured by Query Store using the **QUERY_CAPTURE_POLICY** options.

- We plan to add Query Store hints and support for read replicas in SQL Server 2022.

- Finally, and the most important reason, some new IQP scenarios would *require* Query Store. This statement really caught my eye. I remember saying something like "Say that again?" You will see what we mean by requiring Query Store when you read about new IQP scenarios for SQL Server 2022 in this and the next chapter.

This is all nice, but I'm sure you are reading this and still may be asking, "Is there any impact to my application?"

The answer as with any general question like this is "It depends." All the reasons Joe and Pedro gave me previously make me feel comfortable telling anyone that the impact to any application with Query Store enabled could be negligible.

Having said that here are a few thoughts in my personal opinion to consider:

- We only enable Query Store for newly created databases in SQL Server 2022. Any databases restored from a previous version of SQL Server will only have Query Store enabled if it was already turned on.

- I always recommend to any customer to test their application with any system or program that is capturing telemetry. This includes third-party applications, use of Dynamic Management Views (DMVs), Extended Events, or Query Store.

- We have had Query Store on by default for Azure SQL Database for several years with no report of customer workloads being impacted.

- New capture policies allow you to "capture what you need," therefore decreasing overall impact to the system.

- We still recommend for some production workloads the use of trace flag 7745 to avoid impact of shutdown. You can read more about this trace flag and all the best practices for Query Store at `https://docs.microsoft.com/sql/relational-databases/performance/best-practice-with-the-query-store`.

Query Store Hints

In the summer of 2021, we introduced the concept of Query Store hints for Azure SQL Database. The concept of Query Store hints is to shape query execution plans without changing application code.

Note   You can read about the original launch of Query Store hints in this episode of Data Exposed with Anna Hoffman and Joe Sack: `https://youtu.be/pYB6Uik_Q7A`.

The concept of a *query hint* is not new, and you may use them already today. By adding an OPTION clause to your T-SQL statement, you can influence the query optimizer on the building of a query plan. Two common query hints I've seen used are RECOMPILE (for a compilation each time a query is executed) and MAXOP (control the max degree of parallelism at the query level). You can read about all the possible query hints and examples at `https://docs.microsoft.com/sql/t-sql/queries/hints-transact-sql-query`.

If you are not using query hints, don't be concerned. Query hints are designed for scenarios where for some reason your application is not working well with the query plan compiled by the query processor by default.

However, there are practical reasons when these hints are needed for production workloads. Query hints require the ability to change the T-SQL statement. But what if the T-SQL statement is called in application code and it is not practical or not possible to change application code to apply the hint? This is where Query Store hints can be beneficial because the query optimizer can apply the hint based on what is stored in Query Store without changing application code.

How Do You Use Query Store Hints?

Here is how you would use a Query Store hint assuming Query Store is enabled for read/write:

- A query is executed, and the plan is stored in Query Store.

- You find the **query_id** using Query Store catalog views for the query to which you want to apply the hint.

- You execute the stored procedure **sys.sp_query_store_set_hints** specifying the **query_id** and the hint you want to apply.

- You can view existing Query Store hints with the view **sys.query_store_query_hints.**

We save the hint in Query Store so the query processor will use the hint provided for the next execution of the query. Because the hint is persisted, it will survive restarts and plan cache eviction.

Not all query hints are supported with Query Store. For a complete list of supported query hints, check the documentation at `https://docs.microsoft.com/sql/relational-databases/system-stored-procedures/sys-sp-query-store-set-hints-transact-sql`. There are also some scenarios where the query optimizer cannot use a query hint you specify based on the compilation rules for a given query. This is called a Query Store hint *failure* and will be logged in the view **sys.query_store_query_hints**.

The documentation has a very nice end-to-end example for using Query Store hints at `https://docs.microsoft.com/sql/relational-databases/performance/query-store-hints?#examples`. I'll show you an example of a system-generated Query Store hint in Chapter 5 called **cardinality estimation (CE) model feedback**.

When Should I Use a Query Store Hint?

While query hints could be a useful feature for you to use long-term with your application, most of the uses of query hints I've seen are a temporary measure. Therefore, Query Store hints can be an extremely useful feature when you want to temporarily apply a query hint and not change (or can't change) application code. Query Store hints are also nice in situations where you want to override a query hint in a query from the application code.

Note   There are some aspects of using Query Store hints you should understand before using them, which you can read about at `https://docs.microsoft.com/sql/relational-databases/performance/query-store-hints?#query-store-hints-and-feature-interoperability`.

Before you use a Query Store hint, confirm that the problem you are trying to solve can't be done another way. For example, many have used the RECOMPLIE or OPTIMIZE FOR hint to solve the classic problem of Parameter-Sensitive Plans. In SQL Server 2022, we have a new solution for this problem that may allow you to avoid the use of those query hints. You can read more about Parameter-Sensitive Plan (PSP) optimization in Chapter 5.

How Is This Different Than Plan Guides?

Like Query Store hints, plan guides provide a method to shape query plans without changing application code. Plan guides have been in SQL Server for many versions. Query store hints provide a much simpler interface to shape query plans mainly because you only need to add a query hint(s) to an existing query stored in Query Store.

Plan guides can be created by providing the original SQL text of the query from the application or by using a plan handle from a plan in cache. Therefore, Query Store hints have the advantage of being a simpler method for implementation and can be used for queries persisted over time. One advantage plan guides have over Query Store hints is that they do not require Query Store to be enabled.

Query Store Support for Secondary Replicas

While Query Store has been a great innovation for SQL Server, a frequently requested enhancement is to support collecting performance execution statistics for queries run against secondary read replicas for Always On Availability Groups.

Note   You can see how popular this request has been on our `https://aka.ms/sqlfeedback` site at `https://feedback.azure.com/d365community/idea/eade91be-4e25-ec11-b6e6-000d3a4f0da0`.

With SQL Server 2022, you can now configure an Always On Availability Group to support capturing statistics if queries are directed at a read replica.

I think the best way to dive deeper into this new capability is to answer some "how" questions.

How to Do You Configure It?

Once Query Store is enabled on the primary replica of the Always On Availability Group, you can run the following T-SQL in the context of the primary database:

```
ALTER DATABASE CURRENT FOR SECONDARY SET QUERY_STORE = ON ( OPERATION_MODE =
READ_WRITE);
```

Note   At the time of the writing of the book before General Availability, trace flag 12606 was required to enable this feature. Please consult the documentation at General Availability to see if this trace flag is still required. When you enable this feature, Query Store information is captured for all secondary replicas in the availability group. There is no method to control this per secondary replica.

Once you execute this statement, any query executed against *any* secondary replica will be captured in Query Store.

But if the query is run against a secondary replica, how can Query Store capture information about the query if the replica database is read-only? Let's see how it works.

How Does It Work?

When you enable Query Store and performance information is captured for a query, it is first recorded in a set of memory structures. Asynchronously, Query Store information is flushed to disk (to a collection of system tables in the user database). Runtime statistics are flushed to disk based on a configuration value called **DATA_FLUSH_INTERVAL_SECONDS**. You can read more about how Query Store collects information at https://docs.microsoft.com/sql/relational-databases/performance/how-query-store-collects-data.

If you have enabled Query Store capture for secondary replicas, Query Store information is captured in memory structures on the secondary replica, but not flushed to the disk for the secondary replica database (because the database is read-only). Instead, the information is sent back to the primary replica where it is flushed to disk. Always On Availability Group replicas have a *channel* to communicate with each other, and we simply use that channel to send data back to the primary. The SQL Server 2022 engine has been enhanced to understand this new type of information sent back to the primary and then adds the data to Query Store on the primary replica as seen in Figure 4-2.

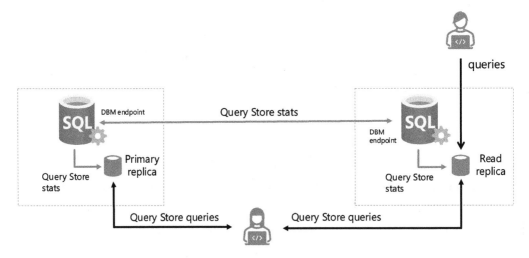

Figure 4-2. *Query Store and secondary replicas*

Let's explore more the flow of how this works. Let's assume you have an Always On Availability Group set up and configured for Query Store on secondaries. When a user issues a query against the secondary read replica, the engine will collect Query Store stats in memory. These stats are not persisted on the secondary because the database is read-only.

- Background tasks will queue these stats in memory in the secondary replica engine. At *some point* (an internal implementation detail), these stats will be sent on the same communication channel used for availability group log changes (the dbm endpoint). We try to make sure that these performance stats have a lower priority than log changes so as not to disrupt replica of log changes.

Note   As I was writing this chapter, our team was investigating whether we could enable the system stored procedure **sp_query_store_flush_db** to force the sending of stats from the secondary to the primary.

- On the primary replica, background tasks will receive these Query
  Store stats and persist them to disk, tracking the replica details
  along with the stats. Since these stats are stored in the database and
  are logged changes, they are also sent to secondary replicas like all
  logged changes.

- Now, any user can run queries or reports for Query Store stats against
  the primary replica or secondary replicas.

In order to distinguish the difference between queries on the primary and secondary
replicas, a new column has been added to Query Store view **sys.query_store_runtime_
stats** called **replica_group_id**. This maps to a new view called **sys.query_store_replicas**,
which contains all the replica names, roles, and their ID value.

There are a few things I think you should know about the expected behavior of this
capability:

- If you enable this feature, you may need to increase the value of
  MAX_STORAGE_SIZE_MB, especially if you have multiple secondary
  replicas where you are executing queries.

- The results do not show up on the primary replica immediately.
  Since we use the same channel for replicating changes to replicas, we
  don't want to negatively impact transaction changes. Therefore, we
  send back data to the primary in a delayed fashion. Today there is no
  configuration value to adjust this time. In my experience, it can take
  several minutes for query performance information to appear on the
  primary after executing a query on a secondary replica.

- Even with this delay, if your application is sensitive to changes to be
  replicated in your Always On Availability Group, you should test this
  option carefully to ensure the use of the standard communication
  channel for replica changes is not impacted. Throughput can also
  depend on how often you execute queries on secondary replicas and
  how many secondary replicas are in the availability group.

- The only Query Store views that capture the **replica_group_id** are
  sys.query_store_runtime_stats and **sys.query_store_wait_stats**. If
  you want to find out information in the *plan store* (i.e., **Sys.query_
  store_query**) specific to a replica, you will need to join to one of

these views (using the **plan_id** as the join column). In other words, if you only query **sys.query_store_plan**, you will not be able to tell whether plans were captured from the primary or secondary replicas.

- At the time of the writing of this chapter, we were still working out what features that use Query Store may or may not be supported for read replicas. This includes Query Store hints, optimized plan forcing, DOP feedback, and CE feedback. You can keep track of all the latest updates with this feature in the documentation at `https://docs.microsoft.com/sql/relational-databases/performance/monitoring-performance-by-using-the-query-store?#query-store-for-secondary-replicas`.

How Do You Use It?

Since we are just enhancing the existing Query Store functionality, you can now use Query Store like you do today to analyze query performance. And because all the data is in the primary replica, any backup of the primary replica database includes all the information from all replicas.

Store for IQP

Since Query Store data is persisted in the database, it survives restarts, contains important telemetry information, and therefore serves as a perfect "store" for new IQP features.

In addition, since Query Store has persistent storage, the query processor can save specific information in Query Store to enable new capabilities. Furthermore, Query Store implementation in the engine has background tasks, which can be used to perform analysis to avoid impacting query execution.

For example, Query Store background tasks can be used to record query performance statistics and *feedback* data for queries that are eligible for **degree of parallelism (DOP) feedback**. This data is persisted in Query Store tables and can be used by the query processor when determining the degree of parallelism (DOP) for a query. You can read more about the details of DOP feedback in Chapter 5.

Because specific IQP features rely on Query Store, it is even more important to maintain and configure Query Store properly. You should treat Query Store as a *production* set of data (even though it is a collection of system tables within the user database).

Therefore, be sure to review these documentation pages on best practices and maintenance of Query Store:

- https://docs.microsoft.com/sql/relational-databases/ performance/best-practice-with-the-query-store.

- https://docs.microsoft.com/sql/relational-databases/ performance/monitoring-performance-by-using-the-query- store?#Scenarios

IQP Nextgen Defaults

When you upgrade to SQL Server 2022, several IQP features are simply "turned on" without any dbcompat change required. This means that you could be using a dbcompat level from versions of SQL Server prior to when IQP "was born," like SQL Server 2016 (dbcompat 130), and take advantage of new IQP features. This includes approximate percentile and optimized plan forcing. Let's explain how each of these features works and how you can take advantage of them.

Approximate Percentile

In SQL Server 2019, we introduced a new T-SQL function called **APPROX_COUNT_ DISTINCT** to allow you to get an approximation for the number of distinct values for a query. Even though this is not as accurate as using a SELECT COUNT DISTINCT, it can perform much faster and have an accuracy of around 97%. We have found that this type of function can greatly improve the performance of analytic workloads. You can read more about APPROX_COUNT_DISTINCT at https://docs.microsoft.com/sql/t-sql/ functions/approx-count-distinct-transact-sql.

SQL Server includes two functions to help an analytic workload calculate a *percentile* of a range of values: PERCENTILE_CONT (which you can read about at https:// docs.microsoft.com/sql/t-sql/functions/percentile-cont-transact-sql) and PERCENTILE_DISC (which you can read about at https://docs.microsoft.com/sql/ t-sql/functions/percentile-disc-transact-sql).

SQL Server 2022 provides *approximate* equivalent to these two functions: **APPROX_PERCENTILE_CONT** and **APPROX_PERCENTILE_DISC**. These can be extremely useful for analytic workloads with exceptionally large sets of data. These functions will perform faster, and the implementation guarantees up to a 1.33% error rate within a 99% probability. Here is a T-SQL example for APPROX_PERCENTILE_CONT:

```
SELECT DeptId,
APPROX_PERCENTILE_CONT(0.10) WITHIN GROUP(ORDER BY Salary) AS 'P10',
APPROX_PERCENTILE_CONT(0.90) WITHIN GROUP(ORDER BY Salary) AS 'P90'
FROM tblEmployee
GROUP BY DeptId;
```

The argument for APPROX_PERCENTILE_CONT is the *percentile* to compute for the range of data.

You can read more about how to use APPROX_PERCENTILE_CONT at https://docs.microsoft.com/sql/t-sql/functions/approx-percentile-cont-transact-sql and APPROX_PERCENTILE_DISC at https://docs.microsoft.com/sql/t-sql/functions/approx-percentile-disc-transact-sql.

I spoke with Balmukund Lakhani, Senior Program Manager at Microsoft, about why T-SQL users should consider using these new functions:

> *In SQL Server 2022, we have the newest member in approximate query processing family: approximate percentile functions (APPROX_PERCENTILE_CONT for continuous and APPROX_PERCENTILE_DISC for discrete). These are aggregate functions which can be used in place of earlier analytic percentile functions (PERCENTILE_CONT for continuous and PERCENTILE_DISC for discrete) when faster performance is desirable at the cost of minimal error in output. Imagine a table of temperature sensor data which has millions of rows and you want to find 99th percentile quickly with acceptable rank based error bound to take quick decisions. These functions can give output in a single pass with less CPU and memory usage.*

Optimized Plan Forcing

Optimized plan forcing is a new capability in SQL Server 2022 intended to reduce the time it takes to compile certain queries if the query plan is forced in Query Store.

> **Note**   Forcing a query plan in Query Store is different than using query plan hints. Forcing a query plan allows you to take a specific query plan in Query Store and "tell" the optimizer to use the plan vs. creating a new plan on compilation. You use the system procedure **sp_query_store_force_plan** to force a query plan.

The Background

By 2019, our engineering team along with CSS had noticed a pattern of performance problems for some customers called a *compile storm*. In these situations, all query plans were evicted from cache due to some unforeseen event (e.g., failover, restart, memory pressure). Then the application would immediately generate a large number of concurrent connections, each with queries that required compilation in a truly brief period.

The typical symptom of this problem was a significant amount of CPU utilization across all processors (e.g., 100% CPU utilization or "pegged"). Applications were effectively halted as all users were running queries that required query compilation of significant duration. Query compilation is almost an entirely CPU-bound operation, and certain query patterns can take a prolonged period of time to compile and generate a query plan.

For several of these examples, the problem could occur even if the customer were using Query Store to force a specific query plan. Even when a query plan is forced in Query Store, the query still must go through compilation when the plan is not in cache.

How Does It Work?

In SQL Server 2022, we have enhanced Query Store and the query processor to shortcut the time of compilation for forced query plans if we believe compilation of the query can take a significant amount of time. We call this concept **optimized plan forcing**.

Here is how optimized plan forcing works:

- If Query Store is enabled when a query is compiled, it is eligible to have a *compilation script* generated if query compilation takes a significant amount of time. What is significant? We don't document the threshold for this or allow you to change it, but it effectively means the *compilation phase* for query execution is affecting the overall query duration. You will see in the next section titled "**See It in Action**" an example. In addition, only queries that require "full optimization" (i.e., queries that don't have trivial plans) are eligible. You can review all the different considerations that determine what queries are eligible for optimized plan forcing at `https://docs.microsoft.com/sql/relational-databases/performance/optimized-plan-forcing-query-store?#considerations`.

- The compilation script is binary data encoded into the binary representation of the XML query plan stored in Query Store as represented by the **query_plan** column from the **sys.query_store_plan** view. You will not see this information if you "cast" the **query_plan** column to XML. It is a binary format that is not documented and not part of the showplan XML schema.

- We also mark the query plan as having a compilation script by setting the column **has_compile_replay_script** to **1** as seen in the **sys.query_store_plan** view.

All of this happens by default in SQL Server 2022 for any dbcompat level if Query Store is enabled with READ_WRITE for the database. If you use **sp_query_store_force_plan** to force a plan that has a compilation script, the next time we need to compile the query, we will use the compilation script to shorten compile time. This will occur as long as the query plan is marked as forced in Query Store.

When I've presented this concept, I have been asked, "Why would we need this feature if the query plan is forced?" A forced query plan simply "locks in" a specific query plan when a query is compiled. It doesn't mean we don't have to compile the query's plan. If we can shortcut the time to compile the plan, it can end up saving a lot of CPU cycles, especially during these "compile storm" scenarios.

See It in Action

I must admit I was struggling to produce scenarios to trigger a compilation script. When I researched some of the background of our design for this feature, we sometimes used queries from the TPC-H benchmark to test it. As it turns out, anyone can run a workload that *simulates* TPC-H by using HammerDB (`www.hammerdb.com`). I followed the instructions in the HammerDB documentation for TPC-H for SQL Server (using the smallest size possible). I then enabled Query Store (capture mode = ALL) and ran a sample workload. Several queries showed up in **sys.query_store_plan** with a column value of **1** for **has_compile_replay_script**.

I looked over several of these queries and noticed this pattern:

- Most of these queries had fairly larger SQL text than most other queries.

- Many of these queries involved joins for many tables.

I was able then to construct my own demonstration using the **WideWorldImporters** sample database.

Here are the prerequisites to run this example:

- SQL Server 2022 Evaluation Edition.

- Virtual machine or computer with minimum of four CPUs and 8Gb RAM (it may be possible to see this in action with fewer CPUs, but this is the minimum I used for the test).

- SQL Server Management Studio (SSMS). The latest 18.x or 19.x build will work.

- A copy of the scripts from the GitHub repo of this book from the **ch4_builtinqueryintelligence\opf** directory.

Here are the steps you can use to see this for yourself:

1. Copy the sample backup for **WideWorldImporters** from https://aka.ms/WideWorldImporters. The restore script in the next steps assumes a location for the backup in **c:\sql_sample_databases**.

2. Execute the script **restorewwi.sql**. Edit the file locations per your needs. The script executes the following T-SQL statements:

```
USE master;
GO
DROP DATABASE IF EXISTS WideWorldImporters;
GO
RESTORE DATABASE WideWorldImporters FROM DISK = 'c:\sql_sample_
databases\WideWorldImporters-Full.bak' with
MOVE 'WWI_Primary' TO 'c:\sql_sample_databases\
WideWorldImporters.mdf',
MOVE 'WWI_UserData' TO 'c:\sql_sample_databases\
WideWorldImporters_UserData.ndf',
```

```
    MOVE 'WWI_Log' TO 'c:\sql_sample_databases\WideWorldImporters.ldf',
    MOVE 'WWI_InMemory_Data_1' TO 'c:\sql_sample_databases\
    WideWorldImporters_InMemory_Data_1',
    stats=5;
    GO
    ALTER DATABASE WideWorldImporters SET QUERY_STORE CLEAR ALL;
    GO
```

3. Execute the script **bigjoin.sql**. The query should take
    around ~7–10 seconds to complete. The script executes the
    following T-SQL:

```
    USE WideWorldImporters;
    GO
    ALTER DATABASE SCOPED CONFIGURATION CLEAR PROCEDURE_CACHE;
    GO
    SET STATISTICS TIME ON
    GO
    SELECT o.OrderID, ol.OrderLineID, c.CustomerName,
    cc.CustomerCategoryName, p.FullName, city.CityName,
    sp.StateProvinceName, country.CountryName, si.StockItemName
    FROM Sales.Orders o
    JOIN Sales.Customers c
    ON o.CustomerID = c.CustomerID
    JOIN Sales.CustomerCategories cc
    ON c.CustomerCategoryID = cc.CustomerCategoryID
    JOIN Application.People p
    ON o.ContactPersonID = p.PersonID
    JOIN Application.Cities city
    ON city.CityID = c.DeliveryCityID
    JOIN Application.StateProvinces sp
    ON city.StateProvinceID = sp.StateProvinceID
    JOIN Application.Countries country
    ON sp.CountryID = country.CountryID
    JOIN Sales.OrderLines owl
    ON ol.OrderID = o.OrderID
```

```
JOIN Warehouse.StockItems si
ON ol.StockItemID = si.StockItemID
JOIN Warehouse.StockItemStockGroups sisg
ON si.StockItemID = sisg.StockItemID
UNION ALL
SELECT o.OrderID, ol.OrderLineID, c.CustomerName,
cc.CustomerCategoryName, p.FullName, city.CityName,
sp.StateProvinceName, country.CountryName, si.StockItemName
FROM Sales.Orders o
JOIN Sales.Customers c
ON o.CustomerID = c.CustomerID
JOIN Sales.CustomerCategories cc
ON c.CustomerCategoryID = cc.CustomerCategoryID
JOIN Application.People p
ON o.ContactPersonID = p.PersonID
JOIN Application.Cities city
ON city.CityID = c.DeliveryCityID
JOIN Application.StateProvinces sp
ON city.StateProvinceID = sp.StateProvinceID
JOIN Application.Countries country
ON sp.CountryID = country.CountryID
JOIN Sales.OrderLines ol
ON ol.OrderID = o.OrderID
JOIN Warehouse.StockItems si
ON ol.StockItemID = si.StockItemID
JOIN Warehouse.StockItemStockGroups sisg
ON si.StockItemID = sisg.StockItemID
ORDER BY OrderID;
GO
```

Notice the amount of SQL text, multiple joins, and UNION ALL
clause. The procedure cache for the database is cleared to make
sure the query is compiled for each execution. This may not be a
beautifully written query, but it represents an example of a query
where the compile time can represent a sizable percentage of the
CPU time required to execute the query.

Use the **Messages** tab in the SSMS results window and scroll down to the bottom. Your result should look similar to the following:

```
SQL Server parse and compile time:
   CPU time = 353 ms, elapsed time = 353 ms.

(916540 rows affected)

 SQL Server Execution Times:
   CPU time = 2531 ms,  elapsed time = 7827 ms.
```

You can see in this example that the compile time is ~13% of the overall CPU time for query execution.

4. Now let's see if this query is a candidate for optimized plan forcing. Execute the script **find_query_in_query_store.sql**. The script uses the following T-SQL:

```
USE WideWorldImporters;
GO
SELECT query_id, plan_id, avg_compile_duration/1000 as avg_
compile_ms,
last_compile_duration/1000 as last_compile_ms, is_forced_plan,
has_compile_replay_script,
cast(query_plan as xml) query_plan_xml
FROM sys.query_store_plan;
GO
```

The results should look like the following (I flipped the results to show each field vertically):

```
query_id                       2
plan_id                        1
avg_compile_ms                 353.088
last_compile_ms                353
is_forced_plan                 0
has_compile_replay_script      1
query_plan_xml                 <ShowPlanXML...>
```

166

The **query_id** and **plan_id** could be different, and your compile times could vary. However, they should be somewhere around 10–15% of the overall CPU time for the execution of the query. The key is the value of **has_compile_replay_script** is **1**.

If you "click" in SSMS on the **query_plan_xml** output, SSMS will open a new window and show XML text. If you look closely at the line starting with <StmtSimple… and scroll to the right, you will see these two values:

```
QueryCompilationReplay="1" StatementOptmLevel="FULL"
```

This means that this query is a candidate for optimized plan forcing. The "script" or "compile steps" have been baked into the plan XML in Query Store. These steps will be used the next time this query is compiled, but only if the query plan is forced in Query Store.

5. Let's try it. Load the script **forceplan.sql**. Edit the script to put in the **query_id** and **plan_id** values from the results in step 4. Execute the script. The script uses the following T-SQL:

```
EXEC sp_query_store_force_plan @query_id = <n>, @plan_id = <n>;
GO
```

6. Verify the query plan is forced by executing the script **find_query_in_query_store.sql** again. You should see a value for **is_forced_plan** of **1**.

7. The next time this query is compiled, we should see a significant reduction in compilation time. Run the script **bigjoin.sql** again (be sure to run the entire script as it forces a new compile). Using the Messages tab again, observe the compile time vs. overall CPU time. Your result should look similar to the following:

```
SQL Server parse and compile time:
   CPU time = 38 ms, elapsed time = 38 ms.

(916540 rows affected)

 SQL Server Execution Times:
   CPU time = 2672 ms,  elapsed time = 7636 ms.
```

You can see from these results that the time to compile the query is now ~1% of the overall CPU time.

8. To see the new values in Query Store views, first, flush data to Query Store so we can see all the recent statistics using the script **flush_query_store.sql**. This script uses the following T-SQL:

```
USE WideWorldImporters;
GO
EXEC sys.sp_query_store_flush_db;
GO
```

9. Now look at the latest statistics in Query Store by executing the script **find_query_in_query_store.sql** again. The **last_compile_ms** should match the value of the latest "SQL Server parse and compile time" from step 7.

Considerations for Using Optimized Plan Forcing

We enabled this feature by default for new databases in SQL Server 2022 because there is really no harm in using it. It does require Query Store to be enabled. If you are forcing query plans, any of the plans that are eligible for a compilation script will simply compile faster. There is no real overhead in using it.

Having said that, you can disable optimized plan forcing using the following methods:

- Set the ALTER DATABASE SCOPED CONFIGURATION statement using the option **OPTIMIZED_PLAN_FORCING** to OFF. (You can also use this option to turn it back on.)

- You can disable optimized plan forcing when you force a query plan with the system stored procedure **sp.query_store_force_plan** by using the **@disable_optimized_plan_forcing** option.

- You can use a query hint called **DISABLE_OPTIMIZED_PLAN_ FORCING**.

> **Tip**   When you want to get a list of all possible query hints (i.e., USE HINT), execute the system procedure **sys.dm_exec_valid_use_hints**.

Keep up with all the latest information on optimized plan forcing in our documentation at `https://docs.microsoft.com/sql/relational-databases/ performance/optimized-plan-forcing-query-store`.

IQP Nextgen with dbcompat 140+

Based on the previous section, you can see that if you upgrade to SQL Server 2022 with any supported dbcompat level, you are eligible to gain performance from these features:

- Approximate percentile

- Optimized plan forcing

For example, if you upgraded from SQL Server 2016 and kept the dbcompat level at 130, you would able to take advantage of these features (provided you meet the criteria for each).

But let's say you upgrade from SQL Server 2017 or 2019 and have dbcompat set at 140 or 150. What additional features can you use to improve performance? First, remember that any IQP features that shipped in 2017 and 2019 are available to you depending on dbcompat 140 or 150.

> **Note**   Approximate distinct was added to SQL Server 2019 independent of dbcompat level. You can read more at `https://docs.microsoft.com/sql/t- sql/functions/approx-count-distinct-transact-sql`.

In SQL Server 2022, if you are using dbcompat 140 or greater, then you can take advantage of enhancements for **memory grant feedback**.

In Chapter 2 of *SQL Server 2019 Revealed*, I provided a detailed background and explanation of memory grant feedback. Let me summarize here the key points I made in that chapter about memory grant feedback.

There are certain operators in a query plan that require their own memory allocation such as hash joins and sorts. When a query is compiled, SQL Server will decide how much memory is needed for these types of operators; this is called a *memory grant*. I love this detailed blog post by one of our longtime developers Jay Choe on memory grants: `https://docs.microsoft.com/en-us/archive/blogs/sqlqueryprocessing/understanding-sql-server-memory-grant`. Memory grants are also known as *query memory*.

A frequent problem I saw in support over the years occurred when the memory grant was not accurate compared with the memory actually required for the operator. This problem could come in two forms:

- If the memory grant was too small for query execution, then a *spill* could occur. Effectively, if during query execution the memory grant allocated up front at the start of the query was not enough, the engine would have to use tempdb as a *paging file*. Even the fastest disk for tempdb is not as fast as if the entire memory required was in RAM. As a result, a spill would result in slower performance of the query.

- If the memory grant was too large for query execution, other queries could be forced to wait, especially if multiple queries needed memory grants of a certain size. The symptom would be a wait_type = RESOURCE_SEMAPHORE.

Inaccurate memory grants can occur for many reasons. One of the most common is inaccurate cardinality estimations for operators that feed something like a hash join or sort. It could simply be that statistics are out of date.

Like any other problem, our support team would work with customers to provide workarounds. There were many options such as query hints or resource governor settings. But nothing really solved the underlying problem. Users would struggle to do a deep investigation on why the memory grant was not accurate.

In SQL Server 2017, we created a feedback model for memory grants for batch-mode operations (only columnstore at the time) if you used dbcompat 140. In SQL Server 2019, we enhanced the feedback system if dbcompat 150 was enabled to include row-mode operations (but batch mode was also introduced in SQL Server 2019 to be used without columnstore).

> **Note**   Read through the following about batch- and row-mode operations for SQL Server at `https://techcommunity.microsoft.com/t5/azure-sql-blog/introducing-batch-mode-on-rowstore/ba-p/386256`.

The concept of the feedback system was to evaluate how memory was *actually used* compared with the initial memory grant at the start of execution. On the next execution, if the memory used was significantly higher than the initial grant, the memory grant would be increased. If memory used was lower, the grant would be decreased.

SQL Server effectively *learns* from previous executions to make future executions more efficient. This innovation for me personally was groundbreaking. All those support cases over the years where customers struggled with spills or blocking problems could be solved automatically by the engine.

However, we discovered two areas of improvement from what we shipped in SQL Server 2017 and 2019:

Volatility

We baked into the initial design the ability to disable memory grant feedback if we discovered we were constantly having to adjust the memory grant for the same query over time. Parameter-Sensitive Plans (PSPs) are a notable example of this type of scenario. You could see if we needed to disable memory grant feedback by looking at the **IsMemoryGrantFeedbackAdjusted** attribute in the query plan and discovering a value of **No: Feedback disabled**.

Persistence

The feedback system works for most workloads but unfortunately is not persisted to disk. Therefore, if the server is restarted or the query plan is evicted from cache, all feedback is lost.

Memory Grant Percentiles

To improve the volatility problem with the initial design, memory grant feedback in SQL Server 2022 uses a percentile-based approach instead of disabling memory grant feedback. Rather than using the previous used memory from query execution, we consider a history of previous memory used to adjust a memory grant that is applicable across many query executions.

This approach favors avoiding spills, so it is possible that more memory may be granted than is required. If we use this approach for memory grants, you can observe this in the **IsMemoryGrantFeedbackAdjusted** attribute in the query plan with a value of **Yes: Percentile Adjusting**.

This behavior is on by default for SQL Server 2022 if you are using dbcompat 140 or greater. If you want to disable this feature, set the database-scoped configuration option **MEMORY_GRANT_FEEDBACK_PERCENTILE** to OFF.

Memory Grant Feedback Persistence

If you are using dbcompat 140 or greater with SQL Server 2022 and Query Store is enabled for READ_WRITE, we will persist memory grant feedback details to Query Store. This allows any memory grant feedback to survive server restart or plan cache eviction.

What better way to learn than through an exercise? I'm all about efficiency, so I'll reuse the example for memory grant feedback I introduced in *SQL Server 2019 Revealed* in Chapter 2 with a few additions.

A quick comment about this example before you go through it: I'm inducing the conditions where memory grant feedback is needed by forcing a hash join on a query and simulating cardinality problems. But the innovation here is real. This capability is solving real-world problems faced by applications every day that are not worried about whether a hash join is used by the query processor or don't even know what a memory grant is. That is the intention of IQP. Just make it work!

Prerequisites

The prerequisites for using this example are as follows:

- SQL Server 2022 Evaluation Edition.

- Virtual machine or computer with minimum of two CPUs with 8Gb RAM.

- SQL Server Management Studio (SSMS). The latest 18.x or 19.x build will work.

- A copy of the scripts from the GitHub repo of this book from the **ch4_ builtinqueryintelligence\persistedmgf** directory.

Follow These Steps for the Exercise

Follow these steps to see memory grant feedback with persistence on SQL Server 2022:

1. Download the **WideWorldImportersDW** database backup from https://github.com/Microsoft/sql-server-samples/releases/download/wide-world-importers-v1.0/ WideWorldImportersDW-Full.bak. The restore script in the next steps assumes the backup is located in **c:\sql_sample_databases**. There is a customized backup available with extended data preloaded you can use at https://github.com/microsoft/ sqlworkshops-sql2022workshop/releases.

2. Restore this database to your SQL Server 2022 instance. Execute the script **restorewwidw.sql**. You may need to change the directory paths for the location of your backup and where you will restore the database files. This script runs the following T-SQL statements:

```
USE master;
GO
DROP DATABASE IF EXISTS WideWorldImportersDW;
GO
RESTORE DATABASE WideWorldImportersDW FROM DISK = 'c:\sql_sample_
databases\wideworldimportersdw-full.bak'
WITH MOVE 'wwi_primary' TO 'c:\sql_sample_databases\
wideworldimportersdw.mdf',
MOVE 'wwi_userdata' TO 'c:\sql_sample_databases\
wideworldimportersdw_userdata.ndf',
MOVE 'wwi_log' TO 'c:\sql_sample_databases\
wideworldimportersdw.ldf',
MOVE 'wwidw_inmemory_data_1' TO 'c:\sql_sample_databases\
wideworldimportersdw_inmemory_data'
GO
```

3. In order to run some of the examples, you will need a larger
    table than what exists by default in WideWorldImportersDW that
    does not have a columnstore index. Therefore, execute the script
    extendwwidw.sql to create a larger table. Extending this database
    will increase its size, including the transaction log, to about 8Gb
    overall. This script runs the following T-SQL statements:

```
USE WideWorldImportersDW;
GO

-- Build a new rowmode table called OrderHistory based off
of Orders
--
DROP TABLE IF EXISTS Fact.OrderHistory;
GO

SELECT 'Buliding OrderHistory from Orders...'
GO
SELECT [Order Key], [City Key], [Customer Key], [Stock Item Key],
[Order Date Key], [Picked Date Key], [Salesperson Key], [Picker
Key], [WWI Order ID], [WWI Backorder ID], Description, Package,
Quantity, [Unit Price], [Tax Rate], [Total Excluding Tax], [Tax
Amount], [Total Including Tax], [Lineage Key]
INTO Fact.OrderHistory
FROM Fact.[Order];
GO

ALTER TABLE Fact.OrderHistory
ADD CONSTRAINT PK_Fact_OrderHistory PRIMARY KEY
NONCLUSTERED([Order Key] ASC, [Order Date Key] ASC)WITH(DATA_
COMPRESSION=PAGE);
GO

CREATE INDEX IX_Stock_Item_Key
ON Fact.OrderHistory([Stock Item Key])
INCLUDE(Quantity)
WITH(DATA_COMPRESSION=PAGE);
GO
```

```
CREATE INDEX IX_OrderHistory_Quantity
ON Fact.OrderHistory([Quantity])
INCLUDE([Order Key])
WITH(DATA_COMPRESSION=PAGE);
GO

-- Table should have 231,412 rows
SELECT 'Number of rows in Fact.OrderHistory = ', COUNT(*) FROM
Fact.OrderHistory;
GO

SELECT 'Increasing number of rows for OrderHistory...';
GO
-- Make the table bigger
INSERT Fact.OrderHistory([City Key], [Customer Key], [Stock Item
Key], [Order Date Key], [Picked Date Key], [Salesperson Key],
[Picker Key], [WWI Order ID], [WWI Backorder ID], Description,
Package, Quantity, [Unit Price], [Tax Rate], [Total Excluding
Tax], [Tax Amount], [Total Including Tax], [Lineage Key])
SELECT [City Key], [Customer Key], [Stock Item Key], [Order Date
Key], [Picked Date Key], [Salesperson Key], [Picker Key], [WWI
Order ID], [WWI Backorder ID], Description, Package, Quantity,
[Unit Price], [Tax Rate], [Total Excluding Tax], [Tax Amount],
[Total Including Tax], [Lineage Key]
FROM Fact.OrderHistory;
GO 4
-- Table should have 3,702,592 rows
SELECT 'Number of rows in Fact.OrderHistory = ', COUNT(*) FROM
Fact.OrderHistory;
GO
```

4. Set up the demo by executing the script **setup.sql**. This script runs
    the following T-SQL statements:

```
USE [WideWorldImportersDW];
GO
ALTER DATABASE [WideWorldImportersDW] SET COMPATIBILITY_
LEVEL = 150;
```

```
GO
ALTER DATABASE SCOPED CONFIGURATION CLEAR PROCEDURE_CACHE;
GO
ALTER DATABASE WideWorldImportersDW SET QUERY_STORE CLEAR ALL;
GO
```

This script will set the dbcompat to 150 to allow memory grant feedback for row mode to be enabled. Query Store is already enabled for this database, so we simply need to clear the procedure cache (to ensure we get a new fresh compile) and Query Store statistics so we can focus only on this query.

5. To easily simulate a problem where a memory grant is not accurate based on incorrect cardinality, execute the script **set_stats.sql**. This script executes the following T-SQL statements:

```
USE WideWorldImportersDW;
GO
UPDATE STATISTICS Fact.OrderHistory
WITH ROWCOUNT = 1000;
GO
```

6. In a query editor in SSMS, select Query ➤ Include Actual Execution Plan (you can also enable it with Ctrl+M). Then execute the script **execute_query.sql**, which will take ~30 seconds to complete (the row results are irrelevant to this example). This script executes the following T-SQL statements:

```
USE WideWorldImportersDW;
GO
SELECT fo.[Order Key], fo.Description, si.[Lead Time Days]
FROM  Fact.OrderHistory AS fo
INNER HASH JOIN Dimension.[Stock Item] AS si
ON fo.[Stock Item Key] = si.[Stock Item Key]
```

```
WHERE fo.[Lineage Key] = 9
AND si.[Lead Time Days] > 19;
GO
```

7.   Select the **Execution Plan** tab from the results window. You will
     see a graphical showplan output that looks like Figure 4-3.

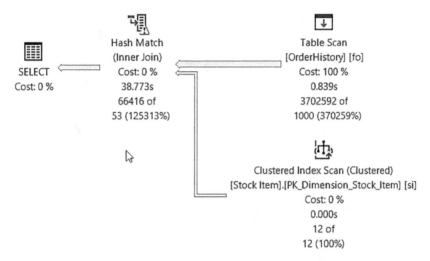

Figure 4-3. *Query plan with spill*

Notice the yellow warning on top of the Hash Match operator. If
you move your cursor over this operator, you can see a warning
about a spill to tempdb that looks like Figure 4-4.

177

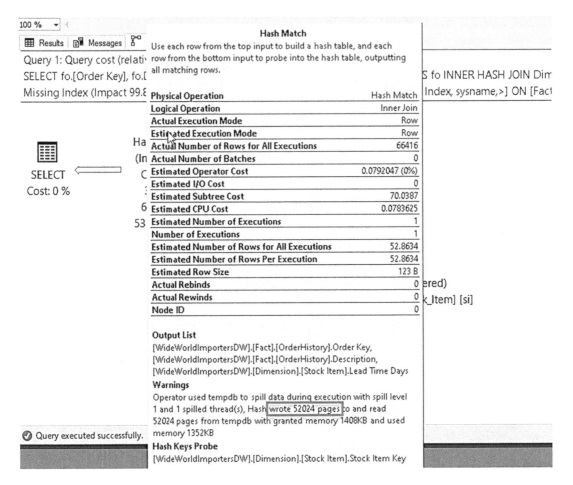

Figure 4-4. Spill warning in the query plan

You can see that the hash join required ~426Mb (52024*8192) of memory and the original grant was only for ~1.4Mb.

8. If you move your cursor over the SELECT operator, you can confirm the memory grant was ~1.4Mb as seen in Figure 4-5.

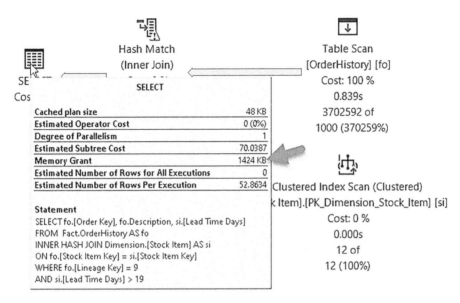

Figure 4-5. *Memory grant for spill*

If you right-click the SELECT operator and select Properties, you can expand the MemoryGrantInfo property as shown in Figure 4-6.

Memory Grant	1424 KB
⊟ MemoryGrantInfo	
DesiredMemory	1424
GrantedMemory	1424
GrantWaitTime	0
IsMemoryGrantFeedbackAdjusted	NoFirstExecution
LastRequestedMemory	0
MaxQueryMemory	990808
MaxUsedMemory	1352
RequestedMemory	1424
RequiredMemory	1024
SerialDesiredMemory	1424
SerialRequiredMemory	1024

Figure 4-6. *Memory grant feedback on first execution*

IsMemoryGrantFeedbackAdjusted = NoFirstExecution means that the query has been executed for the first time, so no feedback adjustment occurred. Note the MaxUsedMemory value doesn't reflect the tempdb spill of pages.

9. Since we are using SQL Server 2022, after the execution of this
    query, feedback is stored in Query Store. You can see this feedback
    by executing the script **get_plan_feedback.sql**. This script
    executes the following T-SQL statements:

```
USE WideWorldImportersDW;
GO
SELECT qpf.feature_desc, qpf.feedback_data, qpf.state_desc,
qt.query_sql_text, (qrs.last_query_max_used_memory * 8192)/1024 as
last_query_memory_kb
FROM sys.query_store_plan_feedback qpf
JOIN sys.query_store_plan qp
ON qpf.plan_id = qp.plan_id
JOIN sys.query_store_query qq
ON qp.query_id = qq.query_id
JOIN sys.query_store_query_text qt
ON qq.query_text_id = qt.query_text_id
JOIN sys.query_store_runtime_stats qrs
ON qp.plan_id = qrs.plan_id;
GO
```

Your results should look like the following (I flipped the results
vertically so you could see them line up for each column):

```
feature_desc       Memory Grant Feedback
feedback_data
[{"NodeId":"0","AdditionalMemoryKB":"624504"}]
state_desc         FEEDBACK_VALID
query_sql_text
SELECT fo.[Order Key], fo.Description, si.[Lead Time
Days]  FROM Fact.OrderHistory AS fo  INNER HASH JOIN Dimension.
[Stock Item] AS si   ON fo.[Stock Item Key] = si.[Stock Item
Key]  WHERE fo.[Lineage Key] = 9  AND si.[Lead Time Days] > 19
last_query_memory_kb        1424
```

The **feedback_data** column shows the new memory grant that will be used for the next execution of the same query, which should be plenty based on the tempdb spill from the first execution.

10. Execute the **execute_query.sql** script again. You should see the query complete now in just a few seconds.

If you look at the graphical query plan, you will notice there is no warning for the hash join operator. If you move your cursor over the SELECT operator, you should see a memory grant like Figure 4-7.

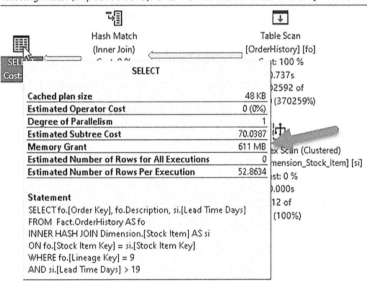

Figure 4-7. Memory grant after feedback

If you right-click the SELECT operator and select Properties, you can expand the MemoryGrantInfo and see details like Figure 4-8.

Memory Grant	611 MB
MemoryGrantInfo	
DesiredMemory	625528
GrantedMemory	625528
GrantWaitTime	0
IsMemoryGrantFeedbackAdjusted	YesAdjusting
LastRequestedMemory	1424
MaxQueryMemory	996072
MaxUsedMemory	494408
RequestedMemory	625528
RequiredMemory	1024
SerialDesiredMemory	625528
SerialRequiredMemory	1024

Figure 4-8. *Memory grant feedback adjusted*

IsMemoryGrantFeedbackAdjusted = YesAdjusting means that feedback has been applied from the previous execution to adjust the memory grant. No tempdb spill results in a significantly faster execution time.

11. Execute the script **get_plan_feedback.sql** again. You will see in the results the value for **last_query_memory_kb** will reflect the new, larger memory grant.

12. At this point, the behavior of this scenario is exactly like SQL Server 2019, except previously the memory grant feedback was only stored in the cached query plan. Now you can see that the feedback is persisted in Query Store. Execute the script **clear_ proc_cache.sql** to clear the plan cache. This script uses the following T-SQL statements:

```
USE [WideWorldImportersDW];
GO
ALTER DATABASE SCOPED CONFIGURATION CLEAR PROCEDURE_CACHE;
GO
```

13. Execute the script **execute_query.sql** again. You will see the query finishes in a few seconds and uses the same memory grant as stored in the feedback_data column in Query Store.

You can disable memory grant feedback persistence by using the following database-scoped configuration option:

```
ALTER DATABASE SCOPED CONFIGURATION SET MEMORY_GRANT_FEEDBACK_
PERSISTENCE = OFF
```

You can also disable memory grant feedback persistence at the query hint level using the option **DISABLE_MEMORY_GRANT_FEEDBACK_PERSISTENCE.**

Now memory grant feedback will support a wider variety of workloads using percentiles and persist feedback to Query Store to survive server restarts and plan cache eviction.

Keep track of all the latest information about memory grant enhancements for SQL Server 2022 at `https://docs.microsoft.com/sql/relational-databases/performance/intelligent-query-processing-details?#percentile-and-persistence-mode-memory-grant-feedback`.

The Intelligent Query Processor

In this chapter you explored what built-in query intelligence means. Simply put, it's faster queries with no code changes. It leverages enhancements to Query Store, with the built-in store for query performance statistics now on by default for new databases and enhancements for hints and read replicas. It is about nextgen IQP capabilities to get you better performance using approximate percentile, optimized plan forcing, and enhancements to memory grant feedback. You can get all of these improvements even without using the new dbcompat level 160 for SQL Server 2022.

I asked Kate Smith, Senior Program Manager over the IQP space, about her thoughts on the significance of built-in query intelligence in SQL Server 2022:

> *In my opinion, query processing is the beating heart at the center of SQL Server's capabilities. All queries leverage it, and all benefit from our efforts there. The latest work in Intelligent Query Processing continues this trend – by allowing the optimizer to self-tune to a customer's specific needs, we expand the scope of what is possible from requiring manual intervention and move towards a self-regulating system. The features released in SQL 22 expand the capabilities in many ways – addressing previous challenges in memory grant feedback, introducing the ability for the optimizer to use different CE models with cardinality estimation feedback, creating parameter*

sensitive plans, and even adjusting the degree of parallelism for a query without user input. What's more, these features can all work together, seamlessly. So while before SQL 22 a problematic query might have required multiple iterations of manual tuning, that same query can now be adjusted, on the fly, across many dimensions, without any user action. These adjustments can be persisted across restarts and can apply across different replicas. Taken together, the latest IQP features will greatly reduce headaches for SQL Server DBAs everywhere. I'm thrilled to see these features land, and I'm excited for users to start seeing their benefit. Be warned though: we are not done! This team is always looking to the future, and what more we can deliver. So, stay tuned.

If you are ready for more, the story gets better in the next chapter. If you are ready to move to dbcompat 160, read on to the next chapter about how built-in query intelligence evolves even further with solutions to three age-old problems: Parameter-Sensitive Plans, cardinality estimation model issues, and degree of parallelism.

CHAPTER 5

Built-In Query Intelligence Gets Even Better

In Chapter 4 you learned the history behind built-in query intelligence and its promise: getting you faster performance with no code changes. You learned about new SQL Server 2022 capabilities like the new Query Store, memory grant feedback persistence, and others. None of these require a change to the new dbcompat level 160 for SQL Server 2022.

What if you want all of what you read in Chapter 4 and more? If you change your dbcompat level to 160, you will definitely get more. This includes the following:

- Parameter-Sensitive Plan (PSP) optimization
- Cardinality estimation (CE) model feedback
- Degree of parallelism (DOP) feedback

In this chapter you will learn about each of these, including what problem we are trying to solve, how they work, and examples on how to use them. The story begins by trying to save the world from parameter sniffing.

Parameter-Sensitive Plan (PSP) Optimization

I believe the query processor in SQL Server is one of the most robust and best parts of the engine. Our investments in IQP show that we are committed to adapting to all types of workloads, gaining performance with no code changes. But for years there's been a particular type of scenario that has been a painful problem for our users.

© Bob Ward 2022
B. Ward, *SQL Server 2022 Revealed*, https://doi.org/10.1007/978-1-4842-8894-8_5

What Is a Parameter-Sensitive Plan?

Consider the scenario where you build a stored procedure and use a parameter as input. You then use the parameter in T-SQL statements to filter data (i.e., in a WHERE clause). When a query is first compiled, the optimizer will determine the *value* of the parameter to make decisions on what query plan is best for the statement. This query plan is then used for *any* subsequent execution of the stored procedure regardless of the parameter value passed in, until the procedure is recompiled. Only one query plan can exist for a single statement in the plan cache. Therefore, the plan is sensitive to the value of the parameter when the query is first compiled. This problem is known as *parameter sniffing*.

Note   Many in the SQL community have said I'm the person who many years ago coined the term *parameter sniffing*. Some have said it was Conor Cuningham. I guess it will just remain a mystery.

For many workloads and datasets, this scenario does not pose a problem. But what if the query plan that was built for a particular parameter value is not the best plan for execution of the query with other parameter values? *Some* users may experience poor or inconsistent performance. The problem typically happens when the data involved in the query to be filtered with the parameter is *skewed* – in other words, is not evenly distributed across values that match the parameter.

I have personally seen this problem cause performance issues for customers for almost my entire three-decade career at Microsoft. You can read a few resources describing this problem further and the various workarounds you can try if you encounter this problem including

https://docs.microsoft.com/sql/relational-databases/query-processing-architecture-guide?#parameter-sensitivity and https://docs.microsoft.com/azure/azure-sql/identify-query-performance-issues?#resolving-queries-with-suboptimal-query-execution-plans

But SQL Server 2022 has a better solution, one that is built into the query processor and does not require any code changes.

Learn PSP Through a Scenario

Here is a simple visual sequence of a scenario where PSP can cause a problem as seen in Figure 5-1.

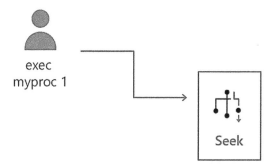

Figure 5-1. *Stored procedure execution results in a plan with an index seek*

In this first scenario, a user executes a stored procedure with a parameter value of 1 (could be based on user input from an application). The query in the procedure that uses this parameter value to filter rows is compiled, and a query plan uses an index seek operator because there are only a few rows in the table that match a value of 1. This query probably runs extremely fast.

Let's say for circumstances outside of anyone's control, memory pressure causes the query plan to be evicted from the plan cache. Now what if another user comes in at this time and executes the same stored procedure with a parameter of 10, as seen in Figure 5-2?

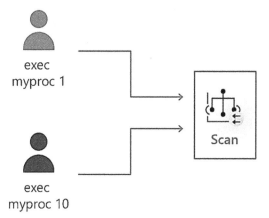

Figure 5-2. *Same stored procedure with a different parameter generates a plan with index scan*

If many rows match a value of 10 as a filter for the table, when compiling the new plan, the optimizer instead might use a clustered index scan (and even uses parallelism). This is perfectly normal, and for a user who is executing the procedure with a value of 10, the performance could be considered normal. Both users are now tied into the plan with a scan.

What about the first user who now executes the procedure with a parameter of 1? As you can see in Figure 5-3, this situation is likely not good.

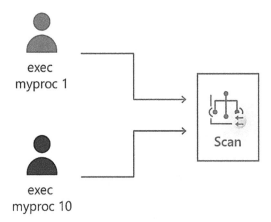

Figure 5-3. *First user experiences performance degradation due to PSP*

A query that only needs to find a few rows could now be scanning millions of rows to get the result. The behavior could easily cause degradation in performance. Most likely, a user of the application using this procedure would simply say, "It just got slow all of a sudden." Sounds familiar?

The problem all stems from the fact that only one plan can be in cache for a specific T-SQL statement. And a skew of data may mean that one plan cannot meet the needs of various parameter values. And as a developer of the stored procedure, it is not your fault the data is skewed. So instead of all the workarounds and performance tuning madness that you may encounter, let's look at a solution to this problem in SQL Server 2022 that is quite frankly a "game changer."

How It All Started

In early 2020 I was in the Microsoft offices in Irving, Texas. In those days I had an actual office in the building where the CSS team lived. Since I had worked for CSS for so many years, when I joined the engineering team, they let me keep my office. And by then one of my former CSS colleagues, Jack Li, had also joined engineering as a developer. He kept a cube in the Irving office for his job as well. It was pretty late in the day, and I was going to head out when I stopped by Jack's cube to see if he was in. It was my good luck he was, so we chatted a bit about family, some fun stories together from CSS, and how each of our jobs was going with engineering. And then I said to Jack, *"Hey*, what are you working on these days?" He is such a humble person, but he said, *"Well*, something pretty big actually. I'm working on some code to solve parameter sniffing." I stopped for a second to take that in, and I said something like *"You are kidding m*e. I want to know more." Much to the chagrin of probably both of our wives, we spent the next 2 hours talking about this project staying late. When we were done, I remember saying to him, *"Jack, this is keynote*-worthy demo material. The SQL world will freak out when you deliver this."

And as you can imagine from the timeline, the world kind of blew up, and I lost track of talking to Jack about this. Fast forward to spring of 2021, and I got an email from Jack: *"Hey*, Bob, remember the parameter sniffing project on which I was working? Well, it is going to happen, and we think we can put this in project Dallas." Jack called the solution **Parameter-Sensitive Plan (PSP) optimization**. My work stopped that day. I called him immediately to get the scoop on the details. When we were done talking, I knew I really did have a keynote-worthy demo and a major highlight for a feature for SQL Server 2022.

Note   The reality of doing this in a keynote did happen at the PASS Community Summit in 2021. And thanks to Jack for giving a demo I could use for the keynote. The keynote was virtual, but it was still great to do it. Check out this video at `https://youtu.be/Ydlg1KpmrKU` and fast forward to about 17 minutes in. Peter Carlin introduced me to demonstrate this new capability, and of course the Conor and Bob show had to exist even if we were not in the same room or city!

How Does PSP Optimization Work?

The concept of PSP optimization is simple but powerful.

Note   I will say to you up front we really don't know if we will solve all PSP problems. We know there are limits to the first version of this work. But we do believe it has a real possibility to make a difference for applications that are affected by parameter sniffing.

To implement PSP optimization, we have built new concepts in the query processor for query plans. A *dispatcher* query plan is a parent query plan for a *parameterized* SQL statement and is stored in the plan cache. A parameterized statement can be in a stored procedure, parameterized by an application, or even auto-parameterized by the SQL Server engine. You can read more about parametrization at `https://docs.microsoft.com/sql/relational-databases/performance/parameter-sensitivity-plan-optimization?#understanding-parameterization`.

A dispatcher plan itself is not used for execution. Rather, a dispatcher plan can have more than one *variant* plan. Variant plans are created based on buckets or ranges of values for *predicates* or filters used in parameterized queries. Figure 5-4 shows a visual of how dispatchers and variants work.

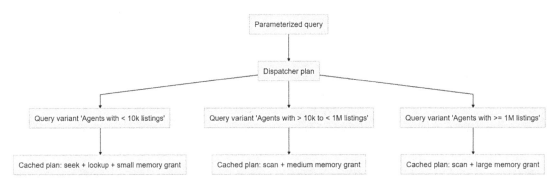

Figure 5-4. *Dispatcher and query variants with PSP optimization*

In this figure you can see there are three variants, each for a query that covers a certain "range" (i.e., bucket) of values that match a predicate or filter. What is interesting about this concept is that it can also help resolve some of the memory grant issues I discussed in Chapter 4. This is because each variant plan is "its own plan" in the plan cache and can contain a different memory grant even if two variants use a similar *plan shape* (e.g., an index scan).

Note   Figure 5-4 is a diagram showing the concepts of a dispatcher and variants. The design of how many variants or buckets we can use for a dispatcher is internal and not documented.

When a query is first compiled, the query processor can identify a parameterized statement to see if it is eligible for a dispatcher and query variants. The first execution will result in a dispatcher and variant. If the same statement is executed with a different parameter that falls into another bucket, a new variant plan can be compiled and stored into cache.

The dispatcher and variant plans are not persisted. They exist only in the plan cache but can be rebuilt on new compilation as needed. Variant plans can be recompiled as needed on their own.

Let's look back at the visual scenario earlier in this section showing a PSP problem. In that same scenario, if dbcompat 160 was enabled, the story now looks like Figure 5-5.

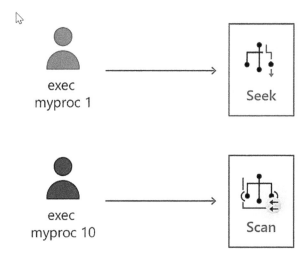

Figure 5-5. *PSP optimization allows for more than one plan in cache*

With no code changes, the optimizer can use variants to have more than one plan in cache for a stored procedure or parameterized statement. There is no better way to learn more about how PSP optimization works than to try it out.

Let's See PSP Optimization in Action

There is a long set of steps for this exercise, but I think you will find it worth it.

Prerequisites

To go through this exercise, you will need the following prerequisites:

- SQL Server 2022 Evaluation Edition.

- Virtual machine or computer with minimum of two CPUs with 8Gb RAM.

- SQL Server Management Studio (SSMS). The latest 18.x or 19.x build will work.

- Download **ostress.exe** from `https://aka.ms/ostress`. Install using the RMLSetup.msi file that is downloaded. Use all defaults. Only download this tool on Windows systems. Part of the following exercise will only work on Windows systems.

- A copy of the scripts from the GitHub repo of this book from the **ch05_builtinqueryintelligence_getsbetter\pspopt** directory.

Follow These Steps for the Exercise

Follow these steps to see how PSP optimization works:

1. Download a copy of the backup of WideWorldImporters from `https://aka.ms/WideWorldImporters`. The script in the next step assumes a location of the backup at **c:\sql_sample_databases**. There is a customized backup available with extended data preloaded you can use at `https://github.com/microsoft/ sqlworkshops-sql2022workshop/releases`.

2. Restore the WideWorldImporters sample backup. You can edit and use the **restorewwi.sql** script. This script was designed for a SQL Server on Azure Virtual Machines marketplace image, which has separate disks for data and log files. Edit this file to match your file paths. This script contains the following T-SQL statements:

```
USE master;
GO
```

```
DROP DATABASE IF EXISTS WideWorldImporters;
GO
-- Edit the locations for files to match your storage
RESTORE DATABASE WideWorldImporters FROM DISK = 'c:\sql_sample_
databases\WideWorldImporters-Full.bak' with
MOVE 'WWI_Primary' TO 'e:\data\WideWorldImporters.mdf',
MOVE 'WWI_UserData' TO 'e:\data\WideWorldImporters_UserData.ndf',
MOVE 'WWI_Log' TO 'f:\log\WideWorldImporters.ldf',
MOVE 'WWI_InMemory_Data_1' TO 'e:\data\WideWorldImporters_
InMemory_Data_1',
stats=5;
GO
```

3. Execute the **populatedata.sql** script to load more data into the
   Warehouse.StockItems table. This script will take 5–10 minutes
   to run (timing depends on how many CPUs and the speed of
   your disk). This script executes the following T-SQL statements
   (no apologies for my favorite sports team in the exercise), which
   add data to the Warehouse.StockItems table to create a data skew
   scenario:

```
USE WideWorldImporters;
GO
-- Add StockItems to cause a data skew in Suppliers
--
DECLARE @StockItemID int;
DECLARE @StockItemName varchar(100);
DECLARE @SupplierID int;
SELECT @StockItemID = 228;
SET @StockItemName = 'Dallas Cowboys Shirt'+convert(varchar(10),
@StockItemID);
SET @SupplierID = 4;
DELETE FROM Warehouse.StockItems WHERE StockItemID >=
@StockItemID;
SET NOCOUNT ON;
BEGIN TRANSACTION;
WHILE @StockItemID <= 4000000
```

```
BEGIN
INSERT INTO Warehouse.StockItems
(StockItemID, StockItemName, SupplierID, UnitPackageID,
OuterPackageID, LeadTimeDays,
QuantityPerOuter, IsChillerStock, TaxRate, UnitPrice,
TypicalWeightPerUnit, LastEditedBy
)
VALUES (@StockItemID, @StockItemName, @SupplierID, 10, 9, 12, 100,
0, 15.00, 100.00, 0.300, 1);
SET @StockItemID = @StockItemID + 1;
SET @StockItemName = 'Dallas Cowboys Shirt'+convert(varchar(10),
@StockItemID);
END;
COMMIT TRANSACTION;
SET NOCOUNT OFF;
GO
DECLARE @StockItemID int;
DECLARE @StockItemName varchar(100);
DECLARE @SupplierID int;
SELECT @StockItemID = 4000001;
SET @StockItemName = 'Dallas Cowboys Mug'+convert(varchar(10),
@StockItemID);
SET @SupplierID = 5;
DELETE FROM Warehouse.StockItems WHERE StockItemID >=
@StockItemID;
SET NOCOUNT ON;
BEGIN TRANSACTION;
WHILE @StockItemID <= 8000000
BEGIN
INSERT INTO Warehouse.StockItems
(StockItemID, StockItemName, SupplierID, UnitPackageID,
OuterPackageID, LeadTimeDays,
QuantityPerOuter, IsChillerStock, TaxRate, UnitPrice,
TypicalWeightPerUnit, LastEditedBy
)
```

```
VALUES (@StockItemID, @StockItemName, @SupplierID, 10, 9, 12, 100,
0, 15.00, 100.00, 0.300, 1);
SET @StockItemID = @StockItemID + 1;
SET @StockItemName = 'Dallas Cowboys Mug'+convert(varchar(10),
@StockItemID);
END;
COMMIT TRANSACTION;
SET NOCOUNT OFF;
GO
```

4. Rebuild an index associated with the table using the script
   rebuild_index.sql.

Important   If you miss this step, you will not be able to see the performance improvement for PSP optimization. This script uses the following T-SQL statements:

```
USE WideWorldImporters;
GO
ALTER INDEX FK_Warehouse_StockItems_SupplierID ON Warehouse.
StockItems REBUILD;
GO
```

---

5. Create a new procedure to be used for the exercise using the script
   proc.sql. This script uses the following T-SQL statements:

```
USE WideWorldImporters;
GO
CREATE OR ALTER PROCEDURE [Warehouse].[GetStockItemsbySupplier]
@SupplierID int
AS
BEGIN
SELECT StockItemID, SupplierID, StockItemName, TaxRate,
LeadTimeDays
FROM Warehouse.StockItems s
```

```
WHERE SupplierID = @SupplierID
ORDER BY StockItemName;
END;
GO
```

You can see the stored procedure takes in a single parameter, @SupplierID, and will use this parameter as a predicate or filter to find rows in the StockItems table.

6. Execute the script **setup.sql** using SSMS. This will ensure the WideWorldImporters database is at dbcompat 150 (so PSP is not initially enabled) and clear Query Store. This script uses the following T-SQL statements:

```
USE WideWorldImporters;
GO
ALTER DATABASE current SET COMPATIBILITY_LEVEL = 150;
GO
ALTER DATABASE current SET QUERY_STORE CLEAR;
GO
```

7. In SSMS open a new query editor window (I like to select Databases in Object Explorer and use the File ➤ New ➤ Database Engine Query menu) and choose the button on the menu for Include Actual Execution Plan. Execute the script **query_plan_seek.sql** twice in a query window in SSMS. The script uses the following T-SQL statements:

```
USE WideWorldImporters;
GO
SET STATISTICS TIME ON;
GO
USE WideWorldImporters;
GO
-- The best plan for this parameter is an index seek
EXEC Warehouse.GetStockItemsbySupplier 2;
GO
```

Note the query execution time is fast (< 1 second). Check the timings from SET STATISTICS TIME ON from the second execution (use the last set of timings). The query is run twice, so the second execution will not require a compile. This is the time we want to compare. If you select the **Messages** tab and scroll down for the last set of timings, your results should look similar to the following (your timings may vary, but it should be fairly close to these):

```
SQL Server Execution Times:
   CPU time = 15 ms,  elapsed time = 34 ms.

 SQL Server Execution Times:
   CPU time = 15 ms,  elapsed time = 34 ms.
```

If you select the Execution Plan tab in the results window, you can see the query plan uses an index seek as seen in Figure 5-6.

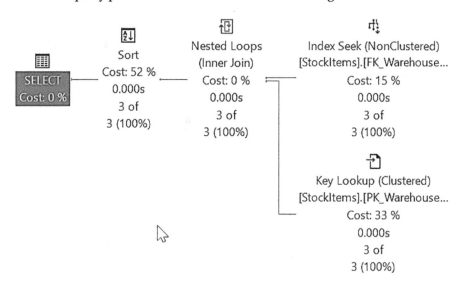

Figure 5-6. *Index seek plan for a stored procedure parameter*

8. In a different query window, choose the menu button for Include Actual Execution Plan in SSMS. Execute the script **query_plan_ scan.sql**. The execution can take up to ~30 seconds. This script uses the following T-SQL statements:

```
USE WideWorldImporters;
GO
ALTER DATABASE SCOPED CONFIGURATION CLEAR PROCEDURE_CACHE;
GO
-- The best plan for this parameter is an index scan
EXEC Warehouse.GetStockItemsbySupplier 4;
GO
```

This script will simulate a plan cache eviction so that when the
stored procedure is executed, the query processor will have to
compile a new query plan. If you select the Execution Plan tab in
the results window, you will see a query plan similar to Figure 5-7.

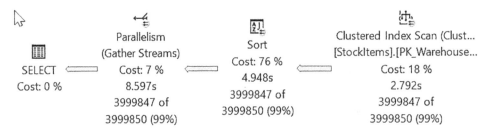

Figure 5-7. *Clustered index scan for a different parameter*

You can see that the new query plan uses a clustered index scan
and parallelism.

9. Run the script **query_plan_seek.sql** again. The elapsed time
   is still fast (< 1 second), but if you look at the timings in the
   Messages tab, you will see it is significantly slower. If you select the
   Execution Plan tab, you will now see this query is using the new
   plan with a clustered index scan. This is because only one plan
   can be in cache for the statement in the same stored procedure.

Note   If you want to just see PSP optimization from a single execution, you
have the option here to execute the script **dbcompat160.sql** and then repeat the
preceding steps with **query_index_seek.sql** and **query_index_scan.sql**. You
will see each execution can have its own plan. To see the workload impact for PSP
optimization, proceed to the next steps. If you try out PSP optimization with these

SQL scripts and want to proceed to next steps, run setup.sql to reset the exercise. **These next steps will only work on Windows systems, but you could change the scripts to run ostress.exe on a Windows system connecting to SQL Server on Linux or a container.**

---

10. Launch Windows Performance Monitor (you can just type **perfmon** from a command prompt). Leave the default counter of **% Processor Time**. Add the counter **SQL Server:SQL Statistics Batch Requests/Sec**. I like to use batch requests/sec as a simple measure of workload throughput. I recommend you change the colors for one of the counters. I also like to increase the width of the counter to make it more readable (color and width are available by right-clicking a counter and selecting Properties).

11. Examine the script **workload_index_seek.cmd**. This script will use ostress.exe to simulate multiple users repeatedly executing the stored procedure with a value that will ideally use an index seek in the query plan. The script assumes a connection to a local server and Windows authentication. Change the script per your needs. The script uses the following command:

```
"c:\Program Files\Microsoft Corporation\RMLUtils\
ostress" -E -Q"EXEC Warehouse.GetStockItemsbySupplier
2;" -n%1 -r200 -q –dWideWorldImporters
```

   - The -n parameter is number of users (ostress uses threads). This is a value you provide when you execute the script. On a two-CPU machine, ten users are enough. You may want to increase this number on machines with more CPUs to see more impact.

   - The -r parameter is number of iterations.

   - The -q parameter is "quiet mode" to throw away results because we just want to see how fast this will run.

12. Execute the script **workload_index_seek.cmd 10** from a command prompt. The command should finish in a second or two. Take note of the values in perfmon. Your results should look similar to Figure 5-8.

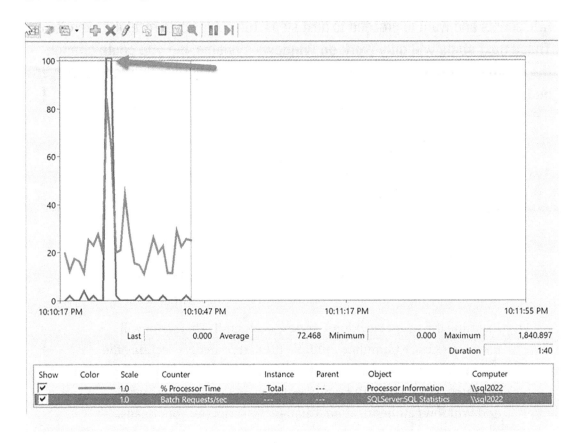

Figure 5-8. *Workload throughput with an initial index seek plan*

13. Execute the script **workload_index_scan.cmd** from a command prompt. This should take longer but still complete in a few seconds. This script uses the following commands:

```
"c:\Program Files\Microsoft Corporation\RMLUtils\
ostress" -E -Q"ALTER DATABASE SCOPED CONFIGURATION
CLEAR PROCEDURE_CACHE;" -n1 -r1 -q -oworkload_wwi
_regress -dWideWorldImporters
"c:\Program Files\Microsoft Corporation\RMLUtils\
ostress" -E -Q"EXEC Warehouse.GetStockItemsbySupplier
4;" -n1 -r1 -q -oworkload_wwi_regress -dWideWorldImporters
```

This script simulates plan cache eviction and executes the stored procedure that will cause a query plan to be compiled into cache using a clustered index scan.

14. Execute the script ***workload_index_seek.cmd 10*** from a command prompt again. Notice the command does not complete after a few seconds. Look at perfmon and compare it with the previous execution. You will see a severe drop in batch requests/ sec and a jump to 100% CPU utilization as shown in Figure 5-9.

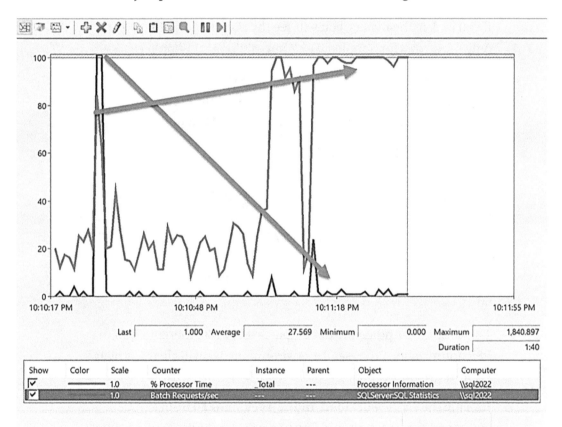

Figure 5-9. *Workload throughput drops due to PSP*

This example demonstrates the overall impact of the change to a plan with a clustered index scan. Multiple users are now all scanning the table using parallelism at the same time.

15. Before you look at the solution, execute the script **suppliercount. sql** from SSMS. This script uses the following T-SQL statements:

```
USE WideWorldImporters;
GO
SELECT SupplierID, count(*) as supplier_count
FROM Warehouse.StockItems
GROUP BY SupplierID;
GO
```

If you look at the results, you will see the skew in data. There are only a few rows for SupplierID = 2 but millions for SupplierID = 4.

16. Now let's see how SQL Server 2022 can solve this problem with no code changes. Execute the SQL script **dbcompat160.sql** in SSMS. This script uses the following T-SQL statements:

```
USE WideWorldImporters;
GO
ALTER DATABASE CURRENT SET COMPATIBILITY_LEVEL = 160;
GO
ALTER DATABASE SCOPED CONFIGURATION CLEAR PROCEDURE_CACHE;
GO
ALTER DATABASE CURRENT SET QUERY_STORE CLEAR;
GO
```

This script will update the dbcompat level to 160, thereby enabling PSP optimization. To reset the environment, we will clear the plan cache and Query Store.

17. Execute the script **workload_index_seek.cmd 10** from a command prompt. It should finish in a few seconds. Next, execute **workload_index_scan.cmd** from a command prompt. Finally, execute **workload_index_seek.cmd 10** from a command prompt again. Notice both executions finish at approximately the same time. Perfmon should also show consistent results from both executions as seen in Figure 5-10.

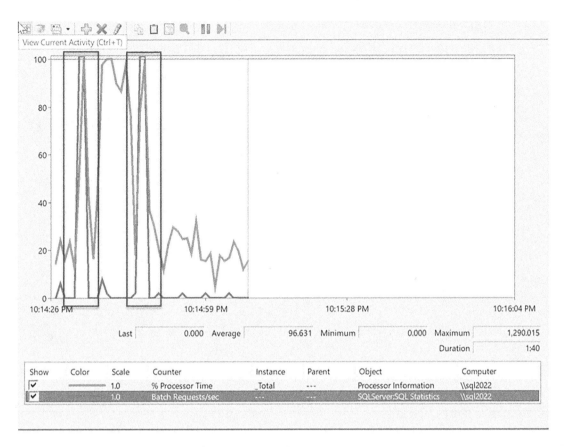

Figure 5-10. *Consistent performance with PSP optimization*

The two rectangular shapes in purple represent the consistent performance between both executions of workload_index_seek. cmd with PSP optimization enabled.

You can see that with PSP optimization, you can now achieve consistent performance with no code changes.

18. With Query Store enabled, we can get insights into the different plans, dispatcher, and variants.

Note   Query Store is not required for PSP optimization but can be useful to get insights into query performance.

Using SSMS, select from Query Store in Object Explorer the **Top Resource-Consuming Queries** report. Figure 5-11 shows the query variant plan using the clustered index scan for the query from the stored procedure.

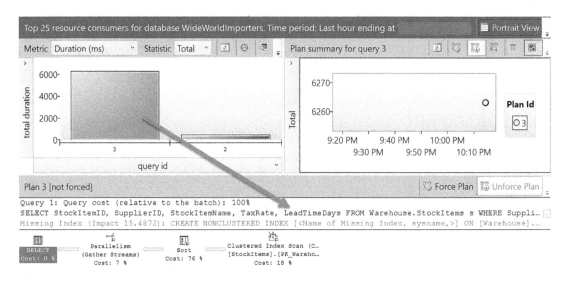

Figure 5-11. *Clustered index scan query variant plan*

Figure 5-12 shows another query_id using the index seek but for the same query text.

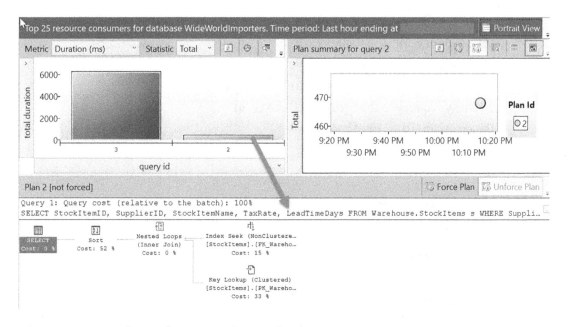

Figure 5-12. *Index seek query variant plan*

I said PSP optimization allows for multiple plans for the same
query, but why does Query Store think there are two "queries"?
Let's look further using Query Store metadata.

19. Execute the script **query_store_plans.sql**. This script executes the
following T-SQL statements:

```
USE WideWorldImporters;
GO
-- Look at the queries and plans for variants
-- Notice each query is from the same parent_query_id and the
query_hash is the same
SELECT qt.query_sql_text, qq.query_id, qv.query_variant_query_id,
qv.parent_query_id,
qq.query_hash,qr.count_executions, qp.plan_id, qv.dispatcher_plan_
id, qp.query_plan_hash,
cast(qp.query_plan as XML) as xml_plan
FROM sys.query_store_query_text qt
JOIN sys.query_store_query qq
ON qt.query_text_id = qq.query_text_id
```

```
JOIN sys.query_store_plan qp
ON qq.query_id = qp.query_id
JOIN sys.query_store_query_variant qv
ON qq.query_id = qv.query_variant_query_id
JOIN sys.query_store_runtime_stats qr
ON qp.plan_id = qr.plan_id
ORDER BY qv.parent_query_id;
GO
```

If you look at the results, you will see the following interesting things:

- The **query_hash** value is the same for both **query_id** values.

- There are two **query_variant_id** values with the same **parent_query_id** (dispatcher). These values come from a new DMV in Query Store called **sys.query_store_query_variant**.

- If you expand the **query_sql_text** values, you will see the SELECT statement from the stored procedure but with an added option like **option (PLAN PER VALUE(ObjectID = 1835153583, QueryVariantID = 1, predicate_range([WideWorldImporters]. [Warehouse].[StockItems].[SupplierID] = @SupplierID, 100.0, 1000000.0)))**

  and

  option (PLAN PER VALUE(ObjectID = 1835153583, QueryVariantID = 3, predicate_range([WideWorldImporters].[Warehouse].[StockItems]. [SupplierID] = @SupplierID, 100.0, 1000000.0))).

  This added text is why there are technically two queries that *hash* to the same query_hash value.

  The implementation details of how we decide query variants and the predicate_range() function are internal-only at present. We don't want anyone relying on these details because as we improve PSP optimization, we may change them.

But I'll give you a few insights:

The concepts of variants and predicate_range are based on how I described PSP optimization concepts in the section titled "**How Does PSP Optimization Work?**" and Figure 5-4.

For this parent plan, there are three possible variants based on cardinality and predicate matches: those with <=100 rows, those with rows between 100 and 1M, and those with rows >= 1M.

- If you look at the details of the **xml_plan** column for each query variant, a new section called `<Dispatcher>` contains a `QueryVariantID` in the section `<QueryPlan>` with details of the variant and predicate_range.

20. Execute the script **query_store_parent_query.sql**. This script uses the following T-SQL statements:

```
USE WideWorldImporters;
GO
-- Look at the "parent" query
-- Notice this is the SELECT statement from the procedure with no
OPTION for variants.
SELECT qt.query_sql_text
FROM sys.query_store_query_text qt
JOIN sys.query_store_query qq
ON qt.query_text_id = qq.query_text_id
JOIN sys.query_store_query_variant qv
ON qq.query_id = qv.parent_query_id;
GO
```

The results will be the SQL statement text for the query in the stored procedure *without* the options for variants like the following:

```
(@SupplierID int)SELECT StockItemID, SupplierID, StockItemName,
TaxRate, LeadTimeDays  FROM Warehouse.StockItems s  WHERE
SupplierID = @SupplierID  ORDER BY StockItemName
```

21. Execute the script **query_store_dispatcher_plan.sql**. This script uses the following T-SQL statements:

```
USE WideWorldImporters;
GO
-- Look at the dispatcher plan
-- If you "click" on the SHOWPLAN XML output you will see a
"multiple plans" operator
SELECT qp.plan_id, qp.query_plan_hash, cast (qp.query_plan as XML)
as dispatcher_plan
FROM sys.query_store_plan qp
JOIN sys.query_store_query_variant qv
ON qp.plan_id = qv.dispatcher_plan_id;
GO
```

If you click the value of the **dispatcher_plan**, you will see a graphical showplan operator like in Figure 5-13.

Query 1: Query cost (relative to the batch): 100%
SELECT StockItemID, SupplierID, StockItemName, TaxRate, LeadTimeDays FROM Warehouse.StockItems s WHERE SupplierID = @SupplierID ORDER BY StockItemName

Figure 5-13. *A dispatcher plan operator*

This is a new operator for a dispatcher plan that doesn't execute a query but is the parent of variant query plans.

I know that was a long exercise to go through, but I hope you found it worth it! This example showed you the power of PSP optimization as well as some insights on how it works.

What Other Details About PSP Optimization Should I Know?

Here are some other details I think you will find useful about PSP optimization.

Check the Latest Information

First, be sure to check in on all the latest information in our documentation about PSP optimization at `https://aka.ms/pspopt`.

Known Limitations

There are limitations for PSP optimization in the initial release with SQL Server 2022:

- We only support predicates in WHERE clauses using an "=" operator.

- We do support multiple parameters, but there are limits on the number and how many we can support in a stored procedure.

- You cannot configure the number of variants, buckets, or predicate ranges with PSP optimization except to enable or disable it. Because of the limited number of predicates per plan, your plan cache should not become "bloated." The possible downside is that you may experience situations within a variant where multiple parameter values may still have issues with *one plan per variant*.

- If you have disabled "parameter sniffing" in SQL Server, we will not use PSP optimization. Parameter sniffing can be disabled with trace flag 4136, the database-scoped configuration PARAMETER_SNIFFING, or the query hint USE HINT('DISABLE_PARAMETER_SNIFFING').

- If you use a RECOMPILE hint or option, we don't consider this "cacheable," so we will not use PSP optimization for the query.

- If you use the OPTIMIZE FOR query hint, which is a workaround used by some for PSP problems, we will not use PSP optimization for the query.

- PSP optimization *is supported* for queries against temporary tables.

- One issue we have discovered as we built out the feature during the preview is tracking performance information between stored procedures and statements in the procedure. For example, it can now be difficult to tie in statements and procedures together for performance using DMVs like sys.dm_exec_query_stats and sys.

dm_exec_procedure_stats. In addition, in Query Store to associate statements with stored procedures, you will need to use sys. query_store_query_variant, which has information associating the dispatcher plan (stored procedure) with query variants (statements in the procedure). We do store the object_id in the query SHOWPLAN and in the statement text of the variant saved in Query Store.

One reality of letting PSP optimization work is to "let go" of some of the things you have done in the past to avoid this problem. It could be something you have to do in phases (e.g., use workarounds at a query level vs. at a database-scoped level) until you can see how much PSP optimization will solve your problems without requiring other solutions.

Use the Diagnostics

We have Extended Events to help you look further at PSP optimization including the following:

parameter_sensitive_plan_optimization_skipped_reason

If you believe PSP optimization should be working but it is not, enable this event. The **reason** for the event gives more context on why PSP was not used. The two reason values you might find valuable are

> **NonCacheable** – A query that cannot be saved into the plan cache. It could be you are using hints for RECOMPILE that could cause this state, which has been a common workaround for the PSP problem.

> **SkewnessThresholdNotMet** – This means there is not enough "data skew" to enable PSP optimization. We do not document the threshold. You can see in the example I used "millions" of rows, but the threshold doesn't necessarily have to be that. Note also that if statistics are not up to date, you might encounter this problem even if you have data skew because we rely on statistics.

parameter_sensitive_plan_optimization

This is a *debug* channel-only event but can show that the query processor is using query variants.

You can intentionally *disable* PSP optimization by (other than the workarounds listed previously that disable its use)

- Using dbcompat level < 160

- Using the database-scoped configuration PARAMETER_SENSITIVE_ PLAN_OPTIMIZATION = OFF (and you can enable it again with this option)

PSP Optimization Is a Powerful Innovation

I personally think the innovation here will help so many people avoid expensive and time-consuming query performance problems. For me, PSP optimization is clearly one of the best things to come out of SQL Server 2022. Jack Li summed it up best when I asked him his perspective on PSP optimization: *"When it comes to parameterized queries involving scenarios such as data skewness, having one plan per* query makes it impossible for optimizer to pick a plan that will meet the needs for all conditions. By allowing multiple plans per query, Parameter Sensitive Plan Optimization enables the ability to choose plans based on cardinality of predicates to achieve optimal performance."

Cardinality Estimation (CE) Model Feedback

I vividly remember back before SQL Server 2014 shipped, I was in Redmond for what was called a "milestone review" for the release. I was working in CSS in those days and often found myself meeting "early" on a release internally to give a supportability and customer perspective to the engineering team. This is when I first learned about a new cardinality estimation (CE) model to be introduced in SQL Server 2014.

I understood the concept. We needed to update our query processor assumptions about cardinality. We were using assumptions from 1998, when SQL Server 7.0 was released, and we created a new query processor from the old Sybase code. But I had my "support hat" on for those meetings, so even though I understood this was probably the right thing to do, I made sure to ask for a way to "turn it off" in case of problems.

Unfortunately, the need to disable this new "model" for queries over the years happened far more than we thought. Let's first look more at exactly what a "CE model" is and why it has resulted in problems for customers.

What Is the CE Model Problem?

Cardinality is pretty well described in my opinion in our documentation at `https://docs.microsoft.com/sql/relational-databases/performance/cardinality-estimation-sql-server`. Here is a quote I like from this documentation:

> *The Query Optimizer determines the cost of executing a query plan based on two main factors:*
>
> *The total number of rows processed at each level of a query plan, referred to as the cardinality of the plan.*
>
> *The cost model of the algorithm dictated by the operators used in the query.*
>
> *The first factor, cardinality, is used as an input parameter of the second factor, the cost model. Therefore, improved cardinality leads to better estimated costs and, in turn, faster execution plans.*

Cardinality estimation (CE) is a process for the query optimizer to estimate the uniqueness of any part of an operator when compiling a plan. Sometimes it is obvious and easy. Sometimes it is not so easy.

The *CE model* dictates how the query optimizer in SQL Server makes certain assumptions about cardinality when it is not so easy. In SQL Server 7.0, we redesigned the assumptions of the CE model as we built a new query processor. The types of assumptions fall into areas described in our documentation at `https://docs.microsoft.com/sql/relational-databases/performance/cardinality-estimation-sql-server?#versions-of-the-ce`. In this documentation, we introduce the concept of CE *versions*. There are two CE versions: (1) the CE model we introduced in SQL Server 7.0 and (2) a new CE model we introduced in SQL Server 2014. The documentation also talks about different CE model scenarios including **independence**, **uniformity**, **containment**, and **inclusion**.

In all of these scenarios, there is no right or wrong answer. It is a classic "it depends" situation. The SQL Server 7.0 CE model, known as the *legacy* CE model, made certain assumptions. In SQL Server 2014, we made changes to the CE model to what we believed were more in line with "modern" workloads. Concepts like *correlation* and *containment* were updated. Correlation is one of the more interesting problems and is how the optimizer decides how columns are *related* to each other (or not related).

We believed we were making the optimizer more "accurate." And in many cases we were spot on. In fact, in many cases we improved the performance of queries with this new model. If you used a dbcompat level of 120 (the default for SQL Server 2014), the *new* CE model took effect.

Unfortunately, there are assumptions this new model makes that don't work for every workload. Although we were trying to make a model more accurate, that didn't always lead to the same or better performance and sometimes resulted in performance regressions.

We introduced trace flags, query hints, and even database options to use the *legacy* CE model. These topics in themselves can be detailed and difficult to read even for a seasoned SQL professional. I encourage you to read two additional resources to learn more:

- A blog we wrote on why we built a new CE model at `https://cloudblogs.microsoft.com/sqlserver/2014/03/17/the-new-and-improved-cardinality-estimator-in-sql-server-2014/`

- An incredible detailed whitepaper written by the famous Joe Sack at `https://download.microsoft.com/download/d/2/0/d20e1c5f-72ea-4505-9f26-fef9550efd44/optimizing%20your%20query%20plans%20with%20the%20sql%20server%202014%20cardinality%20estimator.docx`

The bottom line is that customers would tell us they upgraded to SQL Server 2014 and used the new dbcompat 120 level and "it just got slower." It was not a prevalent complaint but enough to cause a problem. As a result, customers over the years have become accustomed to using the legacy CE model along with the latest dbcompat levels.

Along comes **CE feedback** to try and help resolve some of these conflicts.

How Does CE Feedback Work?

CE feedback is a coordination between the query optimizer and Query Store to recognize query patterns that fit the CE model problem and then use query hints to rectify the issue.

The optimizer will go through the process of compiling a query. If it recognizes a CE model pattern that is a candidate for CE model feedback, it will save a query hint that could make the query faster. We are conservative with this approach, and the query must be run a certain number of times with the same query text before we attempt to *analyze* for CE feedback.

Once we have analyzed for CE feedback, then on the next query execution, we attempt to apply the query hint and perform a *validation* if the hint made the CPU time of the query better or worse (it could be slightly better, which is not considered good enough to continue to use the hint). If the validation is successful, we save the query hint and feedback in Query Store. If not successful, it is considered a regression, and we will not use or save the hint. We also record the fact that the feedback caused a regression in Query Store.

Try Out an Exercise

Let's do an exercise of CE feedback to try and solve a scenario involving **correlation**.

Prerequisites

In order to try this exercise, you will need the following perquisites:

- SQL Server 2022 Evaluation Edition.

- Virtual machine or computer with minimum of two CPUs with 8Gb RAM.

Note   The timings for this example are *very CPU sensitive*. I've used several virtual machines and computers that allow you to see the problem, but older CPUs with slower speeds may not allow you to see CE feedback in action with this specific exercise. For my tests I used an Azure Virtual Machine Standard_D2ds_v5 (two vCPUs, 8Gb memory). Our documentation for Azure says this VM size uses a third-generation Intel® Xeon® Platinum 8370C (Ice Lake) processor reaching an all-core turbo clock speed of up to 3.5 GHz. I think one of the keys is to use a *dedicated* VM or computer. Any CPU cycles from other programs can disrupt a pure CPU workload.

- SQL Server Management Studio (SSMS). The latest 18.x or 19.x build will work.

- A copy of the scripts from the GitHub repo of this book from the **ch05_builtinqueryintelligence_getsbetter\cefeedback** directory.

Follow These Steps for the Exercise

Follow these steps to see CE feedback in action:

1. Download the AdventureWorks2016_EXT sample backup
   from https://github.com/Microsoft/sql-server-samples/
   releases/download/adventureworks/AdventureWorks2016_EXT.
   bak. The restore scripts assume a directory of **c:\sql_sample_
   databases**.

2. Restore the AdventureWorks_EXT sample backup using the script
   restore_adventureworks_ext.sql. Edit the file path per your
   needs. This script runs the following T-SQL statements:

```
USE master;
GO
DROP DATABASE IF EXISTS AdventureWorks_EXT;
GO
RESTORE DATABASE AdventureWorks_EXT FROM DISK = 'c:\sql_sample_
databases\AdventureWorks2016_EXT.bak'
WITH MOVE 'AdventureWorks2016_EXT_Data' TO 'c:\sql_sample_
databases\AdventureWorks2016_Data.mdf',
MOVE 'AdventureWorks2016_EXT_Log' TO 'c:\sql_sample_databases\
AdventureWorks2016_log.ldf',
MOVE 'AdventureWorks2016_EXT_Mod' TO 'c:\sql_sample_databases\
AdventureWorks2016_EXT_mod'
GO
```

   Query Store is already enabled after restoring this backup.

3. Execute the script **create_xevent_seassion.sql** to create and start
   an Extended Events session to view feedback events. Use SSMS
   in Object Explorer to view the session with Watch Live Data. The
   script uses the following T-SQL statements:

```
IF EXISTS (SELECT * FROM sys.server_event_sessions WHERE name =
'CEFeedback')
DROP EVENT SESSION [CEFeedback] ON SERVER;
GO
```

```
CREATE EVENT SESSION [CEFeedback] ON SERVER
ADD EVENT sqlserver.query_feedback_analysis(
    ACTION(sqlserver.query_hash_signed,sqlserver.query_plan_hash_
    signed,sqlserver.sql_text)),
ADD EVENT sqlserver.query_feedback_validation(
    ACTION(sqlserver.query_hash_signed,sqlserver.query_plan_hash_
    signed,sqlserver.sql_text))
WITH (MAX_MEMORY=4096 KB,EVENT_RETENTION_MODE=NO_EVENT_LOSS,MAX_
DISPATCH_LATENCY=1 SECONDS,MAX_EVENT_SIZE=0 KB,MEMORY_PARTITION_
MODE=NONE,TRACK_CAUSALITY=OFF,STARTUP_STATE=OFF);
GO
-- Start XE
ALTER EVENT SESSION [CEFeedback] ON SERVER
STATE = START;
GO
```

4. Execute the script **create_index_on_city.sql** to add an index on
    the City column for the Person.Address table. This script uses the
    following T-SQL statements:

```
USE [AdventureWorks_EXT];
GO
CREATE NONCLUSTERED INDEX [IX_Address_City] ON [Person].[Address]
(
    [City] ASC
);
GO
```

5. Execute the script **dbcompat160.sql** to turn on dbcompat 160 and
    clear Query Store and cache. This script uses the following T-SQL
    statements:

```
USE master;
GO
ALTER DATABASE [AdventureWorks_EXT] SET COMPATIBILITY_LEVEL = 160;
GO
ALTER DATABASE [AdventureWorks_EXT] SET QUERY_STORE CLEAR ALL;
```

```
GO
USE [AdventureWorks_EXT];
GO
ALTER DATABASE SCOPED CONFIGURATION CLEAR PROCEDURE_CACHE;
GO
```

6. Execute the script **cefeedbackquerybatch.sql** to *prime* CE feedback. This script uses the following T-SQL statements:

```
USE AdventureWorks_EXT;
GO
SELECT AddressLine1, City, PostalCode FROM Person.Address
WHERE StateProvinceID = 79
AND City = 'Redmond';
GO 15
```

The script should finish in seconds. Here is the classic correlation example. Is the city of Redmond correlated to be in the state where StateProvinceID = 79? Which assumption should the optimizer make about correlation? We will see later what CE feedback does. The script is run 15 times to ensure we run a query at a minimum level of times before trying to provide feedback. This number is not documented, so do not rely specifically on the magic number of 15.

7. Now execute the script **cefeedbackquery.sql**, which runs the same query one more time. If you check the Extended Events live data, you should see an event called **query_feedback_analysis**. The output should look something like Figure 5-14.

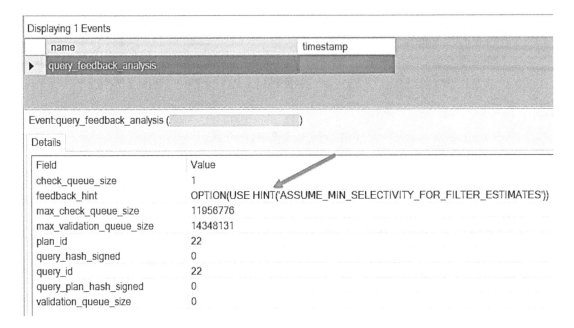

Figure 5-14. *CE feedback analysis*

One of the key columns is the **feedback_hint**. You will learn more about this over the rest of the exercise.

8. Execute the query **check_query_hints_and_feedback.sql**. This script uses the following T-SQL statements:

```
USE AdventureWorks_EXT;
GO
SELECT * from sys.query_store_query_hints;
GO
SELECT * from sys.query_store_plan_feedback;
GO
```

sys.query_store_query_hints is where all query hints are stored whether you supply a hint or the system does. **sys.query_store_plan_feedback** is used to show any feedback the system is providing for query processing. You saw examples of this in Chapter 4 for memory grant persistence.

Your output should look similar to the following for the second query (I flipped the results vertically but left out the datetime values):

```
plan_feedback_id        2
plan_id                 22
feature_id              1
feature_desc            CE Feedback
feedback_data           {"Feedback hints":""}
state                   2
state_desc              PENDING_VALIDATION
```

This data indicates that CE feedback is eligible to be provided, but validation is needed. The validation is to ensure the feedback doesn't make the query slower (more specially, the feedback hint doesn't lead to a plan that uses more CPU). The first query doesn't return any rows because we have not "locked" in the hint to be used for CE feedback.

9. Execute the script **cefeedbackquery.sql** again.

10. Check the Extended Events live data. Now an event has fired called **query_feedback_validation**. Your results should be similar to Figure 5-15.

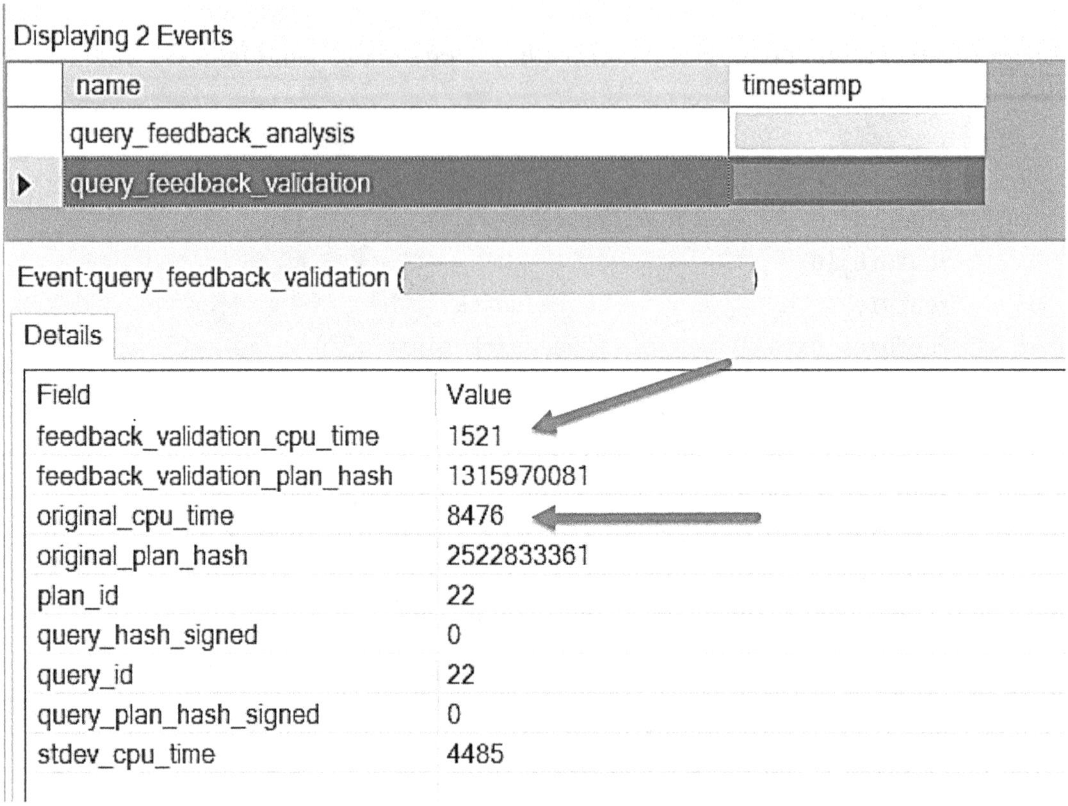

Displaying 2 Events

name	timestamp
query_feedback_analysis	
▶ query_feedback_validation	

Event:query_feedback_validation (   )

Details

Field	Value
feedback_validation_cpu_time	1521
feedback_validation_plan_hash	1315970081
original_cpu_time	8476
original_plan_hash	2522833361
plan_id	22
query_hash_signed	0
query_id	22
query_plan_hash_signed	0
stdev_cpu_time	4485

Figure 5-15. *CE feedback validation*

Notice the value of **feedback_validation_cpu_time** is less than **original_cpu_time**. This means the hint we are using requires less CPU for the query.

11. Run the script **check_query_hints_and_feedback.sql** again. You should see results now like the following for the first query from **sys.query_store_query_hints:**

```
query_hint_id                            1
query_id                                 22
query_hint_text
OPTION(USE HINT('ASSUME_MIN_SELECTIVITY_FOR_FILTER_ESTIMATES'))
last_query_hint_failure_reason           0
last_query_hint_failure_reason_desc      NONE
query_hint_failure_count                 0
```

```
source                              1
source_desc                         CE feedback
comment                             NULL
```

And results for the second query from **sys.query_store_plan_feedback** should look like

```
plan_feedback_id    2
plan_id             22
feature_id          1
feature_desc        CE Feedback
feedback_data
{"Feedback hints":"Min selectivity"}
state               5
state_desc          VERIFICATION_PASSED
```

Note   If the validation fails, you will see a **state_desc** value of VERIFICATION_
REGRESSED. The typical reason is that during validation the hint resulted in higher
CPU time for the query.

A query hint has been automatically applied to make the query run faster. But what
does the hint 'ASSUME_MIN_SELECTIVITY_FOR_FILTER_ESTIMATES' mean? Back in
the previous section titled "**What Is the CE Model Problem**?" I described one of the CE
model issues related to how to deal with correlation. The ASSUME_MIN_SELECTIVITY_
FOR_FILTER_ESTIMATES hint assumes *full correlation*. You can find more details in
our documentation at https://docs.microsoft.com/sql/t-sql/queries/hints-
transact-sql-query. The following is the quote for this hint:

*Causes SQL Server to generate a plan using minimum selectivity when esti-
mating AND predicates for filters to account for full correlation. This hint
name is equivalent to trace flag 4137 when used with cardinality estimation model of SQL Server 2012 (11.x) and earlier versions and has similar
effect when trace flag 9471 is used with cardinality estimation model of SQL
Server 2014 (12.x) or higher.*

12.   Run the script **cefeedbackquerybatch.sql** again to compare the times from the first run.

13.   Use Query Store reports in SSMS to see the differences. Use the **Top Resource-Consuming Queries report** from Object Explorer to see the differences in CPU time. There are two plans for the query. The original plan that takes longer is as shown in Figure 5-16.

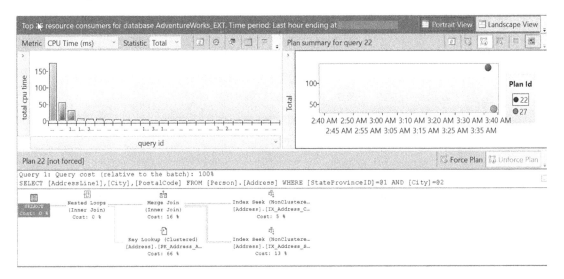

Figure 5-16. *Original query plan before CE feedback hint*

Notice this plan uses several joins over several indexes. Part of the reason is the optimizer is using the "new" CE model to make the assumption that there is no correlation or only partial correlation. Figure 5-17 shows the new plan after applying the new hint with CE feedback.

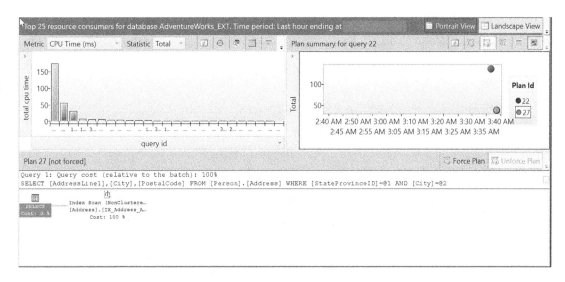

Figure 5-17. *New plan with CE feedback hint*

This plan runs faster and consumes less CPU. The new plan
uses a single index scan to get the data. If you move your cursor
over the index scan operator, you can see the scan is using a
filtered predicate to resolve the two predicate values as seen in
Figure 5-18.

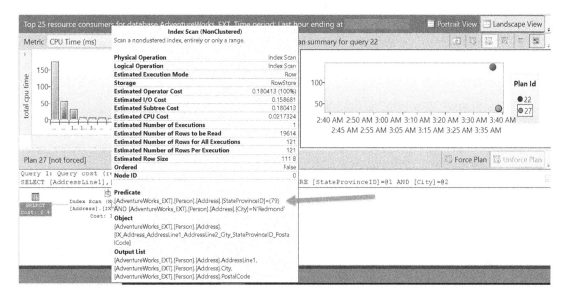

Figure 5-18. *Predicate pushdown with the new query plan*

This scenario is called *predicate pushdown*. The idea is that the optimizer can "scan and filter" at the same time on an index. There is a great explanation of this concept in this blog post by the famous Pedro Lopes at `https://techcommunity.microsoft.com/t5/sql-server-blog/predicate-pushdown-and-why-should-i-care/ba-p/385946`. Since the optimizer is now using the hint 'ASSUME_MIN_SELECTIVITY_FOR_FILTER_ESTIMATES', it can easily decide to use this technique since it assumes full correlation.

Pretty nifty, right? And since the feedback and hint is persisted in Query Store, it will be used even if the plan is evicted from cache.

Limits and More Details About CE Feedback

Stay up to date with all the latest on CE feedback at `https://aka.ms/cefeedback`.

When you look at the actual execution plan XML for a query that has used CE feedback, you will find these properties have been added to the `<StmtSimple>` clause:

`QueryStoreStatementHintId="1`

This will match the **sys.query_store_query_hints.query_hint_id**:

`QueryStoreStatementHintText="OPTION(USE HINT('ASSUME_MIN_SELECTIVITY_FOR_FILTER_ESTIMATES'))" QueryStoreStatementHintSource="CE feedback"`

CE feedback will not be used under the following situations:

- You are using a dbcompat level < 160.

- You are using your own Query Store hints.

- You are forcing the plan in Query Store.

- You execute the following T-SQL to turn off CE feedback for the database: ALTER DATABASE SCOPED CONFIGURATION SET CE_FEEDBACK = OFF.

- You are executing a query that doesn't meet the pattern under the category of correlation, join containment, or optimizer row goal as outlined in our docs at `https://aka.ms/cefeedback`.

- You are using the query hint DISABLE_CE_FEEDBACK.

I expect there will be variability in how CE feedback works for applications and workloads. Since we apply the "do not harm policy" by using a validation process, my hope is that customers will observe that it is helping their workloads after they move to dbcompat 160.

Degree of Parallelism (DOP) Feedback

At its deepest level, the SQL Server engine is powered by a series of worker threads coordinated by SQLOS. We have designed the engine to make smart decisions to partition out work for certain operations using multiple threads concurrently. These operations range from creating database backups and rebuilding indexes to running queries that retrieve data using SELECT statements. When the engine uses multiple threads to perform some of these operations in parallel, we use the term *degree of parallelism* (DOP). DOP refers to the number of threads that run concurrently to perform a task. A task could be building an index, or it could be an operator used to execute part of a query plan for a SELECT statement. The history of using parallel threads for query execution dates all the way back to SQL Server 7.0 when we built a new query processor from the SQL 6.X versions.

Note   Step back in time. I found the original SQL Server 7.0 docs on our announcement of this new feature at https://docs.microsoft.com/en-us/ previous-versions//cc917537(v=technet.10)?redirectedfrom=M SDN. Also, take a look at this slide deck built by Lubor Kollar, who was one of the original architects of query parallelism in SQL Server: www.slideserve.com/ gilon/parallel-query-processing-in-sql-server-powerpoint-ppt-presentation.

I remember working in support when this new feature came out. It definitely helped boost the performance for certain workloads, especially those with analytic-type queries. But it came with a cost. In support, we started noticing customers contacting us with problems where all CPUs were "pegged" at 100% for minutes at a time, hampering performance for all users. When we introduced this feature in SQL Server 7.0, we built into the query processor heuristics to decide when to use parallelism and to dynamically decide what the maximum degree of parallelism should be for a query. We introduced a **sp_configure** setting called **'max degree of parallelism'**. The default value was 0, which means "let the engine decide." And most of the time, this means use all available processors. For the one query that uses parallelism, that's great. But for all other users, this can spell trouble.

Keith Elmore, Robert Dorr, and I were working in support in those days, and we found ourselves starting to recommend to customers to set 'max degree of parallelism' to a value other than 0 (our recommendation was complicated because this setting is an advanced setting and originally required a server restart). But what value should we tell them to use? For the most extreme critical problems, some customers would set this value to 1, which means do not allow any queries to use parallelism. I was hesitant to recommend this because it effectively means disabling a feature of the product. For the most part, we would recommend some setting that was lower than the total number of available processors.

In later releases, SQL Server would support NUMA architectures, resource governor, database-scoped configuration, and query hints, which can affect how to set MAXDOP. We built knowledge base articles with guidance. All of this experience has led to the following documentation page for guidance on setting MAXDOP: `https://docs.microsoft.com/sql/database-engine/configure-windows/configure-the-max-degree-of-parallelism-server-configuration-option`.

Even with this guidance and all of these options, our users continually fight a battle to decide how best to set this value to allow some queries to benefit from parallelism while not greatly affecting the overall application workload. Along comes the concept of **DOP feedback**. DOP feedback is designed to dynamically adjust the DOP used by operators in a query plan. Let's look at the background of the project and how it works, go through an example, and understand considerations for using this feature.

Why Did We Build DOP Feedback?

If you read and study how parallelism works, you can see a certain amount of CPU cycles are required to run many different threads in parallel and coordinate between them. What may not be clear in some cases is whether a query could run with a lower number of threads and achieve the same overall final execution duration, therefore using less CPU resources.

Back in 2019 (before SQL Server 2019 shipped), I remember seeing a new project launched by Slava Oks and Pedro Lopes called *Gaia*. The concept was to build a new service that would be able to observe telemetry from the engine and provide *feedback* to certain core engine components. The Gaia service would run outside the engine and maintain its own database with the purpose of collecting telemetry and providing feedback. As Pedro Lopes tells it, *"..the purpose is to be the all-encompassing framework for product internal feedback telemetry, it's just like Gaia in Greek mythology, where she is t*he mother of all life."

A real-world scenario was needed to test out Gaia, and one of the early ones was DOP. The concept of Gaia is still around as a project, but the decision was made for SQL Server 2022 to take the concept of DOP feedback and infuse this into the engine using data captured in Query Store.

What Is DOP Feedback?

I looked back at some of our original design docs and found this statement that summarizes our goal: "Improve system throughput by lowering MAXDOP for parallel queries to *reduce CPU usage* while maintaining the Do No Harm principle in regard to performance."

So the question becomes: How do you know if a lower degree of parallelism for the query will achieve a good enough result? You need a way to execute the query and get feedback on trying lower DOP values. That is effectively what DOP feedback does. DOP feedback is a coordination between the query processor and Query Store to execute, try, and validate DOP values for an *eligible* query until the lowest possible DOP value is found that reduces CPU usage and achieves the "no harm" principle over time.

Note   One of the interesting aspects I found in the design of the feature was the use of workloads like TPC-H to see what kind of optimal DOP values across various queries in the benchmark could still achieve a great result. We also looked at telemetry we see in Azure to find out what typical DOP values were used across many different queries over time.

How Does DOP Feedback Work?

DOP feedback can be used no matter what dbcompat setting is used for the database. But, in order for DOP feedback to be enabled, a database-scoped option must be turned on like the following:

```
ALTER DATABASE SCOPED CONFIGURATION SET DOP_FEEDBACK = ON
```

If this option is enabled, when a query is executed that can use parallelism, the query processor will engage in a *feedback system* within the engine to determine if DOP feedback can be used. Figure 5-19 shows an architecture of the DOP feedback system.

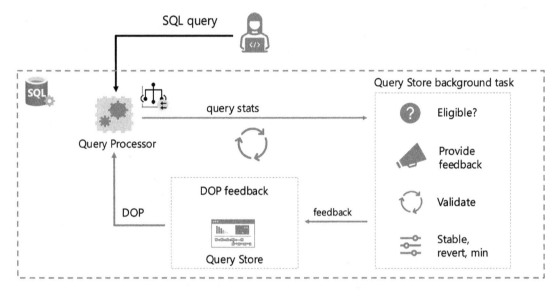

SQL query

Query Processor

query stats

DOP

DOP feedback

Query Store

feedback

Query Store background task

? **Eligible?**

Provide feedback

Validate

Stable, revert, min

Figure 5-19. *The DOP feedback system*

Let's dive into the flow of the DOP feedback system:

- When a query is executed and the query processor determines it will use parallelism, it will look to see if any *DOP feedback* exists to adjust what DOP to use (assuming the database option DOP_FEEDBACK is enabled).

- For the DOP feedback system to work, the query processor will send query statistics to a Query Store background task. Query Store by its nature only collects performance statistics aggregated. This would not provide enough detail for DOP feedback, so we use a Query Store background task to accept detailed query statistics and aggregate them internally in memory within the task.

- The Query Store background task will always look to see if a query is *eligible* for DOP feedback. Eligibility is somewhat complicated, but the primary concept is to see if a query would not significantly run slower with a lower DOP and use less CPU resources. Eligibility also includes a factor of how many times a query has executed, a query that has a *fairly long* duration, and *parallel efficiency.* Parallel efficiency measures how efficient it is to use parallelism vs. the cost of CPU to execute the query. We do not document these factors, but you will see how SQL Server 2022 behaves in the next section with an example.

Note   A query is not eligible if the query hint option **DISABLE_DOP_FEEDBACK** is used.

- If the query is eligible, background tasks will *provide feedback* to lower the DOP of the query. Lowering the DOP happens in a *stepdown* fashion typically in increments of 4 and 2. So if the *original DOP* was 8, feedback will be provided for 6, then 4, and finally 2, which is the minimum DOP level. The *baseline* DOP is based on your configuration settings for the instance, database, resource group, and query. I've provided more details on DOP precedence in the section titled "**What Else Should I Know About DOP Feedback?**"

- When feedback is provided, the system will go into a *validation phase.* The query processor feeds the background tasks statistics to validate if the query performs with a *similar* duration as the original execution and less CPU resources. This validation phase can take several query iterations. If the feedback fails on the **first** attempt at validation for an eligible query, the feedback is considered *reverted.* This means the baseline DOP of the query when it became eligible will be used. Any new compilation of the query without persisted feedback would be considered for eligibility and validation again.

- If the query passes the validation phase, feedback is considered *stable.* When stabilization occurs, feedback is persisted in Query Store.

- This cycle will continue until a DOP feedback value is used that fails validation from the last stable value or hits the "minimum" stable value, which is 2 regardless of the number of CPUs or any configuration settings.

In summary, the process of DOP feedback is to see if a query is eligible and then perform a loop of feedback and validation until feedback is reverted, the lowest best stable value is found, or the minimum feedback value of 2 is encountered.

All of this takes place without any recompilation required for the query. The query processor looks at DOP feedback as part of deciding which DOP value to use for parallelism for a specific query execution.

The overall goal of DOP feedback is to increase parallel efficiency without causing any significantly longer duration for the query. The less workers required to execute a query with the same duration results in lower CPU usage, so the entire system benefits.

DOP feedback always attempts to lower DOP and never increase it. SQL Server includes several different diagnostic options to view how DOP feedback works including DMVs, XML plan details, and Extended Events. You will see how these work in the next section for an example of DOP feedback.

Let's Try DOP Feedback

Here are the prerequisites to run this example:

- SQL Server 2022 Evaluation Edition.

- VM or computer with eight CPUs and at least 24Gb RAM.

Note   This exercise is very CPU sensitive. You should execute this exercise on a VM or computer that is "dedicated" to SQL Server and has fast I/O storage. Slower CPU speeds or other processes running may affect the ability to see the results of this exercise. I used an Azure Virtual Machine Standard+E8ads_v5 (eight vCPUs, 64Gb memory) for this exercise. I've also had success with this example using a D32ds_v5 Azure Virtual Machine with DOP for the instance lowered from 32 down to 12.

- SQL Server Management Studio (SSMS). The latest 18.x or 19.x build will work.

- Download **ostress.exe** from https://aka.ms/ostress. Install using the RMLSetup.msi file that is included, and use all defaults.

- A copy of the scripts from the GitHub repo of this book from the **ch05_builtinqueryintelligence_getsbetter\dopfeedback** directory.

Follow these steps to see DOP feedback in action:

1. Download a copy of the backup of WideWorldImporters from `https://aka.ms/WideWorldImporters`. The script in the next step assumes a location of the backup at **c:\sql_sample_databases**. There is a customized backup available with extended data preloaded you can use at `https://github.com/microsoft/sqlworkshops-sql2022workshop/releases`.

2. Restore the WideWorldImporters sample backup. You can edit and use the **restorewwi.sql** script. This script was designed for a SQL Server on Azure Virtual Machines marketplace image, which has separate disks for data and log files. Edit this script to match your file paths. This script contains the following T-SQL statements:

```
USE master;
GO
DROP DATABASE IF EXISTS WideWorldImporters;
GO
-- Edit the locations for files to match your storage
RESTORE DATABASE WideWorldImporters FROM DISK = 'c:\sql_sample_
databases\WideWorldImporters-Full.bak' with
MOVE 'WWI_Primary' TO 'e:\data\WideWorldImporters.mdf',
MOVE 'WWI_UserData' TO 'e:\data\WideWorldImporters_UserData.ndf',
MOVE 'WWI_Log' TO 'f:\log\WideWorldImporters.ldf',
MOVE 'WWI_InMemory_Data_1' TO 'e:\data\WideWorldImporters_
InMemory_Data_1',
stats=5;
GO
```

3. Execute the script **configmaxdop.sql**. This runs the following T-SQL statements:

```
sp_configure 'show advanced', 1;
go
reconfigure;
go
```

```
sp_configure 'max degree of parallelism', 0;
go
reconfigure;
go
```

In order to start the baseline correctly, I set MAXDOP to the
instance at 0 to use all available CPUs. No other MAXDOP setting
is configured.

4. Execute the **populatedata.sql** script to load more data into the
    Warehouse.StockItems table. This script will take ~15 minutes
    to run (timing depends on how many CPUs and the speed of your
    disk). This script executes the following T-SQL statements (no
    apologies for my favorite sports team in the exercise):

```
USE WideWorldImporters;
GO
-- Add StockItems to cause a data skew in Suppliers
--
DECLARE @StockItemID int;
DECLARE @StockItemName varchar(100);
DECLARE @SupplierID int;
SELECT @StockItemID = 228;
SET @StockItemName = 'Dallas Cowboys Shirt'+convert(varchar(10),
@StockItemID);
SET @SupplierID = 4;
DELETE FROM Warehouse.StockItems WHERE StockItemID >=
@StockItemID;
SET NOCOUNT ON;
BEGIN TRANSACTION;
WHILE @StockItemID <= 20000000
BEGIN
INSERT INTO Warehouse.StockItems
(StockItemID, StockItemName, SupplierID, UnitPackageID,
OuterPackageID, LeadTimeDays,
QuantityPerOuter, IsChillerStock, TaxRate, UnitPrice,
TypicalWeightPerUnit, LastEditedBy
)
```

```
VALUES (@StockItemID, @StockItemName, @SupplierID, 10, 9, 12, 100,
0, 15.00, 100.00, 0.300, 1);
SET @StockItemID = @StockItemID + 1;
SET @StockItemName = 'Dallas Cowboys Shirt'+convert(varchar(10),
@StockItemID);
END
COMMIT TRANSACTION;
SET NOCOUNT OFF;
GO
```

5. Execute the script **rebuild_index.sql** to rebuild the index for
    added data. This script runs the following T-SQL statements:

```
USE WideWorldImporters;
GO
ALTER INDEX FK_Warehouse_StockItems_SupplierID ON Warehouse.
StockItems REBUILD;
GO
```

6. Execute the script **dopfeedback.sql** to enable DOP feedback, set
    dbcompat to 160, and clear settings for the exercise. This script
    executes these T-SQL statements:

```
USE WideWorldImporters;
GO
-- Make sure QS is on and set runtime collection lower
than default
ALTER DATABASE WideWorldImporters SET QUERY_STORE = ON;
GO
ALTER DATABASE WideWorldImporters SET QUERY_STORE (OPERATION_MODE
= READ_WRITE, DATA_FLUSH_INTERVAL_SECONDS = 60, INTERVAL_LENGTH_
MINUTES = 1, QUERY_CAPTURE_MODE = ALL);
GO
ALTER DATABASE WideWorldImporters SET QUERY_STORE CLEAR ALL;
GO
-- You must change dbcompat to 160
```

```
ALTER DATABASE WideWorldImporters SET COMPATIBILITY_LEVEL = 160;
GO
-- Enable DOP feedback
ALTER DATABASE SCOPED CONFIGURATION SET DOP_FEEDBACK = ON;
GO
-- Clear proc cache to start with new plans
ALTER DATABASE SCOPED CONFIGURATION CLEAR PROCEDURE_CACHE;
GO
```

Notice we don't have to change dbcompat for this database
(which is set to 130). I also set the INTERVAL_LENGTH_MINUTES
to 1 so that I could show detailed query statistics at a more
granular level when looking at Query Store and reports. This is
not a recommended Query Store configuration for a production
environment.

7. Execute the script **proc.sql** to create a stored procedure to query
    data that will use a query plan with parallelism. This script
    executes the following T-SQL statements:

```
USE WideWorldImporters;
GO
CREATE OR ALTER PROCEDURE [Warehouse].[GetStockItemsbySupplier]
@SupplierID int
AS
BEGIN
SELECT StockItemID, SupplierID, StockItemName, TaxRate,
LeadTimeDays
FROM Warehouse.StockItems s
WHERE SupplierID = @SupplierID
ORDER BY StockItemName;
END;
GO
```

Note   You may recognize this example from Parameter-Sensitive Plan (PSP) optimization. I'll be completely transparent: this exercise uses this procedure and code where I first built PSP optimization. I realized that part of that example uses a query plan with parallelism. So you are seeing DOP feedback first, but it was "born" from my work first on PSP optimization. Imagine both of these features actually working in harmony to improve performance "all up."

8. Execute the script **dopxe.sql** to set up an Extended Events session to track the status of DOP feedback. This script runs the following T-SQL statements:

```
IF EXISTS (SELECT * FROM sys.server_event_sessions WHERE name =
'DOPFeedback')
DROP EVENT SESSION [DOPFeedback] ON SERVER;
GO
CREATE EVENT SESSION [DOPFeedback] ON SERVER
ADD EVENT sqlserver.dop_feedback_eligible_query(
    ACTION(sqlserver.query_hash_signed,sqlserver.query_plan_hash_
    signed,sqlserver.sql_text)),
ADD EVENT sqlserver.dop_feedback_provided(
    ACTION(sqlserver.query_hash_signed,sqlserver.query_plan_hash_
    signed,sqlserver.sql_text)),
ADD EVENT sqlserver.dop_feedback_reverted(
    ACTION(sqlserver.query_hash_signed,sqlserver.query_plan_hash_
    signed,sqlserver.sql_text)),
ADD EVENT sqlserver.dop_feedback_stabilized(
    ACTION(sqlserver.query_hash_signed,sqlserver.query_plan_hash_
    signed,sqlserver.sql_text)),
ADD EVENT sqlserver.dop_feedback_validation(
    ACTION(sqlserver.query_hash_signed,sqlserver.query_plan_hash_
    signed,sqlserver.sql_text))
WITH (MAX_MEMORY=4096 KB,EVENT_RETENTION_MODE=NO_EVENT_LOSS,MAX_
DISPATCH_LATENCY=1 SECONDS,MAX_EVENT_SIZE=0 KB,MEMORY_PARTITION_
MODE=NONE,TRACK_CAUSALITY=OFF,STARTUP_STATE=OFF);
```

```
GO
-- Start XE
ALTER EVENT SESSION [DOPFeedback] ON SERVER
STATE = START;
GO
```

Right-click the new Extended Events session in Object Explorer in SSMS and select Watch Live Data.

9. Run the script **workload_index_scan_users.cmd** from the command prompt. This script takes about 15 minutes to complete. This script executes the procedure you have created in a repeated loop.

Note   This script assumes a local server connection with Windows authentication.

---

10. When this script completes, you can observe DOP feedback using the live data from Extended Events. You should see a series of events like Figure 5-20.

name	timestamp	feedback_dop	query_dop	avg_adjusted_elapsed_time_ms	avg_cpu_time_ms	feedback_state
dop_feedback_eligible_query		NULL	8	NULL	NULL	NULL
dop_feedback_provided		6	8		16991	35023 NULL
dop_feedback_validation		6	NULL		13626	30077 PendingValidationTest
dop_feedback_validation		6	NULL		14070	30347 PendingValidationTest
dop_feedback_validation		6	NULL		13879	30361 Stable
dop_feedback_provided		4	6		13933	30430 NULL
dop_feedback_validation		4	NULL		12054	26080 PendingValidationTest
dop_feedback_validation		4	NULL		12243	26040 PendingValidationTest
dop_feedback_validation		4	NULL		12430	25592 Stable
dop_feedback_provided		2	4		12417	25591 NULL
dop_feedback_validation		2	NULL		13837	23466 PendingValidationTest
dop_feedback_stabilized		4	NULL		12417	25591 NULL

Figure 5-20. *DOP Extended Events sequence*

Within the Live Data Viewer in SSMS, you can add columns to the default view to see the sequence of feedback (right-click any field in the Details pane and select Show Column in Table). Over time you can see the **feedback_dop** lowering and the decrease in elapsed time and CPU time for the query. You can also see the iterations for validations with a feedback_state of PendingValidationTest and also Stable. Whenever Stable is reached, the feedback is persisted to Query Store.

Let's focus on the last two events as in Figure 5-21.

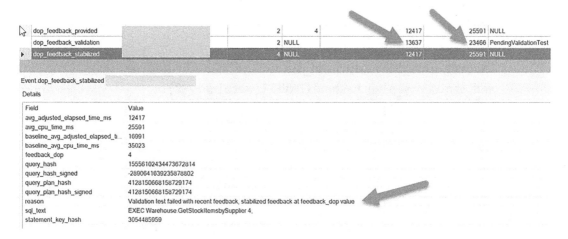

Figure 5-21. *DOP feedback stabilization event*

Notice that the **dop_feedback_stabilized** event is fired after feedback_dop is attempted at 2 but not stable. The elapsed time goes up after trying DOP feedback of 2, but CPU goes down. In order to adhere to our "do not harm" policy, we have to stop at DOP of 4. The **dop_feedback_stabilized** event shows the reason for stabilization. In this case, the validation for DOP 2 fails because the query duration is longer. This ends the feedback loop as we have found the best and lowest possible DOP value of 4. However, remember that when feedback is provided and feedback state is **Stable**, the feedback is persisted to Query Store. This allows the stable state to be persisted even though it could be lowered with further feedback.

I've run this test and scenario several times, and in some cases I've seen DOP feedback lower to 2 and stabilize at that number.

11. Execute the script **dop_query_stats.sql**. This script runs the following T-SQL statements:

```
USE WideWorldImporters;
GO
-- The hash value of 4128150668158729174 should be fixed for the
plan from the workload
SELECT qsp.query_plan_hash, avg_duration/1000 as avg_duration_ms,
```

```
avg_cpu_time/1000 as avg_cpu_ms, last_dop, min_dop, max_dop, qsrs.
count_executions
FROM sys.query_store_runtime_stats qsrs
JOIN sys.query_store_plan qsp
ON qsrs.plan_id = qsp.plan_id
and qsp.query_plan_hash = CONVERT(varbinary(8),
cast(4128150668158729174 as bigint))
ORDER by qsrs.last_execution_time;
GO
```

Looking at the results, you should see the progression of lower duration (elapsed) time and CPU as DOP is lowered based on feedback. But notice when the value of last_dop = 2, the duration is higher, which is why DOP feedback is considered stable at 4.

12. Execute the script **check_query_feedback.sql.** This script runs the following T-SQL statements:

```
USE WideWorldImporters;
GO
SELECT * from sys.query_store_plan_feedback;
GO
```

Your results should look similar to the following (I flipped the results vertically for readability and did not include the datetime columns):

```
plan_feedback_id        1
plan_id                 1
feature_id              3
feature_desc            DOP Feedback
feedback_data
{"BaselineStats":{"dop":"8","avg_cpu_time_ms":"35023","avg_
elapsed_time_ms":"16995","avg_wait_time_ms":"4578"},"LastGoodFe
edback":{"dop":"4","avg_cpu_time_ms":"25591","avg_elapsed_time_
ms":"12440","avg_wait_time_ms":"23"}}
State                   7
state_desc              FEEDBACK_VALID
```

The **feedback_data** shows the DOP feedback persisted to use **LastGoodFeedback** for subsequent executions of this query by the query engine, with the feedback surviving any restarts or plan cache eviction. Persistence in Query Store is the key, which makes DOP feedback effective over time.

13.   Look at the **Top Resource-Consuming Queries** report in SSMS. Change the Statistic to Avg for Duration. You should see a report like in Figure 5-22.

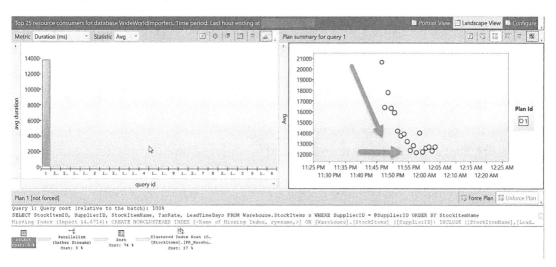

Figure 5-22. *Avg duration for DOP feedback*

Notice the drop in duration over time until stabilization is reached when it flattens out. Not all scenarios will result in a decrease in duration. The key is that DOP feedback should at least result in similar duration values over time.

Use the same report but change for Metric CPU Time with Statistic Avg. You should see a report like in Figure 5-23.

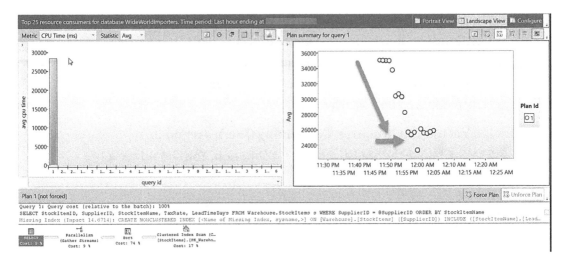

Figure 5-23. *Avg CPU for DOP feedback*

> This report shows the *true power of DOP feedback*: a significant
> reduction in CPU resources required to achieve a similar or lower
> duration for the query.

Note   If you were to look at actual query execution plans (such as from the
Extended Event **query_post_execution_plan_profile**) while this workload was
running, you would see an XML property of DOPFeedbackAdjusted="Yes:
Adjusting" and then eventually "Yes: Stable" once DOP feedback was
stabilized.

What Else Should I Know About DOP Feedback?

There are several key points about DOP feedback you need to know as you take
advantage of this feature:

- If you set the database-scoped configuration value **DOP_FEEDBACK**
  = **OFF** and feedback has not been persisted, it will be lost, and you
  have effectively "reset the system." If feedback is persisted, then
  queries will revert to "default" DOP behavior, but feedback is not lost.
  If you turn it ON again, DOP feedback will be used.

- If feedback is not persisted, then any recompile causes a reset to "start over." If feedback is persisted, then feedback survives a restart or recompile, which is the benefit of using Query Store to save feedback.

- The current context of the database where a query is executed is the basis for considering DOP feedback. Therefore, if you execute a query that crosses multiple databases, the database context in which you executed the query is used if DOP_FEEDBACK is ON for that database.

- Queries using temporary tables are eligible for DOP_FEEDBACK. I modified the preceding exercise to use a temporary table in the stored procedure and ran through the entire exercise. It behaved the same as when using a user table.

- I mentioned earlier about the original DOP and precedence order for using DOP feedback. Assuming that the database option DOP_FEEDBACK is ON and you are not using the DISABLE_DOP_FEEDBACK query hint, we will "start" the baseline DOP to use for feedback consideration on your settings for a query hint, resource group, database-scoped configuration, or instance configuration.

  As an example, if you are not using query hints or any other configuration value except you have 'max degree of parallelism' set to 8, we will start the baseline for DOP feedback at 8 (even if you have more CPUs than 8).

- In SQL Server 2017, we introduced the concept of Automatic Plan Correction (APRC), which also leverages Query Store. The concept is to automatically revert to a "last known good" plan if a regression has occurred. If you have APRC enabled, that takes precedence over using DOP feedback. You can learn more about APRC at `https://docs.microsoft.com/sql/relational-databases/automatic-tuning/automatic-tuning?#automatic-plan-correction.ack`.

Keep up to date with all the latest documentation and updates for DOP feedback at `https://aka.ms/dopfeedback`.

An Engine That Works for You

Think about all the innovation that is now poured into built-in query intelligence in SQL Server 2022.

Starting in **SQL Server 2016**, we introduced Query Store, and now it is more powerful and useable than ever in SQL Server 2022 with hints, support for read replicas, and integration with IQP.

In **SQL Server 2017** we introduced these IQP capabilities:

- Adaptive joins

- Interleaved execution

- Memory grant feedback for batch mode

Then in **SQL Server 2019** we added

- Memory grant feedback for row mode

- Batch mode for row mode (non-columnstore queries)

- Scalar UDF inlining

- Table variable deferred compilation

- Approximate count distinct

And now in **SQL Server 2022**, along come

- Approximate percentile

- Optimized plan forcing

- DOP feedback

- Memory grant percentiles and persistence

- Parameter-Sensitive Plan optimization

- CE feedback

I know I'm biased, but for me this is an engine that works for you. Aside from coding up examples for approximate functions, every one of these features doesn't require any code changes. And these are not special add-on features. They are built into the core of the engine, everywhere SQL exists. They are some of the brightest areas of innovation in our product based on real-world scenarios, scenarios that you see every day.

I think Hanuma Kodavalla, Technical Fellow at Microsoft, summed it up best when he told me

The power of the query is what distinguishes relational databases from others and SQL Server provides one of the most sophisticated query processing engines in the industry. SQL Server engineers and program managers routinely use the telemetry collected from millions of cloud databases, of varying sizes – a few GB to a hundred TB, running a large spectrum of workloads – OLTP, Datawarehouse, HTAP – to understand common query patterns and design features that improve query performance. Stemming from that effort are many SQL Server 2202 features – Parameter-Sensitive Plans, Cardinality Estimate feedback, Approximate Query Processing, Optimized Plan Forcing, QDS on readable secondaries, improvements to QDS hints, Memory Grant Feedback, and intelligent selection of Degree of Parallelism. In all of these features, a constant theme is to develop innovative algorithms that adapt to the various query patterns and system load at run-time to come up with better plans and improve query execution. Due to these features, workloads often see dramatic performance improvements without requiring any changes to the application. Further, all of these features are deployed to the cloud and tested on mission-critical workloads before releasing to the SQL Server 2022 customers, so they are all ready to be used in production.

CHAPTER 6

The Meat and Potatoes of SQL Server

Several years ago I was preparing for one of the famous "Conor and Bob" shows for the PASS Summit keynote. I created this elaborate idea involving machine learning, analytics, and other types of new features. I showed this to Conor, and he simply said, *"Bob, I think we should stick to the meat and potatoes for our show."* Being from Texas I knew what he meant. Highlight the *core engine* capabilities of SQL Server.

Of course, SQL has core capabilities for things like machine learning and analytics, but what Conor really meant was security, scalability (performance), and availability. For every major release, we have to invest in these three areas, or we really don't have an engine.

The Core Engine Is the Meat and Potatoes of SQL Server

This chapter is all about the core engine areas of security, scalability (performance), and availability – plus some other "stuff" that doesn't quite fit those categories. Built-in query intelligence is certainly a part of the core engine, but it deserved its own chapters. Here I'll cover all the new features to help:

- Secure your application and data.

- Ensure your application can scale and perform.

- Ensure your application is highly available.

© Bob Ward 2022
B. Ward, *SQL Server 2022 Revealed*, https://doi.org/10.1007/978-1-4842-8894-8_6

And then a list of features that are just "pure goodness" for the engine. You may start reading this chapter and feel that this is "just a list of features." But every new enhancement in this chapter has a story and a reason behind it. I'll try to give you those details for many of these new features. These categories are not in a particular order, but I usually start with security.

Security

I've always felt our engineering team deeply cares about security, not just because we are the least vulnerable database in the industry for well over a decade (we didn't produce this – you can see for yourself from the National Institute of Standards and Technology Comprehensive Vulnerability Database) but because we pour in new features to help keep applications and data more secure.

For SQL Server 2022, this includes enhancements for data integrity, encryption, and authorization. The story all starts with a revolutionary innovation called Ledger for SQL Server.

Note   I consider Azure Active Directory (AAD) authentication, Microsoft Purview policy management, and Microsoft Defender all "security" features. But these are covered in more detail in Chapter 3 of the book.

Ledger for SQL Server

Ledger for SQL Server is a tamper-evident record of data stored in a SQL Server database. Blockchain technology was invented to provide a *digital ledger* using crypto hashes to ensure transactions are valid and can be trusted. The original blockchain concept was brought into the public eye in the late 2000s to support cryptocurrency bitcoin. In fact, when I've talked to some people about the term *blockchain*, they seem to think blockchain = bitcoin. The concept of a digital ledger has so many applications other than supporting bitcoin trading. One of the major benefits of a blockchain is the ability for multiple parties to participate in a transaction system where no one party can be trusted to manage the authenticity of the data. One of the challenges for many blockchain implementations is that they are decentralized, requiring distributing algorithms that often cause performance issues and hinder data management capabilities. Performance and data management capabilities are two things at which SQL Server excels.

Background of Ledger for SQL Server

In 2018, Microsoft began to explore whether the worlds of blockchain and relational databases could converge into a digital ledger solution. According to Panagiotis Antonopoulos, Principal Software Engineer at Microsoft

> *In 2018, together with Microsoft Research, we started the effort to identify an architecture that would bridge the gap between blockchains and relational databases to provide the benefits of both technologies. We evaluated different design options where SQL Server would run in a decentralized configuration, using the advanced consensus algorithms of blockchains, or in a centralized environment, more aligned with the traditional SQL Server setup. We analyzed the technical feasibility of these options but also talked to a large number of blockchain customers to understand the challenges they were facing when adopting the technology. This was a very educational exercise and made it clear for us that decentralization, despite its security benefits, was making blockchains expensive and complex to develop and manage, causing significant friction to their adoption by enterprise customers.*

Note   If you recognize the name Panagiotis Antonopoulos, he is one of the lead developers for the incredible cool technology Accelerated Database Recovery (ADR) we introduced in SQL Server 2019. He just builds great software!

This research effort led to the development of Ledger for SQL Server. The work first started in Azure SQL Database. You can read about the original project at `https://aka.ms/sqlledgerpaper`.

Ledger for SQL Server uses proven blockchain techniques like cryptographic data structures such as hash-chains and Merkle trees. (The whitepaper goes into the details of what a Merkle tree is for those of you who are interested.) One of the keys to Ledger for SQL Server is to leverage…well, SQL Server. Ledger for SQL Server is built into the product itself requiring no application changes, special provider, or code. Just use T-SQL.

Panagiotis summed up the power of Ledger for SQL Server: *"Although the data is stored centrally, individual organizations can use these digests to verify the data integrity. The simplicity and transparency of this solution allows u*s to commoditize blockchains and enable all SQL users to leverage their benefits at a very low cost and complexity."

Because of this capability, I like to think of Ledger as a form of **data integrity**. Let's learn how it works to see why.

How Does It Work

Ledger for SQL Server is made up of the following components:

Ledger tables

Users use an extension of the CREATE TABLE syntax to create a ledger table. Ledger tables can either be *updateable* or *append-only*. Updateable ledger tables are perfect for auditing scenarios. Append-only tables only allow INSERT statements, which can be a great solution for multi-party trust scenarios.

Ledger history tables

Updateable ledger tables have a built-in history like a temporal table but with additional transaction information that ties into which SQL principal initiated the change.

Ledger views

When you create a ledger table, we automatically build a view, which joins the ledger table with the ledger history table to provide a consolidated view.

Database ledger

The *database ledger* is a set of system tables, which contains transaction details, crypto hashes, and Merkle trees of all transactions for all ledger tables in the database. This is one of the key components to provide a tamper-evident record of data.

Digests

The hash of the latest block in the database ledger is called the database **digest**. It represents the state of all ledger tables in the database at the time when the block was generated. I like to think of a digest like a *checksum* of the blockchain in the database. A digest is the other key component for a tamper-evident record because a digest is generated and stored *outside* of SQL Server.

Figure 6-1 shows how these components work together for an updateable ledger table.

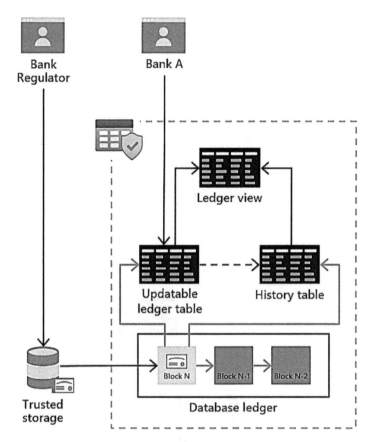

Figure 6-1. *Ledger for SQL Server with updateable ledger tables*

In this example for a company such as a bank, they could create an updateable ledger table by simply using this extension to CREATE TABLE:

```
WITH
(
  SYSTEM_VERSIONING = ON,
  LEDGER = ON
);
```

Automatically, SQL Server will create a history table and a ledger view corresponding to the ledger table.

When any modifications are made to the table (INSERT, UPDATE, or DELETE), audits and crypto hashes of each transaction are recorded in the database ledger as well as blocks for the blockchain.

Digests (which are effectively JSON data) can be generated manually or automatically in a separate storage location. This allows someone like a bank regulator to use the digests to verify the integrity of the ledger at any point in time.

Figure 6-2 shows the components for an append-only ledger table.

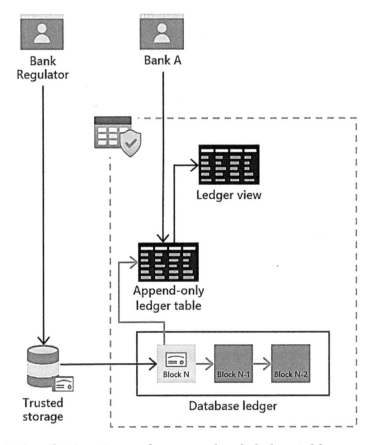

Figure 6-2. *Ledger for SQL Server for append-only ledger tables*

Append-only ledger tables don't need a history table since you can only perform INSERT statements. Append-only ledger tables are great for multi-party scenarios because no one party can "update" the ledger table. Only a history of new records is allowed (even a DBA with sysadmin rights can't make an update to fake the ledger).

With these components in mind, here is how Ledger provides data integrity, trust, and tamper-evident records of data:

- Ledger tables have built-in auditing, so you can see the exact datetime and SQL principal for every modification to the table.

- Append-only ledger tables will only allow an "addition to the record" by only allowing INSERT statements.

- At any time you can verify that no one has tampered with ledger tables (say under the covers of the engine) through crypto hashes in the database ledger.

- Digests, stored outside the ledger, can be used to verify no one has tampered with the database ledger.

To understand in more detail how these components work, let's try out an example.

Exercise to Use Ledger for SQL Server

Let's walk through an exercise to see how Ledger works. There are four parts to this exercise: using an updateable ledger table, using an append-only ledger table, protection from dropping a ledger table, and an interesting example when I tried to "hack" the ledger.

Prerequisites

- SQL Server 2022 Evaluation Edition. **You must configure SQL Server for mixed-mode authentication**.

- Virtual machine or computer with minimum of two CPUs and 8Gb RAM.

- SQL Server Management Studio (SSMS). The latest SSMS 18.x will work, but SSMS 19.x has a new visualization for ledger tables, so the examples in this exercise were done with the latest SSMS 19.x build.

- Get the scripts for this exercise from the book samples at **ch06_meatandpotatoes\security\sqlledger**.

Note   Any name of identifiable information in this exercise is purely fictional and does not represent any real person.

Setting Up the Exercise

We will create two new SQL logins and a database for the exercise:

1. Execute the script **addsysadminlogin.sql** to add a sysadmin SQL login. This script executes the following T-SQL statements:

```
USE master;
GO
-- Create a login for bob and make him a sysadmin
IF EXISTS (SELECT * FROM sys.server_principals WHERE NAME = 'bob')
BEGIN
DROP LOGIN bob;
END
CREATE LOGIN bob WITH PASSWORD = N'StrongPassw0rd!';
EXEC sp_addsrvrolemember 'bob', 'sysadmin';
GO
```

2. Log in with the SQL login **bob** you created in step 1. Create the database and add a login for an "app" by executing the script **createdb.sql**. This script executes the following T-SQL statements:

```
USE master;
GO
-- Create the ContosoHR database
--
DROP DATABASE IF EXISTS ContosoHR;
GO
CREATE DATABASE ContosoHR;
GO
USE ContosoHR;
GO
-- Create a login for the app
IF EXISTS (SELECT * FROM sys.server_principals WHERE NAME = 'app')
BEGIN
DROP LOGIN app;
END
```

```
CREATE LOGIN app WITH PASSWORD = N'StrongPassw0rd!', DEFAULT_
DATABASE = ContosoHR;
GO
-- Enable snapshot isolation to allow ledger to be verified
ALTER DATABASE ContosoHR SET ALLOW_SNAPSHOT_ISOLATION ON;
GO
-- Create an app user for the app login
CREATE USER app FROM LOGIN app;
GO
EXEC sp_addrolemember 'db_owner', 'app';
GO
```

Exercise 1: Using an Updateable Ledger Table

Connect with the SQL login bob for all steps in this first exercise.

1. Create an updateable ledger table for Employees by executing
    the script **createemployeeledger.sql**. This script executes the
    following T-SQL statements:

```
USE ContosoHR;
GO
-- Create the Employees table and make it an updatetable
Ledger table
DROP TABLE IF EXISTS [dbo].[Employees];
GO
CREATE TABLE [dbo].[Employees](
      [EmployeeID] [int] IDENTITY(1,1) NOT NULL,
      [SSN] [char](11) NOT NULL,
      [FirstName] [nvarchar](50) NOT NULL,
      [LastName] [nvarchar](50) NOT NULL,
      [Salary] [money] NOT NULL
      )
WITH
(
  SYSTEM_VERSIONING = ON,
  LEDGER = ON
);
GO
```

If you are using SSMS 19.X, then you can see the visual properties of ledger tables and the corresponding history table name as in Figure 6-3.

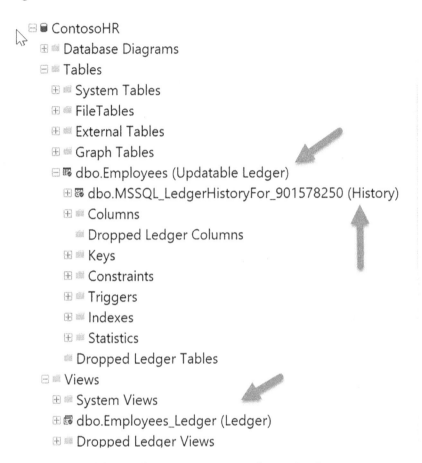

Figure 6-3. *Ledger tables and views in SSMS Object Explorer*

2. Populate initial employee data using the script
    populateemployees.sql. This script executes the following T-SQL
    statements:

```
USE ContosoHR;
GO
-- Clear Employees table
DELETE FROM [dbo].[Employees];
GO
```

-- Insert 10 employees. The names and SSN are completely fictional
and not associated with any person
DECLARE @SSN1 char(11) = '795-73-9833'; DECLARE @Salary1 Money =
61692.00; INSERT INTO [dbo].[Employees] ([SSN], [FirstName],
[LastName], [Salary]) VALUES (@SSN1, 'Catherine', 'Abel',
@Salary1);
DECLARE @SSN2 char(11) = '990-00-6818'; DECLARE @Salary2 Money =
990.00; INSERT INTO [dbo].[Employees] ([SSN], [FirstName],
[LastName], [Salary]) VALUES (@SSN2, 'Kim', 'Abercrombie',
@Salary2);
DECLARE @SSN3 char(11) = '009-37-3952'; DECLARE @Salary3 Money =
5684.00; INSERT INTO [dbo].[Employees] ([SSN], [FirstName],
[LastName], [Salary]) VALUES (@SSN3, 'Frances', 'Adams',
@Salary3);
DECLARE @SSN4 char(11) = '708-44-3627'; DECLARE @Salary4 Money =
55415.00; INSERT INTO [dbo].[Employees] ([SSN], [FirstName],
[LastName], [Salary]) VALUES (@SSN4, 'Jay', 'Adams', @Salary4);
DECLARE @SSN5 char(11) = '447-62-6279'; DECLARE @Salary5 Money =
49744.00; INSERT INTO [dbo].[Employees] ([SSN], [FirstName],
[LastName], [Salary]) VALUES (@SSN5, 'Robert', 'Ahlering',
@Salary5);
DECLARE @SSN6 char(11) = '872-78-4732'; DECLARE @Salary6 Money =
38584.00; INSERT INTO [dbo].[Employees] ([SSN], [FirstName],
[LastName], [Salary]) VALUES (@SSN6, 'Stanley', 'Alan', @Salary6);
DECLARE @SSN7 char(11) = '898-79-8701'; DECLARE @Salary7 Money =
11918.00; INSERT INTO [dbo].[Employees] ([SSN], [FirstName],
[LastName], [Salary]) VALUES (@SSN7, 'Paul', 'Alcorn', @Salary7);
DECLARE @SSN8 char(11) = '561-88-3757'; DECLARE @Salary8 Money =
17349.00; INSERT INTO [dbo].[Employees] ([SSN], [FirstName],
[LastName], [Salary]) VALUES (@SSN8, 'Mary', 'Alexander',
@Salary8);
DECLARE @SSN9 char(11) = '904-55-0991'; DECLARE @Salary9 Money =
70796.00; INSERT INTO [dbo].[Employees] ([SSN], [FirstName],
[LastName], [Salary]) VALUES (@SSN9, 'Michelle', 'Alexander',
@Salary9);

```
DECLARE @SSN10 char(11) = '293-95-6617'; DECLARE @Salary10 Money =
96956.00; INSERT INTO [dbo].[Employees] ([SSN], [FirstName],
[LastName], [Salary]) VALUES (@SSN10, 'Marvin', 'Allen',
@Salary10);
GO
```

3. Examine the data in the Employees table using the script
   getallemployees.sql. This script executes the following T-SQL
   statements:

```
USE ContosoHR;
GO
-- Use * for all columns
SELECT * FROM dbo.Employees;
GO
-- List out all the columns
SELECT EmployeeID, SSN, FirstName, LastName, Salary,
ledger_start_transaction_id, ledger_end_transaction_id,
ledger_start_sequence_number,
ledger_end_sequence_number
FROM dbo.Employees;
GO
```

Notice there are "hidden" columns that are not shown if you
execute a SELECT *. Some of these columns are NULL or 0
because no updates have been made to the data. You normally
will not use these columns, but you can use the ledger view to see
information about changes to the Employees table.

4. Look at the Employees ledger view by executing the script
   getemployeesledger.sql. This script executes the following T-SQL
   statements:

```
USE ContosoHR;
GO
SELECT * FROM dbo.Employees_Ledger;
GO
```

This is a view that uses the Employees table and the ledger *history* table. Notice the ledger has the transaction information from hidden columns in the table plus an indication of what type of operation was performed on the ledger for a specific row.

5. Let's look at the definition of the ledger view by executing the script **getemployeesledgerview.sql**. This script executes the following T-SQL statements:

```
USE [ContosoHR];
GO
sp_helptext 'Employees_ledger';
GO
```

The results of this query should look like the following T-SQL code:

```
CREATE VIEW [dbo].[Employees_Ledger] AS
SELECT [EmployeeID], [SSN], [FirstName], [LastName], [Salary],
[ledger_start_transaction_id] AS [ledger_transaction_id], [ledger_
start_sequence_number] AS [ledger_sequence_number], 1 AS [ledger_
operation_type], N'INSERT' AS [ledger_operation_type_desc]
FROM [dbo].[Employees]
UNION ALL
 SELECT [EmployeeID], [SSN], [FirstName], [LastName], [Salary],
[ledger_start_transaction_id] AS [ledger_transaction_id], [ledger_
start_sequence_number] AS [ledger_sequence_number], 1 AS [ledger_
operation_type], N'INSERT' AS [ledger_operation_type_desc]
FROM [dbo].[MSSQL_LedgerHistoryFor_901578250]
UNION ALL
SELECT [EmployeeID], [SSN], [FirstName], [LastName], [Salary],
[ledger_end_transaction_id] AS [ledger_transaction_id], [ledger_
end_sequence_number] AS [ledger_sequence_number], 2 AS [ledger_
operation_type], N'DELETE' AS [ledger_operation_type_desc] FROM
[dbo].[MSSQL_LedgerHistoryFor_901578250]
```

Let's break down how the view constructs its results. Any rows in the Employees ledger table are an INSERT. Any UPDATE in the history table (**MSSQL_LedgerHistoryFor_901578250**) is an

INSERT and a DELETE, and any DELETE appears in the history table as a DELETE. Note that the history table will always be MSSQL_LedgerHistoryFor_<object id> where <object id> is the object_id of the base ledger table. A UNION ALL is used to bring these together.

6. Let's use the ledger view to get more auditing information about transactions associated with the ledger table by executing the script **viewemployeesledgerhistory.sql**. This script executes the following T-SQL statements:

```
USE ContosoHR;
GO
SELECT e.EmployeeID, e.FirstName, e.LastName, e.Salary,
dlt.transaction_id, dlt.commit_time, dlt.principal_name,
e.ledger_operation_type_desc, dlt.table_hashes
FROM sys.database_ledger_transactions dlt
JOIN dbo.Employees_Ledger e
ON e.ledger_transaction_id = dlt.transaction_id
ORDER BY dlt.commit_time DESC;
GO
```

I've introduced a new system table in this query (which is really a view) called **database_ledger_transactions**. We can use the transaction ID from the ledger view to join to this table to gain more insights. From this system table, we can see when a transaction was executed, who was the SQL principal to execute the change, and a crypto hash value for the transaction. You can see that "bob" inserted all the rows for the ledger table. You can see a complete definition of this system table at https://docs.microsoft.com/sql/relational-databases/system-catalog-views/sys-database-ledger-transactions-transact-sql.

7. Let's generate a digest to ensure we can verify the ledger by executing the script **generatedigest.sql**. This script executes the following T-SQL statements:

```
USE ContosoHR;
GO
EXEC sp_generate_database_ledger_digest;
GO
```

The result of this procedure is JSON data. You could verify the ledger at this point, but instead we will run this again after an update to verify the ledger, so you don't need to save the output of this query.

8. You can see the generated blockchain in the database ledger by executing the script **getledgerblocks.sql**. This script executes the following T-SQL statements:

```
USE ContosoHR;
GO
SELECT * FROM sys.database_ledger_blocks;
GO
```

The system table **database_ledger_blocks** (which is really a view) represents the internal blockchain in the database ledger.

9. Try to update Jay Adam's salary to see how Ledger can track changes by executing the script **updatejayssalary.sql**. This script executes the following T-SQL statements:

```
USE ContosoHR;
GO
UPDATE dbo.Employees
SET Salary = Salary + 50000
WHERE EmployeeID = 4;
GO
```

10. Execute the script **getallemployees.sql** again. If you didn't know anything about what the original data was in the Employees table, you would not know if any updates had occurred.

11. Execute the script **viewemployeesledgerhistory.sql** again. Now the results show what we need. We can see the original INSERT for Jay Adam's salary, but we also see someone named bob tried to update it (INSERT/DELETE combo) directly.

Generate another digest by executing the script **generatedigest.sql** again. Save this output value (including the brackets) to be used for verifying the ledger.

12. You can now verify the ledger (1) after initial population of data and (2) after the update was made to Jay Adam's salary. Verify the current state of the ledger by first editing the script **verifyledger.sql**. Put in your most recent saved digest JSON inside the N' ' quotes. This script executes the following T-SQL statements:

```
USE ContosoHR;
GO
EXECUTE sp_verify_database_ledger
N'<saved digest JSON>'
GO
```

Execute the script. Your output should list the same block_id as in the digest JSON data.

You have now verified the ledger tables match crypto hashes, the blockchain, and the saved digest. You can now trust the ledger data is accurate in that bob is the one who updated Jay Adam's salary.

Exercise 2: Using an Append-Only Ledger

While Ledger for SQL Server is great for auditing which SQL principal makes any transaction change, what about scenarios where an application uses an "application login" to execute all SQL queries? How will you know the original application user that initiated an operation that led to a change of data?

For this scenario, we will build an append-only ledger table, which records information from the application including the user-initiated application operations that lead to SQL changes. With one exception noted in this exercise, execute all queries while connected with the **bob** login created in the first exercise.

1. Create an append-only ledger table for auditing the application by executing the script **createauditledger.sql**. This script executes the following T-SQL statements:

```
USE ContosoHR;
GO
-- Create an append-only ledger table to track T-SQL commands from
the app and the "real" user who initiated the transaction
DROP TABLE IF EXISTS [dbo].[AuditEvents];
GO
CREATE TABLE [dbo].[AuditEvents](
      [Timestamp] [Datetime2] NOT NULL DEFAULT (GETDATE()),
      [UserName] [nvarchar](255) NOT NULL,
      [Query] [nvarchar](4000) NOT NULL
      )
WITH (LEDGER = ON (APPEND_ONLY = ON));
GO
```

The application has been enhanced to insert a row in this table for any transaction executed against the Employees table. Notice you do not need the SYSTEM_VERSIONING clause.

2. Now log into a new connection using the **app** login created in the first exercise (this login was created in the **createdb.sql** script). Execute the script **appchangemaryssalary.sql**. This script executes the following T-SQL statements:

```
USE ContosoHR;
GO
UPDATE dbo.Employees
SET Salary = Salary + 50000
WHERE EmployeeID = 8;
GO
INSERT INTO dbo.AuditEvents VALUES (getdate(), 'bob', 'UPDATE
dbo.Employees SET Salary = Salary + 50000 WHERE EmployeeID = 8');
GO
```

This script simulates what the application would do if a user tried to update Mary's salary.

3. Using the connection for the sysadmin login **bob**, execute the script **viewemployeesledgerhistory.sql**. You can see from the results that the **app** login changed Mary's salary. This is accurate, but who really initiated the change?

4. Execute the script **getauditledger.sql**. This script executes the following T-SQL statements:

```
USE ContosoHR;
GO
SELECT * FROM dbo.AuditEvents_Ledger;
GO
```

You can see that the application registered that **bob** initiated a query (the **app** login records the query) that resulted in Mary's salary change. Since the table is append-only, no other user could go in and try to erase any record of what the application did.

Exercise 3: Protect Ledger Objects

In this exercise, you will learn how SQL Server protects ledger objects.

1. Execute the script **getledgerobjects.sql** to see a history of what ledger tables and columns have been created. This script executes the following T-SQL statements:

```
USE ContosoHR;
GO
SELECT * FROM sys.ledger_table_history;
GO .
SELECT * FROM sys.ledger_column_history;
GO
```

2. Try to alter or drop ledger objects. Execute the script **admindropledger.sql**. This script executes the following T-SQL statements:

```
USE ContosoHR;
GO
-- You cannot turn off versioning for a ledger table
ALTER TABLE Employees SET (SYSTEM_VERSIONING = OFF);
GO
```

```
-- You cannot drop the ledger history table
DROP TABLE dbo.MSSQL_LedgerHistoryFor_901578250;
GO
-- You can drop a ledger table
DROP TABLE Employees;
GO
-- But we keep a history of the dropped table
SELECT * FROM sys.objects WHERE name like '%DroppedLedgerTable%';
GO
```

You can see from the output you cannot turn off versioning for a ledger table (there is no syntax to set LEDGER = OFF). You cannot drop the history table either. You can drop the ledger table, but we keep a record of what was dropped. And you can't drop the "dropped" ledger table. Furthermore, even if you drop a ledger table, the transactions associated with this table remain in the database ledger (system tables). The only way to remove the existence of dropped ledger tables would be to drop the database.

You can also execute the script **getledgerobjects.sql** again to see the drop history. SSMS in Object Explorer can also show you what ledger tables were dropped.

Exercise 4: What Does a Tampered Ledger Look Like?

When I first heard about Ledger, I thought to myself, "I know internals pretty well. Can I beat the system?" So I went on a journey of trying to *tamper* with the ledger.

I can't share the details of what I did, but effectively after a basic T-SQL update, I attempted ways that were *outside the boundaries* of supported SQL to *hack* the ledger. I attempted to conceal an update to a ledger table by manipulating the database ledger system tables in an extremely undocumented way. I actually found a way to get this working until Panagiotis said to me, "What about the digest?" Got me! I literally could hack my way into SQL Server to make it look like my update never existed, but the digest is on separate storage, so I couldn't hack that. You can see the results of my early tries at this in the T-SQL notebook **ledger.ipynb** in the samples directory. You can also see me do this live with Buck Woody at the 2022 SQLBits keynote at https://youtu.be/_R9FE2ZclVk (start at about 12 minutes in).

What Else Should You Know?

Ledger for SQL Server is amazing technology in so many ways. For me, what I've realized is that SQL now provides solutions for industry problems like multi-party trust scenarios, which are not traditional solutions for SQL.

In fact, very early on we had customers start to embrace this technology to solve real problems. Lenovo saw an opportunity to build trust into their supply chain. Their supply chain spans multiple parties, but who oversees the data? That is the power of Ledger. You can read Lenovo's story at `https://customers.microsoft.com/story/1497685499820529889-lenovo-manufacturing-azure-SQL-database-ledger`.

As a team, we are committed to finding new and innovative ways to bring Ledger into the market where SQL was never thought of as a solution.

One very nice feature added to Ledger for SQL Server is automatic digest storage. In the example, you learned how to manually generate and use a digest. SQL Server 2022 can be configured to automatically save a digest to Azure Blob Storage. You can read all the details at `https://docs.microsoft.com/sql/relational-databases/security/ledger/ledger-how-to-enable-automatic-digest-storage`.

As with any feature, there are some limits, and Ledger is no different. Keep up to date with all the limits at `https://docs.microsoft.com/sql/relational-databases/security/ledger/ledger-limits`.

As I worked on Ledger, I built up my own set of questions that I worked on with Panagiotis and Pieter Vanhove, our lead program manager over Ledger:

- How is this different from a temporal table?

  Ledger uses temporal table functionality for updateable ledger tables, but unlike temporal tables it has built-in auditing and supports append-only tables.

- How is this different from SQL Server Audit?

  Ledger has auditing baked into transaction changes, and all the audits are stored in the database. Furthermore, all changes are tracked with crypto hashes and separate digest storage. Once a ledger is created, you can't undo it where system admins with the right privilege can erase audits. The only way to erase ledger tables once created is to completely drop the database, but even then, separate digests exist.

- How often do I need to save the digest?

  Digests are the primary mechanism to verify the ledger from tampering. Theoretically, you would need to generate a separate digest for every transaction, but that is not practical. Save digests as often as you need to verify the ledger for your business needs. Automatic digest management saves a digest every 30 seconds.

- Does Ledger require more space?

  Updateable ledger tables require pretty much the same extra space as a temporal table. Each transaction requires separate system table rows for crypto hash. There is minimal space required for the internal blockchains, but it all depends on how long you keep the ledger. Digests are small in nature, and again you need to keep a history as long as you keep the database with ledger tables.

- Is there any performance impact?

  We have not run specific performance benchmarks with Ledger because we believe the impact will be minimal. Consider that append-only ledger tables should not see any impact. Updateable ledger tables could see the same impact as temporal tables.

Keep up with all the latest information on Ledger for SQL Server at `https://aka.ms/sqlledger`.

Encryption Enhancements

Encryption of data is a key aspect to security, and SQL Server provides several different capabilities to encrypt data end-to-end. End-to-end means from a connection to SQL Server, data in the SQL Server engine, and data stored at rest. To read about the complete lineup of encryption capabilities of SQL Server, check our documentation at `https://docs.microsoft.com/sql/relational-databases/security/encryption/sql-server-encryption`.

In SQL Server 2022 we have a few enhancements around encryption including enhancements for Always Encrypted, crypto enhancements, and enhancements for connection encryption.

Always Encrypted Enhancements

In SQL Server 2016 we introduced a new concept for end-to-end encryption called Always Encrypted. The concept is that data is encrypted at the client application and always encrypted in the SQL Server engine (hence the name). Furthermore, the keys to unencrypt the data are owned by the application. As a result, administrators of SQL Server cannot unencrypt the data; only the application can do this. If you are not familiar with Always Encrypted, you can read about how to configure and use it at `https://docs.microsoft.com/sql/relational-databases/security/encryption/always-encrypted-database-engine`.

Because data can never appear in *plaintext* inside the SQL Server engine, there were limitations with the original design. For example, queries using operators such as LIKE won't work because the engine would need to unencrypt the data into plaintext to perform the operation.

In SQL Server 2019 we enhanced Always Encrypted with a concept called *secure enclaves*. A secure enclave is a secure region of memory inside the SQL Server engine. Even in the database engine, code cannot see data in plaintext in the enclave. Enclave technologies provide a method for SQL Server to pass keys from the application to the enclave to perform any operations required in plaintext such as pattern matching operations. SQL Server 2019 supports a concept called virtualized enclaves or VBS enclaves (Azure supports hardware enclaves through Intel Software Guard Extensions (Intel SGX)). Since decryption happens on the server, I have personally found that using secure enclaves can also boost performance for almost any operation on columns that are encrypted with Always Encrypted.

You can read the complete story of Always Encrypted with secure enclaves at `https://docs.microsoft.com/sql/relational-databases/security/encryption/always-encrypted-enclaves`.

In SQL Server 2022 we have enhanced Always Encrypted with secure enclaves with the following new capabilities:

- SQL Server 2022 can use multi-threads and key caching inside the VBS secure enclave to further boost performance.

- SQL Server 2022 can support new join types and ORDER BY and GROUP BY operations. This support is in line with Azure SQL Database support.

Crypto Enhancements

We want to make sure SQL Server is up to date with the latest standards for cryptography or crypto. SQL Server uses crypto for many different types of capabilities in the engine including certificate and key support. According to Shoham Dasgupta, Senior Program Manager for security for SQL, *"We wanted to enhance default cryptography in SQL Server to meet/exceed industry standards and protect customer's confidential data to meet the evolving threat landscape."*

One of the enhancements we made internally that is not visibly seen by customers is a strengthening of our algorithms to align with the current National Institute of Standards and Technology (NIST) including the following:

- All system-generated certificates have a minimum strength of RSA-3072, a bit key size recommended by NIST.

- Enhance our internal hashing algorithm used for signature generation to use SHA-2 512, a more secure method than SHA-1.

Another investment to strengthen security to today's standards is support for personal information exchange (PFX) format. SQL Server supports the ability to create a certificate inside the database engine to secure objects, connections, and data. SQL Server 2022 now supports creating certificates for PFX. PFX or PKCS#12 is a modern format for certificates, and SQL Server now supports using a PFX file to create a certificate in SQL Server with the CREATE CERTIFICATE statement. You can read more about how to create a certificate with a PFX file at `https://docs.microsoft.com/sql/t-sql/statements/create-certificate-transact-sql`.

The final enhancement for crypto is to support backup and restore for keys to and from Azure Blob Storage. A database master key is often used to secure a credential such as used for external data sources. But you often need to back up this key separate from the database. SQL Server 2022 allows you now to back up or restore one of these keys to or from Azure Blob Storage instead of a local or network file path. You can read how to use the new URL syntax at `https://docs.microsoft.com/sql/t-sql/statements/backup-master-key-transact-sql`. The same support exists for SYMMETRIC keys, which you can read about at `https://docs.microsoft.com/sql/t-sql/statements/backup-symmetric-key-transact-sql`.

Strict Connected Encryption

The Tabular Data Stream (TDS) is the *data protocol* used for applications to connect to and transfer data to and from SQL Server. TDS has been around for as long as SQL Server has been a product. As time has gone by, TDS has been enhanced and changed using a version numbering system. Typically, as new versions of TDS were released, applications would need to use a provider or driver to support it. Microsoft changed the major version of TDS to 7.0 when SQL Server 7.0 was released in 1998. Since then, minor version changes have come with the latest, TDS 7.4, supporting SQL Server 2012 and later. Users, admins, and developers don't need to know the details of the TDS protocol, just the features it supports with changes or the need to use updated drivers. As a support engineer for many years at Microsoft, I often needed the details of TDS to solve complex customer problems. You can read all the details yourself at `https://docs.microsoft.com/openspecs/windows_protocols/ms-tds/b46a581a-39de-4745-b076-ec4dbb7d13ec`.

SQL Server 2022 introduces a new major version of TDS, TDS 8.0. Drivers and providers using TDS 7.4 are still fully supported. New drivers understand TDS 8.0 and can use this protocol. The main reason behind this new version is connecting encryption. SQL Server has supported encryption of the communication between an application and SQL Server for years. Like many applications, SQL Server uses Transport Layer Security (TLS) to implement communication encryption. SQL Server has always allowed applications to make decisions on whether they want to encrypt communications with SQL Server using connection string options called **Encrypt** and **TrustServerCertificate**. You also have the ability on the server side to force encryption for client connections. The combination of these two connection strings is significant, and you can read more details at `https://docs.microsoft.com/dotnet/framework/data/adonet/connection-string-syntax#using-trustservercertificate`.

TDS 8.0 introduces the concept of **strict connection** encryption. If an application uses a value of **Encrypt = strict**, then the TDS 8.0 protocol is enabled. One of the significant changes here is that if strict connection encryption is used, then the communication between the client and SQL Server **must** be encrypted (hence the term *strict*). The other significance is how TDS 8.0 handles connection encryption. Prior to TDS 8.0, SQL Server would perform a handshake or prelogin with the client that was not encrypted. Now with TDS 8.0, that handshake is completely encrypted with TLS. This works with all TLS versions. This is very significant because it aligns with the standards of protocols like HTTPS and allows network appliances to safely pass through SQL communication. The latest providers are required to be able to use TDS 8.0. You can learn more at `https://docs.microsoft.com/sql/relational-databases/security/networking/tds-8-and-tls-1-3#strict-connection-encryption`.

In addition, but independent of TDS 8.0, SQL Server 2022 now supports the latest version of TLS 1.3. TLS 1.3 is the most secure TLS version. You can read more about differences between TLS 1.2 and 1.3 at `https://docs.microsoft.com/sql/relational-databases/security/networking/tds-8-and-tls-1-3?#differences-between-tls-12-and-tls-13`.

Note   We are also looking into ways to enforce this option at the server level when the product becomes generally available.

Security Permission Enhancements

In SQL Server 2022 we also have introduced some enhancements for authorization or permission scenarios. This includes new fixed server-level roles and a new permission for dynamic data masking.

New Fixed Server-Level Roles

Up until SQL Server 2022, the product came with a certain set of *fixed* server-level roles. They are fixed because you cannot change the access level or definition of the role. They are server-level because they apply to the entire SQL Server instance, not just a single database.

You are probably familiar with some of these like **sysadmin**, **securityadmin**, **dbcreator**, and **public**. You can view the complete list of these roles at `https://docs.microsoft.com/sql/relational-databases/security/authentication-access/server-level-roles`.

One request we have seen from customers for some time is for *more granularity* of roles we provide with the product – in other words, more fixed roles that have fewer privileges for specific tasks. My colleague at Microsoft, Andreas Wolter, wrote an interesting blog on the topic of *least privilege* at `https://techcommunity.microsoft.com/t5/azure-sql-blog/security-the-principle-of-least-privilege-polp/ba-p/2067390`.

SQL Server 2022 now provides built-in new fixed server-level roles that follow this principle. You can see the complete list at `https://docs.microsoft.com/sql/relational-databases/security/authentication-access/server-level-roles?#fixed-server-level-roles-introduced-in-sql-server-2022`.

I picked out a few I found interesting:

##MS_DefinitionReader##

A member of this role is granted permissions to view catalog views that require the VIEW ANY DEFINITION or VIEW DEFINITION permission with a database (assuming they have a user account in the database). It is a great way to give someone the right to "view" important information about a server or database without allowing them to make changes.

##MS_ServerStateReader##

A member of this role is granted permissions to view Dynamic Management Views (DMVs) or functions that require the VIEW SERVER STATE or VIEW DATABASE state within a database (assuming they have a user account within the database).

##MS_ServerPerformanceStateReader##

This is similar to the previous fixed role but is more focused on viewing specific performance information from Dynamic Management Views (DMVs). Users in this fixed role are granted the same permission as objects that require the VIEW SERVER PERFORMANCE STATE permission.

Imagine a situation where you want to hire a consultant to come in and view important information about the system and database to provide you with an analysis. You don't want to give access to any user data for privacy reasons, nor do you want to allow them to make changes. Adding them as members to these two roles could help you achieve this, whereas before you would have to use a fixed server-level role that had more privileges than necessary or set up custom permissions to their account for the instance and in all databases for which you need their consultation.

You will also love that SSMS 19 has been enhanced to support these new fixed server-level roles as you can see in Figure 6-4.

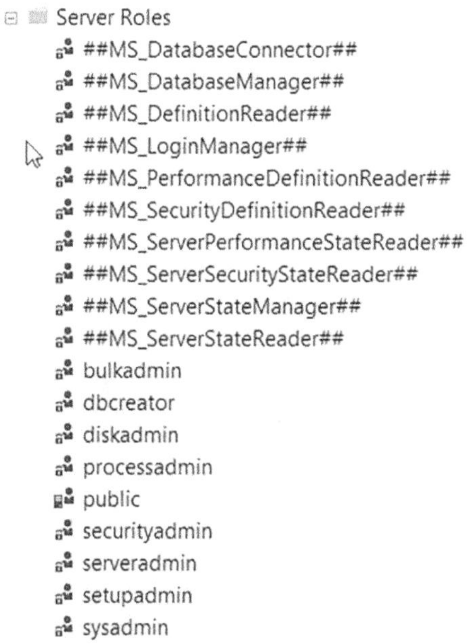

☐ ▨ Server Roles
   ⚙ ##MS_DatabaseConnector##
   ⚙ ##MS_DatabaseManager##
   ⚙ ##MS_DefinitionReader##
   ⚙ ##MS_LoginManager##
   ⚙ ##MS_PerformanceDefinitionReader##
   ⚙ ##MS_SecurityDefinitionReader##
   ⚙ ##MS_ServerPerformanceStateReader##
   ⚙ ##MS_ServerSecurityStateReader##
   ⚙ ##MS_ServerStateManager##
   ⚙ ##MS_ServerStateReader##
   ⚙ bulkadmin
   ⚙ dbcreator
   ⚙ diskadmin
   ⚙ processadmin
   ⚙ public
   ⚙ securityadmin
   ⚙ serveradmin
   ⚙ setupadmin
   ⚙ sysadmin

Figure 6-4. *SQL Server 2022 fixed server-level roles*

I did a quick test to see the difference for membership in the
##MS_ServerPerformanceStateReader## role vs. just the public role. If you have just
the public fixed role, you are allowed to see your session only when you query **sys.dm_
exec_requests**. But if you are a member of the **##MS_ServerPerformanceStateReader##**
role, you can see all sessions from **sys.dm_exec_requests**. An example of a DMV that
would require **##MS_ServerStateReader##** or **##MS_ServerSecurityStateReader##**
membership is the **sys.dm_server_audit_status** DMV. Anyone in just the **##MS_
ServerPerformanceStateReader##** would not have access to this DMV. Effectively what
we have done here is separate **##MS_ServerStateReader##** into two different roles:
##MS_ServerPerformanceStateReader## and **##MS_ServerSecurityStateReader##**.

Dynamic Data Masking Enhancements

Dynamic data masking is the concept of providing logic within a table schema to
mask data when viewed by a user (think of masking an email address with characters
like xxxx@xxxx). We introduced this concept in SQL Server 2016, and it was quite
popular. Prior to this feature, applications would have to put masking logic in their
code. If the masking logic needed to be changed, the application would have to be
changed and deployed. Dynamic data masking provides a way to define mask rules

when defining columns in a table. If you are new to dynamic data masking, start with our documentation at https://docs.microsoft.com/sql/relational-databases/ security/dynamic-data-masking.

One nice aspect of dynamic data masking is that we provide built-in functions for common mask scenarios. So a column definition like this

```
Email    varchar(100) MASKED WITH (FUNCTION = 'email()') NOT NULL
```

would result in any value stored in this column seen by users as XXX@XXXX.com.

You can see a complete list of functions for dynamic data masking at https:// docs.microsoft.com/sql/relational-databases/security/dynamic-data- masking?#defining-a-dynamic-data-mask.

In SQL Server 2022 we added a new function for datetime column types. You can mask all or part of the datetime values such as year, month, day, hour, minute, or second.

The original implementation of dynamic data masking by default did not allow "non-admin" users to see unmasked data. However, we provided a T-SQL command option called GRANT UNMASK so that a user could be granted the ability to see data unmasked. The problem with this original design is that the unmasking permission was for any masked rule in the database.

In 2021, we introduced the concept of granular UNMASK to Azure so that this permission could be applied at the schema, table, or column level. You can see the original announcement at https://azure.microsoft.com/updates/general- availability-dynamic-data-masking-granular-permissions-for-azure-sql-and- azure-synapse-analytics/.

SQL Server 2022 simply brings this implementation from the cloud to SQL Server. You can see examples for granular unmasking at https://docs.microsoft.com/sql/ relational-databases/security/dynamic-data-masking?#granular.

Performance and Scalability

I always love to see the innovation and enhancements in any SQL Server release for performance and scalability. One of the reasons is that almost everything in this area comes from tuning exercises, real customer stories, or research we do for benchmarking. SQL Server 2022 comes with a variety of investments in performance and scalability across the entire spectrum of workload and engine components.

Columnstore and Batch Mode Improvements

SQL Server 2022 comes with enhancements to boost performance for columnstore indexes and batch-mode operations (which do not require columnstore in SQL Server 2019 and later).

Ordered Clustered Columnstore Index

Both Azure Synapse Analytics and SQL Server support columnstore indexes. An entire book could be devoted to columnstore indexes and why they can be beneficial to applications. I still find this an underused feature of SQL Server. Almost any customer I encounter who doesn't know columnstore immediately sees how they can use them once they understand how they work. If you don't know columnstore, go right to the documentation to get started at `https://docs.microsoft.com/sql/relational-databases/indexes/columnstore-indexes-overview`.

Azure Synapse Analytics added an option to create a clustered columnstore index as *ordered*. While building an ordered clustered columnstore index can take longer, the performance benefits to certain queries can be significant. SQL Server 2022 now supports ordered clustered columnstore indexes. Learn more at `https://docs.microsoft.com/azure/synapse-analytics/sql-data-warehouse/performance-tuning-ordered-cci`.

Columnstore String Improvements

We don't have specific documentation on this one, but when I chatted with Ryan Stonecipher, the veteran SQL engineer about this, his quote to me was "Simply rebuild your indexes and we will maintain min/max values for deep data (e.g., *char and *binary + guid). Furthermore, we now support LIKE pushdown operations on column stores and a fast string-equal implementation."

Vector Extension to Improve Batch Mode

In SQL Server 2016 we added code to take advantage of special processor instructions called **vector**-based hardware capabilities. Vector-based hardware capabilities allow programs to simply process data faster and in more parallel manner due to vector registers in the processor. If you would love to read some very deep content on this topic, here is a nice article: `www.techspot.com/article/2166-mmx-sse-avx-explained`.

SQL Server 2016 could recognize two different types of vector capabilities, namely, SEE and AVX, and use them to speed up columnstore operations especially when using batch mode. Robert Dorr outlines how we did this in this blog post: `https://docs.microsoft.com/archive/blogs/bobsql/sql-2016-it-just-runs-faster-columnstore-uses-vector-instructions-sseavx`.

The latest vector hardware technology is AVX-512, and SQL Server 2022 can recognize this new hardware capability to gain even more performance specifically for batch-mode operators for columnstore and rowstore. I was curious what led us to looking into AVX-512 and found this interesting quote from Conor Cunningham:

> *During the pandemic, I found an academic paper that explained how to use AVX-512 instructions to do a fast quicksort. These instructions essentially do N operations at a time instead of one, meaning that it can potentially speed up performance-critical code substantially. I implemented the sort from the paper and started making it better than the paper. Eventually I wanted to start playing with implementing something in SQL's code. There is logic that we have that uses the prior generation of vector instructions (AVX2) and I looked at that code and figured out how to write an equivalent version that used the newer, wider vectors as a side project. When I had it finished, we got good performance gains on our key analytics benchmark (TPC-H). The fun part is that I did not tell anyone I was doing this until one day I showed up and just gave this present to the team – it wasn't a formally funded effort that was intended for SQL Server 2022, but we prioritized it once we realized what value it delivered for customers.*

At the time of the writing of this book, we were keeping this enhancement under a trace flag, and it is possible we will launch the product with this still requiring a trace flag – mostly because the use of this capability is an advanced concept and not for everyone. Check out the documentation at `https://aka.ms/sqlserver2022docs` for the latest information.

One aspect of this work is a new ERRORLOG entry you may see that looks like this:

```
CPU vectorization level(s) detected:  SSE SSE2 SSE3 SSSE3 SSE41 SSE42 AVX
AVX2 POPCNT BMI1 BMI2
```

These monikers are various vector CPU capabilities we have detected in the processor. AVX-512 would appear if you are using a chipset that supports this new vector model.

Columnstore Segment Elimination Enhancements

Columnstore index columns are organized into segments. Columnstore includes a concept called segment elimination so that segments can be eliminated or not ready depending on the query. Prior to SQL Server 2022, only columns with data types of numeric, date, and time and datetimeoffset with scale less than or equal to two were candidates for segment elimination. Now in SQL Server 2022, we have extended segment elimination to new data types including string, binary, and guid data types and the datetimeoffset data type for scale greater than two.

Scalability Improvements

There are several improvements to help scalability of your queries, workload, and use of SQL Server. The last thing you want is to invest in revised application design, new servers, or infrastructure only to have SQL Server prevent you from scaling. All the work in this area is a direct result of customer cases or benchmark and testing we do internally or with our partners.

Buffer Pool Parallel Scan

If you look at my site for all my talks (I'm an open source presenter), `https://aka.ms/ bobwardms`, you will find a folder called SQL PASS 2013. At the PASS Community Summit in 2013, I gave a half-day talk on memory. If you look at this deck, you will see that I have some internals on the buffer pool of SQL Server. As part of these slides, I talk about a BUF hash table and BUF structure. BUF structures point to pages, and a BUF hash table is a way to organize all the BUF structures to easily find a page. Therefore, finding a specific page is not all that hard using a lookup of the BUF hash table.

Unfortunately, some operations in SQL Server must scan all the BUF structures. Think of this like scanning a clustered index vs. using an index seek. And like a clustered index scan, if you only need a few rows, it still may take a very long time to get the results if the clustered index is large.

The same problem can occur for certain operations with the buffer pool, and we would see this type of scenario with customers. They would have a server with, say, 1TB of RAM and allow the buffer pool to consume most of this memory. Then they would go perform some maintenance operation, and even against a very small database, it would take an unusually long time. This is because we would scan the entire ~1TB of

BUF structures to finish the operation. We even added ERRORLOG messages to warn the user this condition was happening. See the article `https://docs.microsoft.com/troubleshoot/sql/performance/buffer-pool-scan-runs-slowly-large-memory-machines` for more information. This is a classic problem of an architecture that for years didn't cause problems, but as hardware technology became vastly bigger, this design needed to be updated.

We took a look at this problem and said something to the effect, "If queries can run in parallel to obtain a faster result, why can't we do this when scanning the buffer pool?" (This is not an exact quote; it's my paraphrasing when I read the design documents for this.)

The result of this work is buffer pool parallel scan, which is enabled by default in SQL Server 2022 for systems with large amounts of memory. My colleague David Pless at Microsoft worked on this feature and explains how it works at `https://cloudblogs.microsoft.com/sqlserver/2022/07/07/improve-scalability-with-buffer-pool-parallel-scan-in-sql-server-2022`.

David shows some great numbers we've seen for improvements in SQL Server 2022. In addition, check out his Data Exposed episode where he shows even more details with a nifty demonstration at `https://youtu.be/4GvU106Xiag`. I have included an example of the results David found in a T-SQL notebook you can view with Azure Data Studio in the example **ch06_meatandpotatoes\scalability\Buffer_pool_parallel_scan_BPP_notebook_quick.ipynb**.

Purvi's List

I have encountered so many talented, kind, and wonderful people at Microsoft over the years who work behind the scenes with no fanfare. They just do their job, do it well, and are incredibly nice and friendly. One of those people is Purvi Shah. Purvi is a senior software engineer in the SQL team, but her role is larger than that title. Purvi works in our "performance" team and literally spends her time finding ways to make SQL Server and Azure SQL faster – but faster on a level that most of us don't understand. Her and the team's work can be felt in so many ways that you may never see because it is often enhancements into the engine that are not a "feature."

Note   One notable example she worked on for SQL Server 2019 was PFS page concurrency for tempdb, which was huge!

For this release I reached out to Purvi and asked her to share her list of scalability enhancements that I want our readers to know about. Here is her list:

- **Reduced buffer pool I/O promotions** – There were cases where we would cause system issues by taking a single page read and promoting it to an eight-page I/O. Turns out this wasn't really helping performance and could overload an I/O system, so we tuned this algorithm. This is simply tuning our engine to be smarter when performing I/O operations.

- **Enhanced some of our core spinlock algorithms** – Spinlocks are a huge part of the consistency inside the engine for multiple threads. We are always looking to tune these algorithms to ensure the engine is running at its best in all types of workloads. We made some internal adjustments to make spinlocks more efficient, and the improvements are so deep into the engine it is hard to quantify its effect (Purvi and the team do this at a very deep level to ensure their work actually makes everything better and not worse).

- **Improved Virtual Log File (VLF) algorithms** – Virtual Log File (VLF) is an abstraction of the physical transaction log. Having a high number of small VLFs based on log growth can affect the performance of operations like recovery. We changed the algorithm for how many VLFs we create during certain log grow scenarios to reduce these types of problems. You can read about how we have changed this algorithm in our docs at `https://docs.microsoft.com/sql/relational-databases/sql-server-transaction-log-architecture-and-management-guide?#virtual-log-files-vlfs`.

- **Instant File Initialization (IFI) for log file growth** – Up until SQL Server 2022, we could not use Instant File Initialization (IFI) on the transaction log because we didn't think we could properly detect the "end of the log." With SQL Server 2022 we have determined that when we have to grow the transaction log, we *can* use IFI if the *grow* size is considered "medium," which is up to 64Mb in size. This one could be a big performance win for scenarios where zeroing the log file during grow operations would cause blocking problems. Turns out 64Mb is exactly the default auto growth size for SQL Server data and log files when creating a new database.

Purvi and her team do such great work to keep the SQL Server engine tuned and fast. I asked Purvi more about why she likes her job at Microsoft, and she said, "Keeping both SQL Server and Azure SQL running at its peak performance is part of my job. I strive to do it to best of my abilities. Of course, I love my job! Hope I am able to make a positive contribution to continue our mission."

"Hands-Free" tempdb

As great as a product as SQL Server is, after working with SQL Server for 29 years, I've seen some issues that to this day just keep me pulling my hair out. One of these issues is latch contention with tempdb.

What Is the Challenge?

All database pages in SQL Server need physical protection using latches. Some database pages are called system pages because they have allocation information; these are known as PFS, GAM, and SGAM pages. Any query or operation that requires allocation or deallocation may need to read or write from or to these pages. Reads and writes from and to these pages require a *latch protection scheme*. Latch protection is needed because two threads could be trying to modify or read a page at the same time (that is a very basic description of how latches work).

These pages are at fixed locations within database files. In addition, every table has pages to store data and indexes. Any queries or operations that affect these pages will also require latch protection. Because system tables have pages like any other table, specific DDL statements in SQL will eventually lead to the latch protection and contention for pages for system tables.

Now consider tempdb. Workloads for SQL Server that involve tempdb typically require a great deal of allocation and system table page operations. Temporary tables, table variables, and spills are just a few that invoke these operations. All of these typically require fast and frequent page allocations and system table modifications. Therefore, when many users run queries concurrently that result in these operations within tempdb, there is naturally contention or *pressure* on latches for pages for allocation and system tables. The main symptom of this problem is seeing your request waiting on a PAGELATCH_XX wait type.

Initially, when latches were first introduced in SQL Server 7.0, I would see latch contention for tempdb on PFS, GAM, and SGAM pages because back then the default behavior was a single file for database pages. Typically, what would happen is that an application would use temporary tables across multiple concurrent users, which would result in frequent CREATE and DROP operations, which required allocation and deallocation operations. This naturally put pressure on PFS, GAM, and SGAM pages in a single file.

Solutions Over the Years

When we first started to really see this problem in SQL Server 7.0 and even into SQL Server 2000, many of us in CSS would recommend that customers create multiple files for tempdb data. Why? Because we were naturally *partitioning* latch concurrency for these allocation pages. This is because SQL Server will allocate pages in a round-robin fashion and leverage a proportional fill algorithm across multiple files for data pages. This solution really helped many of these latch contention problems. But then a new problem surfaced. How many files do you need to create to solve the problem? Unfortunately, many people went overboard and suggested that you would need a number of files to match the number of CPUs for SQL Server. I and others in the community, like Paul Randal, thought differently. For example, we knew that for a 64-CPU machine you would probably not need 64 files. Common sense said that it seemed like it could cause more harm than good. I eventually did some detailed research on this topic, which led me to recommend that using eight files for eight CPUs and then adding by four until you see the performance balance for your workload would be the best approach. You can see more details about this approach in a presentation I did way back in the PASS Summit in 2011 at `www.youtube.com/watch?v=SvseGMobe2w`.

Another thing we did is introduce trace flag 1118 so that all allocations for tables used uniform extents to ease pressure on the SGAM pages of files. We also discovered that using multiple files to ease system page latch contention only worked if all the files were the exact same size. As a result, we introduced trace flag 1117 so that any autogrow activities would grow all files to keep them the same size.

Any true bottleneck requires peeling back the layers like an onion. Even with this approach of multiple files, a system could have so many users that PFS, GAM, and SGAM latch contention could still happen, but it paled in comparison to the new main problem: system table page latch contention. We struggled at first to recognize this. We were used to running scripts that would recognize specific pages for latch contention: PFS, GAM, and SGAM.

Once we saw the hot spot was system table pages, we honestly had no recourse but to tell customers to reduce their tempdb workload contention. We did create some solutions that would help called *tempdb caching*. We discovered that we could save metadata about temporary tables, including some pages for patterns that were repeated. You can see more about this concept at `https://docs.microsoft.com/sql/relational-databases/databases/tempdb-database?#performance-improvements-in-tempdb-for-sql-server`. Even with tempdb caching, it did not eliminate the problem, and not all tempdb scenarios can use caching.

In SQL Server 2016 we helped customers ensure multiple files were created for tempdb by including a default configuration within setup to create the number of files to match the number of CPUs detected up to eight. We also removed the need for trace flags 1117 and 1118 by turning these into ALTER DATABASE options and making them the default for tempdb.

Workloads continued to put pressure on tempdb, and we still saw issues. We introduced two big changes in SQL Server 2019 to help the latch problem:

- PFS pages now would no longer have latching problems. We found ways to update PFS pages even under a shared latch.

- We introduced tempdb metadata optimization as a new server option. When this option is enabled (a server restart is required), we convert critical system tables in tempdb to memory-optimized tables. Memory-optimized tables are "latch-free," so any reads or writes from or to these tables do not experience latch contention.

The improvements were huge. With these two enhancements, I saw many workloads no longer experience significant issues due to latch contention. But the core problem could occasionally still be seen with latch contention on SGAM and GAM pages. When I first saw SGAM contention continue to occur, I was puzzled because we changed tempdb to always use uniform extents. However, there is one page that still has to be allocated for temporary tables or indexes that is not with a uniform extent, and that is an IAM page, which tracks allocations for an object.

Why Now "Hands-Free"?

When I saw the initial set of engine improvements for project Dallas, I was very happy to learn that GAM and SGAM concurrencies were enhanced in the same manner that PFS pages had been in SQL Server 2019.

Now tempdb could truly be "hands-free" with regard to latch issues. Consider this:

- PFS, GAM, and SGAM latch contentions are completely gone.

- If you execute this statement `ALTER SERVER CONFIGURATION SET MEMORY_OPTIMIZED TEMPDB_METADATA = ON` and restart SQL Server, critical system tables are memory optimized and won't encounter latch contention.

Note   tempdb latching issues were never about slow I/O. However, you should always make sure to eliminate any I/O issues for tempdb by placing tempdb data and log files on a separate drive from your user data and preferably on a SSD. If you have I/O issues for tempdb, they are typically seen in the form of PAGELATCH_ IO, IO_COMPLETION, and WRITELOG (tempdb log) wait types.

Try It Yourself

If you want to see how we have hopefully forever removed tempdb latch contention for users, go through the following exercise:

Prerequisites

- SQL Server 2022 Evaluation Edition.

- VM or computer with four CPUs and at least 8Gb RAM.

- SQL Server Management Studio (SSMS). The latest 18.x or 19.x build will work.

- Download **ostress.exe** from `https://aka.ms/ostress`. Install using the RMLSetup.msi file that is downloaded. Use all defaults.

- Use the scripts from the book samples as found in the **ch06_ meatandpotatoes\scalability\tempdb** directory.

Note: This exercise will require you to restart the instance multiple times.

Set Up the Exercise

Follow these steps to set up the exercise:

1. Configure perfmon to track **SQL Server SQL Statistics:SQL Statistics/Batch requests/sec** (set Scale to 0.1) and **SQL Server:Wait Statistics/Page latch waits/Waits started per second**.

2. Execute the script **findtempdbdbilfes.sql** and save the output. A script is provided for the end of this demo to restore your tempdb file settings. This script executes the following T-SQL statements:

```
USE master;
GO
SELECT name, physical_name, size*8192/1024 as size_kb,
growth*8192/1024 as growth_kb
FROM sys.master_files
WHERE database_id = 2;
GO
```

3. Start SQL Server in *minimal* mode using the command script **startsqlminimal.cmd**. Minimal mode (/f startup parameter) allows you to remove tempdb files and only have one data file. This script executes the following commands:

```
net stop mssqlserver
net start mssqlserver /f
```

4. Execute the command script **modifytempdbfiles.cmd**. This will execute the SQL script **modifytempdbfiles.sql** to expand the log to 200Mb (avoid any autogrow) and remove all tempdb files other than the first one (tempdev). If you have more than four tempdb files, you need to edit this script to remove all of them except for **tempdev**.

   modifytempdbfiles.cmd executes the following command:

```
sqlcmd -E -imodifytempdbfiles.sql
```

modifytempdbfiles.sql executes the following T-SQL statements:

```
USE master;
GO
ALTER DATABASE tempdb MODIFY FILE (NAME=templog, SIZE = 200Mb,
FILEGROWTH = 65536Kb);
GO
ALTER DATABASE tempdb REMOVE FILE temp2;
GO
ALTER DATABASE tempdb REMOVE FILE temp3;
GO
ALTER DATABASE tempdb REMOVE FILE temp4;
GO
```

Steps for the Exercise

You are now ready to run the exercise, which is comprised of three different tests. In each test you will run the same workload and observe perfmon counters and overall workload duration.

Test 1: Disable tempdb metadata optimization and disable GAM/SGAM enhancements.

The first test shows performance of a workload where no optimizations are enabled. But since we are using SQL Server 2022, even with one file, PFS concurrency enhancements are enabled since this was built into the code in SQL Server 2019. This is why you won't see any latch contention on PFS pages.

1. Run the script **disableoptimizetempdb.cmd**. This script runs the following commands:

    ```
    sqlcmd -E -idisableopttempdb.sql
    net stop mssqlserver
    net start mssqlserver
    ```

    disableopttempdb.sql executes the following T-SQL statements:

    ```
    ALTER SERVER CONFIGURATION SET MEMORY_OPTIMIZED TEMPDB_
    METADATA = OFF;
    GO
    ```

    Even though tempdb metadata optimization is not on by default, we will disable it to confirm.

2. Run the script **disablegamsgam.cmd**. This scripts runs the following commands:

```
net stop mssqlserver
net start mssqlserver /T6950 /T6962
```

These are undocumented trace flags that disable new SQL Server 2022 enhancements. These are not supported and only used for the purposes of this exercise.

Now the server is running with no optimizations except for PFS concurrency carried over from SQL Server 2019.

3. Load the script **pageinfo.sql** into SSMS. When the workload starts, you will run this to see what the latch contention looks like. This script executes the following T-SQL statements:

```
USE tempdb;
GO
SELECT object_name(page_info.object_id), page_info.*
FROM sys.dm_exec_requests AS d
  CROSS APPLY sys.fn_PageResCracker(d.page_resource) AS r
  CROSS APPLY sys.dm_db_page_info(r.db_id, r.file_id,
  r.page_id,'DETAILED')
    AS page_info;
GO
```

This script uses T-SQL built-in functions introduced in SQL Server 2019 to "crack a page" and look at its contents. In addition, it uses a function to get metadata about a page such as the object_id it belongs to and page type.

4. Execute the script **tempsql22stress.cmd** from the command prompt with the following syntax (you only need .\ in PowerShell):

```
.\tempsql22stress.cmd 25
```

Move forward to the next steps but come back after the command is over to look more at the syntax.

This script executes the following command with ostress.exe:

```
"c:\Program Files\Microsoft Corporation\RMLUtils\ostress"
-E -Q"declare @t table (c1 varchar(100)); insert into @t values
('x');" -n%1 -r1000 -q
```

Let's look at the arguments:

-Q is used to run a query. Notice this is a batch to use a table variable. This particular syntax won't allow for temporary table caching, so we are putting a lot of pressure on allocation and system tables.

-n is number of users. We've supplied a value of 25 concurrent users.

-r is the number of iterations of the query each user will run.

-q suppresses all result set processing to make it faster as we don't care about looking at the results.

5.   Execute the **pageinfo.sql** script and observe the results. Notice the latch contention is for pages that belong to system tables in tempdb. There are hardly any latch waits on GAM pages because system table page latch contention is the "hot spot."

6.   Observe perfmon counters. Record the averages and max values to compare with the second and third tests.

7.   Observe the duration of the workload **tempsql22stress.cmd** as displayed by elapsed time. Record this value to compare with the second and third tests.

Test 2: Enable tempdb metadata optimization and disable GAM/SGAM enhancements.

We will run the exact same test, except this time we will enable tempdb metadata optimization and disable the new SQL Server 2022 enhancements.

1. Run the script **optimizetempdb.cmd**. This script will execute
    optimizetempdb.sql, which turns **ON** tempdb metadata
    optimization.

2. Run the script **disablegamsgam.cmd** again to use trace flags to
    disable new GAM/SGAM optimizations.

3. Run **tempsql22stress.cmd 25** as you did in Test 1.

4. Execute **pageinfo.sql** as you did in Test 1. Now you should see that
    the majority of latch contention problems are on GAM pages.

5. Observe perfmon counters and elapsed time. Record these
    numbers to compare them with Test 1.

You should see fewer latch waits started per second, but a lower number of batch
requests/sec and a longer duration. This is because the latch waits are held longer,
causing a drop of throughput from Test 1. If we had multiple files, we could greatly
reduce the GAM contention, and we would get better performance (and feel free to test
this yourself). But with SQL Server 2022, there is another way.

**Test 3: Enable tempdb metadata optimization and enable GAM/SGAM
enhancements (default for SQL Server 2022).**

Since tempdb metadata optimization is already enabled, all we need to do is restart
SQL Server (with no trace flags) to see the built-in enhancements for GAM and SGAM
contention.

1. Execute the script **restartsql.cmd**. This script runs the following
    commands:

    ```
    net stop mssqlserver
    net start mssqlserver
    ```

2. Run **tempsql22stress.cmd 25** again.

3. Execute the **pageinfo.sql** script. You should not see any latches.

4. Observe perfmon counters and elapsed time. Record these values
    to compare them with Tests 1 and 2.

Note   Did you notice one latch started per second on this final test? Why would that occur if there was no latch contention? It is because there are a few system pages, namely, the BOOT and FILE_HEADER pages, that may still have a small amount of latch contention. However, there should be no performance impact, and that is why I said 99.99% latch-free!

Who won the test for you? If all worked as planned, the results – in order of who was faster – should be

1. **Test 3** – Enable tempdb metadata optimization and enable GAM/SGAM concurrency (on by default).

2. **Test 1** – Disable tempdb metadata optimization and disable GAM/SGAM enhancements.

3. **Test 2** – Enable tempdb metadata optimization and disable GAM/SGAM.

Test 3 should win because we have all optimizations turned on.

Test 1 was second because even though system table page latch contention was heavy, latch wait times were shorter for each latch wait.

Test 2 was the worst because latch wait times for GAM pages were very long.

Note   Use the **restoretempdbfiles.cmd** and **restoretempdbfiles.sql** to restore your tempdb configuration.

You may be wondering what the results would look like for Test 3 if you had multiple tempdb files. Just about the same as with one file, which I know may seem amazing after all these years of using multiple files. My advice is to stick with the recommended number of multiple files; just let SQL Server setup configure it for you. It is another reason I'm advocating "hands-free" installation: Run SQL Server setup with the defaults and turn on tempdb metadata optimization. Then just run your workload. Time will tell whether my bold statement will become true for you and the community.

More Concurrency Improvements

Concurrency problems in SQL Server hurt performance and scalability. Ensuring that workloads can run concurrently but not experience blocking or waiting problems is essential to maximize your investments for application and infrastructure for scale.

SQL Server 2022 solves more real-world scenarios including concurrency issues for shrink database and automatic statistics update.

Shrink Database Concurrency

In SQL Server 2014 we added an option for online index builds to take locks at lower priorities called WAIT_AT_LOW_PRIORITY. Even an online index build (see the documentation at `https://docs.microsoft.com/sql/relational-databases/ indexes/how-online-index-operations-work?#source-structure-activities`) has to obtain locks and may have to wait. During this wait period, other operations might be blocked by the online index build that could normally continue. WAIT_AT_LOW_ PRIORITY allows users that would normally be blocked to continue.

It turns out that shrink database and shrink file operations have these same issues. Therefore, in SQL Server 2022 we added a new WAIT_AT_LOW_PRIORITY for DBCC SHRINKDATABASE and DBCC SHRINKFILE. You can see how the new syntax works at `https://docs.microsoft.com/sql/t-sql/database-console-commands/dbcc- shrinkdatabase-transact-sql`. In general, it is recommended to avoid shrinking a database or its files, but sometimes it is a necessity.

Auto-update Stats Concurrency

As we were building out the story for SQL Server 2022 preview launch, one of the developers I know, Parag Paul, reached out to me: *"Bob, have you seen the auto-update stats improvement coming in SQL Server 2022?"* I told Parag I thought I remembered something in Azure SQL about this, but I didn't know much about it or that it would be in SQL Server 2022.

We discussed the details, and I then remembered a blog post by my colleague Dimitri Furman, who not only is one of the top SQL experts in our team but is one of my "go-to" people at Microsoft on Azure SQL. You can read his blog post at `https:// techcommunity.microsoft.com/t5/azure-sql-blog/improving-concurrency-of- asynchronous-statistics-update/ba-p/1441687`.

The problem is that while SQL Server and Azure SQL can be configured for auto-update statistics to happen asynchronously, the background processes doing the updates can cause concurrency issues. Dimitri has a very nice, detailed diagram and explanation of the problem in this blog post. Effectively, the issue is concurrency between queries and background processes needing schema locks on system metadata. We introduced a new database-scope configuration option called **ASYNC_STATS_ UPDATE_WAIT_AT_LOW_PRIORITY**. When you turn this on, the background processes to update stats will wait for all running processes to release locks that could cause a concurrency issue, effectively running at a "lower priority." This option is off by default because it is possible this option could result in statistics not being updated as often as desired (or as often as folks are used to now), which could lead to undesirable query plans. But we added this option because we saw scenarios where the user wanted to favor concurrency over more frequent, timed updates of statistics.

You can read how to configure this database-scoped option at `https://docs. microsoft.com/sql/t-sql/statements/alter-database-scoped-configuration- transact-sql`.

Availability

While all data and workloads need security and performance, any credible production system must have high availability and dependable disaster recovery. In SQL Server 2022 we have a rich set of new features that span Always On Availability Groups, recovery and redo, backup and restore, and replication.

Contained Availability Groups

At the 2018 PASS Summit, I found myself on stage with my former Microsoft colleague Amit Banerjee presenting the latest updates on SQL Server 2019. We had just announced the first Public Preview of SQL Server 2019 at the Microsoft Ignite conference in September of 2018.

For PASS we surprised the audience by announcing that SQL Server 2019 would support instance-level object replication with Always On Availability Groups. So no longer would you have to manually replicate linked servers, SQL Agent jobs, and logins after a failover for a secondary replica. We literally received a standing ovation from the audience because this has been such a long-standing request. Unfortunately, we were premature in making this announcement. I remember when we had to make the decision not to ship this in SQL Server 2019. I was devastated, and I'm sure all the community was as well.

In early 2022 we continued to evaluate what would be in project Dallas. We had already announced the Private Preview, and I remember we discussed about reviving this capability. In comes the heroics of Kevin Farlee, a longtime program manager veteran in our team, and David Liao, Principal Software Engineer on the SQL Server team. They made it their *mission* to complete the work we had started in the past and ship this feature in SQL Server 2022. We would call it **Contained Availability Groups**. We made a small announcement about this at the SQLBits conference in March of 2022 and made it more widely known when we announced SQL Server 2022 CTP 2.0 at Microsoft //build. I asked Kevin about his thoughts on the importance of getting this into the product:

> When we first shipped Always On Availability Groups in SQL Server 2012, it was very well received, and a big step forward in the HA space. However a request quickly popped up and has been upvoted and reinforced to this day: "It's a pain to make sure all of the replica instances in an AG have the users, logins, permissions, agent jobs, and all the rest of the infrastructure configuration in sync." Customers worked around this by creating jobs or manual processes to force synchronization, but that was not a good solution. As it turned out, some of the Azure HA configurations such as Managed Instance as well as Azure Arc-enabled SQL Managed Instance had the same challenges so we combined forces and arrived at a solution to replicate portions of Master and MSDB databases for each AG. This is what we now call Contained AGs when used in the SQL Server product. I am very happy to be able to ship this to customers.

So are we, Kevin!

How Does It Work?

The concept of a Contained Availability Group is to include a version of the master and msdb system databases inside the availability group, along with user databases. If anyone connects to the listener of the availability group or a user database context directly inside the AG, any instance information in master and msdb will be seen from these system databases. Anyone connecting to the instance directly would see the normal master and msdb databases. It is not a copy of the instance master and msdb databases; it is a special version of these databases used in the context of the AG. On creation of a Contained AG, these system databases are empty except any existing admin logins are copied into the *contained AG master* so that an admin can connect to the AG and start adding instance objects.

Figure 6-5 shows the various components of a Contained AG.

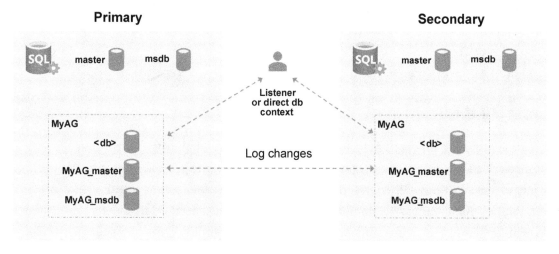

Figure 6-5. *The Contained AG architecture*

When a user creates an availability group, there is a new syntax keyword for the WITH clause called CONTAINED. When this keyword is used, SQL Server will create two databases called **<agname>_master** and **<agname>_msdb** and add these to the availability group. Existing admin logins in the master database of the primary are added to the Contained AG master.

When a user connects to the listener of the AG or a direct database context (i.e., uses the database name in the connection string), this user is considered in the *context* of the Contained AG. Any operation that would normally apply to master or msdb applies to the Contained AG master and msdb. For example, if you were connected to the listener and created a new SQL Server Agent job, that job would exist in <agname>_msdb and NOT in the msdb of the instance of the primary. Since the <agname>_msdb is part of the AG, any logged operations such as adding a new job are replicated to the <agname>_msdb on the secondary.

If a failover occurs, the replicated Contained AG master and msdb will now be used for new primary listener connections.

When I first saw this design, I was puzzled about SQL Server Agent. How could SQL Server Agent know to look for jobs in the Contained AG msdb? Well, turns out we enhanced SQL Server Agent in 2022 to recognize multiple msdb databases that may be needed to use for Agent jobs. Any job in the Contained AG msdb only gets executed on the primary replica.

You can read more about how Contained AGs work at `https://docs.microsoft.com/sql/database-engine/availability-groups/windows/contained-availability-groups-overview`.

I think you will understand further how this works by seeing an example.

Let's Try It Out

Let's walk through an exercise to see how a Contained Availability Group works. For this exercise I'm going to set up a *clusterless* availability group. In other words, I'm not going to use a Windows cluster, so my availability group does not have auto-failover capabilities. A clusterless availability group is the simplest method to show a Contained Availability Group. Because I'm using a clusterless availability group, you can also easily set up this exercise on Linux. You can also set up your own type of availability group and still use most of the examples here.

Caution   The steps for this exercise are very detailed. You need to follow each step carefully, or this exercise will not work.

Prerequisites

- Two Virtual Machines running Windows Server each with four vCPUs and 8Gb RAM. The VMs need to be on the same network and subnet. I used Azure Virtual Machines and put the two VMs in the same resource group, which automatically puts them in the same VNet and subnet. To make my scripts easier, I manually added each IP address for each VM in the C:\windows\system32\drivers\etc\hosts file. This allows me to use server names instead of direct IP addresses. Designate one of the VMs as the primary and one as the secondary. In the following steps, I'll refer to the primary or secondary instance or VM.

- SQL Server Evaluation Editon installed on each VM with mixed-mode authentication enabled (also known as SQL Server and Windows authentication mode). We will use SQL logins to make the exercise simpler. You can do this during install or post install (post install requires an instance restart).

- On each VM, create firewall rules that allow incoming traffic for ports 1433 and 5022.

- Enable the Always On Availability Group feature for each SQL instance using the SQL Server Configuration Manager and restart SQL Server. You can read more about how to do this at `https://docs.microsoft.com/sql/database-engine/availability-groups/windows/enable-and-disable-always-on-availability-groups-sql-server#SQLCM2Procedure` (ignore the instructions about the Windows cluster). This requires an instance restart.

- Use SQL Server Management Studio (SSMS). You can use the latest 18.x build, but 19.x includes new functionality to see Contained Availability Groups in Object Explorer and graphic interfaces to create a Contained AG. We will "do it the hard way" in this exercise using T-SQL, but SSMS 19.X will recognize a Contained AG.

- Get the scripts from the book samples from the **ch06_meatandpotatoes\availability\containedag** directory.

Steps for the Exercise

1. Connected **directly to the instance** using the default sysadmin login from setup, execute the script **sqlsysadminlogin.sql** on both the primary and secondary instances. This script executes the following T-SQL statements:

```
USE master;
GO
CREATE LOGIN sqladmin WITH PASSWORD = '$Strongpassw0rd';
GO
EXEC sp_addsrvrolemember 'sqladmin', 'sysadmin';
GO
```

You will use this login to connect to each instance for the rest of the exercise.

2. Start the SQL Server Agent service on both the primary and secondary VMs.

3. Connect with SSMS on the primary VM to **both** the primary and secondary using the **sqladmin** login.

4. Execute the script **dbmcreds.sql** on both the primary and secondary instances. This script executes the following T-SQL statements:

```
USE master;
GO
CREATE LOGIN dbm_login WITH PASSWORD = '$Strongpassw0rd';
GO
CREATE USER dbm_user FOR LOGIN dbm_login;
GO
```

5. Execute the script **createcert.sql** only on the primary instance. This script executes the following T-SQL statements:

```
USE master;
GO
CREATE MASTER KEY ENCRYPTION BY PASSWORD = '$Strongpassw0rd';
GO
DROP CERTIFICATE dbm_certificate;
GO
CREATE CERTIFICATE dbm_certificate WITH SUBJECT = 'dbm';
GO
BACKUP CERTIFICATE dbm_certificate
TO FILE = 'C:\Program Files\Microsoft SQL Server\MSSQL16.
MSSQLSERVER\MSSQL\DATA\dbm_certificate.cer'
WITH PRIVATE KEY (
FILE = 'c:\Program Files\Microsoft SQL Server\MSSQL16.MSSQLSERVER\
MSSQL\DATA\dbm_certificate.pvk',
ENCRYPTION BY PASSWORD = '$Strongpassw0rd');
GO
```

This script assumes the default installation path for SQL Server on Windows. You will have to modify this script if your install path is different. You will also need to modify this script for Linux to match the correct install path.

6. Copy the files **dbm_certificate.cer** and **dbm_certificate.pvk** from the path of the primary VM into the same exact file path on the secondary VM (the default is C:\Program Files\Microsoft SQL Server\MSSQL16.MSSQLSERVER\MSSQL\DATA).

7. Execute the script **importcert.sql** only on the secondary instance. This script executes the following T-SQL statements (you will need to modify the path if it is not the default as in the following):

```
USE master;
GO
CREATE MASTER KEY ENCRYPTION BY PASSWORD = '$Strongpassw0rd';
GO
CREATE CERTIFICATE dbm_certificate
    AUTHORIZATION dbm_user
    FROM FILE = 'C:\Program Files\Microsoft SQL Server\MSSQL16.
MSSQLSERVER\MSSQL\DATA\dbm_certificate.cer'
    WITH PRIVATE KEY (
    FILE = 'c:\Program Files\Microsoft SQL Server\MSSQL16.
MSSQLSERVER\MSSQL\DATA\dbm_certificate.pvk',
    DECRYPTION BY PASSWORD = '$Strongpassw0rd');
GO
```

8. Execute the script **dbm_endpoint.sql** on **both instances**. This script executes the following T-SQL statements:

```
USE master;
GO
CREATE ENDPOINT [Hadr_endpoint]
    AS TCP (LISTENER_PORT = 5022)
    FOR DATA_MIRRORING (
      ROLE = ALL,
      AUTHENTICATION = CERTIFICATE dbm_certificate,
```

```
        ENCRYPTION = REQUIRED ALGORITHM AES
    );
GO
ALTER ENDPOINT [Hadr_endpoint] STATE = STARTED;
GRANT CONNECT ON ENDPOINT::[Hadr_endpoint] TO [dbm_login];
GO
```

9. Edit the script **createag.sql**. Put in your two VM server names
   (that you put in the hosts file) for <node1> (primary) and <node2>
   (secondary). This script executes the following T-SQL statements:

```
USE master;
GO
CREATE AVAILABILITY GROUP [ag1]
    WITH (CLUSTER_TYPE = NONE, CONTAINED)
    FOR REPLICA ON
        N'<node1>' WITH (
            ENDPOINT_URL = N'tcp://<node1>:5022',
            AVAILABILITY_MODE = ASYNCHRONOUS_COMMIT,
            FAILOVER_MODE = MANUAL,
            SEEDING_MODE = AUTOMATIC,
            SECONDARY_ROLE (ALLOW_CONNECTIONS = ALL)
            ),
        N'<node2>' WITH (
            ENDPOINT_URL = N'tcp://<node2>:5022',
            AVAILABILITY_MODE = ASYNCHRONOUS_COMMIT,
            FAILOVER_MODE = MANUAL,
            SEEDING_MODE = AUTOMATIC,
            SECONDARY_ROLE (ALLOW_CONNECTIONS = ALL)
            );
GO
ALTER AVAILABILITY GROUP [ag1] GRANT CREATE ANY DATABASE;
GO
```

Notice the use of the option CLUSTER_TYPE = NONE (clusterless) and CONTAINED. Any type of availability group will support CONTAINED. I'm just using a clusterless type to simplify the exercise.

For my system, my script looks like this:

```
USE master;
GO
CREATE AVAILABILITY GROUP [ag1]
    WITH (CLUSTER_TYPE = NONE, CONTAINED)
    FOR REPLICA ON
        N'bwsql2022vm1' WITH (
            ENDPOINT_URL = N'tcp://bwsql2022vm1:5022',
            AVAILABILITY_MODE = ASYNCHRONOUS_COMMIT,
            FAILOVER_MODE = MANUAL,
SEEDING_MODE = AUTOMATIC,
            SECONDARY_ROLE (ALLOW_CONNECTIONS = ALL)
            ),
        N'bwsql2022vm2' WITH (
            ENDPOINT_URL = N'tcp://bwsql2022vm2:5022',
            AVAILABILITY_MODE = ASYNCHRONOUS_COMMIT,
            FAILOVER_MODE = MANUAL,
            SEEDING_MODE = AUTOMATIC,
            SECONDARY_ROLE (ALLOW_CONNECTIONS = ALL)
            );
GO
```

10. Execute the script **joinag.sql** on the secondary instance. This script executes the following T-SQL statements:

```
USE master;
GO
ALTER AVAILABILITY GROUP [ag1] JOIN WITH (CLUSTER_TYPE = NONE);
GO
ALTER AVAILABILITY GROUP [ag1] GRANT CREATE ANY DATABASE;
GO
```

11. You should now have a Contained Availability Group up and running. Let's make sure it is working by using Object Explorer in SSMS. If you expand the folder for Availability Groups, you should see something like Figure 6-6.

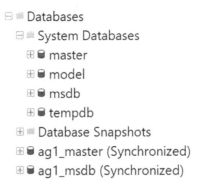

Figure 6-6. *A Contained Availability Group in SQL Server 2022*

You can see the availability group is made up of the Contained AG master and msdb. SSMS 19 has new icons to recognize a Contained AG.

12. Since you are directly connected to the instance (not through a listener or direct db context), you can see these databases as user databases. Expand the Databases folder in Object Explorer. You should see something like Figure 6-7.

```
□ ▦ Databases
  □ ▦ System Databases
    ⊞ 🛢 master
    ⊞ 🛢 model
    ⊞ 🛢 msdb
    ⊞ 🛢 tempdb
  ⊞ ▦ Database Snapshots
  ⊞ 🛢 ag1_master (Synchronized)
  ⊞ 🛢 ag1_msdb (Synchronized)
```

Figure 6-7. *Contained AG master and msdb databases*

When using the listener or direct db context, you will see that we have a different view.

13. Execute the script **createdb.sql** on the **primary instance** to create a new database and back it up. This script executes the following T-SQL statements (change the file path for the backup to your system needs):

```
CREATE DATABASE letsgomavs;
GO
ALTER DATABASE letsgomavs SET RECOVERY FULL;
GO
BACKUP DATABASE letsgomavs
TO DISK = N'c:\Program Files\Microsoft SQL Server\MSSQL16.
MSSQLSERVER\MSSQL\Backup\letsgomavs.bak' WITH INIT;
GO
```

At the time I created this demo, my beloved Dallas Mavericks were in the heat of battle for the NBA Western Conference playoffs, so I couldn't resist using their name here. Sadly, they lost to the eventual champions, Golden State, in the Conference finals.

14. Execute the script **dbjoinag.sql** against the primary instance to join the new database to the availability group. This script executes the following T-SQL statements:

```
USE master;
GO
ALTER AVAILABILITY GROUP [ag1] ADD DATABASE letsgomavs;
GO
```

If you refresh the availability group in SSMS, you will see the database letsgomavs is now part of the AG.

15. Now it gets interesting. Connect to the primary instance **using a direct database context**. I find it easiest to launch another copy of SSMS and connect to the primary instance. But this time on the SSMS login screen, select Options and the Connection Properties tab. Put in letsgomavs in the Connect to database field like in Figure 6-8.

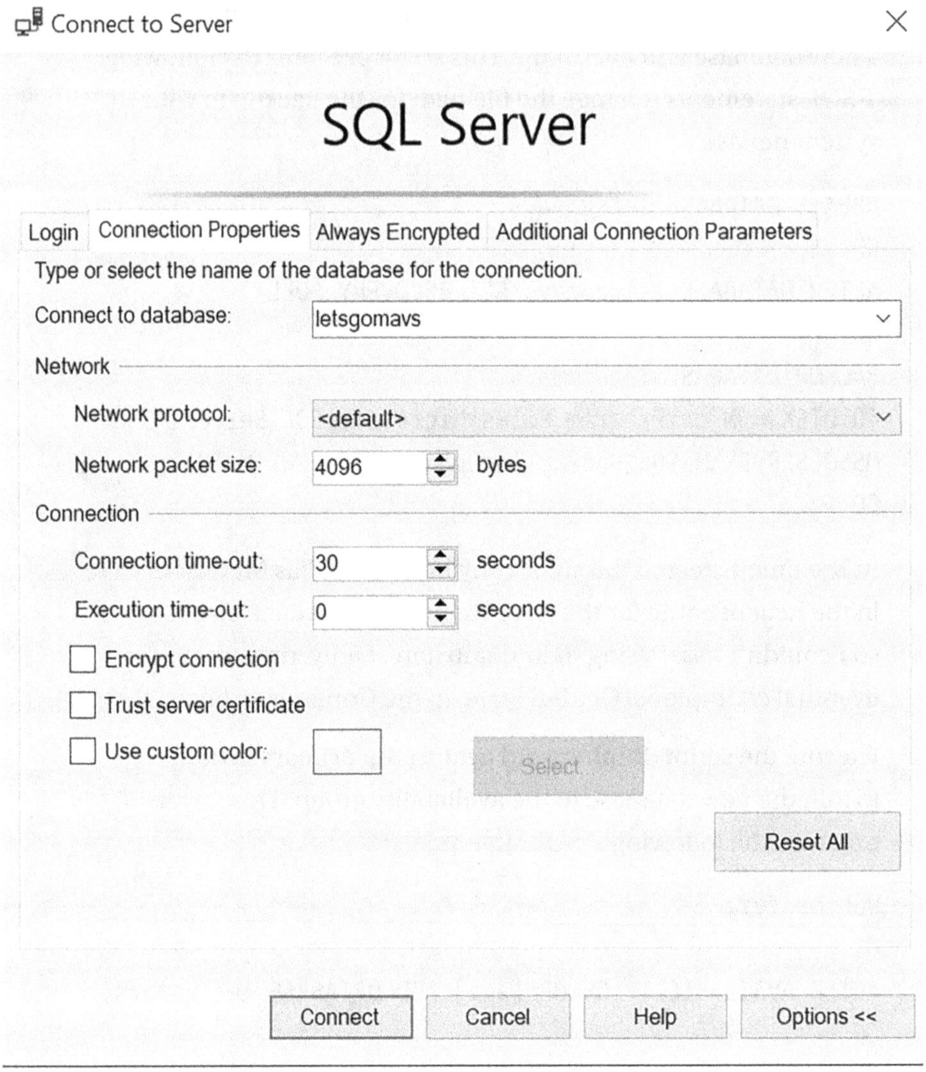

Figure 6-8. *Connect to the primary instance with a database context*

You can achieve the same concept by using a listener. Since I'm using a clusterless availability group, I'll just connect using the database context.

16. Use SSMS to look at the list of databases. You will only see letsgomavs, and if you expand system tables, you will see master and msdb. These are the Contained AG master and msdb databases.

17. While you are connected to the primary instance, use SSMS to create a SQL Server Agent job. It doesn't matter what is in the job. I just used the Object Explorer interface to create a new job called testjob with no steps.

18. Launch another SSMS that is directly connected to the instance. Use Object Explorer to expand the list of jobs for SQL Server Agent. You will not see the job there because it is in the Contained AG msdb database.

19. Connect to the secondary instance using the same technique with SSMS to connect with the letsgomavs database. Expand the jobs for SQL Server Agent in Object Explorer, and you will see the job you created previously. This demonstrates that jobs are replicated to secondary instances.

20. Let's try a failover. Using SSMS **directly connected to the primary instance (not using the database context)**, right-click the availability group and select Failover like in Figure 6-9.

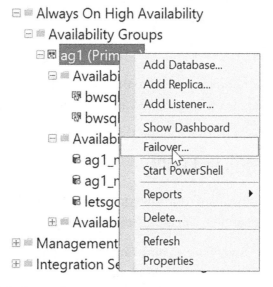

Figure 6-9. *Manual failover for a Contained AG*

Follow the steps in the wizard to fail over to the secondary instance. When connecting to the secondary, use the instance connection (do not provide the database context) and **use the**

sqladmin SQL login created earlier in this exercise. Since we are using a clusterless AG with a manual failover, you will get warnings about data loss. Ignore these to complete the failover and click the option to confirm you know there may be data loss.

21. When the failover is complete, you can use SSMS connected directly to the primary or secondary instance to see the switch in roles. You can also connect using a database context to the *new primary* to see your database and SQL Server Agent job ready to use.

Items to Consider

There are a few limits and considerations for Contained AGs. For example, replication is not supported for databases that are in a Contained AG. But features like CDC, log shipping, and TDE are supported with some special instructions for use. You can learn more about these in our documentation at `https://docs.microsoft.com/sql/database-engine/availability-groups/windows/contained-availability-groups-overview#interactions-with-other-features`.

Other AG Enhancements

We have made other minor enhancements to the core of Always On Availability Groups including reliability fixes, diagnostics, and enhancements for Distributed Availability Groups.

AG Reliability and Supportability

We shored up some reliability issues for Always On Availability Groups (no changes required for you; these are built in) including the following:

- The database recovery task is now run with a higher deadlock priority to avoid being chosen as a deadlock victim with user transactions.

- We fixed a problem where a replica database would get stuck in a recovery pending state.

- Ensured data movement is not paused to replicas due to internal log block errors.

- Eliminated schema lock contention problems on secondary replicas (this problem is also fixed in SQL Server 2019).

We also introduced several diagnostic changes in SQL Server 2022, which were also included in the latest cumulative update for SQL Server 2019:

- Capture the sp_server_diagnostics event in case of errors in the Alwayson_health Extended Events session.

- Add error information in the Alwayson_health Extended Events session for scenarios where the worker pool of threads was exhausted for availability groups.

- Add a new Extended Event, hadr_trace_message, to the Alwayson_health Extended Events session for detailed tracing.

- Increase the default size and number of files retained for the Alwayson_health Extended Events session.

- Remove unnecessary ERRORLOG entries for Always On Availability Group activity.

- Add more diagnostics to the Alwayson_health Extended Events session for connection timeout errors.

You can see that the majority of diagnostic improvements are related to the Alwayson_health Extended Events session. You can read more about the Alwayson_health session and its importance for debugging issues at `https://docs.microsoft.com/sql/database-engine/availability-groups/windows/always-on-extended-events#BKMK_alwayson_health`.

Distributed Availability Group (DAG) Enhancements

In SQL Server 2016 we introduced the concept of a Distributed Availability Group (DAG). A DAG effectively is two availability groups connected together, typically over a long distance. A common scenario in which you might use a DAG is for disaster recovery. You configure an availability group (AG) in your primary location. You configure a second AG in a remote location. You then use a DAG to tie them together but with async commit. If you want to learn the fundamentals of DAG, you can start at `https://docs.microsoft.com/sql/database-engine/availability-groups/windows/distributed-availability-groups`.

A DAG also supports sync commit. You should carefully consider this option depending on the connectivity to the secondary AG that is part of the DAG. By default, even a sync replica model for a single AG does not wait for a transaction to be committed on the secondary before allowing a transaction on the primary to continue. It only waits for the log records to be hardened on the secondary. However, in SQL Server 2017 we introduced an option called REQUIRED_SYNCHRONIZED_SECONDARIES_TO_ COMMIT. This option allows you to set a minimum number of synchronous secondary replicas required to commit before the primary commits a transaction. The default is 0. Previously this option was only allowed on an availability group. In SQL Server 2022 you can configure this option for a Distributed Availability Group.

Another subtle, yet important, change for DAG is that we can use multiple TCP connections to improve throughput for latency-sensitive connections. We found out we can improve our own Azure geo-replication with this design, so we have brought it to SQL Server. No additional configuration is required. We internally decide how to use this to improve throughput.

Recovery Enhancements

The time it takes to recover a SQL Server database is usually not something you spend much time thinking about until (a) an event requires recovery and (b) it takes a long time to recovery, thereby causing you to have unexpected downtime.

We have two areas we have enhanced in SQL Server 2022 for recovery-related operations: Accelerated Database Recovery (ADR) and parallel redo operations.

Accelerated Database Recovery (ADR) Enhancements

I believe one of the most important new capabilities for SQL Server 2019 was Accelerated Database Recovery (ADR). No longer will you encounter transaction log size growing out of control, long rollbacks causing downtime, or recovery taking forever (I encourage you to read my article from 2019 on the topic at www.linkedin.com/pulse/sql-server-2019-how-saved-world-from-long-recovery-bob-ward). And if you want to dig deeper, check out the whitepaper at https://aka.ms/sqladr.

ADR has so many benefits, but there is always room for improvement. As such, in SQL Server 2022 we have made a few enhancements that fall under two categories:

- Cleanup enhancements

- These enhancements include more efficient cleanup inside user transactions, more efficient cleanup to reduce page footprint, and multi-threaded version cleanup, including a thread per database. We have a new **sp_configure** option called **"ADR Cleaner Thread Count,"** which allows more cleanup threads per database. This option may be useful for larger databases or those with a high rate of change.

- Versioning enhancements

- These enhancements include reducing the memory footprint to track versions and a reduction in the growth required for the Persisted Version Store (PVS).

You can read all about these improvements in SQL Server 2022 in more detail at https://docs.microsoft.com/sql/relational-databases/accelerated-database-recovery-concepts#adr-improvements-in-.

Parallel Redo Enhancements

In SQL Server 2016, my colleague Bob Dorr and I started our own grassroots campaign called "It just runs faster," calling out enhancements in SQL Server 2016 that were built into the engine and just made your application and queries *run faster*. One of the features was called **parallel redo**. The concept is that for redo operations during recovery, we can safely redo committed transactions in parallel with multiple threads.

To see this in action, I went to the *video vault* and found about a session I did titled **SQL Server 2016 It just runs faster** on a virtual webinar series originally hosted by Brent Ozar called GroupBy. You can find the video at https://youtu.be/pTEDfmQnpzA. You can watch the entire talk, or for parallel redo fast forward to about 22 minutes into the presentation. You can also get the deck and demos I used for that talk at https://aka.ms/bobwardms. Look for the **GroupBy Org Jan 2017** folder.

Note   Fun fact: My camera for this video presentation was at my office at Microsoft in Irving, Texas, way back in 2017. It is definitely an archive, as the building has been redesigned and that office does not exist anymore.

In the presentation I explained how parallel redo can really boost recovery performance. However, we limited the worker pool for parallel threads to 100, so for systems with a large number of databases running recovery, some would not be able to take advantage of parallel redo threads (and you cannot configure which databases can).

In SQL Server 2022, we no longer limit this thread pool, so all databases can take advantage of parallel redo. We have also introduced a concept of *batching* with parallel redo to increase concurrency and speed up all operations. None of these improvements require any change or configuration on your part. It just works.

Backup/Restore Enhancements

We have made several enhancements to backup and restore operations core to the engine including cross-platform snapshots, hardware offloading for compression, and improved backup metadata.

Note   Chapter 7 covers new capabilities to back up and restore to and from S3 object storage providers.

Cross-Platform SNAPSHOT Backup

Let's say you have a very large database to back up. SQL Server by default *streams* the backup by reading the database and log files and copying the data to the backup target. A very long time ago (I had to check my records because this goes back to SQL Server 7.0), we introduced the concept of a Virtual Device Interface (VDI) for backup and restore. The concept is that a developer could write code based on published libraries to accept a backup stream (or send a stream for restore) and process this backup stream in whatever way they wanted to (e.g., send the stream to a special storage device). The T-SQL language was extended to support a VIRTUAL_DEVICE target in addition to what we already supported (DISK, TAPE, PIPE; I know TAPE and PIPE. Crazy!). When a VDI target was used, SQL Server would engage in a protocol with the VDI program to back up or restore a database, log, or file. As part of this protocol, data would be streamed to the VDI program for backup or restore.

With the introduction of VDI came the ability to perform a database *backup snapshot*. If the VDI program was working in coordination with a device that could simply "copy the files," a snapshot backup could be significantly faster than a streaming backup. This required a new syntax for BACKUP (WITH SNAPSHOT) and a new protocol with VDI programs. The key to making a snapshot work is that the SQL Server engine has to *freeze* all I/O for the database so that the database backup snapshot is consistent.

We also introduced on Windows the ability to use the Windows Volume Snapshot Service (VSS) to work in coordination with a program called SQL Writer to perform database backup snapshots, and you can read more at `https://docs.microsoft.com/sql/relational-databases/backup-restore/sql-server-vss-writer-backup-guide`.

In SQL Server 2016 we introduced the ability to store database and log files in Azure Blob Storage, which allowed us to support file-based snapshot backups in Azure Virtual Machines. Read more at `https://docs.microsoft.com/sql/relational-databases/backup-restore/file-snapshot-backups-for-database-files-in-azure`.

With all this context in mind, we wanted a simpler way to allow snapshot backups both in Azure Virtual Machines and across operating systems without requiring a VDI application or Windows VSS. As Ravinder Vuppula, Principal Software Engineer on the Azure Data team, tells it:

> *SQL Server has allowed users to perform snapshot backups for some time. However, it required users to either write a custom VDI client (complex) or use SQLWriter (less flexible) to perform snapshot backups. Starting with SQL Server 2016, users could also perform T-SQL based snapshot backups with FILE_SNAPSHOT feature but it was limited to files stored on Azure Blob Storage. Furthermore, users were limited to performing snapshot backup of one database at a time even when there could be multiple databases placed on the same underlying storage The snapshot backups feature in SQL Server 2022 is designed to remove these restrictions. We were in pursuit of a solution that was easy to use, storage agnostic (as long as the underlying storage allowed snapshots), OS agnostic (wherever SQL Server can run), API agnostic (flexibility to use either VDI client or just T-SQL without any dependency on the API calls to the underlying storage). Of course, we wanted the solution to be reliable (prevent any kind of deadlocks) but also offered the ability to perform snapshot backup of either a single database or multiple databases at the same time.*

How Does It Work?

This new capability uses a combination of T-SQL commands and the underlying storage layer for your database and log files to capture a snapshot of the files.

Here is the basic sequence for how this works:

Tip   Want to test this yourself on a disk system that doesn't have underlying snapshot support? Start SQL Server with the undocumented trace flag 3661. This allows SQL Server to "share" database and log files. It will allow you to use a standard file copy once you have suspended I/O. This trace flag is not documented, not supported, and definitely not recommended for production. But it gives us a nice and easy way to test this new capability.

---

1. A user executes a new T-SQL statement like the following:

   ```
   ALTER DATABASE <db>
   SET SUSPEND_FOR_SNAPSHOT_BACKUP = ON
   ```

   SQL Server will freeze I/O at this point. Note that in my testing, most write operations from user transactions are blocked on log writes, so you will see WRITELOG wait types.

   A new Dynamic Management View, **sys.dm_server_suspend_status**, shows more details on the status of any suspended databases for snapshot backups.

2. You can then use a supported storage provider that supports snapshots (or a system like Azure storage, which supports taking disk snapshots).

Note   You can see a sample PowerShell script that supports the new backup snapshot support on Azure at `https://github.com/microsoft/sql-server-samples/blob/master/samples/features/t-sql-snapshot-backup/snapshot-backup-restore-azurevm-single-db.ps1`.

---

3. To "unfreeze" I/O, a user would execute the following T-SQL
   statement to back up metadata information about the backup:

```
BACKUP DATABASE <db>
TO DISK='<path>\<db>.bkm'
WITH METADATA_ONLY, FORMAT
```

If the snapshot failed, you could also unfreeze the database with
the following T-SQL statement:

```
ALTER DATABASE <db>
SET SUSPEND_FOR_SNAPSHOT_BACKUP = OFF
```

You will use the .bkm file when doing a snapshot restore.

There are some interesting options with this new capability, including the ability to
perform a backup snapshot of databases into groups and even suspend all databases at
the instance level.

Read all about the new T-SQL-based snapshot backups at `https://docs.microsoft.`
`com/sql/relational-databases/backup-restore/create-a-transact-sql-`
`snapshot-backup`.

Intel QuickAssist (QAT) Backup Compression

When any software performs operations like compression or encryption, the instructions
to support these are very CPU intensive. When SQL Server creates a backup with
compression or encryption, the threads that perform the backup run code that chews up
CPU cycles on the main CPU cores.

Our engineering team at Microsoft is always looking for hardware innovations that
can assist in offloading the CPU resources required for operations like these for main
CPU cycles. We call this concept *hardware offloading*.

One of the partners we work closely with is Intel. Most recently, our engineering
team worked with Intel to integrate a technology called **Intel QuickAssist (QAT)** that
can perform hardware offloading for compression and encryption needs. You can read
more about how **Intel QuickAssist** works at `www.intel.com/content/www/us/en/`
`architecture-and-technology/intel-quick-assist-technology-overview.html`. You
can see from their documentation that in some cases the technology is built into the main
CPU structure and in other cases you can install a separate hardware card (in addition,
this technology has what is called *software mode*, which does use core CPU cycles).

To perform this integration for backup and restore (decompress/unencrypt), we needed to do the following:

- Build an infrastructure to load *accelerators* for hardware offloading.

- Determine how to make the right API calls to use **Intel QuickAssist** technologies (aka drivers) and load this into SQL Server.

- Add configuration options to allow hardware offloading and specific accelerators.

- Enhance the BACKUP and RESTORE syntax to support COMPRESSION options for a new algorithm called **QAT**.

While we have both observed in some cases better backup throughput and better compression using **QAT**, the big key to this technology is offloading CPU resources from SQL Server so queries and workloads can maximize available CPU resources.

QAT does come with a *software mode*, in which the drivers are used but hardware is not. This will *not* help reduce CPU resources since it is all built into the software, but it can be more effective than the default compression used today by SQL Server. By default, SQL Server uses the XPRESS compression library and algorithms. You can read more about XPRESS compression at `https://docs.microsoft.com/windows/win32/cmpapi/-compression-portal`.

I've included a T-SQL notebook created by David Pless that shows you all the different syntax options and configurations for QAT and hardware offloading in the samples at **ch06_meatandpotatoes\availability\ Intel_QuickAssistTech_SQLServer2022.ipynb**. You can view this notebook with Azure Data Studio or a web browser.

You can read performance information using QAT for backups that Intel observed at `https://community.intel.com/t5/Blogs/Tech-Innovation/Data-Center/Accelerate-your-SQL-Server-2022-database-backups-using-Intel/post/1335102`.

David did share some interesting observations with me:

- If your system is idle (no CPU load from SQL workloads), you usually won't get a huge benefit of **QAT** in hardware mode. This all depends on the available compute and memory of your device as compared with the server on which SQL Server is running.

- You get the most out of **QAT** in hardware mode when you back up to multiple files (because we will use different threads all doing compression) and you have a fairly CPU-intensive workload. Additionally, the file count increases the buffercount, which can have a significant impact on backup performance.

- **QAT** in software mode will usually outperform the default XPRESS compression in various combinations.

Tip   From David Pless: If you install the drivers and no **QAT** hardware is detected, you are allowed to install in software mode. The latest **QAT** drivers can be found at `www.intel.com/content/www/us/en/developer/topic-technology/ open/quick-assist-technology/overview.html`.

Backup Metadata

Have you ever found yourself wondering when you can perform the most recent point-in-time restore (PITR) of a database? We now have a nice addition to the **msdb. backupset** table, the column named **last_valid_restore_time**. With this column you can determine exactly the last valid time to which you can perform a PITR. You can find this column now documented for the **msdb.backupset** table at `https://docs.microsoft. com/sql/relational-databases/system-tables/backupset-transact-sql`.

Multi-write Replication

One interesting enhancement for SQL Server replication is multi-write replication with Last Writer Wins (LWW). This enhancement is specifically targeted for peer-to-peer replication. Peer-to-peer replication allows for multiple writers and readers against the same set of data across SQL instances (read all the details of peer-to-peer replication at `https://docs.microsoft.com/sql/relational-databases/replication/ transactional/peer-to-peer-transactional-replication`.) Any type of system like this needs *conflict resolution*. If two users update the same row at the same time, who wins? Prior to these enhancements, conflict resolution effectively paused the entire system, and a manual intervention was required that was not logical (based on node ID). With this enhancement, conflict detection is automatic, and the last user to make the change (based on a synchronized timestamp) wins the conflict.

As we designed project Dallas, we decided that this feature should also be included in an update to SQL Server 2019, so this is not technically new to SQL Server 2022. Check out more details in this blog post by Kevin Farlee at `https://techcommunity.microsoft.com/t5/sql-server-blog/replication-enhancements-in-the-sql-server-2019-cu13-release/ba-p/2814727`.

Other Engine "Stuff"

We have other engine enhancements that target specific customer challenges with solutions based on our experiences over the years or directly from user feedback. It's possible that one of the improvements listed in the following is one you have been looking to see in SQL Server.

XML Compression

XML native data types are popular among some developers, but XML data can get quite large. Features like SQL Server row compression don't affect XML data types, and XML indexes cannot be compressed. Now in SQL Server 2022, we have introduced the ability to compress an XML column, which can greatly reduce the size of your data that uses XML data types. We enhanced the CREATE TABLE statement to support an XML_COMPRESSION keyword. You can read more at `https://docs.microsoft.com/sql/t-sql/statements/create-table-transact-sql`.

The same concept exists to compress an index that contains an XML column, which you can read about at `https://docs.microsoft.com/sql/t-sql/statements/create-index-transact-sql`.

We also support XML_COMPRESSION for both ALTER TABLE and ALTER INDEX statements.

In-Memory OLTP Memory Management

We built enhancements in SQL Server 2022 to improve our memory management for In-Memory OLTP operations. Most of these are specific improvements to avoid out-of-memory (OOM) scenarios and don't require any action from you; they are just built into the engine.

We also introduced a new system procedure in SQL Server 2019, which is also available in SQL Server 2022, called **sys.sp_xtp_force_gc**. This procedure takes as input a database name to release unused memory on demand, without memory pressure, for memory-optimized table data.

Auto-drop Statistics

Here is an interesting enhancement to help with a long-standing problem. Let's say SQL Server auto-creates statistics on a column based on a query or a third-party software program creates statistics on a column. If you try to then drop the column these statistics are based on (or make other schema changes that affect the column), you may encounter an error like this:

```
Msg 5074, Level 16, State 1, Line 20
The statistics '<stats name> is dependent on column '<column name>'.
```

You then need to go and drop the statistics first. Now you can create statistics using the WITH AUTO_DROP = ON option. In the preceding scenario, the statistics would be automatically dropped and not block the schema change. Auto-created statistics are not enabled with auto-drop by default.

Resumable Add Table Constraints

In SQL Server 2017 and 2019 we added the ability to create and rebuild indexes with a *resumable* option. This means if an error occurs during the build of an index (or you pause it), we can resume "where we left off" vs. having to start over.

This is quite a nice feature for index builds that take a very long time. You can read more about resumable indexes at https://docs.microsoft.com/sql/relational-databases/indexes/guidelines-for-online-index-operations?#resumable-index-considerations.

We realize though that many indexes are added as constraints, so we have enhanced the syntax for ALTER TABLE ADD CONSTRAINT to support resumable operations. You can read the exact syntax at `https://docs.microsoft.com/sql/relational-databases/security/resumable-add-table-constraints`.

New Wait Types

With each new release of SQL Server, we add new wait types as part of building new features. I found around ~300 new wait types in SQL Server 2022 vs. SQL Server 2019.

One observation I had when reviewing these new types is that there are new PREEMPTIVE_* wait types for SQL Server 2022. Wait types with this name indicate places in our code where a worker is switched to "preemptive" mode and no longer part of SQLOS scheduling. This is because we are typically calling an API or running code where we can't control thread scheduling. Two new wait types that indicate preemptive scheduling are PREEMPTIVE_SYNAPSESTREAMING_HTTP_EVENT_WAIT and PREEMPTIVE_AAD_HTTP_EVENT_WAIT, which can show up when using Synapse Link or Azure Active Directory (AAD) authentication.

New Extended Events

Almost every new feature has a set of new Extended Events, and you have already seen some related to IQP features in Chapters 4 and 5 as well as several in this chapter.

My incredible colleague and longtime friend Robert Dorr told me about one interesting new event, not related to a feature but one he added to help with query performance troubleshooting and debugging. The name of the event is **query_abort** (it is a debug channel event). This event includes the session, the input buffer, and even a callstack and fires whenever a query is aborted for any reason. If you are seeing queries that are canceled, aborted, or timed out and are not sure why, this new event can probably help.

An Industry-Proven Engine

The #sqllegend David Campbell once told me, *"Bob, if we don't innovate in the engine, we don't have a product."* I think you can see from this chapter that we have provided plenty of innovation into security, scalability, and availability. Think about what you have seen in this chapter: Ledger for SQL Server, "hands-free" tempdb, and Contained Availability Groups just to name a few.

My colleague David Pless spent maybe more than anyone on our team across the new SQL Server 2022 engine features. I asked him for his perspective:

I have been thinking about the theme around what we have accomplished in this release, especially thinking back over the previous releases. In SQL Server 2016, it was "It's just faster" and we said in SQL Server 2017 it was "all about choice." In this release it is a "return to performance," but more than that – what we have done is made a firm commitment to scalability. The commitment for scalability is more than a single feature, but several features that give SQL Server 2022 the ability to take the most advantage of our largest systems for our most critical workloads. We did it with buffer pool parallel scan by allowing customers to be able to scale up to the largest memory servers available and get the full performance they would expect for SQL Server. We did it with concurrent GAM and SGAM updates improving tempdb performance at a factor that we are even questioning whether we still need the tempdb best practices that have stood true for nearly a quarter of a century. And both of these major improvements are on by default – you just have to get your data on SQL Server 2022 and let the scalable SQL Server engine do the rest. And there is so much more. Accelerated Database Recovery improvements recovers our databases faster than ever. Additionally, our partnership with Intel introduces a brand-new feature to help SQL Server not only improve backup capacity and throughput – but with Intel QuickAssist Technology hardware we can protect the CPU of the host machine by offloading the compute overhead of the backup process away from the host SQL Server system. I am proud of this team; I am proud of what we have accomplished with this release.

CHAPTER 7

Data Virtualization and Object Storage

As far back as SQL Server 7.0, we provided a way to query data *outside* of SQL Server, even for data sources that were not SQL Server. We called this capability linked servers. We used OLE-DB as a mechanism to allow the query processor to push a query to another data source and bring the results back into SQL Server. There were even OLE-DB drivers to query "file" data such as Excel spreadsheet files. In a way, the concept of a linked server query is *data virtualization*. Data virtualization means accessing data "where it lives" vs. copying data into SQL Server. Linked server queries were baked into normal SQL statements like SELECT but also through a new T-SQL function called **OPENROWSET()**. You will see later in this chapter that OPENROWSET() is still alive and well.

In SQL Server 2016, we introduced a concept that was first implemented with Parallel Data Warehouse called **Polybase**. Polybase was brought to Parallel Data Warehouse by David Dewitt and the Microsoft research team. The concept was to use the T-SQL language to execute queries against a Hadoop file system, all from the database engine. In SQL Server 2016, we implemented the Polybase concept with Hadoop calling it Polybase services. Polybase services included separate Windows services that were integrated with the SQL Server engine. Polybase services would take T-SQL requests from the engine and translate them into Hadoop MapReduce jobs using Java. Users accessed files from Hadoop systems through T-SQL statements like CREATE EXTERNAL TABLE and OPENROWSET(). This feature has been removed in SQL Server 2022.

In SQL Server 2019, we expanded the concept of data virtualization and Polybase by adding the ability to use ODBC data sources for accessing data through external tables and OPENROWSET(). We even included built-in *connectors* with drivers like Oracle, MongoDB, Teradata, and SQL Server and *generic* ODBC drivers (in other words, any ODBC driver). SQL Server had truly become a **data hub**. You could use the power of

317

© Bob Ward 2022
B. Ward, *SQL Server 2022 Revealed*, https://doi.org/10.1007/978-1-4842-8894-8_7

T-SQL and query to just about any data source, without using ETL or copying the data. This functionality continues to exist in SQL Server 2022.

Both of these capabilities were transforming. We realized customers didn't always have their data in SQL Server and didn't want to have to build expensive ETL applications to copy data, often out of date. However, the Polybase design using services outside the engine had its downsides. We started to look for another method to continue the vision of data virtualization but implemented in a different way. We also recognized a trend in the industry for data storage. The trend was the expansion of companies offering object storage using the Simple Storage Service **(S3)** protocol.

Data Virtualization in SQL Server 2022

Back in the early days of project Dallas, I had a meeting with James Rowland-Jones (we all called him JRJ) about what he was working on. He brought up the name *project Gravity*. Project Gravity was effectively *Polybase v3,* as JRJ called it. Version 1 was our original support for Hadoop using Java. Version 2 was the inclusion of ODBC drivers in SQL Server 2019. JRJ told me project Gravity, version 3, would use REST APIs to access data. One of the biggest targets for this project was object storage providers using S3.

REST, Azure Storage, and S3

Representational state transfer (REST) is an interface for software components to communicate, typically over a remote or Internet connection. REST has been around a long time and uses typical HTTP methods to send and receive data between software components. I think Wikipedia has a good description of REST at `https://en.wikipedia.org/wiki/Representational_state_transfer`, but also there is a good summary in Azure documentation at `https://docs.microsoft.com/rest/api/azure/devops/?view=azure-devops-rest-7.1`. In the Azure docs I really like this description of REST: "Representational State Transfer (REST) APIs are service endpoints that support sets of HTTP operations (methods), which provide create, retrieve, update, or delete access to the service's resources."

REST has many benefits. It is lightweight and uniform, uses HTTP(S), and is portable. It pretty much works across all operating systems, platforms, and clouds. I don't always find it intuitive, but once you get used to the use of HTTP *verbs*, it becomes more natural.

One of the benefits of REST is that systems like Azure storage (including Azure Data Lake) and Amazon Simple Storage Service (S3) can be accessed via a known set of REST commands. Instead of requiring an ODBC driver, any client that can submit HTTP(S) to these providers can send and receive data.

Given that we already know in the engine how to send HTTP(S) requests (that is how we back up to URL), we decided to implement the next set of Polybase innovation using REST inside the engine, instead of through Polybase services.

I will admit while Azure Blob Storage and Azure Data Lake Storage support REST, a big motivator to innovate with REST was S3. Simple Storage Service (S3) from Amazon originates as far back as 2006 (`https://en.wikipedia.org/wiki/Amazon_S3`). One of the things that Amazon did was "open up" the protocol to access S3 *object storage*. S3 is called object storage because objects are files and metadata that describes the files. Objects are collected in *buckets* or containers for files. The core concepts of how object storage, files, and buckets work can be found at `https://docs.aws.amazon.com/AmazonS3/latest/userguide/Welcome.html#CoreConcepts`. Amazon S3 object storage is accessed using a specific set of REST API as documented at `https://docs.aws.amazon.com/AmazonS3/latest/userguide/RESTAPI.html`. Since Amazon launched S3, several companies have come forward to offer *S3-compatible object storage services*. Provided you follow the S3 REST API protocol, you can set up an object storage endpoint and allow clients to use it. We have seen a proliferation in providers offering S3 object storage. Therefore, we decided to add to our REST API story for Polybase by implementing the ability to query files from S3 object endpoints.

Project Gravity Becomes Polybase v3

With this context in mind, SQL Server 2022 changes the Polybase model entirely. The SQL engine now includes the ability to leverage external data source *connectors* for the following storage providers:

- Azure Blob Storage (**abs**)

- Azure Data Lake Storage Gen2 (**adls**)

- S3 compatible object storage (**s3**)

Note   Azure SQL Managed Instance also supports **abs** and **adls**.

The monikers for each of these connectors are used as part of the syntax for LOCATION when creating an external data source. ODBC driver–based connectors use monikers like **oracle**, **teradata**, **mongodb**, **sqlserver**, and **odbc**.

ODBC driver–based connectors run in the context of Polybase services. REST API connectors run inside the SQL Server engine.

Note   Even though REST API connectors run inside the engine and don't technically require Polybase services, in SQL Server 2022, you still must enable the Polybase feature, which installs these services.

Hugo Queiroz, Senior Program Manager at Microsoft over Polybase, helped me build the following visual to show the connector architecture as seen in Figure 7-1.

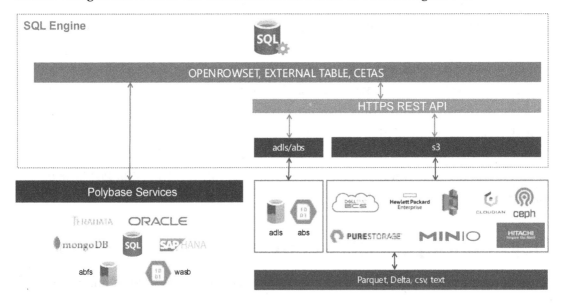

Figure 7-1. *Data virtualization in SQL Server 2022*

In this figure, T-SQL operations like OPENROWSET and CREATE EXTERNAL TABLE are used to access external data sources from connectors. On the left-hand side of this figure, ODBC connectors are accessed by the engine connecting with Polybase services (which are actual Windows services). On the right-hand side of the figure, the SQL Server engine communicates with **abs**, **adls**, and **s3** connectors through REST APIs to access files that are **text/csv** (you provide the format) or **parquet/delta** (the format is baked into the file). I'll describe more about the types of file formats like parquet and delta in the next section of this chapter.

You might be wondering what is the difference between using abs and adls. Azure Blob Storage (abs) is a general-purpose storage system where Azure Data Lake Storage (adls) is specifically built for data analytic workloads. You can read further a detailed comparison at `https://docs.microsoft.com/azure/data-lake-store/data-lake-store-comparison-with-blob-storage`. Both Azure Blob Storage and Azure Data Lake Storage are considered object storage systems like S3.

I've already mentioned the T-SQL statements OPENROWSET and CREATE EXTERNAL TABLE. CETAS stands for CREATE EXTERNAL TABLE AS SELECT. The concept comes from Polybase via Azure Synapse and allows you to create an external table as the result of a SELECT statement in SQL Server. While OPENROWSET and EXTERNAL TABLE are "read" operations, CETAS allows you to "export" data from SQL Server into files and record the metadata of an external table.

Polybase v3 File Formats

You probably know what a CSV (comma-delimited) or text (any format you want) file format is, but you may not be familiar with parquet or delta. Let's review these file formats and discuss why they have become popular to use.

Parquet

Parquet files are a formatted file founded by an Apache project that was started in 2013. The Apache project website at `https://parquet.apache.org` has a simple definition: "Apache Parquet is an open source, column-oriented data file format designed for efficient data storage and retrieval." Column-oriented makes parquet an efficient format for analytic workloads, like columnstore indexes in SQL Server. Parquet is a binary formatted file as opposed to CSV or text. It contains metadata inside the file about the columns and data types. Even though parquet uses a binary format, there is documentation on the details, so developers know how to read and write the format. You can read the format details at `https://parquet.apache.org/docs/file-format/`.

Parquet has become one of the most popular file formats to use for analytics from ground to cloud. Its popularity is one of the reasons we chose to support parquet as a native format for data virtualization in SQL Server 2022. SQL Server 2022 natively supports reading parquet files and writing out SQL data as formatted parquet files.

Delta

Parquet files are static files to read and write as an entire file unit. An open source project was created by several companies called **Delta Lake** to support a *lakehouse* of data based on **delta tables**. Delta tables are effectively a collection of parquet formatted files with *transaction log type* capabilities through JSON files. I found this interesting article by Databricks on the internals of the "transaction log" for delta at `https://databricks.com/blog/2019/08/21/diving-into-delta-lake-unpacking-the-transaction-log.html`.

You can read about the Delta Lake project and all resources at `https://delta.io`. Since Delta Lake is a complete open source project (the GitHub project is at `https://github.com/delta-io/delta`), you can read all the details of how delta tables are formatted, but most users create and use delta tables through interfaces such as Spark. For example, you can see at `https://docs.delta.io/latest/delta-batch.html#-ddlcreatetable` how to use T-SQL with Spark to create a new delta table.

SQL Server 2022 supports natively reading delta tables, but you cannot export data in SQL Server to delta tables. You can export SQL data to parquet files. Spark offers functionality to convert parquet to delta should you need to do that.

Using parquet files offers no capabilities to use predicate pushdown or push your "filter" to a file to get only the data you need. Delta tables do offer this type of capability through a concept called a *partition column*. You will see in this chapter examples of how to use both parquet and delta with SQL Server 2022.

Using the New Polybase v3

To use Polybase v3 or REST API–based data virtualization, you will use a series of T-SQL statements to create objects as seen in Figure 7-2.

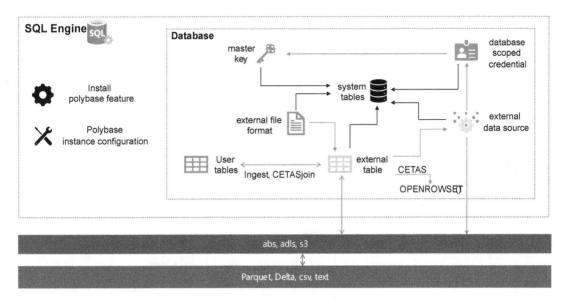

Figure 7-2. *Using REST API data virtualization in SQL Server 2022*

Let's go through this figure to see how to use REST API data virtualization in SQL Server 2022. You will see an example of each of these steps in the section titled "**Try Out Polybase v3.**"

Install and Configure Polybase

Even though REST APIs do not use Polybase services in SQL Server 2022, you must install the Polybase Query Service for External Data feature (or add the feature). You must also enable Polybase setting the **sp_configure** 'polybase enabled' option to 1. If you plan to use CETAS, you will also need to set 'allow polybase export' to 1.

Set Up Credentials and Data Sources

The next step, within the *context of a user database,* is to create a database-scoped credential using the CREATE DATABASE SCOPED CREDENTIAL statement and external data source using the CREATE EXTERNAL DATA SOURCE statement (which requires the credential). You will need to do this for each connector you plan to use. You must first create a master key before you can create a database-scoped credential using the CREATE MASTER KEY statement, but you only need to do this once no matter how many credentials and data sources you want to create in the database. These objects are stored as metadata in system tables in the user database.

Query Files Directly with OPENROWSET( )

With an external data source created, you can directly query files using the OPENROWSET() T-SQL function with the BULK option. File formats such as PARQUET and DELTA don't require any options for column names or types; CSV and text files will require this.

Create an External Table

You can also create an external table using the CREATE EXTERNAL TABLE statement. The external table requires an external data source and can be mapped directly to files for connectors using LOCATION. You must first create a file format, using the CREATE EXTERNAL FILE FORMAT statement, for use with the external table. The file format can be for a "known" format like **ParquetFileFormat** or for a CSV file, which will require you to provide more details. The external table can provide all the column names from the source file or a subset. No data is stored for an external table, only metadata in system tables, which is the same for file formats.

You can also use the CREATE EXTERNAL TABLE AS SELECT (CETAS) syntax to create an external table and store the results from a user table in the LOCATION target. It is a method to "export" data to REST API connectors. You can even use CETAS with the source of a query to OPENROWSET().

Once you create an external table, you can query the external table like any other SQL table (and even assign permissions to it). You can join with other user tables or other external tables and execute OPENROWSET() queries. You can use standard T-SQL like INSERT..SELECT or SELECT INTO to take data from external tables and populate user tables (i.e., ingestion).

Try Out Polybase v3

Let's go through some examples to see REST API–based data virtualization using an S3 object provider.

Note   If you do not want to install non-Microsoft software required for this exercise, you can review the results of the exercise in the SQL notebook files **queryparquet.ipynb** and **querydelta.ipynb**, which can be found with the sample files and scripts in the **ch07_datavirt_objectstorage\datavirt\parquet** and

ch07_datavirt_objectstorage\datavirt\delta folders. You will need to install Azure Data Studio to use these notebooks, or you can view the notebooks in the GitHub repo with a browser.

Prerequisites

To go through this exercise, you will need the following prerequisites:

- SQL Server 2022 Evaluation Edition with the database engine and the Polybase Query Service for External Data feature installed.

Note   For Linux, install the Polybase packages at `https://docs.microsoft.com/sql/relational-databases/polybase/polybase-linux-setup`.

- Virtual machine or computer with minimum of two CPUs with 8Gb RAM.

- SQL Server Management Studio (SSMS). The latest 18.x or 19.x build will work.

- The latest build of Azure Data Studio (ADS). **This is optional**. I have included a SQL notebook with the results of this exercise, so if you do not want to install non-MSFT software, you can review the results with ADS.

Note   The following prerequisites are for non-Microsoft software. The use of this software does not represent any official endorsement from Microsoft. This software is not supported by Microsoft, so any issues using this software are up to the user to resolve.

- The **minio** server for Windows, which you can download at `https://min.io/download#/windows`. For the demo I assume you have created a directory called **c:\minio** and have downloaded the minio. exe for Windows into that directory.

- **openssl** for Windows, which you can download at `https://slproweb.com/products/Win32OpenSSL.html`. I chose the Win64 OpenSSL v3.0.5 MSI option. Set the system environment variable OPENSSL_CONF=C:\Program Files\OpenSSL-Win64\bin\openssl.cfg and put c:\Program Files\OpenSSL-Win64\bin in the system path.

Note   This exercise can also work with Linux and containers. You will need to use the minio server for Linux. openssl comes with Linux or is available by installing an optional package. Check your Linux documentation.

- A copy of the scripts and files from the GitHub repo of this book, from the **ch07_datavirt_objectstorage\datavirt\parquet** directory.

Set Up minio for the Exercise

To use minio.exe with SQL Server, TLS is required. In order to use TLS, you must have a valid certificate. For testing purposes, we will generate a self-signed certificate.

Follow these steps to set up minio for the exercise:

1. Generate a private key by running the following command from the c:\minio directory at the command prompt:

   ```
   openssl genrsa -out private.key 2048
   ```

2. Copy the supplied **openssl.conf** file to c:\minio. Edit this file by changing the **IP.2** to your local IP address and **DNS.2** to your local computer name.

3. Generate a self-signed certificate by running the following command from the c:\minio directory at the command prompt:

   ```
   openssl req -new -x509 -nodes -days 730 -key private.key -out
   public.crt -config openssl.conf
   ```

4. For Windows users, double-click the public.crt file and select Install Certificate. Choose Local Machine and then Place all certificates in the following store. Browse and select Trusted Root Certification Authorities.

Note   Self-signed certificates are great for testing but *not* secure. I recommend you delete the certificate via Manage User Certificates in Control Panel when you are finished with this exercise.

5. Copy the files **private.key** and **public.crt** from the c:\minio directory into the %%USERPROFILE%%\mino\certs directory.

6. From a command prompt, navigate to the c:\minio directory. Then start the minio program by running the following command (cmd.exe users don't need the .\):

    ```
    .\minio.exe server c:\minio --console-address ":9001"
    ```

    This program starts and runs until you quit with Ctrl+C. Your output in the command prompt should look something like this:

```
MinIO Object Storage Server
Copyright: 2015-2022 MinIO, Inc.
License: GNU AGPLv3 <https://www.gnu.org/licenses/agpl-3.0.html>
Version: RELEASE.2022-07-30T05-21-40Z (go1.18.4 windows/amd64)
Status:          1 Online, 0 Offline.
API: https://<local IP>:9000  https://127.0.0.1:9000
RootUser: <user>
RootPass: <password>
Console: https://<local IP>:9001 https://127.0.0.1:9001
RootUser: <user>
RootPass: <password>
Command-line: https://docs.min.io/docs/minio-client-
quickstart-guide
    $ mc.exe alias set myminio https://<local IP>:9000 <user>
    <password>
Documentation: https://docs.min.io
```

7. Test your connection to minio by using a web browser on the local computer for `https://127.0.0.1:9001`. You should be presented with a login screen like Figure 7-3. Use the RootUser and RootPass from the preceding minio server output.

Figure 7-3. *The minio console login screen*

8. On the left-hand side menu, click Identity and Users. Select Create User. Create a user and password. Select the readwrite policy for the user. Note down this user and password. This is the user and password that you will use for the **SECRET** value in the **creates3creds.sql** script later in this exercise.

9. Select the menu option for Buckets. Select Create Bucket. Use a bucket name of *wwi*. Leave all the defaults and click Create Bucket. Your screen should now look like Figure 7-4.

Figure 7-4. *A new bucket in S3 storage*

Learn to Use REST API to Access Parquet Files on S3

With an S3 provider ready to use, we can now access S3 compatible storage with SQL Server. Follow these steps for the exercise for basics of REST API data virtualization to access parquet files on an S3 object provider. The next section has an exercise to access delta files.

1. Copy the **WideWorldImporters** sample database from https://
    aka.ms/WideWorldImporters to a local directory (the restore
    script assumes c:\sql_sample_databases).

2. Edit the **restorewwi.sql** script to specify the correct path for the
    backup and where data and log files should go.

3. Execute the script **restorewwi.sql.** This script executes the
    following T-SQL statements:

```
USE master;
GO
DROP DATABASE IF EXISTS WideWorldImporters;
GO
RESTORE DATABASE WideWorldImporters FROM DISK = 'c:\sql_sample_
databases\WideWorldImporters-Full.bak' with
MOVE 'WWI_Primary' TO 'c:\sql_sample_databases\
WideWorldImporters.mdf',
```

```
MOVE 'WWI_UserData' TO 'c:\sql_sample_databases\
WideWorldImporters_UserData.ndf',
MOVE 'WWI_Log' TO 'c:\sql_sample_databases\WideWorldImporters.ldf',
MOVE 'WWI_InMemory_Data_1' TO 'c:\sql_sample_databases\
WideWorldImporters_InMemory_Data_1',
stats=5;
GO
ALTER DATABASE WideWorldImporters SET QUERY_STORE CLEAR ALL;
GO
```

4. Execute the script **enablepolybase.sql** to configure instance-level settings to allow Polybase features to execute and export data from Polybase to S3. This script executes the following T-SQL statements:

```
EXEC sp_configure 'polybase enabled', 1;
GO
RECONFIGURE;
GO
EXEC sp_configure 'allow polybase export', 1;
GO
RECONFIGURE;
GO
```

5. Edit the script **createmasterkey.sql** to put in a password. Execute the script to create a master key to protect the database-scoped credential. This script executes the following T-SQL statements:

```
USE [WideWorldImporters]
GO
IF NOT EXISTS (SELECT * FROM sys.symmetric_keys WHERE name =
''##MS_DatabaseMasterKey##'')
      CREATE MASTER KEY ENCRYPTION BY PASSWORD = '<password>';
GO
```

6. Edit the script **creates3creds.sql** to put in the user and password
   you created in the minio console for SECRET. Execute the script
   to create a database-scoped credential. This script executes the
   following T-SQL statements:

```
IF EXISTS (SELECT * FROM sys.database_scoped_credentials WHERE
name = 's3_wwi_cred')
    DROP DATABASE SCOPED CREDENTIAL s3_wwi_cred;
GO
CREATE DATABASE SCOPED CREDENTIAL s3_wwi_cred
WITH IDENTITY = 'S3 Access Key',
SECRET = '<user>:<password>';
GO
```

7. Edit the script **creates3datasource.sql** to substitute in your local
   IP address for the minio server. Execute the script to create an
   external data source. This script executes the following T-SQL
   statements:

```
IF EXISTS (SELECT * FROM sys.external_data_sources WHERE
name = 's3_wwi')
      DROP EXTERNAL DATA SOURCE s3_wwi;
GO
CREATE EXTERNAL DATA SOURCE s3_wwi
WITH
(
 LOCATION = 's3://<your local IP>:9000'
,CREDENTIAL = s3_wwi_cred
);
GO
```

Tip   You could put in the bucket name here after the port number so that the data
source is focused only on a specific bucket. We will instead use the bucket when
specifying location for queries.

8. Create a file format for parquet by executing the script **createparquetfileformat.sql**. This script executes the following T-SQL statements:

```
USE [WideWorldImporters];
GO
IF EXISTS (SELECT * FROM sys.external_file_formats WHERE
name = 'ParquetFileFormat')
    DROP EXTERNAL FILE FORMAT ParquetFileFormat;
CREATE EXTERNAL FILE FORMAT ParquetFileFormat WITH(FORMAT_TYPE =
PARQUET);
GO
```

9. Let's first learn how to export data in parquet format to the wwi bucket by executing the script **wwi_cetas.sql**. In SSMS, select the Include Actual Execution Plan option. This script executes the following T-SQL statements:

```
USE [WideWorldImporters];
GO
IF OBJECT_ID('wwi_customer_transactions', 'U') IS NOT NULL
    DROP EXTERNAL TABLE wwi_customer_transactions;
GO
CREATE EXTERNAL TABLE wwi_customer_transactions
WITH (
    LOCATION = '/wwi/',
    DATA_SOURCE = s3_wwi,
    FILE_FORMAT = ParquetFileFormat
)
AS
SELECT * FROM Sales.CustomerTransactions;
GO
```

Let's examine this script. The LOCATION is the bucket name. The LOCATION value can be a bucket name or even a series of folders and even a specific filename. In this case, because the external data source didn't specify a specific bucket, I need to specify that here. Since I only specified the bucket, the query will place all files in the parent folder. There is no predicate pushdown with parquet files and REST API connectors. Any filtering is done inside SQL Server (even if you specify a WHERE clause).

The DATA_SOURCE is the external data source we created to connect to the minio server. The file format matches up to parquet. Notice we do not have to specify anything about the format other than just parquet. We can also include column names with this definition, but we don't need to. Using the AS SELECT part of the statement will create a single parquet file with column names, types, and data.

In the Messages tab, you should see 97147 rows affected. In the Execution Plan tab you should see a plan like Figure 7-5.

Figure 7-5. *Query execution plan for CETAS*

Notice the **Put** operator, which is used to export data to the s3 connector as a parquet file.

Tip   One observation I have had using CETAS is there is no "duplicate" detection. If you run the preceding command twice, two parquet files will be created.

---

10. Use the minio console to browse the wwi bucket and confirm the parquet file has been added. Your results should look like Figure 7-6.

Figure 7-6. *Parquet file added to S3 bucket through CETAS*

11. Query the new external table by executing the script
     querywwiexternaldata.sql. This script executes the following
     T-SQL statements:

```
USE [WideWorldImporters];
GO
SELECT c.CustomerName, SUM(wct.OutstandingBalance) as
total_balance
FROM wwi_customer_transactions wct
JOIN Sales.Customers c
ON wct.CustomerID = c.CustomerID
GROUP BY c.CustomerName
ORDER BY total_balance DESC;
GO
```

Notice in this example the script joins the external table (stored in
parquet in S3) with a local table in the user database. Your results
should display 263 rows. One common use case for an example
like this is to build a VIEW on top of this query and only give users
access to the view. They will be *abstracted* from the source of the
data, whether it be in SQL Server or a parquet file.

12. Use SSMS with Object Explorer to see the column definitions for
     the table created through CETAS. Your results should look like
     Figure 7-7.

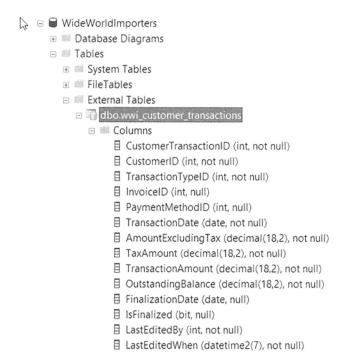

Figure 7-7. *Columns created automatically with parquet through CETAS*

Notice the column names and types match the original table in the database; this demonstrates the power of parquet including metadata.

13. Let's use OPENROWSET() to run an "ad hoc" query from the generated parquet file stored in S3 by executing the script **querybyopenrowset.sql**. In SSMS, select the Include Actual Execution Plan option. This script executes the following T-SQL statements:

```
USE [WideWorldImporters];
GO
SELECT *
FROM OPENROWSET
     (BULK '/wwi/'
     , FORMAT = 'PARQUET'
     , DATA_SOURCE = 's3_wwi')
as [wwi_customer_transactions_file];
GO
```

It turns out the BULK option is not just about the BULK insert of data; it can also be used to "open a rowset" on a file.

In the Messages tab you should see 97147 rows affected, which is the same number of rows in the original table, Sales. CustomerTransactions. If you look at the Execution Plan tab, you should see a query execution plan like Figure 7-8.

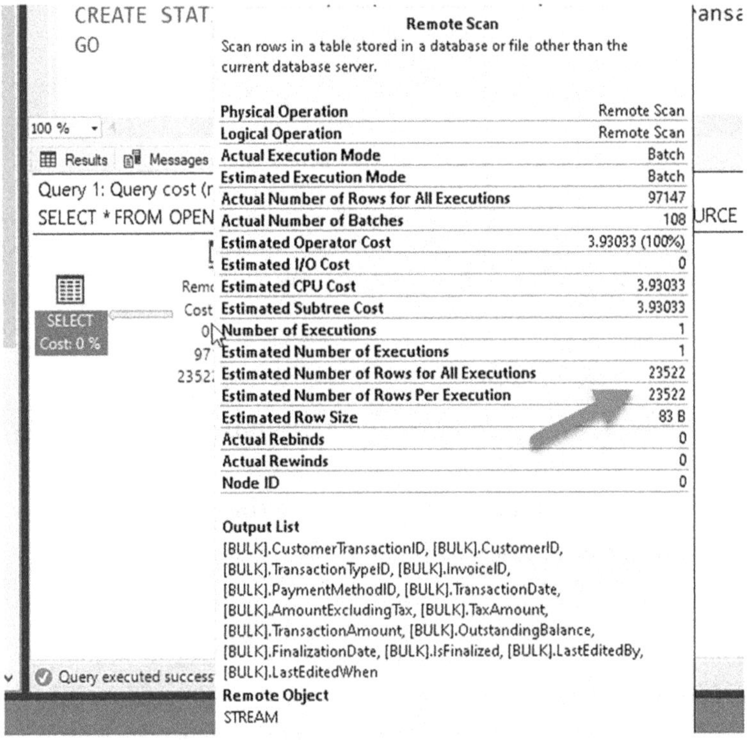

Figure 7-8. *Query execution plan for OPENROWSET()*

Notice that the estimated number of rows is roughly 30% of the total actual rows. This is because the optimizer doesn't have any statistics from the parquet file itself. This is opposite from **wwi_customer_transactions**, which was created as an external table. You can manually create statistics on an external table, or if you have the database option AUTO_CREATE_STATISTICS set to ON (the default), statistics will be automatically created when you query the external table. The estimates will be accurate if these statistics are available. OPENROWSET() query performance may or may not be adversely affected without statistics.

As I've mentioned earlier in the chapter, there is no predicate pushdown for parquet files. If you add a WHERE clause to the preceding SQL statement

```
USE [WideWorldImporters];
GO
SELECT *
FROM OPENROWSET
     (BULK '/wwi/'
     , FORMAT = 'PARQUET'
     , DATA_SOURCE = 's3_wwi')
as [wwi_customer_transactions_file]
WHERE wwi_customer_transactions_file.CustomerTransactionID = 2;
```

the query processor in the engine must bring the results of the parquet file(s) in this bucket parent folder and then filter within the engine to produce the final result.

You can help reduce the amount of data that SQL Server has to read and filter by partitioning your parquet files with a folder structure within the bucket and then specify only the folder you need with the BULK syntax or LOCATION for external tables.

14. Another nice feature for external tables is the ability to create one based on a subset of columns in the parquet file. Execute the script **querybyexternaltable.sql** to see an example of this. This script executes the following T-SQL statements:

```
IF OBJECT_ID('wwi_customer_transactions_base', 'U') IS NOT NULL
     DROP EXTERNAL TABLE wwi_customer_transactions_base;
GO
CREATE EXTERNAL TABLE wwi_customer_transactions_base
(
     CustomerTransactionID int,
     CustomerID int,
     TransactionTypeID int,
     TransactionDate date,
     TransactionAmount decimal(18,2)
)
```

```
WITH
(
        LOCATION = '/wwi/'
    , FILE_FORMAT = ParquetFileFormat
    , DATA_SOURCE = s3_wwi
);
GO
SELECT * FROM wwi_customer_transactions_base;
GO
```

You will see the same number of rows from the wwi_customer_transactions external table, but only with the columns you specified. The columns don't have to be in any specific order.

15. As I mentioned earlier, you can manually create statistics on any number of columns in an external table. Execute the script **creatstats.sql** for an example. This script executes the following T-SQL statements:

```
USE WideWorldImporters;
GO
CREATE STATISTICS wwi_ctb_stats ON wwi_customer_
transactions_base (CustomerID) WITH FULLSCAN;
GO
```

The statistics are stored in user database system tables.

16. I previously mentioned in this chapter that many of the objects for data virtualization are stored in system tables. Execute the script **exploremetadata.sql** to see what data is stored for external data sources, file formats, and external tables. This script executes the following T-SQL statements:

```
USE [WideWorldImporters];
GO
SELECT * FROM sys.external_data_sources;
GO
```

```
SELECT * FROM sys.external_file_formats;
GO
SELECT * FROM sys.external_tables;
GO
```

17. SQL Server also provides system procedures to explore metadata in files like parquet. Execute the script **getparquetmetadata. sql** to see an example. This script executes the following T-SQL statements:

```
EXEC sp_describe_first_result_set N'
SELECT *
FROM OPENROWSET
      (BULK ''/wwi/''
      , FORMAT = ''PARQUET''
      , DATA_SOURCE = ''s3_wwi'')
as [wwi_customer_transactions_file];';
GO
```

18. OPENROWSET also provides a nice feature to gather metadata about the source parquet files. Execute the script **getfilemetadata. sql** to see an example. The script executes the following T-SQL statements:

```
USE [WideWorldImporters];
GO
SELECT TOP 1 wwi_customer_transactions_file.filepath(),
wwi_customer_transactions_file.filename()
FROM OPENROWSET
      (BULK '/wwi/'
      , FORMAT = 'PARQUET'
      , DATA_SOURCE = 's3_wwi')
as [wwi_customer_transactions_file];
GO
```

Learn How to Use Delta Files

This next exercise assumes you have completed all the prerequisites for the previous exercise with parquet. Furthermore, it assumes you have completed all the steps in the previous exercise to restore the WideWorldImporters database, configure Polybase, and create a master key, database-scoped credential, external data source, and external file format. You can leave the previous wwi bucket. You will create a new bucket as part of this exercise.

All *new* scripts and files specifically for this exercise can be found in the **ch07_ datavirt_objectstorage\datavirt\delta** folder. If you don't want to go through the exercise to use minio for delta, you can view the results in the notebook **querydelta.ipynb**.

Note   The people-10m delta table is a sample delta table from a sample dataset from Databricks as found at `https://docs.microsoft.com/azure/ databricks/data/databricks-datasets#sql`. This dataset contains names, birthdates, and SSN, which are all fictional and don't represent actual people. This dataset falls under the Creative Commons license at `http:// creativecommons.org/licenses/by/4.0/legalcode` and can be shared and provided in this book. My colleague Hugo Queiroz wrote a Spark job to grab the delta table from this dataset and downloaded it into all the files that make up the delta table. Hugo also provided many of the queries and ideas for this exercise. I could not have written this chapter without his help!

---

1. Use the minio console to create a new bucket called **delta**. Use the Upload folder option in the console to upload the folder from the example files called **people-10m**. This will create a folder under the delta bucket called people-10m with several parquet files and a folder called **_delta_log**.

2. Query the delta table by executing the script **querydeltatable.sql**. This script executes the following T-SQL statements:

```
USE [WideWorldImporters];
GO
```

```
SELECT * FROM OPENROWSET
(BULK '/delta/people-10m',
FORMAT = 'DELTA', DATA_SOURCE = 's3_wwi') as [people];
GO
```

There are 10 million rows in the delta table spread across all the
parquet formatted files. It will take around 1 minute to bring back
all the results. Pay attention to the various columns in the table.
Most of the query execution time is spent displaying all the rows
in SSMS, not actually reading the data.

3.   By default, the delta table was partitioned by the **id** column. Let's
     run a query to filter rows on a column that is not partitioned.
     Execute the script **querybyssn.sql**. This script executes the
     following T-SQL statements:

```
USE [WideWorldImporters];
GO
SELECT * FROM OPENROWSET
(BULK '/delta/people-10m',
FORMAT = 'DELTA', DATA_SOURCE = 's3_wwi') as [people]
WHERE [people].ssn = '992-28-8780';
GO
```

This query only returns one row but takes around 4 seconds. SQL
Server had to read all 10 million rows from the delta table, but it
used a Filter operator to only return the one row based on **ssn**.

4.   Now let's run a query and filter by the id column. Execute the
     script **querybyid.sql**. This script executes the following T-SQL
     statements:

```
USE [WideWorldImporters];
GO
SELECT * FROM OPENROWSET
(BULK '/delta/people-10m',
FORMAT = 'DELTA', DATA_SOURCE = 's3_wwi') as [people]
WHERE [people].id = 10000000;
GO
```

I specifically chose an id value that is "at the end" of one of the files. Notice the query comes back in ~1 second. That is because the delta table is partitioned by the id column; it is a form of predicate pushdown that can make queries faster.

Note   When you look at a query execution plan, the optimizer does not know the partition column for delta. The power is within the REST API calls to get the data from the delta table. Therefore, you may see a Filter operator after a remote scan. But only one row is returned from the REST API calls, so the Filter operator is not indicative of any performance issues. In the future, we plan to investigate how to make the optimizer more efficient in conjunction with delta-partitioned columns.

---

5. One of the concepts I mentioned with CETAS is the ability to create an external table based on an OPENROWSET() query. Let's look at an example and at the same time use a folder within S3 to narrow what data to query.

6. Create a new set of parquet files as an external table in a new folder for a subset of the delta table by executing the script **createparquetfromdelta.sql**. This script executes the following T-SQL statements:

```
USE [WideworldImporters];
GO
IF EXISTS (SELECT * FROM sys.objects WHERE NAME = 'PEOPLE10M_60s')
      DROP EXTERNAL TABLE PEOPLE10M_60s;
GO
CREATE EXTERNAL TABLE PEOPLE10M_60s
WITH
(   LOCATION = '/delta/1960s',
    DATA_SOURCE = s3_wwi,
    FILE_FORMAT = ParquetFileFormat)
AS
SELECT * FROM OPENROWSET
```

```
(BULK '/delta/people-10m', FORMAT = 'DELTA', DATA_SOURCE = 's3_
wwi') as [people]
WHERE YEAR(people.birthDate) > 1959 AND YEAR(people.
birthDate) < 1970;
GO
```

This script will create a new folder called 1960s under the delta
bucket. It will generate parquet files only for people in the delta
table who were born in the 1960s (chosen because that is my birth
decade).

To be clear about the flow here, SQL Server executes the
OPENROWSET() query against the delta table to bring back all
10 million rows, but then filters out rows based on the WHERE
clause. It takes those results and creates a set of parquet files in the
/delta/1960s folder and stores the metadata about the table and
columns in system tables.

7. Use the minio console to browse the **1960s** folder under the delta
   bucket to see the new parquet files created.

8. Query the new external table by executing the script
   query1960speople.sql. This script executes the following T-SQL
   statements:

```
USE [WideWorldImporters];
GO
SELECT * FROM PEOPLE10M_60s
ORDER BY birthDate;
GO
```

You have now seen several examples of how to query parquet files and delta tables
using the new REST API interfaces for S3. You have also seen some interesting ways to
export SQL data or results of OPENROWSET queries into parquet formatted files.

What Else Do You Need to Know

Going through these exercises has allowed you to see various aspects of using Polybase v3 with new REST API connectors.

There are a few details that are worth noting as you consider using this innovative technology:

- There are other options I didn't show you for CREATE EXTERNAL TABLE like "reject options" to handle data that doesn't match columns and data types. You can get a complete set of options and limitations when using external tables at `https://docs.microsoft.com/sql/t-sql/statements/create-external-table-transact-sql`.

- There are some limits when using S3 compatible storage such as the number of files. You can read the complete set of limits and requirements for using S3 at `https://docs.microsoft.com/sql/relational-databases/polybase/polybase-configure-s3-compatible`.

- The focus of the exercises was how to use S3. You can see an example of how to use delta tables on **abs** and **adls** at `https://docs.microsoft.com/sql/relational-databases/polybase/virtualize-delta`.

Backup and Restore with S3 Compatible Object Storage

A long-standing best practice for SQL Server is to separate the storage of backups from your data. A very long time ago, customers would put backups in separate drives, network file shares, or tapes (yikes!). Then SANs came along, and separate SAN storage could be used.

With the innovation of Azure, SQL Server embraced the ability to store backups in the cloud by writing directly to Azure storage starting in SQL Server 2012. We enhanced the BACKUP and RESTORE T-SQL syntax to support the URL option, and we still support this today. you can see all the details about how to use Azure storage as offsite storage at `https://docs.microsoft.com/sql/relational-databases/backup-restore/sql-server-backup-to-url`. Inside the SQL engine, we use REST API calls through HTTPS to send and receive data for backups to Azure.

And since we have figured out how to use REST APIs to support S3 object storage for data virtualization, why not just enhance the storage engine to support a database backup and restore to any S3-compatible storage?

How Does It Work?

When you back up or restore a database, you have the option of using the URL syntax for a backup:

```
BACKUP DATABASE WideWorldImporters
TO URL = 'https://<mystorageaccountname>.blob.core.windows.
net/<mycontainername>/WideWorldImporters.bak';
```

SQL Server will take the data from the data file, and instead of streaming this to a local disk, it will stream the data over REST API calls to a .bak file in Azure Blob Storage. Notice the **https** keyword.

This is all completely supported in SQL Server 2022. For S3, we simply extended the URL syntax to support S3:

```
BACKUP DATABASE WideWorldImporters
TO URL = 's3://<endpoint>:<port>/<bucket>/wwi.bak'
```

If the engine detects the keyword s3 as part of the URL syntax, it will use code built to support the S3 protocol to send data to an S3-compatible object storage provider.

What is great about this feature is that just about anything you can do with BACKUP and RESTORE works with S3, just like backup and restore to Azure storage. Full database, differential, log, and file backups are all supported. And most of the RESTORE options work as well including VERIFYONLY, HEADERONLY, and FILELISTONLY.

There are some limits and caveats to consider, such as maximum size, and some backup options are not supported. One of the biggest factors to consider is that the S3 object provider will store the backup file internally into multiple parts, which then affects the maximum backup size. But there are options like MAXTRANSFERSIZE to help. Read more about parts, file sizes, and limitations at https://docs.microsoft.com/sql/relational-databases/backup-restore/sql-server-backup-to-url-s3-compatible-object-storage.

Let's Look at an Example

Using the same minio server setup (including the restore of WideWorldImporters) with the data virtualization example in this chapter, use scripts from **ch07_datavirt_objectstorage\s3objectstorage** to see a basic backup and restore with S3. You do not have to configure Polybase to use backup and restore with S3.

If you have not set up minio and just want to see the results of this exercise, you can use the Azure Data Studio notebook **backuprestores3.ipynb**.

1. Use the minio console to create a new bucket called **backups**.

2. Edit the script **creates3creds.sql** to enter your local IP, user, and password (without the <>) from the minio setup earlier in this chapter. Create a credential for the backup by executing the script **creates3creds.sql.** This script executes the following T-SQL statements:

```
USE MASTER
GO
CREATE CREDENTIAL [s3://<local IP>:9000/backups]
WITH IDENTITY = 'S3 Access Key',
SECRET = '<user>:<password>';
GO
```

You cannot use the same database-scoped credential that was used in the data virtualization example. This credential is specifically created against the S3 storage and is created in the context of the master database.

3. Edit the script **backupdbtos3.sql** and enter in your local IP in all instances. You can review basic BACKUP commands to S3 by executing the script **backupdbtos3.sql**. This script executes the following T-SQL statements:

```
USE MASTER;
GO
ALTER DATABASE WideWorldImporters SET RECOVERY FULL;
GO
BACKUP DATABASE WideWorldImporters
```

```
TO URL = 's3://<local IP>:9000/backups/wwi.bak'
WITH CHECKSUM, INIT, FORMAT;
GO
BACKUP DATABASE WideWorldImporters
TO URL = 's3://<local IP>:9000/backups/wwidiff.bak'
WITH CHECKSUM, INIT, FORMAT, DIFFERENTIAL
GO
BACKUP LOG WideWorldImporters
TO URL = 's3://<local IP>:9000/backups/wwilog.bak'
WITH CHECKSUM, INIT, FORMAT
GO
BACKUP DATABASE WideWorldImporters
FILE = 'WWI_UserData'
TO URL = 's3://<local IP>:9000/backups/wwiuserdatafile.bak'
WITH CHECKSUM, INIT, FORMAT;
GO
```

4. Use the minio console to browse the **backups** bucket to see the new backup files stored in S3.

Tip   Another way to look at files for any S3-compatible storage is to use the free tool S3 Browser at `https://s3browser.com`.

---

5. Edit the script **restoredbfroms3.sql** to enter your local IP in all instances. Let's restore the full database backup to another database name by executing the script **restoredbfroms3.sql**. This script executes the following T-SQL statements:

```
USE MASTER;
GO
RESTORE VERIFYONLY FROM URL = 's3://<local IP>:9000/backups/
wwi.bak';
GO
RESTORE HEADERONLY FROM URL = 's3://<local IP>:9000/backups/
wwi.bak';
GO
```

```
RESTORE FILELISTONLY FROM URL = 's3://<local IP>:9000/backups/
wwi.bak';
GO
DROP DATABASE IF EXISTS WideWorldImporters2;
GO
RESTORE DATABASE WideWorldImporters2
FROM URL = 's3://<local IP>:9000/backups/wwi.bak'
WITH MOVE 'WWI_Primary' TO 'c:\sql_sample_databases\
WideWorldImporters2.mdf',
MOVE 'WWI_UserData' TO 'c:\sql_sample_databases\
WideWorldImporters2_UserData.ndf',
MOVE 'WWI_Log' TO 'c:\sql_sample_databases\
WideWorldImporters2.ldf',
MOVE 'WWI_InMemory_Data_1' TO 'c:\sql_sample_databases\
WideWorldImporters2_InMemory_Data_1';
GO
```

6. Since this is implemented in the engine, all the standard
    backup and restore history exists in the **msdb** database such as
    backupmediafamily, **backupset**, and **restorehistory**. You can
    browse these system tables to see the results from this exercise.

Migration from AWS

In the spring of 2022, as I was studying the concept of backup and restore with S3 object
storage, something dawned on me on an afternoon walk (I am one of those strange
people who comes up with ideas about SQL Server while I walk and exercise).

If AWS invented S3 and SQL Server 2022 supports restoring a database from S3,
then (wait for it)...I should be able to migrate a SQL Server database from AWS into SQL
Server using the new RESTORE from S3, right?

Right. I did it. I don't have a specific exercise for you, but I'll share the steps I took:

-   I deployed an AWS RDS SQL Server database using a version of SQL
    Server 2019.

-   I created an S3 bucket in AWS for storage. I used the following
    documentation from AWS to do this: https://docs.aws.amazon.
    com/AmazonS3/latest/userguide/setting-up-s3.html.

- I enabled on-demand backup/restore for AWS RDS using the following instructions: `https://docs.aws.amazon.com/AmazonRDS/latest/UserGuide/Appendix.SQLServer.Options.BackupRestore.html`.

- I created a new database in AWS RDS and backed it up to the S3 bucket.

- I obtained the AWS Access Key ID and Secret Key for the S3 storage.

- I created a credential against the S3 bucket using a T-SQL statement against SQL Server 2022 (my S3 URL is based on the region where my S3 bucket was created):

```
IF EXISTS (SELECT * FROM sys.credentials WHERE [name] = 's3://
s3.us-east-1.amazonaws.com/bwsqlbackups')
BEGIN
        DROP CREDENTIAL [s3://s3.us-east-1.amazonaws.
        com/<bucket>];
END
GO
CREATE CREDENTIAL    [s3://s3.us-east-1.amazonaws.com/<bucket>]
WITH
        IDENTITY    = 'S3 Access Key'
,       SECRET      = '<Access Key ID>:<Secret Key>;
GO
```

- I then ran the following T-SQL statement against SQL Server 2022 to restore the database:

```
RESTORE DATABASE <db> FROM URL = 's3://s3.us-east-1.amazonaws.
com/<bucket>/<backupfile>.bak'
```

That was it. I completed a very simple offline migration by restoring a full backup from AWS RDS into SQL Server 2022. Pretty cool, right?

SQL Server Is a Data Hub

I made the claim with SQL Server 2019 that SQL Server had become a data hub. I have to admit I borrowed that term from my Vice President Rohan Kumar. I remember him using this term as we talked about SQL Server and its future capability to connect to just about any data source *without moving the data*. That is, in a nutshell, the concept of data virtualization. Point your application to SQL Server using T-SQL, and the power of the SQL engine will access just about any data source for any type of data. Our innovations in SQL Server 2022 expand this capability by connecting with REST API connectors including S3 object storage. We also added innovations to allow SQL backups to be stored and restored with S3 object storage. I asked Hugo Queiroz to sum up his thoughts about data virtualization and SQL Server 2022. Hugo said, *"One of our major goals for SQL Server 2022 is to make Data Virtualization more flexible and* easier for everyone to use. Less dependencies, less complexity, less code, and a broader range of supported file types and connectors. To make this happen changing to a Rest-API implementation was fundamental, it allows SQL Server 2022 to be used as a data hub and leverage in-database analytics."

CHAPTER 8

New Application Scenarios with T-SQL

Transact-SQL (T-SQL) may just be the most popular query language in the world. T-SQL is compliant with industry standards (read the details at `https://docs.microsoft.com/en-us/openspecs/sql_standards/ms-sqlstandlp/89fb00b1-4b9e-4296-92ce-a2b3f7ca01d2`) and has a very rich extension from standard Data Manipulation Language (DML) and Data Definition Language (DDL) statements. You can see the complete T-SQL reference guide at `https://aka.ms/tsql`.

One of the areas that T-SQL excels at is providing a rich set of *built-in* functions (`https://aka.ms/tsqlfunc`). This includes categories for analytics, conversion, cryptography, mathematics, security, spatial, string, and statistics. Think of this like the programmer's library of SQL functions. In SQL Server 2022 we made a conscious effort to expand T-SQL function support and enhance the language in other areas. It may be the biggest set of additions we have made to the language in several releases. We felt we needed to expand the language to ensure it enhanced the developer experience. We even built a new team within SQL engineering to focus on this. This team reports to architect Conor Cunningham. Conor talked to me about this team and their charter:

After SQL Server 2019, I was looking to try my hand at something different professionally and I had been discussing starting an engineering team where I live in Austin, Texas. As part of that process, I put together a proposal for an initial charter for the team and what deliverables it might have. I decided to focus on extending the T-SQL language for a couple of reasons. First, in the era of cloud databases, there is a greater need for improving the developer experience to make it easier and faster to write cloud applications. Second, we had accumulated a number of requests from customers for improving the syntax in specific areas. Finally, we didn't have anyone actively funding this area so it was a great opportunity for a team to step in and work mostly independently (during a pandemic). It

© Bob Ward 2022
B. Ward, *SQL Server 2022 Revealed*, https://doi.org/10.1007/978-1-4842-8894-8_8

*turned out that a number of these T-SQL customer asks were great opportu-
nities to teach early-in-career engineers how to do the kinds of low-level,
performance-sensitive systems programming, and the team has really
enjoyed the challenge to build their own features as their first projects at
Microsoft.*

In this chapter I'll explore and show you enhanced and new T-SQL functions and
extensions to make you more productive. These enhancements fall into three categories:

- **JSON** – Enhanced and new T-SQL functions to process JSON data.

- **"Surface area"** – These are core functions and enhancements to the
  T-SQL language spread across several areas.

- **Time series** – These are new T-SQL functions to process time
  series data.

JSON Functions

By SQL Server 2016 we knew the popularity of processing and storing data as JSON was
important to new applications and developers. So we added into the T-SQL language
functions to process JSON data stored as strings in SQL Server tables. This included
functions to test the existence of JSON, extract JSON values, modify JSON parts, and even
format results of SQL row data into JSON documents. You can see a complete list of these
functions at `https://docs.microsoft.com/sql/relational-databases/json/json-data-sql-server`.

In SQL Server 2022, we have enhanced and added new functions to process
JSON. This includes testing existence of JSON and functions to generate JSON arrays and
objects. JSON functions do not require a specific dbcompat level.

I turned to the longtime SQL veteran Umachandar Jayachandran (UC) to find out our
motivation to do this new work for JSON. UC told me:

*SQL Server currently has support for manipulating and querying JSON
data. This approach is based on built-in functions, OPENJSON & FOR
JSON operators. This functionality implements a subset of features specified in JSON specification (RFC 8259) and ANSI SQL standard (Part 2:
SQL/Foundation) specification. The JSON enhancements in SQL Server
2022 provide functionality for some of the additional features in these specifications. The ISJSSON function now supports an optional JSON type*

constraint parameter that can be used to test if the input string is a valid JSON scalar, value, array, or object per RFC 8259. The new JSON_PATH_ EXISTS function provides a compatible syntax for the JSON_EXISTS predicate in the ANSI SQL standard and allows for testing existence of a specific SQL/JSON path in a JSON document. The JSON value constructors – JSON_OBJECT and JSON_ARRAY provide ANSI SQL compatible functionality for construction of JSON object or array. The JSON value constructors also allow construction of complex structures in a JSON document that require workarounds or string manipulation in older versions of SQL Server. Together, the new JSON enhancements provide rich functionality to manipulate JSON data and is a small step towards providing more standard compatible functionality in future version(s) of SQL Server.

The easiest way to see how these new T-SQL statements work is to go through some exercises. I've provided prerequisites first for the exercises. Then I'll combine some of the JSON functions together in two different exercises.

Prerequisites for Exercises

- SQL Server 2022 Evaluation Edition.

- Virtual machine or computer with at least two CPUs and at least 8Gb RAM.

- SQL Server Management Studio (SSMS). The latest 18.x build or 19.x build will work.

- There is no user database required for these exercises. They all work from any database context including master.

- Scripts from the book samples from the **ch08_tsql\json** folder.

JSON_ARRAY and ISJSON

While the FOR JSON clause of a SELECT statement allows you to return formatted JSON data, in SQL Server 2022 we have introduced a new function to produce JSON array text using an expression, which can be from columns in tables. In addition, even though we have had the ISJSON function to test for the existence of valid JSON, in SQL Server 2022 we added an option to look for a valid JSON array, object, or scalar.

Let's look at an exercise:

1. Open up the script **json_array.sql** to follow multiple steps as
    outlined in the comments of the script.

2. Execute the T-SQL statements for **Step 1**, which in the script are
    the following:

```
-- Step 1: Show a simple JSON array
USE master;
GO
SELECT s.session_id, JSON_ARRAY(s.host_name, s.program_name)
FROM sys.dm_exec_sessions AS s
WHERE s.is_user_process = 1;
GO
```

Your results will vary based on how many user requests are active
and your host. For my system the results looked like Figure 8-1.

	session_id	(No column name)
1	54	["BW-SQL2022","Microsoft SQL Server Management Studio - Query"]
2	59	["BW-SQL2022","SQLServerCEIP"]
3	81	["BW-SQL2022","Microsoft SQL Server Management Studio"]

Figure 8-1. *Basic JSON_ARRAY results*

You can see for the second column the results are a JSON text
array from several columns from the DMV **sys.dm_exec_
requests**.

3. Execute the statements for **Step 2**, which in the script are the
    following:

```
-- Step 2: Create a table based on a JSON array
USE master;
GO
DROP TABLE IF EXISTS sql_requests_json_array;
GO
```

```
SELECT r.session_id, JSON_ARRAY(r.command, r.status, r. database_
id, r.wait_type, r.wait_resource, s.is_user_process) as json_
array, r.command
INTO sql_requests_json_array
FROM sys.dm_exec_requests r
JOIN sys.dm_exec_sessions s
ON r.session_id = s.session_id
ORDER BY r.session_id;
GO
SELECT * FROM sql_requests_json_array;
GO
```

In this scenario you created a new table, which includes three columns. Two of the columns are strings, but only one is formatted as a JSON array based on a combination of columns from the DMV.

Your results will vary, but here is a portion of the results from my system as seen in Figure 8-2.

	session_id	json_array	command
47	47	["XTP_THREAD_POOL","background",6,"DISPATCHER_QUEUE_SEMAPHORE","",false]	XTP_THREAD_POOL
48	48	["XTP_THREAD_POOL","background",6,"DISPATCHER_QUEUE_SEMAPHORE","",false]	XTP_THREAD_POOL
49	49	["XTP_THREAD_POOL","background",6,"DISPATCHER_QUEUE_SEMAPHORE","",false]	XTP_THREAD_POOL
50	50	["XTP_THREAD_POOL","background",6,"DISPATCHER_QUEUE_SEMAPHORE","",false]	XTP_THREAD_POOL
51	51	["UNKNOWN TOKEN","background",0,"XTP_PREEMPTIVE_TASK","",false]	UNKNOWN TOKEN
52	52	["XTP_THREAD_POOL","background",6,"DISPATCHER_QUEUE_SEMAPHORE","",false]	XTP_THREAD_POOL
53	53	["XTP_THREAD_POOL","background",0,"DISPATCHER_QUEUE_SEMAPHORE","",false]	XTP_THREAD_POOL
54	54	["SELECT INTO","running",1,"",true]	SELECT INTO
55	55	["TASK MANAGER","sleeping",1,"",false]	TASK MANAGER
56	56	["TASK MANAGER","sleeping",1,"",false]	TASK MANAGER
57	57	["TASK MANAGER","sleeping",1,"",false]	TASK MANAGER
58	58	["TASK MANAGER","sleeping",1,"",false]	TASK MANAGER
59	60	["TASK MANAGER","sleeping",1,"",false]	TASK MANAGER

Figure 8-2. *Creating a table with a JSON array string*

4. Let's use ISJSON to see which strings in the table are a valid JSON
    array. Execute **Step 3** in the script, which contains the following
    T-SQL statements:

```
-- Step 3: Use ISJSON to test if JSON data exists in the array or
other columns
USE master;
GO
SELECT ISJSON(json_array) as is_json, ISJSON(json_array, OBJECT)
as is_json_object, ISJSON(json_array, ARRAY) as is_json_array,
ISJSON(command) as is_json
FROM sql_requests_json_array;
GO
-- Cleanup the table
DROP TABLE IF EXISTS sql_requests_json_array;
GO
```

You can see from these statements that we test whether the json_
array column is JSON, a JSON object, or a JSON array. We also test
whether the column command is JSON.

On my system you can see a portion of the results as in Figure 8-3.

	is_json	is_json_object	is_json_array	is_json
1	1	0	1	0
2	1	0	1	0
3	1	0	1	0
4	1	0	1	0
5	1	0	1	0
6	1	0	1	0
7	1	0	1	0
8	1	0	1	0
9	1	0	1	0
10	1	0	1	0

Figure 8-3. *Testing for a valid JSON array*

You can see that the json_array column is valid JSON and a valid
JSON array but not a JSON object. The command column is a
string and not valid JSON.

You can learn more about JSON_ARRAY at https://docs.microsoft.com/sql/
t-sql/functions/json-array-transact-sql and ISJSON at https://docs.microsoft.
com/sql/t-sql/functions/isjson-transact-sql.

JSON_OBJECT and JSON_PATH_EXISTS

Now let's look at JSON objects with T-SQL using another exercise:

1. Load the script **json_object.sql** to follow multiple steps as
   outlined in the comments of the script.

2. Execute **Step 1** in the script, which uses the following statements:

   ```
   -- Step 1: Create a JSON object using same data
   USE master;
   GO
   DROP TABLE IF EXISTS sql_requests_table_json_object;
   GO
   SELECT JSON_OBJECT('command': r.command, 'status': r.status,
   'database_id': r.database_id, 'wait_type': r.wait_type, 'wait_
   resource': r.wait_resource, 'user': s.is_user_process) as json_
   object, r.command
   INTO sql_requests_table_json_object
   FROM sys.dm_exec_requests r
   JOIN sys.dm_exec_sessions s
   ON r.session_id = s.session_id
   ORDER BY r.session_id;
   GO
   SELECT * FROM sql_requests_table_json_object;
   GO
   ```

   This time we used the exact same columns previously used to
   build an array and instead built a JSON object with a series of
   fields matching the columns from the DMV. Figure 8-4 shows a
   portion of the results on my system.

	json_object	command
49	{"command":"XTP_THREAD_POOL","status":"background","database_id":6,"wait_type":"DISPATCHER_QUEUE_SEMAPHO...	XTP_THREAD_POOL
50	{"command":"UNKNOWN TOKEN","status":"background","database_id":0,"wait_type":"XTP_PREEMPTIVE_TASK","wait_res...	UNKNOWN TOKEN
51	{"command":"XTP_THREAD_POOL","status":"background","database_id":6,"wait_type":"DISPATCHER_QUEUE_SEMAPHO...	XTP_THREAD_POOL
52	{"command":"XTP_THREAD_POOL","status":"background","database_id":0,"wait_type":"DISPATCHER_QUEUE_SEMAPHO...	XTP_THREAD_POOL
53	{"command":"SELECT INTO","status":"running","database_id":1,"wait_type":null,"wait_resource":"","user":true}	SELECT INTO
54	{"command":"TASK MANAGER","status":"sleeping","database_id":1,"wait_type":null,"wait_resource":"","user":false}	TASK MANAGER
55	{"command":"TASK MANAGER","status":"sleeping","database_id":1,"wait_type":null,"wait_resource":"","user":false}	TASK MANAGER
56	{"command":"TASK MANAGER","status":"sleeping","database_id":1,"wait_type":null,"wait_resource":"","user":false}	TASK MANAGER

Figure 8-4. *Creating a table with a JSON object*

You can see from this result the difference between the JSON array and object. The array was just a list of values, where the object has a <field>:<value> pair.

3. Now execute **Step 2** in the script, which uses the following statements:

```
-- Step 2: See if status exists in the json path of the object
USE master;
GO
SELECT JSON_PATH_EXISTS(json_object, '$.status'), JSON_PATH_
EXISTS(command, '$.status')
FROM sql_requests_table_json_object;
GO
```

The results should be 1 for the first column and 0 for the second. This is because the field status exists in the json_object column but not in the string from the command column.

You can learn more about JSON_OBJECT at https://docs.microsoft.com/sql/t-sql/functions/json-object-transact-sql and JSON_PATH_EXISTS at https://docs.microsoft.com/sql/t-sql/functions/json-path-exists-transact-sql.

T-SQL Surface Area

There are several new T-SQL functions and enhancements to the language that cross several areas. Therefore, I decided to call this section of the chapter "T-SQL Surface Area," since we are expanding several areas of coverage of the T-SQL language. Each following section covers a range of these new enhancements. As with JSON, the best way to learn these is through exercises.

Prerequisites

Here are the prerequisites for all the exercises in this section of the chapter:

- SQL Server 2022 Evaluation Edition.

- Virtual machine or computer with at least two CPUs and at least 8Gb RAM.

- SQL Server Management Studio (SSMS). The latest 18.x build or 19.x build will work.

- Scripts from the book samples from the **ch08_tsql\ surfacearea** folder.

- For the exercise on **IS [NOT] DISTINCT FROM**, you will need to restore the WideWorldImporters sample backup from `https://aka. ms/WideWorldImporters`. All other exercises do not require a user database.

- For the exercise on the new **WINDOW** clause, you will only *examine* the example queries and not execute the exercise.

DATETRUNC

Based on requests from our customers and response to other database products, we added the DATETRUNC function to T-SQL in SQL Server 2022. Aashna Bafna is a software engineer on Conor's team and told me the story behind DATETRUNC. Aashna said, "We decided to implement this feature in response to numerous customer requests to eliminate the need for complex date truncation workarounds and continue our efforts to make T-SQL queries faster and more user-friendly. Additionally, this feature will enable easier migrations to SQL from other competitors which already have a date truncation feature."

Use these steps to see an exercise for DATETRUNC. There is no user database required for this exercise. Any database context can be used including master.

1. Load the script **datetrunc.sql** to execute multiple steps in the script.

2. Execute **Step 1** in the script, which uses the following T-SQL statements:

```
-- Step 1: Truncate just the year from a date with a variable
USE master;
GO
DECLARE @d date = '2022-05-14';
SELECT DATETRUNC(year, @d);
GO
```

DATETRUNC returns the data type of the source, so a date value of 2022-01-01 should be your returned result.

3. Execute **Step 2** in the script, which uses the following T-SQL statements:

```
-- Step 2: Truncate the hour from a granular datetime value
USE master;
GO
SELECT DATETRUNC(hour, '1963-12-29 02:04:23.1234567');
GO
```

Since the source is a full datetime type, your result should be

```
1963-12-29 02:00:00.0000000
```

This is the rounded-down hour for the datetime value but returned as a full datetime value.

4. Execute **Step 3** in the script, which uses the following T-SQL statements:

```
-- Step 3: Truncate to the day of the year
USE master;
GO
SELECT DATETRUNC(dayofyear, '1996-03-27 08:05:30');
GO
```

The result should be the following, which is a truncation to midnight of the datetime value:

```
1996-03-27 00:00:00.0000000
```

5. Execute **Step 4** in the script, which uses the following T-SQL statements:

```
-- Step 4: Truncate to the quarter of the year using a date type
USE master;
GO
DECLARE @date date = '1993-08-30'
SELECT DATETRUNC(Quarter, @date);
GO
```

Since we are using a date type, the result should be the start of the quarter for this date, which is 1993-07-01.

The DATETRUNC function does not require a specific dbcompat level, and you can learn more at https://docs.microsoft.com/sql/t-sql/functions/datetrunc-transact-sql.

WINDOW Clause

SQL Server has supported powerful analytic T-SQL capabilities through functions so users can let the engine do more. One of these T-SQL statements is the OVER clause to support a *window*. You can read more about how to use the OVER clause with examples at https://docs.microsoft.com/sql/t-sql/queries/select-over-clause-transact-sql.

I noticed in the enhancements for SQL Server 2022 something called a WINDOW clause but was not sure how it could be used. So I reached out to Sharanya Bhat, a software engineer on Conor's team, to find out. Sharanya explained it this way: "Without the support for Window clause, our customers were facing the inconvenience of redefining specifications in OVER clause for every window function in the select list, even if the specifications are identical. There were numerous requests from them for this feature and so we decided to implement it in SQL Server 2022."

Sharanya provided me an example script, which if you restore the AdventureWorks sample database you can try yourself. I've provided the script **window.sql** so you can examine the difference before and after using the WINDOW clause.

Here is an example script using OVER without the WINDOW clause:

```
-- Without the WINDOW clause
SELECT SalesOrderID, ProductID, OrderQty
    ,SUM(OrderQty) OVER (PARTITION BY SalesOrderID ORDER BY SalesOrderID,
    ProductID ) AS Total
    ,AVG(OrderQty) OVER (PARTITION BY SalesOrderID ORDER BY SalesOrderID,
    ProductID) AS "Avg"
    ,COUNT(OrderQty) OVER (PARTITION BY SalesOrderID ORDER BY SalesOrderID,
    ProductID) AS "Count"
FROM Sales.SalesOrderDetail
WHERE SalesOrderID IN(43659,43664);
GO
```

Here is the same query now using the new WINDOW clause:

```
-- With the WINDOW clause
SELECT SalesOrderID, ProductID, OrderQty
    ,SUM(OrderQty) OVER win1 AS Total
    ,AVG(OrderQty) OVER win1 AS "Avg"
    ,COUNT(OrderQty) OVER win1 AS "Count"
FROM Sales.SalesOrderDetail
WHERE SalesOrderID IN(43659,43664)
WINDOW win1 AS (PARTITION BY SalesOrderID ORDER BY SalesOrderID,
ProductID );
GO
```

The new WINDOW clause requires dbcompat 160 to be used, or you will get a syntax error. You can learn more about using the WINDOW clause at https://docs. microsoft.com/sql/t-sql/queries/select-window-transact-sql.

GREATEST and LEAST

Trying to find values that are the highest or lowest among a list and returning a result has typically involved a complex use of T-SQL CASE statements. In April of 2021, we introduced the T-SQL functions GREATEST and LEAST to Azure SQL Database and Azure SQL Analytics. You can read this announcement at https://techcommunity. microsoft.com/t5/azure-sql-blog/introducing-the-greatest-and-least-t-sql-functions/ba-p/2281726. We are now bringing these functions into SQL Server 2022.

Let's see how they work from an exercise. There is no user database required for this exercise. Any database context can be used including master.

1. Load the script **greatest_least.sql**, which contains multiple steps for the exercise.

2. Execute **Step 1** in the script, which uses the following T-SQL statements:

```
-- Step 1: A simple set of numbers
USE master;
GO
SELECT GREATEST(6.5, 3.5, 7) as greatest_of_numbers;
GO
```

This is a very simple example as the highest of these numbers is 7.

3. Execute **Step 2** in the script, which uses the following T-SQL statements:

```
-- Step 2: Does it work even if datatypes are not the same?
USE master;
GO
SELECT GREATEST(6.5, 3.5, N'7') as greatest_of_values;
GO
```

The result is still 7, but it is interesting SQL Server can recognize a 7 as higher even when it is a character value (it assumes you were comparing all numbers).

4. Execute **Step 3** in the script, which uses the following T-SQL statements:

```
-- Step 3: What about strings?
USE master;
GO
SELECT GREATEST('Buffalo Bills', 'Cleveland Browns', 'Dallas
Cowboys') as the_best_team
GO
```

This shows that the engine can compare strings and determine the highest character order. It is amazing that SQL Server knows the Dallas Cowboys are the best team!

5. Execute **Step 4** in the script, which uses the following T-SQL statements:

```
-- Step 4: Use it in a comparison
USE master;
GO
CREATE TABLE dbo.studies (
    VarX varchar(10) NOT NULL,
    Correlation decimal(4, 3) NULL
);
INSERT INTO dbo.studies VALUES ('Var1', 0.2), ('Var2', 0.825),
('Var3', 0.61);
GO
DECLARE @PredictionA DECIMAL(4,3) = 0.7;
DECLARE @PredictionB DECIMAL(4,3) = 0.65;
SELECT VarX, Correlation
FROM dbo.studies
WHERE Correlation > GREATEST(@PredictionA, @PredictionB);
GO
```

Here is an example where GREATEST can be used to do a comparison to a column in a WHERE clause. The results for this query should be one row with the following values:

```
VarX     Correlation
Var2     0.825
```

6. Let's look at a simple example for LEAST. Execute **Step 5** in the script, which uses the following T-SQL statements:

```
-- Step 5: Simple LEAST example
USE master;
GO
SELECT LEAST(6.5, 3.5, 7) as least_of_numbers;
GO
```

Your result should be 3.5.

7. Execute **Step 6** in the script, which uses the following T-SQL statements:

```
-- Step 6: Combine with variables
USE master;
GO
DECLARE @VarX decimal(4, 3) = 0.59;
SELECT VarX, Correlation, LEAST(Correlation, 1.0, @VarX) AS
LeastVar
FROM dbo.studies;
GO
-- Clean up table
DROP TABLE IF EXISTS studies;
GO
```

This is an example of using variables with the LEAST function. Your results should have three rows like this:

```
VarX     Correlation    LeastVar
Var1     0.200          0.200
Var2     0.825          0.590
Var3     0.610          0.590
```

GREATEST and LEAST do not require a specific dbcompat level. You can learn more about GREATEST at https://docs.microsoft.com/sql/t-sql/functions/logical-functions-greatest-transact-sql and LEAST at https://docs.microsoft.com/sql/t-sql/functions/logical-functions-least-transact-sql.

IS [NOT] DISTINCT FROM

There may be many who use SQL who think the introduction of a NULL value could have been the worst mistake in the history of the language because NULL means *unknown*. Rather than debate that here in the book, let's see an example where we are trying to help with some interesting scenarios involving NULL values. We have introduced a new syntax called IS [NOT] DISTINCT FROM. What better person to turn to for how this new syntax helps with NULL than the famous Itzik Ben-Gan. Itzik may be the most knowledgeable person on T-SQL I know in or out of Microsoft. He wrote the following blog post talking about new SQL Server 2022 T-SQL enhancements at https://sqlperformance.com/2022/08/sql-server-2022/additional-t-sql-improvements-in-sql-server-2022. In this article he talked about the complexity of handling NULL values with examples of this problem.

I took the examples in Itzik's blog post and made some tweaks. The result is an exercise so you can see how our new syntax will help you query for NULL values but also achieve a good execution plan.

As I mentioned in the beginning of this section, you will need to restore the WideWorldImporters sample database backup from https://aka.ms/WideWorldImporters in order to go through this exercise.

1. Execute the script **setup_isnotdistinct.sql** to create a new index on the Sales.Order table for the PickingCompletedWhen column. This script executes the following T-SQL statements:

```
USE [WideWorldImporters];
GO
DROP INDEX IF EXISTS Sales.Orders.pickingdateidx;
GO
CREATE INDEX pickingdateidx ON Sales.Orders (PickingCompletedWhen);
GO
```

2. Load the script **isnotdistinct.sql** to run multiple steps. For each step enable **Include Actual Execution Plan** in SSMS.

3. Execute **Step 1** in the script, which uses the following statements:

```
-- Step 1: Query for a specific value which should yield 35 rows
using an Index Seek for pickingdateidx
USE [WideWorldImporters];
GO
DECLARE @dt datetime2 = '2013-01-01 12:00:00.0000000'
SELECT * FROM Sales.Orders WHERE
PickingCompletedWhen = @dt;
GO
```

This yields 35 rows and uses an index seek for the new index.

4. Execute **Step 2** from the script, which uses the following statements:

```
-- Step 2: Find all the orders where picking was not completed.
This shows 0 rows even though there is ~ 3000 rows with a
NULL value
USE [WideWorldImporters];
GO
DECLARE @dt datetime2 = NULL
SELECT * FROM Sales.Orders WHERE
PickingCompletedWhen = @dt;
GO
```

This shows 0 rows even though there are ~3000 rows with a NULL value.

5. Execute **Step 3** in the script, which uses the following statements:

```
-- Step 3: Try to use ISNULL. Works but requires a scan
USE [WideWorldImporters];
GO
DECLARE @dt AS DATE = NULL;
```

```
SELECT * FROM Sales.Orders
WHERE ISNULL(PickingCompletedWhen, '99991231') = ISNULL(@dt,
'99991231');
GO
```

This works and gives the right results but requires an index scan.

6. Execute **Step 4** in the script, which uses the following statements:

```
-- Step 4: Try to use the new operator. Should yield ~3000 rows
but use an index seek
USE [WideWorldImporters];
GO
DECLARE @dt datetime2 = NULL
SELECT *
FROM Sales.Orders
WHERE PickingCompletedWhen IS NOT DISTINCT FROM @dt;
GO
```

Now we get the right results, but also an index seek is used. Now
with this new operator, we have achieved what Itzik calls a search
argument or SARG, which allows the index to be used.

IS [NOT] DISTINCT FROM does not require a specific dbcompat level. You can read
more about this new syntax at https://docs.microsoft.com/sql/t-sql/queries/is-
distinct-from-transact-sql.

Nicholas Simmons, a software engineer who works on Conor's team who developed
this new enhancement, summarized this important work: "IS [NOT] DISTINCT FROM
allows users to make equality and inequality comparisons between values while
guaranteeing a true or false result. Where NULL = NULL would return unknown,
NULL IS NOT DISTINCT FROM NULL would return true. Where NULL != NULL would
return unknown, NULL IS DISTINCT FROM NULL would return false. This syntax is a
more succinct way to make these comparisons, and it can be used in scenarios where
the ANSI_NULLS setting does not apply. This is the main motivation for the addition
of IS [NOT] DISTINCT FROM in SQL22. It gives users a cleaner way to make these
comparisons, and it can be used anywhere without the limitations involved with making
these comparisons when ANSI_NULLS is set to OFF."

STRING_SPLIT

SQL Server has several T-SQL functions to help you manipulate and search string data inside table data. The complete list of these functions can be found at https://docs. microsoft.com/sql/t-sql/functions/string-functions-transact-sql.

STRING_SPLIT is a function we introduced in SQL Server 2016. It requires dbcompat 130 or higher to be used. STRING_SPLIT is very handy to "split apart" strings into separate string values. One of the limitations of this function is that there is no *ordinal* for the new separate values. In other words, there is no guarantee of what order the values are returned. SQL Server 2022 provides a new enhancement to include an ordinal. I found this excellent blog by the legendary SQL community member Aaron Bertrand (who also was the tech reviewer for *SQL Server 2019 Revealed*): www. mssqltips.com/sqlservertip/7265/sql-server-2022-t-sql-enhancements.

Let's look at an exercise based on what Aaron posted. There is no user database required for this exercise. Any database context can be used including master.

1. Load the script **string_split.sql**, which has multiple steps.

2. Execute **Step 1** in the script, which uses the following statements:

   ```
   -- Step 1: Use STRING_SPLIT to get back a list of NFL teams. There
   is no guarantee for the order but it may work.
   USE master;
   GO
   DECLARE @nflteams NVARCHAR(max) = N'Cowboys,Browns,Seahawks,Bronco
   s,Eagles';
   SELECT value as nfl_team FROM STRING_SPLIT(@nflteams, N',');
   GO
   ```

   Your results may vary because there is no guarantee in the order of the results. You should get back five rows for each string "part" in the @nflteams variable.

3. Execute **Step 2** in the script, which uses the following statements:

   ```
   -- Step 2: Use the new ordinal option to ensure order
   without a sort
   USE master;
   GO
   ```

```
DECLARE @nflteams NVARCHAR(max) = N'Cowboys,Browns,Seahawks,
Broncos,Eagles';
SELECT value as nfl_team, ordinal as rank FROM STRING_SPLIT
(@nflteams, N',', 1)
ORDER BY ordinal;
GO
```

This uses the new ordinal syntax. The third argument to STRING_
SPLIT is a 0 or 1. 1 means to enable ordinals. Then we can use the
keyword **ordinal** as a column in the results. And it makes sense
that SQL Server would once again recognize the ranking order
here with the Cowboys being first and the Eagles being last<g>.

You can read more details with examples about STRING_SPLIT at `https://docs.`
`microsoft.com/sql/t-sql/functions/string-split-transact-sql`.

TRIM Function Extensions

Another set of T-SQL functions can be used to trim characters from strings. This includes
the **TRIM**, **LTRIM**, and **RTRIM** functions. In order to bring our implementation of
these functions up to the latest ANSI standards and other database products, we have
extended these functions. Let's see in an exercise how these new extensions open up
new capabilities.

1. Load the script **trim.sql**, which has multiple steps.

2. Execute **Step 1** in the script, which uses the following statements:

    ```
    -- Step 1: Use new extensions for the TRIM functions
    USE master;
    GO
    -- The first statement is what was previously only supported
    SELECT TRIM('STR' FROM 'STRmydataSTR') as trim_strings;
    SELECT TRIM(LEADING 'STR' FROM 'STRmydataSTR') as leading_string;
    SELECT TRIM(TRAILING 'STR' FROM 'STRmydataSTR') as
    trailing_string;
    -- Same as the previous release behavior but explicitly
    specifying BOTH
    ```

```
SELECT TRIM(BOTH 'STR' FROM 'STRmydataSTR') as both_strings_
trimmed;
GO
```

Notice that before SQL Server 2022, the TRIM function removed spaces or characters from the beginning and end of a string. We added a new argument to specify how you want to trim characters: LEADING (at the front), TRAILING (at the end), and BOTH. BOTH is the same as the default behavior before SQL Server 2022.

3. Execute **Step 2** in the script, which uses the following statements:

```
-- Step 2: Use the new extension to the LTRIM function
USE master;
GO
SELECT LTRIM('STRmydataSTR', 'STR') as left_trimmed_string;
GO
```

LTRIM previously only trimmed leading spaces. Now you can trim spaces or any string expression.

4. Execute **Step 3** in the script, which uses the following statements:

```
-- Step 3: Use the new extension to the RTRIM function
USE master;
GO
SELECT RTRIM('STRmydataSTR', 'STR') as right_trimmed_string;
GO
```

Like LTRIM, RTRIM only supported trimming spaces at the end of a string. Now you can specify a character expression to trim.

These new extensions **require dbcompat 160**. You can read more details about the TRIM function at https://docs.microsoft.com/sql/t-sql/functions/trim-transact-sql. You can read more about LTRIM at https://docs.microsoft.com/sql/t-sql/functions/ltrim-transact-sql and RTRIM at https://docs.microsoft.com/sql/t-sql/functions/rtrim-transact-sql.

Bit T-SQL Functions

In my previous career at Microsoft, debugging SQL Server problems was a daily job. Often I would find myself looking through complex data structures inside the engine including how the source code works. A common programming technique when writing software as complex as SQL Server is to manipulate data using **bit** operators. SQL Server actually has bitwise operators to compare numbers at the bit level, which you can read about at `https://docs.microsoft.com/sql/t-sql/language-elements/bitwise-operators-transact-sql`.

There are other types of bit operators used in programming languages like C++ like bit shift operators and specific bit searching operators. The C++ language has keywords built in to do this. SQL Server 2022 comes with functions to mirror some of this capability, which are called **bit manipulation functions**.

You may be wondering why SQL Server would include operators for these types of bit manipulation functions. Time will tell how T-SQL programmers will use this, but I created a few interesting exercises using data from SQL Server.

Getting Packed Bits

Here is an exercise using the BIT_COUNT and GET_BIT functions to look at a number that is *packed* with bits, meaning different values into one value. Some of the steps in this exercise don't require a database context. The context of master is used in some steps, but the scripts change that context.

1. Load the script **getbits.sql**, which has multiple steps.

Note   The use of DBCC PAGE is not supported, and this script should only be used in test or development environments.

---

2. Execute **Step 1** in the script, which uses the following statements with a bunch of comments to explain the results:

```
-- Step 1: Run DBCC page against the PFS page and look at a member
of the BUF structure
-- Dump out the PFS page in master
-- Look at the BUF structure output
```

```
-- bstat should be 0x9
-- It could be 0xb if someone has made any page allocations and
master has not been checkpointed. For a new installed SQL Server
it should be 0x9
-- If you see 0x109 it could because of an internal bit for
checkpointing but it can be ignored
-- Here are several bstat values packed into this number
/*
BUF_ONLRU = 0x000001
BUF_DIRTY = 0x000002
BUF_IO      0x000004
BUF_HASHED  0x000008
*/
USE master;
GO
-- Checkpoint master to clear any dirty bits for PFS
CHECKPOINT;
GO
DBCC TRACEON(3604);
GO
DBCC PAGE(1,1,1,3);
GO
```

The results of the DBCC PAGE command can be found in the
Messages tab, not the Results tab. If you scroll in these results,
you will find information about a BUFFER: structure. Look at the
output for this string:

```
bstat = 0x9
```

As the comments show, this is an example of packing in multiple
values in a single number. So 0x9 represents several bits to reflect
certain *status* values ON like the following:

```
BUF_ONLRU = 0x000001
BUF_DIRTY = 0x000002
BUF_IO      0x000004
BUF_HASHED  0x000008
```

BUF_ONLRU means the page (in this case a PFS system page) is on a least recently used list.

BUF_DIRTY means the page is modified but not flushed to disk.

BUF_IO means the page is in the middle of I/O read or write (Note this is how we know the difference between a PAGELATCH and PAGEIOLATCH).

BUF_HASHED means the buffer is on a hash list for easy searching.

There are more bstat values than I'm showing here, and in fact in some tests, you may see a value of 0x109. 0x100 is used for internal checkpoint purposes and can be ignored for the purposes of this demonstration.

This technique is a very common programming practice to save storage in memory by packing bits into a single number (instead of having to have a separate field for each status value). You could do the same thing with a status value in a column in a SQL table.

3. Execute **Step 2** in the script, which uses the following statements:

```
-- Step 2: Get a count of bits that are 1 in the value
USE master;
GO
DECLARE @bstat varbinary(4);
SET @bstat = 0x9;
SELECT BIT_COUNT(@bstat);
GO
```

The new BIT_COUNT function can tell us how many bits are ON or 1 in the hex value.

The results for 0x9 should be 2 because two of the bits are ON.

4. Execute **Step 3** in the script, which uses the following statements:

```
-- Step 3: Which bits are on in the packed value
USE master;
GO
```

```
DECLARE @bstat varbinary(4);
SET @bstat = 0x9;
SELECT GET_BIT(@bstat, 3) as "2^3 BUF_HASHED", GET_BIT(@bstat, 2)
as "2^2 BUF_IO", GET_BIT(@bstat, 1) as "2^1 BUF_DIRTY", GET_BIT(@
bstat, 0) as "2^0 BUF_ONLRU";
GO
```

Bits should be read from right to left, so the output of this query should be the following for 0x9 (I flipped the results vertically):

```
2^3 BUF_HASHED     1
2^2 BUF_IO         0
2^1 BUF_DIRTY      0
2^0 BUF_ONLRU      1
```

So the BUF structure for this PFS page is on the LRU list and hashed as is the case for every BUF structure in the system. The buffer is not dirty because it has not been modified and is not in the middle of an I/O read or write.

5. Execute **Step 4** in the script, which uses the following statements:

```
-- Step 4: Combine the packed bits back into the number
USE master;
GO
DECLARE @bstat varbinary(4);
SET @bstat = 0x9;
SELECT GET_BIT(@bstat, 3)*2*2*2+GET_BIT(@bstat, 2)*2*2+GET_BIT(@
bstat, 1)*2+GET_BIT(@bstat, 0)*1;
SELECT cast((GET_BIT(@bstat, 3)*2*2*2+GET_BIT(@bstat, 2)*2*2+GET_
BIT(@bstat, 1)*2+GET_BIT(@bstat, 0)*1) as varbinary(4));
GO
```

To prove that 0x9 represents these bits, let's do 2-based arithmetic. 2^0 should be 1, 2^1 should be 2, 2^2 should 4, and 2^3 should be 8. But bit 1 and bit 2 are OFF or 0, so we really are adding 1+8 to get 9 or 0x9.

6. Let's see what happens if we modify the PFS page indirectly
    through a page allocation. Execute **Step 5** in the script, which uses
    the following:

```
-- Step 5: Create a table in master and see if there are changes
USE master;
GO
DROP TABLE IF EXISTS cowboysrule;
GO
CREATE TABLE cowboysrule (col1 int);
INSERT INTO cowboysrule VALUES (1);
GO
-- bstat should now be 0xb
DBCC TRACEON(3604);
GO
DBCC PAGE(1,1,1,3);
GO
-- BUF_DIRTY is now ON which means the page has been modified but
not written.
-- The PFS page is modified because a page allocation was required
for the new table data
DECLARE @bstat varbinary(4);
SET @bstat = 0xb;
SELECT GET_BIT(@bstat, 3) as "2^3 BUF_HASHED", GET_BIT(@bstat, 2)
as "2^2 BUF_IO", GET_BIT(@bstat, 1) as "2^1 BUF_DIRTY", GET_BIT(@
bstat, 0) as "2^0 BUF_ONLRU";
GO
```

Your results for the BUF structure should now be 0xb. The results
of the new query should show the BUF_DIRTY bit is now 1. So
now if bits 0, 1, and 3 are ON, you get 11, which is also 0xb in hex.

7. Execute **Step 6** in the script, which uses the following statements
    to drop the created table and checkpoint master:

```
-- Step 6: Cleanup the table we created in master and checkpoint
it to clear the dirty bit
USE master;
```

```
GO
DROP TABLE IF EXISTS cowboysrule;
GO
CHECKPOINT;
GO
```

Packing Bits into a Value

This exercise will use the LEFT_SHIFT, RIGHT_SHIFT, and SET_BIT functions to pack multiple values into a single byte. This exercise can be done under any database context.

1. Load the script **packbits.sql**, which has multiple steps.

2. Execute **Step 1** in the script, which uses the following statements:

```
-- Step 1: Pack 6 into the upper bits and 4 into the lower bits
-- The value of 100 is a byte that combines 6 in the upper bits
and 4 in the lower bits
USE master;
GO
DECLARE @x tinyint;
SELECT @x = LEFT_SHIFT(6, 4) + 4;
SELECT @x = (6 << 4 ) + 4;
SELECT @x;
```

My goal here is to pack in the numbers 6 and 4 as *separate* numbers but into the same byte value.

The result should be 100, but how did I produce this? Let me break this down. A tinyint is a single byte or 8 bits. Let's look at the value 100 in binary:

0110 0100

The upper bits (left 4 bits) represent the number 6.

The lower bits (right 4 bits) represent the number 4.

So I used the LEFT_SHIFT function (I also show how to use the << operator, so either one can be used) to shift a 6 to the upper bits, which would now make the number like this in binary:

0110 0000

Now just add a 4, and I get the final result because the 4 will be placed into the lower bits.

Together the value is 100, but if you know the *protocol* here, you know this is really a 6 and a 4. So instead of having two tinyint columns in a table for the 6 and for the 4, I can use just one.

So how do you "extract" the 6 and 4? Go to the next step.

3. Execute **Step 2** in the script, which uses the following statements:

```
-- Step 2: Only give me upper bits from the 100 packed value. The
result should be a 6
USE master;
GO
DECLARE @x tinyint;
DECLARE @y tinyint;
SELECT @x = LEFT_SHIFT(6, 4) + 4;
SELECT @x = (6 << 4 ) + 4;
SELECT @y = RIGHT_SHIFT(@x, 4);
SELECT @y = @x >> 4;
SELECT @y;
```

The answer should be 6. So taking the original 100 value, I can use the RIGHT_SHIFT function (I also show how to use the >> operator, so either one can be used) to shift the 6 into the lower bits (pushing out the 4). The result in binary is now this value:

0000 0110

I can now take the result and do whatever I need to do with the 6 value. Go to the next step to see how you can extract out the value of 4 from the packed byte.

4. Execute **Step 3** in the script, which uses the following statements:

```
-- Step 3: Let's use SET_BIT to clear the upper bits to get the
lower so the result should be a 4
USE master;
GO
```

```
DECLARE @x tinyint;
SELECT @x = LEFT_SHIFT(6, 4) + 4;
SELECT @x = (6 << 4 ) + 4;
SELECT @x = SET_BIT(@x, 4, 0);
SELECT @x = SET_BIT(@x, 5, 0);
SELECT @x = SET_BIT(@x, 6, 0);
SELECT @x = SET_BIT(@x, 7, 0);
SELECT @x;
GO
```

I can now take the value of 100 and just clear the upper bits using the SET_BIT function to get a new value of

0000 0100

which is 4.

You can read more about bit manipulation functions in SQL Server 2022 at `https://docs.microsoft.com/sql/t-sql/functions/bit-manipulation-functions-overview`. These bit manipulation functions do not require a specific dbcompat level.

Time Series

Time series data is data that is time-stamped usually to collect measurements or metrics. Time series data is usually organized into a concept called intervals or buckets. Many IoT devices produce telemetry, which requires time series data processing.

Even though SQL Server doesn't contain an actual time series data type or database, you can use SQL Server tables to store and process time series data. In fact, we built capabilities to use T-SQL to process time series data in Azure SQL Edge for IoT scenarios, which you can read more about at `https://docs.microsoft.com/azure/azure-sql-edge/imputing-missing-values`.

We decided to bring these same T-SQL functions from Edge and enhance them in SQL Server 2022. We recognized that you may have time series data you want to bring directly into the SQL Server engine and would like to use the power of T-SQL to process this type of data.

I asked Kendal Van Dyke, the senior program manager for time series and our EAP, the value of time series in T-SQL. Kendal said, *"We live in a world where data is constantly measured and stored on repeated intervals over time* – stock prices, weather data, retail sales, and factory floor sensor measurements are just a few examples. We then use that data to track changes, look for trends, and build reports with time being one of the axes. The Time Series capabilities in SQL Server 2022 make it easy for analysts, data scientists, and developers to do that work directly in the database, through enhancements to the T-SQL language that are both easy to write and highly performant and using tools with which they are already familiar."

In this section of the chapter, we will look at four T-SQL functions that can be useful for processing time series data stored as SQL Server rows and columns. In each section we will use an exercise to show how the functions work.

Prerequisites

To use the exercises in this section of the chapter, you will need

- SQL Server 2022 Evaluation Edition.

- Virtual machine or computer with two CPUs and at least 8Gb RAM.

- SQL Server Management Studio (SSMS). The latest 18.x build or 19.x build will work.

- Scripts from the book samples from the **ch08_tsql\timeseries** folder.

DATE_BUCKET

You can use the DATE_BUCKET T-SQL function to find an interval or bucket based on a date or time part like year, month, day, quarter, minute, etc. DATE_BUCKET is similar to the new DATETRUNC function you learned about earlier in this chapter, but there are some key differences. If you are looking to generate interval or bucket data for time series, I would recommend DATE_BUCKET.

Let's use an exercise to see how to use DATE_BUCKET. This exercise does not require any specific database context.

1. Load the script **date_bucket.sql**, which has multiple steps.

2. Execute **Step 1** from the script, which uses the following statements:

```
-- Step 1: Calculate DATE_BUCKET with a bucket width of 1 with
various dateparts
USE master;
GO
DECLARE @date DATETIME = '2022-05-14 13:30:05';
SELECT 'Now' AS [BucketName], @date AS [DateBucketValue]
UNION ALL
SELECT 'Year', DATE_BUCKET (YEAR, 1, @date)
UNION ALL
SELECT 'Quarter', DATE_BUCKET (QUARTER, 1, @date)
UNION ALL
SELECT 'Month', DATE_BUCKET (MONTH, 1, @date)
UNION ALL
SELECT 'Week', DATE_BUCKET (WEEK, 1, @date)
UNION ALL
SELECT 'Day', DATE_BUCKET (DAY, 1, @date)
UNION ALL
SELECT 'Hour', DATE_BUCKET (HOUR, 1, @date)
UNION ALL
SELECT 'Minutes', DATE_BUCKET (MINUTE, 1, @date)
UNION ALL
SELECT 'Seconds', DATE_BUCKET (SECOND, 1, @date);
GO
```

Go through the results and see how you extract a date or time unit as a bucket from the original datetime value.

3. Execute **Step 2**, which uses the following statements:

```
-- Step 2: Use a date instead of datetime
USE master;
GO
DECLARE @date DATE = '2022-05-14';
SELECT DATE_BUCKET(week, 1, @date);
GO
```

Here is an example of how DATE_BUCKET will return a value at the data type of input, so the result here is 2022-05-09, which is the beginning of the week (or interval) for 2022-05-14 but returned not as full datetime but a date value.

4. Execute **Step 3**, which uses the following statements:

```
-- Step 3: Generate fixed bucket sizes
USE master;
GO
DECLARE @dt DATETIME = '2022-05-14 13:35:12';
SELECT '5 Minute Buckets' AS [BucketName], DATE_BUCKET
(MINUTE, 5, @dt)
UNION ALL
SELECT 'Quarter Hour', DATE_BUCKET (MINUTE, 15, @dt);
GO
```

This is a nice feature for DATE_BUCKET to create fixed-size buckets based on number of the date part. DATETRUNC does not have this capability. The results for this query are

```
BucketName              (No column name)
5 Minute Buckets        2022-05-14 13:35:00.000
Quarter Hour            2022-05-14 13:30:00.000
```

So for the datetime passed in, a 5-minute interval is 13:35, but the quarter hour is back to 13:30.

You can learn more about DATE_BUCKET at https://docs.microsoft.com/sql/t-sql/functions/date-bucket-transact-sql. DATE_BUCKET does not require a specific dbcompat level.

GENERATE_SERIES

Another concept for time series data is create or generate data, especially a range of values. The GENERATE_SERIES T-SQL function can take as input a series of numbers or number range and automatically generate numbers including within a specified interval.

This is a new function for SQL Server 2022 and not in Azure SQL Edge. Let's go through an exercise. You must run this script in the context of a database that has dbcompat 160. The master database in SQL Server 2022 is automatically set to dbcompat 160.

1. Load the script **generate_series.sql**, which has multiple steps.

2. Execute **Step 1** in the script, which uses the following statements:

```
-- Step 1: Generate a series of integer values with a default
interval of 1
USE master;
GO
SELECT value
FROM GENERATE_SERIES(1, 100);
GO
```

You should get 100 rows with values 1–100. Notice here you can use the keyword **value** to represent the result of the GENERATE_SERIES function.

3. Execute **Step 2** in the script, which uses the following statements:

```
-- Step 2: Generate a series of integer values backwards with an
interval of 5
USE master;
GO
SELECT value
FROM GENERATE_SERIES(100, 1, -5);
GO
```

Here we generate values 100 down to 1 by an interval of 5.

4. Intervals don't have to be whole integers. Execute **Step 3**, which uses the following statements:

```
-- Step 3: Generate a series of decimal values between 0 and
1.0 in increments of 0.05
USE master;
GO
```

```
SELECT value
FROM GENERATE_SERIES(0.0, 1.0, 0.05);
GO
```

Your results should be a series of numbers from 0 to 1 with an
increment of 0.05.

5. Execute **Step 4**, which uses the following T-SQL statements:

```
-- Step 4: Data types must match! The first batch results in
an error
-- To get around this, either explicitly cast to matching data
types or use parameters
USE master;
GO
SELECT value
FROM GENERATE_SERIES(1, 10, 0.5);
GO
DECLARE @start numeric(2,1) = 1;
DECLARE @end numeric(3,1) = 10;
DECLARE @step numeric(2,1) = 0.5;
SELECT value
FROM GENERATE_SERIES(@start, @end, @step);
GO
```

In the first batch, you should get the following error:

```
Msg 8116, Level 16, State 3, Line 3
Argument data type numeric is invalid for argument 3 of generate_
series function.
```

This is followed by a series of other errors. To fix this we will use
variables to ensure all arguments for GENERATE_SERIES use the
same types.

You can learn more about GENERATE_SERIES at https://docs.microsoft.com/
sql/t-sql/functions/generate-series-transact-sql. This function **requires
dbcompat 160**, or you will get a syntax error 208 saying GENERATE_SERIES is an invalid
object name.

Gap Filling with FIRST_VALUE and LAST_VALUE

When working with telemetry or measurement time series data, it is common for there to be *gaps* in the data usually represented by NULL values. SQL Server provides functions to fill in these gaps based on other values in the measurement set called FIRST_VALUE and LAST_VALUE. These functions have been in previous releases of SQL Server, but we now include new options in SQL Server 2022:

IGNORE NULLS – Ignore null values in the dataset when computing the first/last value over a partition.

RESPECT NULLS – Respect null values in the dataset when computing first/last value over a partition.

Let's go through an exercise:

1. Execute the script **setup_gapfilling.sql** to set up the demo, which executes the following T-SQL statements:

```
USE master;
GO
DROP DATABASE IF EXISTS GapFilling;
GO
CREATE DATABASE GapFilling;
GO
USE GapFilling;
GO
DROP TABLE IF EXISTS MachineTelemetry;
GO
CREATE TABLE MachineTelemetry (
      timestamp DATETIME
      , VoltageReading NUMERIC(9, 6)
      , PressureReading NUMERIC(9, 6)
);
GO
```

```
INSERT INTO MachineTelemetry
(
        [timestamp]
        , VoltageReading
        , PressureReading
)
VALUES
('2020-09-07 06:14:50.000', NULL, NULL)
, ('2020-09-07 06:14:51.000', 164.990400, 7.223600)
, ('2020-09-07 06:14:52.000', 162.241300, 93.992800)
, ('2020-09-07 06:14:53.000', 163.271200, NULL)
, ('2020-09-07 06:14:54.000', 161.368100, 93.403700)
, ('2020-09-07 06:14:55.000', NULL, NULL)
, ('2020-09-07 06:14:56.000', NULL, 98.364800)
, ('2020-09-07 06:14:59.000', NULL, 94.098300)
, ('2020-09-07 06:15:01.000', 157.695700, 103.359100)
, ('2020-09-07 06:15:02.000', 157.019200, NULL)
, ('2020-09-07 06:15:04.000', NULL, 95.352000)
, ('2020-09-07 06:15:06.000', 159.183500, 100.748200);
GO
```

You can see from this script we are setting up a measurement table, which contains gaps or NULL values in some of the readings.

2. Execute the script **gapfilling.sql**, which executes the following T-SQL statements:

```
-- Use FIRST_VALUE and LAST_VALUE to fill in gaps
USE GapFilling;
GO
SELECT timestamp
        , VoltageReading
        , FIRST_VALUE (VoltageReading) IGNORE NULLS OVER (
                ORDER BY timestamp ASC ROWS BETWEEN CURRENT ROW AND
                UNBOUNDED FOLLOWING
                ) AS [FIRST_VALUE]
```

```
, LAST_VALUE (VoltageReading) IGNORE NULLS OVER (
        ORDER BY timestamp DESC ROWS BETWEEN UNBOUNDED
        PRECEDING AND CURRENT ROW
        ) AS [LAST_VALUE]
FROM MachineTelemetry
ORDER BY [timestamp];
GO
```

When you look at the results, you can see how FIRST_VALUE and LAST_VALUE could be used to fill in gaps that are NULL depending on your needs.

You can see I used the IGNORE NULLS clause. The syntax is a bit hard to understand, so let's look at the example for FIRST_VALUE:

```
FIRST_VALUE (VoltageReading) IGNORE NULLS OVER (
        ORDER BY timestamp ASC ROWS BETWEEN CURRENT ROW AND
        UNBOUNDED FOLLOWING
        ) AS [FIRST_VALUE]
```

What this means is that the value for a given row will be the first value (ignoring NULL values) based on the current row until the end of all rows ordered by the timestamp column.

Let's look at some of the results to understand them. First, look at the first five rows as in Figure 8-5.

	timestamp	VoltageReading	FIRST_VALUE	LAST_VALUE
1	2020-09-07 06:14:50.000	NULL	164.990400	164.990400
2	2020-09-07 06:14:51.000	164.990400	164.990400	164.990400
3	2020-09-07 06:14:52.000	162.241300	162.241300	162.241300
4	2020-09-07 06:14:53.000	163.271200	163.271200	163.271200
5	2020-09-07 06:14:54.000	161.368100	161.368100	161.368100

Figure 8-5. *Using FIRST_VALUE for gap filling*

You can see the FIRST_VALUE column is based on the current VoltageReading row except IGNORE NULLS is used so the first row is actually the second row's value.

Now look at the next several rows as in Figure 8-6.

6	2020-09-07 06:14:55.000	NULL	157.695700	157.695700
7	2020-09-07 06:14:56.000	NULL	157.695700	157.695700
8	2020-09-07 06:14:59.000	NULL	157.695700	157.695700
9	2020-09-07 06:15:01.000	157.695700	157.695700	157.695700

Figure 8-6. *How FIRST_VALUE handles NULL values*

You can see here that for row 6 we have to use the value in row 9 to generate the "first value" because we are ignoring the NULL values.

This is just an example of how you can use FIRST_VALUE and LAST_VALUE for gap filling. There are other uses for these functions. You can learn more about FIRST_VALUE at `https://docs.microsoft.com/sql/t-sql/functions/first-value-transact-sql` and LAST_VALUE at `https://docs.microsoft.com/sql/t-sql/functions/last-value-transact-sql`. Neither of these functions requires a specific dbcompat level.

T-SQL Is Alive and Well

The T-SQL language has so much functionality and built-in capabilities. Our goal is for developers to push logic into the server vs. application code. It makes your application lighter and allows you to use the full power of the SQL Server engine, even combining these language capabilities with all the other features of SQL Server.

Derek Wilson is a principal program manager in the SQL Server team, and I saw firsthand how he poured his heart and soul into this release. One of his areas of focus was T-SQL, and I asked him about the importance of our investment in this space. Derek said, *"I am most excited about the new T*-SQL language enhancements that are part of this release. We have sprinkled in a few T-SQL delighters, some new functions, and a few extensions to the language in SQL Server 2022. Our intent is to continue to not only bring more language parity for cloud native or SQL developers who have worked with other SQL dialects, but to provide productivity enhancements to the language that can provide a more natural experience when writing SQL statements. I cannot thank the SQL Server community enough for all the support and fantastic feedback that continues to have a tremendous impact on the evolution of SQL Server and the T-SQL language space."*

CHAPTER 9

SQL Server 2022 on Linux, Containers, and Kubernetes

In 2016 we shocked the database industry by announcing we would be releasing SQL Server on Linux operating systems (you can see the original blog post by Scott Guthrie at `https://blogs.microsoft.com/blog/2016/03/07/announcing-sql-server-on-linux`). This announcement led to the release of SQL Server on Linux with SQL Server 2017. We built SQL Server on Linux using an innovative approach with software called the Platform Abstraction Layer (PAL). This allowed us to bring SQL Server on Linux to the marketplace quickly without rewriting the entire engine. The PAL also provided compatibility so that the core engine code remained the same, allowing you to back up and restore databases across operating systems. This means that core engine capabilities like the query processor and columnstore indexes are exactly the same across SQL Server on Windows and Linux. In SQL Server 2019, we shored up most of the features that didn't exist in SQL Server 2017 including replication, CDC, DTC transactions, machine learning, and data virtualization.

We made sure that our approach using the PAL would allow SQL Server to perform as fast as or faster than SQL Server on Windows (you can read the original PAL approach in a blog post by our engineering ream at `https://cloudblogs.microsoft.com/sqlserver/2016/12/16/sql-server-on-linux-how-introduction`). TPC-H results submitted by our partners proved the point (you can see examples of these at `www.tpc.org/tpch/results/tpch_price_perf_results5.asp?resulttype=noncluster&version=3`).

By supporting SQL Server on Linux, we opened up new possibilities with containers and support for Kubernetes. This allowed us to reach new customers and applications, which was never possible before.

SQL Server 2022 continues the support for Linux, containers, and Kubernetes. This chapter is not a deep dive into how SQL Server on Linux works. I actually wrote an entire book on that topic called *Pro SQL Server on Linux*. In this chapter I'll cover differences for SQL Server 2022 but also review with you some of the fundamentals on how you can use and optimize SQL Server on Linux, containers, and Kubernetes.

SQL Server 2022 on Linux

SQL Server 2022 on Linux is very similar to SQL Server 2019 with a few minor differences. This includes the Linux distribution versions we support, enhanced support for DTC transactions, and some features we won't support. For all the latest information on SQL Server Linux, stay connected to `https://aka.ms/sqllinux`.

What's New for SQL Server 2022

SQL Server 2022 is *officially* supported on the following Linux distributions:

- Red Hat Enterprise Linux 8.0–8.5 Server

- Ubuntu 20.04 LTS

- SUSE Linux Enterprise Server (SLES) 15

I often get questions about support for other Linux distributions like CentOS. SQL Server on Linux can run just fine on other Linux distributions, but we only officially support RHEL, Ubuntu, and SLES. These are distributions we have tested, and we have agreements with these companies to provide official production support.

Note We do not support running SQL Server on Linux on Windows Subsystem for Linux (WSL). However, do we support running SQL Server containers with Docker on Windows including WSL integration.

New Capabilities Specific to Linux

One thing that is new for SQL Server 2022 for Linux is managing DTC transactions. We added DTC support for Linux in SQL Server 2019. However, there is limited support for monitoring and managing transactions, especially when there is an issue. In SQL Server 2022 we were able to add WMI support within the PAL to support this new capability. You can read more at `https://docs.microsoft.com/sql/linux/sql-server-linux-configure-msdtc`.

Also, as I described in Chapter 6 of the book, we now support T-SQL snapshot backups, so you can perform snapshot backups on Linux without writing a VDI program or relying on programs like Windows VSS.

There are some new enhancements for SQL Server 2022 that we do not support:

- Azure extension for SQL Server during setup (you can use a different method to install the extension)

- Multiple TCP connections for Distributed Availability Groups

- TLS 1.3

- Intel QAT backup compression

- Microsoft Purview policies

Note   Synapse Link requires the self-hosted integration runtime (SHIR) as you learned in Chapter 3 of the book. SHIR only works on the Windows OS, but you can direct it to connect to a SQL Server on Linux instance.

This was the list at the time of the writing of this book. It is possible that we have added support for these features by the time we ship SQL Server 2022. Keep up with all the latest details at `https://docs.microsoft.com/sql/linux/sql-server-linux-editions-and-components-2022#unsupported-features-and-services`.

I received a question when presenting early on about SQL Server 2022 that went like this: "Bob, it doesn't seem like you are investing much these days on Linux." My response was that we are. We may not be investing in new features that are specific to Linux, but look at all the rich capabilities in the engine that work on both Windows and Linux including cloud-connected features, built-in query intelligence, Ledger for SQL Server, tempdb, Contained AGs, REST-based Polybase, and new T-SQL enhancements. That is the power of the compatible story we built for SQL Server on Linux.

Deploying SQL Server 2022 on Linux

Deploying SQL Server 2022 on Linux is the same as it has been with SQL Server 2017 and 2019. You choose your supported Linux distribution and use the *package managers* that come with the Linux distribution to install SQL Server. This is because we post Linux packages for you to use with RHEL, Ubuntu, and SLES. We provide instructions on how to download a *repo file*, which contains the source on the Web where our packages can be found.

Tip   Did you know you can browse all of our packages at `https://packages.microsoft.com`?

For example, on RHEL, there are two simple commands to install the core SQL Server engine package:

```
sudo curl -o /etc/yum.repos.d/mssql-server.repo https://packages.microsoft.com/config/rhel/8/mssql-server-preview.repo
sudo yum install -y mssql-server
```

Note   The package name will change from mssql-server-preview.repo to a different name like mssql-server-2022.repo when SQL Server becomes generally available. You can stay up to date at `https://docs.microsoft.com/sql/linux/quickstart-install-connect-red-hat`.

It is a very simple install process, and the core engine package has just about everything you need for the fundamentals all built into these steps.

There are a few unique aspects to SQL Server on Linux deployment:

- In order to complete the setup, you must run the following command no matter what distribution you are using:

```
sudo /opt/mssql/bin/mssql-conf setup
```

mssql-conf is a script that can perform configuration operations outside of the SQL instance. The setup option is used to establish the admin password, choose an edition, and other options to complete the setup process.

- Unlike SQL Server on Windows, other features may require you to install additional packages such as tools, full-text search, SSIS, Java extension and ML services, Polybase, and HA (for availability groups). You can get a list of all of these packages on the following site under the Package details section: `https://docs.microsoft.com/sql/linux/sql-server-linux-release-notes-2022#supported-platforms`.

- One interesting aspect of Linux is that each cumulative update (CU) and General Distribution Release (GDR) is a separate package so you could install a CU directly without installing RTM and then have to apply a CU package (which is required for Windows).

What Else Should I Know?

- SQL Server on Linux is installed as a service on Linux. Therefore, you can see the status of SQL Server (running, stopped, etc.) at any time with the following command:

  `systemctl status mssql-server`

- The default directory for data, log, log files, and backups is based on /var/opt/mssql. This directory must always exist, but you can change the default location for your files such as databases and backups.

- SQL Server on Linux allows you to perform uninstalls, upgrades, offline installs, and automatic installs (using environment variables).

- Licensing for SQL Server on Linux is the same as on Windows. You can use your existing SQL Server licenses on either operating system.

Ansible with RHEL

One of the nice capabilities unique to Red Hat Enterprise Linux is **Ansible**. Ansible provides a great platform for *automation*. Therefore, it can be a solution to automate the installation of many computers or virtual machines for SQL Server on Linux through a concept called a *playbook*.

We have worked with Red Hat to include a special role for using playbooks with SQL Server on Linux.

You can learn more about how to do this with the following resources:

- `https://access.redhat.com/documentation/en-us/` `red_hat_enterprise_linux/8/html/administration_and_` `configuration_tasks_using_system_roles_in_rhel/` `assembly_configuring-microsoft-sql-server-using-` `microsoft-sql-server-ansible-role_assembly_updating-` `packages-to-enable-automation-for-the-rhel-system-roles`

- `https://docs.microsoft.com/sql/linux/sql-server-linux-` `deploy-ansible`

How to Connect and Use SQL Server 2022 on Linux

Once you have deployed SQL Server on Linux, you are going to want to connect and start using the instance with T-SQL statements. I've included some brief tips in this section of the chapter. If you are looking for exercises for SQL Server on Linux, you can easily use the scripts from *Pro SQL Server on Linux* (you will need to retrofit package names for SQL Server 2022) from `https://github.com/microsoft/bobsql/tree/master/` `sqllinuxbook`.

ssh vs. rdp

For those in the Windows world used to using Remote Desktop (rdp), Linux has a standard remote shell called secure shell (ssh), which is a command line interface into a bash shell on the computer or VM. There are many ways to use ssh to connect to your Linux computer or VM. Here are some ways I use ssh:

- ssh just comes with PowerShell, so you can use it right from a PowerShell command prompt.

- If you have deployed in Azure, the Azure Cloud Shell comes with a bash shell interface, and ssh is included.

- I personally love using the free tool MobaXterm, which you can download from `https://mobaxterm.mobatek.net`. One thing that is nice about this tool is that there is a graphical interface to upload and download files from your local computer into Linux.

Connecting with Our Tools

Since SQL Server on Linux is a compatible SQL Server engine, you can use your favorite tool that normally connects to SQL Server on Windows such as SSMS.

Azure Data Studio (ADS) has become very popular and works well with Linux. One of the nice advantages of ADS is that it works cross-platform, so it can run on Windows, Linux, or macOS. ADS also comes with the concept of notebooks, which you have seen already in some exercises in this book.

The command line tool sqlcmd works well with SQL Server on Linux. There is a Linux version of the tool, which comes as a separate package to install depending on your Linux distribution.

We also have a cross-platform alternative command line tool called mssql-cli, which you can read more about at `https://docs.microsoft.com/sql/tools/mssql-cli`.

Configuring with mssql-conf

For SQL Server on Windows, you may be used to using the SQL Server Configuration Manager tool. For SQL Server on Linux, the equivalent tool is called mssql-conf. mssql-conf can be used to configure a variety of settings like enabling SQL Server Agent or setting trace flags. You can read more about all the options supported by mssql-conf at `https://docs.microsoft.com/sql/linux/sql-server-linux-configure-mssql-conf`.

Note   Configuration inside SQL Server is still supported by using ALTER SERVER CONFIGURATION or sp_configure.

Active Directory Authentication with adutil

SQL Server on Linux supports both SQL and Active Directory (AD) authentication for logins. When we first shipped SQL Server on Linux for SQL Server 2017 and even 2019, setting up AD authentication was fairly complex. We now have a tool called **adutil** that can simplify this process. The adutil tool works for SQL Server 2019 and 2022 and is also supported for containers. You can read more about how to use adutil at `https://docs.` `microsoft.com/sql/linux/sql-server-linux-ad-auth-adutil-introduction`.

Azure Extension for SQL Server

The Azure extension for SQL Server is not currently included in the setup process for SQL Server on Linux. But you can use a method that has already existed to support SQL Server on Azure Arc–enabled servers for Linux as documented at `https://docs.` `microsoft.com/sql/sql-server/azure-arc/connect`.

As I described in Chapter 3 of the book, the Azure extension for SQL Server is a Windows service that is part of the Azure Arc Agent framework, which also runs as a Windows service. On Linux, these programs run as daemon programs called himds (Arc agent) and SqlServerExtension.Service (SQL extension).

Optimizing SQL Server 2022 on Linux

Besides the typical SQL Server optimization techniques you use such as proper indexes, there are some optimizations to consider for running SQL Server on Linux:

- Since we have shipped SQL Server 2017 with Linux, we have learned across customer experiences and benchmarks how to tune the Linux kernel and SQL Server in very specific ways to achieve optimal performance. There is a very detailed list of these recommendations at `https://docs.microsoft.com/sql/linux/sql-server-linux-performance-best-practices`. If you are just trying out SQL Server on Linux, you may not need to consider any or all of these. However, for the optimal production experience, I highly recommend you read through all of these.

- There are some settings outside SQL Server on Windows like Instant File Initialization (IFI) and Lock Pages in Memory. These settings do not apply to SQL Server on Linux.

- You may notice these two messages appear right after you install SQL Server on Linux:

```
ForceFlush is enabled for this instance
ForceFlush feature is enabled for log durability
```

My longtime colleague Robert Dorr spent a considerable amount of time researching SQL Server I/O consistency and performance on Linux. This work led to a series of configuration options we recommend, which you can read at https://docs.microsoft.com/sql/linux/sql-server-linux-performance-best-practices#linux-os-configuration under the section titled "**SQL Server and Forced Unit Access (FUA) I/O subsystem capability**." And if you love reading the inside story, check out Bob's blog post at https://techcommunity.microsoft.com/t5/sql-server-blog/sql-server-on-linux-forced-unit-access-fua-internals/ba-p/3199102.

- Avoid the OOM killer.

Sounds like a horror movie, right? Well, if you encounter an out-of-memory (OOM) situation that kills your program, it can be horrific. SQL Server does a great job of dynamic memory management, but if it consumes too much memory within Linux, it could be subject to this problem. This is why we created a configuration option called **memorylimitmb**. By default we actually limit the overall memory SQL Server can use on Linux, so this may not be an issue for you. But I encourage you to read more details at https://docs.microsoft.com/sql/linux/sql-server-linux-performance-best-practices#sql-server-configuration under the section titled **Set a memory limit with mssql-conf** to ensure your instance will be stable.

HADR for SQL Server 2022 on Linux

SQL Server comes with powerful high-availability and disaster recovery (HADR) features including failover clustering, Always On Availability Groups (AGs), and a rich set of BACKUP/RESTORE options.

Let's look at how each of these can be used with SQL Server on Linux.

Failover Clustering

On SQL Server on Windows, SQL Server is integrated with Windows Server Failover Cluster (WSFC) to support a shared storage automatic high-availability feature. Since WSFC is not available on Linux, you can use a software package called **Pacemaker** to support a SQL Server failover cluster. You can read more about how to set this up at `https://docs.microsoft.com/sql/linux/sql-server-linux-shared-disk-cluster-configure`.

Always On Availability Groups (AGs)

The core AG software is all built into the SQL Server engine. This is why for SQL Server on Linux (or Windows), you can set up a *clusterless* availability group (if you remember I showed you how to do this in Chapter 6 of the book for a Contained Availability Group). This option doesn't provide automatic failover, but it does provide a replica scheme. We also call this a read-scale availability group because it can be a perfect solution to separate your read-only workloads. You can read more about setting up a read-scale availability group at `https://docs.microsoft.com/sql/linux/sql-server-linux-availability-group-configure-rs`.

We also support a fully automatic failover solution with AGs using Pacemaker supported on RHEL, Ubuntu, and SLES. You can read more about how to set this up for RHEL at `https://docs.microsoft.com/sql/linux/sql-server-linux-availability-group-cluster-rhel`. You can also set up this configuration with Azure Virtual Machines, which you can read about at `https://docs.microsoft.com/azure/azure-sql/virtual-machines/linux/rhel-high-availability-stonith-tutorial`.

HPE Serviceguard

Turns out one of the things we did is take our code to support how SQL Server controls failover for an Always On Availability Group and put it into an open source project, which you can find at `https://github.com/Microsoft/mssql-server-ha`. By doing this we allowed other partners to integrate their failover solution with SQL Server. And one of those solutions is from HPE called Serviceguard. You can read more about how to use HPE Serviceguard with SQL Server at `https://docs.microsoft.com/sql/linux/sql-server-availability-group-ha-hpe`.

BACKUP/RESTORE

All the BACKUP/RESTORE features for SQL Server are available on SQL Server on Linux including backup to Azure storage with the URL syntax and the new S3 object storage backup capabilities with SQL Server 2022.

You also read in Chapter 6 of the book that snapshot backups are supported using T-SQL and don't require you to write a VDI program or rely on Windows VSS. In fact, we also call this feature *cross-platform snapshot backups* because we wanted to support snapshot backups on Linux.

SQL Server 2022 Containers

I remember back around 2010 when it became very popular to run SQL Server on a virtual machine. The power of abstraction from a bare-metal machine plus being able to consolidate multiple machines on one host revolutionized computing in many ways.

In recent years on Linux systems, the concept of a container has become extremely popular for applications, especially for developers. There is nothing fundamentally new for SQL Server containers in SQL Server 2022. But it is worth reviewing why containers can be used, how to use them, and some interesting scenarios where they can be quite powerful.

Keep up to date with all the latest on SQL Server containers at `https://aka.ms/ sqlcontainers`.

Why Containers?

One myth for containers I always have to bust is that they are used to replace virtual machines. That is actually possible, but I've found they typically *complement* virtual machines. One powerful use of containers is to consolidate applications into multiple containers running in a virtual machine.

Containers are actually an instance of an *immutable image* that contains a program(s) that is run in an isolated manner with a complete private file system. A container only includes the files necessary to run the programs in it from the image.

For example, SQL Server does not require every file and process that runs on a Linux system. So now you can deploy multiple SQL Server containers in a virtual machine instead of deploying multiple virtual machines, saving space and resource usage. In fact, running multiple SQL containers is exactly how you can run multiple instances of SQL Server in the same virtual machine or computer for Linux since we don't support named instances.

Another myth about containers is that they don't perform as well as a normal process because they are abstracted from the underlying Linux OS for threads, memory, I/O, etc. This is not true. Containers are just run in the OS in an isolated manner (containers only know about processes inside them) but have direct access to OS resources. So a SQL container running on Linux should have the same performance as SQL Server on Linux.

Note   Make sure you are comparing the right environment with containers. SQL containers on Windows run on a Linux virtual machine hosted by Windows (or WSL). That is a layer of abstraction that is different than running a container directly in a Linux VM hosted by Linux.

Containers are *run* by a container runtime like Docker. Effectively a container runtime like Docker understands how to take a container image and execute the program(s) associated with the container in an isolated manner using native Linux APIs (such as namespaces and cgroups). Container runtimes also understand how to manage containers such as stopping and starting a container.

Containers have other advantages including:

- **Portability** – Containers can run on any operating system that supports a container runtime like Docker, and you can be assured it is the same container image. So SQL Server containers can run on Windows, Linux, or macOS, and you can be assured it is the same SQL Server engine. Linux containers on Windows and macOS have some type of virtualization that allows them to run Linux programs. This portability is huge for development. Instead of trying to maintain a development server for SQL Server that all developers share, just provide them with SQL Server containers to run on their own environment for any OS.

- **Consistency** – Let's say you want all developers to use a specific cumulative update of SQL Server 2019 (or 2022 when we start shipping CU builds) along with a specific database schema and scripts. Containers provide that capability across any OS. Microsoft produces container images for each CU build of a major version of SQL Server: 2017, 2019, and 2022.

- **Efficiency** – Patching SQL Server with a cumulative update on Windows requires you to install a separate program that installs the update on top of the existing RTM build or update. SQL Server on Linux has an upgrade option to upgrade to a newer CU build. Containers do not require any patching. In fact, you can't patch a container. Instead, you *switch* containers. Read more in the section titled "**The Container Switch Method**" to see how it works.

Here is a talk I gave at SQLBits on SQL Server containers to learn more: `https://sqlbits.com/Sessions/Event18/Inside_SQL_Server_Containers`.

Using SQL Server 2022 Containers

I forgot to mention one of the most powerful capabilities of SQL Server containers. SQL Server containers are a preinstalled SQL Server (and by default Developer Edition, so it is free!). We have built our container images for SQL Server so that when you run them, SQL Server just starts up and executes. Part of the magic is that SQLSERVR.EXE was built to run as a standalone program (in effect, a daemon program) and our container image is set up to configure and start the SQL Server engine.

Running a SQL Server Container

I dusted off my exercises from *SQL Server 2019 Revealed* where I showed readers the basics of running a SQL Server container. You can find the SQL Server 2022 version of these scripts at `https://github.com/microsoft/bobsql/tree/master/demos/sqlserver2022/containers`.

How easy is it to run a SQL Server container? If you look at these scripts, you will find the first step is this command:

```
docker run `
 -e 'ACCEPT_EULA=Y' -e 'MSSQL_SA_PASSWORD=Sql2022isfast' `
 --hostname sql2022 `
 -p 1401:1433 `
 -v sql2022volume:/var/opt/mssql `
```

```
--name sql2022 `
-d `
mcr.microsoft.com/mssql/server:2022-latest
```

This is an example using the Docker container runtime on Windows with PowerShell (Docker Desktop on Windows can now use the Windows Subsystem for Linux, which means it is run as a virtualized process and not a full Linux VM). By default images are cached locally on your machine. If you run a container and the image does not exist locally, it is first *pulled* into your local cache. You can pull the image yourself with the docker pull command.

Let's look at the parameters of this command to run a container:

The -e parameters are to set environment variables (you can use any valid SQL Server Linux environment variable such as setting the edition).

The --hostname parameter is nice because this becomes @@SERVERNAME for the container. This will help scenarios like DTC, replication, and linked servers.

The -p parameter is a port mapping so that you can run multiple instances (multiple SQL instances using port 1433 would be a conflict).

The -v parameter is important. It maps the local directory in the container private file system to persisted storage. In this case Docker takes the name sql2022volume and associates this with a directory on the storage of my local computer that will survive any container restart or delete operation. Otherwise, when a container is deleted, the private file system would be deleted, which contains databases.

The --name parameter is a convenient name to use to manage the container with Docker (e.g., stop the container).

The -d parameter runs the program in the background so any stdout would be suppressed. (Without this the stdout of SQLSERVR.EXE would be displayed, which is the ERRORLOG file entries. Removing this parameter can be helpful to debug problems.)

The last parameter is the location of the container image. Microsoft hosts official product container images in the Microsoft Container Repository or mcr.microsoft.com. In this case the image name

```
mcr.microsoft.com/mssql/server:2022-latest
```

is this latest version of SQL Server 2022 images based on Ubuntu. We produce an image for each cumulative update. Using the "latest" tag just gives you the latest version. This was very convenient for me as I just changed 2019-latest to 2022-latest and at the time of the writing of this book, I got the latest preview build of SQL Server 2022.

Note   You can browse a list of container images based on RHEL at `https://mcr.microsoft.com/v2/mssql/rhel/server/tags/list` and Ubuntu at `https://mcr.microsoft.com/v2/mssql/server/tags/list`. To be supported you need to make sure and run a container image that matches the host OS. For example, Docker on Windows with WSL is based on Ubuntu, so only the SQL Server images based on Ubuntu are supported. You can learn more at `https://docs.microsoft.com/troubleshoot/sql/general/support-policy-sql-server#guidelines`.

This base SQL Server container image comes with the core SQL Server engine and tools like sqlcmd.

Get a complete reference for Docker at `https://docs.docker.com/reference`. I've been using Docker for some time, and it is important that you should know that in 2021 Docker announced some changes to their licensing, which could affect your ability to use Docker Desktop for free. Read more at `www.docker.com/blog/updating-product-subscriptions`. SQL Server containers are OCI compliant, so they are supported by other container runtime engines like **podman** (`https://podman.io`).

Since SQL Server containers are based on Linux, all the features supported and not supported by SQL Server on Linux are the same. One exception in SQL Server 2022 is that the Azure extension for SQL Server is not supported with containers.

Connecting to a SQL Server Container

Since this is the SQL Server engine, just connect to the container like you would any SQL Server with tools like SSMS or Azure Data Studio. Remember that if you used port mapping using the -p parameter, you need to use the new port number in the connection string. A simple example to connect to a container with sqlcmd outside the container can be found at `https://github.com/microsoft/bobsql/blob/master/demos/sqlserver2022/containers/deploy/step4_querysql.ps1`.

Since SQL Server containers include sqlcmd in the container image, you can also connect *inside* the container. Here is a script that uses sqlcmd inside the container to restore a database backup: `https://github.com/microsoft/bobsql/blob/master/demos/sqlserver2022/containers/deploy/step3_restoredb.ps1`.

Speaking of backups, you can restore a backup for a SQL Server container from the container file system. You first need to copy the backup file into the container file system. You can see an example with the script at `https://github.com/ microsoft/bobsql/blob/master/demos/sqlserver2022/containers/deploy/step2_ copyintocontainer.ps1`.

Building a Customized Container Image

You can see the power of containers, but what about all the other packages for SQL Server on Linux such as Polybase? How do they run in a SQL Server container? Docker includes the ability to build a new container image *based* on other images and a set of files like packages you install into the image. In fact, the core SQL Server container image is an image we build based on a base Linux OS image combined with our files for SQL Server.

The **docker build** command is used to build container images. You create a text file called a **Dockerfile**, which contains a set of commands on how to build the new image. You can see an example of how to build new packages combining the core SQL Server container image with other SQL Linux packages at `https://github.com/microsoft/ mssql-docker/tree/master/linux/preview/examples`. Docker build doesn't run a container. It is used to build an image that is run as a container with docker run.

This customization capability is very powerful. You can build your own container images that combine the SQL Server core image with your own set of scripts and even database backup files.

One tool to help build a complex set of container images and run them including applications is called **docker-compose** (`https://github.com/docker/compose`). Check out this example I built (thanks to my former colleague Vin Yu) to install SQL Server replication with containers using docker-compose at `https://github.com/microsoft/ bobsql/tree/master/demos/sqlserver2022/containers/replication`.

The Container Switch Method

I mentioned earlier in this chapter that you don't patch SQL Server containers. You *switch* them to apply a cumulative update. Here is how the magic works. When you run a container and specify a persistent volume with the -v command, any files in this volume survive a container restart or delete. If you put your SQL Server database files (including system databases) into a directory that is mapped to persisted storage, you can *point* any SQL Server container to this volume, one at time.

In addition, SQL Server cumulative updates are compatible with each other in a major version. Therefore, I could do the following:

1. Start a SQL Server 2022 RTM container image, pointing it to a persisted volume for /var/opt/mssql.

2. Let's say the first cumulative update for SQL Server 2022 comes out and I want to use it.

3. Stop the SQL Server 2022 RTM container.

4. Then run a new SQL Server container based on SQL Server 2022 CU1, pointing it to the same persisted volume. The new SQL Server will start up and recognize the new master database and user databases. In a manner of minutes, I've updated SQL Server.

5. Let's now say a problem occurs and you want to roll back to the SQL Server 2022 RTM container.

6. Stop the new SQL Server 2022 CU1 container and start the SQL Server 2022 RTM container. Within a few minutes, you have rolled back.

You can see examples of how to do this with SQL Server 2019 from *SQL Server 2019 Revealed* at `https://github.com/microsoft/bobsql/tree/master/sql2019book/ch7_inside_sql_containers/update/dockerpowershell`.

SQL Server 2022 on Kubernetes

Supporting Linux for SQL Server opened up a whole new world for us, including containers. Containers opened up the world to us for Kubernetes. Do you want to learn Kubernetes in a fun way? Nothing compares to The Illustrated Children's Guide to Kubernetes at `https://youtu.be/4ht22ReBjno`.

Why k8s

Kubernetes originated at Google. The founders of Kubernetes like Brendan Burns (who now works for Microsoft) wanted a way to run containers at scale. Linux on its own didn't provide for this, so they built a set of software services on top of Linux called Kubernetes. Brendan has built a really nice playlist of videos explaining Kubernetes at `www.youtube.com/watch?v=daVUONZqn88&list=PLLasXO2E8BPCrIhFrc_ZiINhbRkYMKdPT`.

Since SQL Server supports containers, why not also support Kubernetes? Okay, enough of that long word. Let's use k8s (k<eight letters>s) like the cool kids do. Admittedly the support for SQL Server on k8s is very basic. You can deploy SQL Server, connect to the instance, and store data in persisted storage. But k8s does provide some nice built-in capabilities like load balancers and basic high availability. If you are looking for a complete managed experience using k8s and SQL Server, you should take a look at Azure Arc–enabled SQL Managed Instance (Arc SQL MI) (`https://aka.ms/azurearcsqlmi`).

Keep up to date on the latest with SQL Server on k8s at `https://aka.ms/sqlk8s`. You can also watch a presentation I did for SQLBits to dive deeper at `https://youtu.be/USfCJDoCMr8`

It is worth understanding the basics so you can see how SQL Server on k8s works and whether it could be a platform for you to scale many SQL Server containers.

Deploying SQL Server on k8s

Let's look at the basics of deploying a single SQL Server container on k8s.

What Are the Major Components of k8s?

There a few terms for k8s you need to understand when you see the deployment experience. This is a very basic set of definitions. For a more complete reference to these components and architecture, see the k8s documentation at `https://kubernetes.io/docs/concepts/overview/components`.

Let's review these components through Figure 9-1 (not all components are shown here).

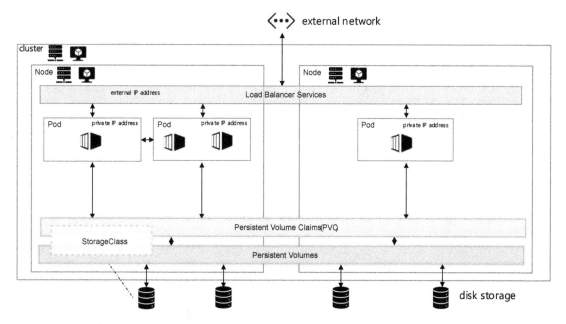

Figure 9-1. *k8s components*

Cluster

Think of a cluster like a host that contains all the k8s internal software and a series of virtual machines or nodes (can be physical servers) to run containers.

Node

Think of a node like a virtual machine (it can be a physical machine) that can help orchestrate other nodes or run user programs as containers.

Control plane

All the internal k8s software that runs the system is called the control plane and runs on every node. For example, k8s is all API based, so the API server can take requests and orchestrate across nodes.

Pod

A pod is defined as one or more containers to execute on a node. It is the smallest component of execution in the k8s system.

Container runtime

Since containers are at the heart of execution of pods, a container runtime like Docker must exist on all nodes to pull container images and run containers.

Namespace

A namespace is a logical group of k8s objects and makes it very convenient to organize projects. Every k8s system has a default namespace, but I recommend you always create other namespaces for your pods and other k8s objects.

Load balancer service

You have seen connection abstraction with SQL Server in the form of a listener. Think of a load balancer service (another type is called a node port) as a listener. A load balancer is a way to abstract a connection to a fixed IP address and port so that if the underlying IP address changes, it will always be directed to the right location.

Storage class and PersistentVolumeClaim

Storage class is a mapping of the storage types on your system. For example, Azure Kubernetes Service has a storage class defined by the system called managed-premium that gives you access to Azure Premium managed disks. Think of a PersistedVolumeClaim (PVC) as a volume of a fixed size from the storage class. The key to using PVC is that your data is stored in the cluster independent of a node. If you store your database files on a PVC, they will be available no matter what node the pod for SQL Server is running.

Replicaset and Statefulset

One of the coolest features of k8s is the ability to declare a form of high availability for our pods. For example, you can *tell* k8s, "I always want one copy of my pod running at any point in time." So if the pod fails (SQL Server crashes) or even the node fails (VM crashes), k8s will automatically try to start the pod again (could be on the same node or another node if one is available).

How Do I Get k8s?

K8s was built as an open source project, and you can deploy your own k8s cluster based on open source. For example, you can use the open source tool kubeadm to install k8s as documented at `https://kubernetes.io/docs/setup/production-environment/tools/kubeadm/create-cluster-kubeadm/`.

Most k8s customers use a licensed product for k8s production such as Azure Stack HCI, Red Hat OpenShift, or Rancher. You can use cloud-based k8s systems such as Azure Kubernetes Service (AKS), Google Kubernetes Engine (GKE), and Amazon Elastic Kubernetes Service (EKS). The big advantage of licensed products is some of the k8s system is managed and you can receive commercial production support.

What Are the Deployment Steps?

We built a simple tutorial for you to try out SQL Server on AKS at `https://aka.ms/sqlk8s`.

I also built a series of scripts to explain the deployment steps in more detail at `https://github.com/microsoft/bobsql/tree/master/demos/sqlserver2022/sqlk8s/deploy`.

The concepts are for you to *declare* to k8s the definition of a pod with a single SQL Server container image. The command line tool **kubectl** is often used to state your declaration to k8s (kubectl uses the k8s API). You also often use a text file called a YAML file to provide details of your declaration.

In the sample scripts, you do the following steps:

1. Create a new namespace for k8s objects.

2. Create a secret for the admin password.

3. Create a new load balancer service mapped to port 1433.

4. Create a PVC from the managed-premium storage class.

5. Use a YAML file to deploy a pod using the SQL Server container image referencing the secret, load balancer, and PVC. In the YAML file, declare a Replicaset of 1 so a SQL Server pod is always running.

Deploying the pod is an asynchronous operation. Container images are pulled if they do not exist in a node and executed. The overall orchestration of pods is far more complex than this. K8s has sophisticated algorithms to decide which nodes to schedule and run pods. It also must have event notifications to look for pod failures or resource limits and take action.

Connecting and Using SQL Server on k8s

On a system like AKS, the load balancer IP address and port are available externally, so a tool like SSMS can be used to connect through the load balancer to the SQL instance running in the pod. In my example script at `https://github.com/microsoft/bobsql/blob/master/demos/sqlserver2022/sqlk8s/deploy/step12_querysql.ps1`, you can see a way to dynamically determine the IP address of the load balancer to connect to SQL Server.

K8s includes built-in services to monitor resource usage to ensure the system remains healthy. One issue we have seen with k8s and SQL Server is that SQL Server can use a lot of memory within the node. It could cause a trigger for k8s to forcefully fail the pod and move it to another node. This is because k8s contains algorithms to detect the amount of memory that should be available within a node to keep it healthy. SQL Server though doesn't know about these algorithms. Famed SQL and Linux community expert Anthony Nocentino has a nice writeup on this scenario at `www.centinosystems.com/posts/2019-09-28-memory-settings-for-running-sql-server-in-kubernetes` including how you can address it.

High Availability with k8s

High availability is critical to a production SQL Server, so it is very nice that k8s provides built-in *basic* high availability within the system.

Basic HA with SQL and k8s

When you deploy a SQL Server pod on k8s and use a load balancer, PVC, and Replicaset, you have already declared to k8s you would like to use basic high availability.

Consider these two scenarios:

Pod failure

If for any reason SQL Server crashes, this is recognized as a pod failure, and k8s will automatically start a new pod, which will start a new SQL Server container typically on the same node if resources are available. Since all databases are on a PVC, this is like persisted storage for a SQL Server container. SQL Server will just run recovery on all databases.

A pod failure can occur within k8s for other reasons, and k8s may decide to start a new pod on a different node. Nodes have private IP addresses, but since you are using a load balancer, your connection is automatically redirected to the new node. And since you are using a PVC, all databases are available even on the new node. This is like a failover cluster with shared storage without you having to set up or configure any failover cluster software.

Node failure

The same situation can occur if a node fails assuming you have deployed multiple nodes when you built your k8s cluster. In fact, I recommend you have *at least* three nodes on any k8s cluster for SQL Server. One node will serve to orchestrate other worker nodes, and you will have at least two worker nodes for redundancy.

Here are my scripts to see HA in action with SQL Server on AKS at `https://github.com/microsoft/bobsql/tree/master/demos/sqlserver2022/sqlk8s/ha`.

Always On Availability Groups and k8s

In the preview of SQL Server 2019, we introduced a concept to deploy an Always On Availably Group integrated with k8s. Unfortunately, that capability did not make the final release of SQL Server 2019. The work we did there did evolve into the built-in AG feature (through the Business Critical service tier) that comes with Azure Arc–enabled SQL Managed Instance.

There is another solution that comes with our partner DH2i (`https://dh2i.com`). You can see how to deploy an AG on k8s with DH2i's solution at `https://docs.microsoft.com/sql/linux/tutorial-sql-server-containers-kubernetes-dh2i`.

Helm Charts

Some find the k8s deployment experience a bit complicated. Along comes the concept of Helm charts (`https://helm.sh`). Think of Helm as a package manager for k8s. You can see how to deploy SQL Server using Helm at `https://docs.microsoft.com/sql/linux/sql-server-linux-containers-deploy-helm-charts-kubernetes`.

The World of Linux, Containers, and k8s

For many SQL Server on Linux has opened up new doors and possibilities. I've spoken to customers who have different parts of their organization use Windows, while others use Linux but need a consistent database platform like SQL Server across them.

But Linux support opens up so many other possibilities. SQL Server containers could change the way your organization builds applications. Imagine developers across your company using the OS of their choice to build applications against the same consistent SQL Server engine and database. In fact, the new Azure SQL Database local development experience (`https://docs.microsoft.com/azure/azure-sql/database/local-dev-experience-overview`) uses SQL Server containers. Or consider the fact that you can consolidate multiple SQL Server instances in a single VM with containers.

With containers comes k8s, and our Azure Arc–enabled SQL Managed Instance proves you can bring the power of Azure managed services to your infrastructure using k8s.

All of these tell the story of choice for SQL Server. Choice with compatibility. Your application doesn't have to change, and databases are interchangeable no matter where SQL Server is deployed.

CHAPTER 10

SQL Server 2022 on Azure Virtual Machines

Today when you deploy SQL Server 2022, you have choices to run SQL Server on a laptop, a "bare-metal" server, or even a container. The most common choice to deploy and run SQL Server is a *virtual machine*. While running SQL Server with virtualization technologies such as Hyper-V and VMWare is extremely popular, many customers are now turning to the cloud to get the Infrastructure-as-a-Service (IaaS) experience. I believe using an **Azure Virtual Machine** provides you with a great experience.

The SQL Server on Azure Virtual Machines experience is constantly evolving and getting better. So while there are no new specific capabilities in Azure Virtual Machines for SQL Server 2022, I thought a chapter devoted to SQL Server on Azure Virtual Machines would be valuable for readers of this book.

In this chapter I'll show how to deploy SQL Server on Azure Virtual Machines as well as using, managing, optimizing, and monitoring it.

What Is SQL Server on Azure Virtual Machines?

You may have an existing SQL Server virtual machine (VM) deployment or may be thinking about a new one. Now, where to host the VM? One of these choices is in Azure called an Azure Virtual Machine. An Azure Virtual Machine is known as an Infrastructure as a Service (IaaS) because Azure provides the hosting infrastructure as a service to you for a virtual machine running Windows or Linux. This means that Azure will host your virtual machine and provide all the hardware including compute, storage, and networking. You will be responsible to manage everything inside the *guest* virtual machine including the operating system and SQL Server. We do certain things to help you manage the guest virtual machine environment, and you will see that in this chapter.

© Bob Ward 2022
B. Ward, *SQL Server 2022 Revealed*, https://doi.org/10.1007/978-1-4842-8894-8_10

Since you have complete control inside the virtual machine, you are free to use either a Windows or Linux operating system (including containers). And SQL Server running in this environment is the complete "box" product including the database engine and all services. Effectively, any SQL Server feature you can run in a VM in your environment can be run in an Azure Virtual Machine. This includes services outside the engine like SQL Server Integration Services (SSIS), SQL Server Analysis Services (SSAS), and SQL Server Reporting Services (SSRS).

Planning for Deployment

Anytime you are going to deploy a new SQL Server instance, a certain healthy amount of planning will save you time, money, and effort. When you plan a new SQL deployment on a Hyper-V virtual machine, you have factors you consider like number of CPUs, CPU type and speed, and memory. What kind of storage capacity, performance, and number of drives are required? You might even work in a company that has data centers where you are required to use a website to request a virtual machine to be provisioned. It would be typical in those scenarios to choose a VM *size*, which dictates the resources you have available for your SQL Server instance.

You also need to know how an application and tools will connect to SQL Server. Will you use Remote Desktop (rdp) to run tools like SSMS inside the VM or remotely? How will you set up the network of your virtual machine to connect to your applications? What about high availability and disaster recovery? All questions to be thought through for any production SQL Server deployment.

These decisions are no different with an Azure Virtual Machine. One big difference is now your virtual machine with SQL Server is being hosted in Azure. This means your choices on possible virtual machine resources are dictated by what Microsoft provides (but you will see the choices are vast).

Let's review some of the important decisions you need to consider to make the overall experience the best possible. You will use these planning decisions to make choices during and after deployment. A big reason I think you should consider these choices before you deploy is you may become blocked on deployment because you are not sure about what choice to make.

- You need an **Azure subscription** to deploy a virtual machine and also to decide what **resource group** to use. Resource groups are a great way to organize multiple Azure resources, but they also can be a convenient method to create your own virtual network in Azure. Read more about resource groups at https://docs.microsoft.com/azure/azure-resource-manager/management/overview#resource-groups.

- **Review the possible virtual machine sizes** available in Azure at https://aka.ms/azurevmsizes. To help you narrow down your choices, check out our advice on Azure VM sizes for SQL Server at https://aka.ms/SQLIaaSSizing. Also take heart, in many cases, you can change your VM size after you have deployed often with a very small amount of downtime.

Tip You will see an issue later in this chapter where the virtual machine size I choose has a cap on storage performance that is less than the disk storage choices for data, log, and tempdb. This can cause an unexpected and hard-to-detect performance problem. Take time reading our documentation at https://docs.microsoft.com/azure/azure-sql/virtual-machines/windows/performance-guidelines-best-practices-checklist to align these choices.

- Are there **trust concerns** about hosting SQL Server and data in Azure? Check out https://aka.ms/azuretrust for more information on Azure privacy, compliance, security layers, and monitoring.

- VM sizes can dictate what type of **storage choices** are available for performance, but also consider the basic decision of what is the maximum size of storage you need for your database(s). For example, you can get storage in Azure for databases with a VM size that would support 2048TB across multiple disks. However, the maximum size to back up a SQL Server database to Azure Blob Storage is 12TB (Azure Premium file shares can support 100TB). Read through our best practices for storage choices first at https://docs.microsoft.com/azure/azure-sql/virtual-machines/windows/performance-guidelines-best-practices-checklist.

- A very important decision to make is which **Azure region** to deploy your virtual machine. An Azure region is a geographical location where Azure data centers exist. What started with just a few data centers years ago has turned into a worldwide force. So much so that we organize Azure regions into *geographies*. You can see the amazing story of just how many choices you have to deploy an Azure virtual machine at `https://azure.microsoft.com/global-infrastructure/ geographies`. Your choice of an Azure region can be based on many factors mostly centered around where your applications will connect to SQL Server in an Azure virtual machine. I think picking the right region for you is important from the beginning, but there are methods to move virtual machines to other regions, which you can read about at `https://docs.microsoft.com/azure/resource-mover/tutorial- move-region-virtual-machines`. Azure virtual machines are considered a *core service*, so whenever we build a new region, you can be assured an Azure virtual machine will be available. However, not all virtual machine sizes may be available in all regions.

- Decide on an **admin account** and password. You will be required to supply an admin account for either Windows or Linux. I've had customers get totally blocked here because there are company standards for admin accounts. If you use a SQL Server marketplace image, we automatically add this admin account as a member of the sysadmin role.

- **How will you deploy?**

  There are several ways to deploy SQL Server on an Azure Virtual Machine. I'll show you later in this chapter a step-by-step process to deploy using the Azure portal, but you can also deploy using scripts and a concept called an **ARM template**.

  You also need to decide if you will use a **marketplace image for SQL Server**, which comes with an operating system and SQL Server preinstalled. We have various choices of OS and SQL Server combinations available. There are advantages with this approach including the automatic installation of the **SQL Server IaaS extension**, which you will learn more about later in this chapter in the section titled "**The SQL Server IaaS Agent Extension.**"

Note   The marketplace images for SQL Server can come with all services including SQL Server Reporting Services (SSRS) and SQL Server Analytics Services (SSAS) installed, or you can choose just the database engine. There are also separate marketplace images for just SSRS or SSAS.

There can be scenarios where you want to install SQL Server yourself. I do this sometimes when I'm installing a specific build of SQL Server. So I will use the Azure marketplace to install just the operating system. Then I copy my SQL install packages into the virtual machine and install SQL Server. One nice feature of using the marketplace images for SQL Server is that we leave the installation binaries inside the virtual machine so you can uninstall and reinstall for a named instance scenario.

No matter what method you use, you will have to decide on **licensing**. Do you have existing SQL Server, Windows, and/or Linux licenses, or will you choose a pay-as-you-go method? Using existing licenses for SQL Server and Windows is called **Azure Hybrid Benefit** (AHUB). You can read more about AHUB at https://azure.microsoft.com/pricing/hybrid-benefit. There is one other license option for **DR** where you can deploy an Azure virtual machine for disaster recovery only and be license free for SQL Server. You can learn more about this at https://docs. microsoft.com/azure/azure-sql/virtual-machines/windows/ business-continuity-high-availability-disaster-recovery- hadr-overview#free-dr-replica-in-azure.

You also have options to save money by using a concept called **reserved instances**, which you can read about at https://azure. microsoft.com/pricing/reserved-vm-instances. Even if you choose options to use existing software licenses for Windows and SQL Server, you will still incur costs for compute and storage.

- Do you need a **Failover Cluster Instance (FCI)** or **Always On Availability Group?**

  If you plan to deploy SQL Server as part of a Failover Cluster Instance (FCI) or Always On Availability Group, then you will need to make certain choices including availability, storage, and networking. See the section titled "**High Availability**" later in this chapter for more details.

There are other choices for deployment to make, but I'll show you those in an exercise in the section later in this chapter titled "**Deploying SQL Server on an Azure Virtual Machine**," which shows you how to deploy using a SQL Server marketplace image through the Azure portal.

The SQL Server IaaS Agent Extension

You have learned in this book the concept of the Azure Arc Agent and extensions like the Azure extension for SQL Server. Azure virtual machines have the same concept through virtual machine extensions. You can read more about the overall extension concept at `https://docs.microsoft.com/azure/virtual-machines/extensions/overview`. The extension architecture is also available for Linux, which you can read about at `https://docs.microsoft.com/azure/virtual-machines/extensions/features-linux`.

What Is the SQL Server IaaS Agent Extension?

For SQL Server we have built an extension for Azure virtual machines called the **SQL Server IaaS Agent Extension**. This extension installs a set of services inside your virtual machine to give you real value in managing your virtual machine and SQL Server including

- Azure portal management

- Automatic SQL database backups

- Automatic security updates

- Licensing and edition management including AHUB

- SQL configuration management such as tempdb

- SQL best practices assessment
- Microsoft Defender for Cloud

Note   At the time of the writing of this book, the SQL Server IaaS Agent Extension did not support Azure Active Directory (AAD) authentication and Microsoft Purview access policies with SQL Server 2022. Our team has plans to add these capabilities in the future.

There is no cost associated with using the SQL Server IaaS Agent Extension.

IaaS Agent Extension Modes

The extension has two different modes and installation methods.

Full

This is the default mode when you use a SQL marketplace image and enables all features.

Lightweight

Lightweight mode does not install the agent software but does give you a limited portal experience including licensing and edition management. For example, you can use this method to use Azure Hybrid Benefit. You can upgrade to full mode at any time because for lightweight mode, we copy the agent binaries into the virtual machine but do not install them.

Installing the Agent Extension

When you deploy SQL Server using Azure marketplace images, we automatically install the Agent Extension in full mode. You also can install the Agent Extension in any mode after you deploy. We call the installation of the extension *registration*. You can read more about how to register the extension on Windows at `https://docs.microsoft.com/azure/azure-sql/virtual-machines/windows/sql-agent-extension-manually-register-single-vm` or Linux at `https://docs.microsoft.com/azure/azure-sql/virtual-machines/linux/sql-iaas-agent-extension-register-vm-linux`.

Registering the extension does not require a restart of the virtual machine. You have options to do a bulk registration of virtual machines and repair and unregister the extension.

Details of the Agent Extension

If you have chosen full mode, you will see programs installed in your Windows virtual machine called the Microsoft Monitoring Agent and the Microsoft SQL Server IaaS Agent. These programs use several different Windows services (or daemon programs on Linux).

For example, if you use Extended Events to trace activity coming into your SQL Server, you will see an application called Microsoft SQL Server IaaS Agent Query Service.

To see more details on the differences for SQL Server on Linux, read this documentation page: `https://docs.microsoft.com/azure/azure-sql/virtual-machines/linux/sql-server-iaas-agent-extension-linux`.

In my experience the Agent Extension does not consume a lot of resources. You always have the option to unregister the extension if you feel it is causing any problems.

There are a few other important points about the extension:

- We only support lightweight mode for a Failover Cluster Instance (FCI), but full mode is supported for Always On Availability Groups.

- We don't support the extension for multiple instances on a SQL Server Windows virtual machine. We only support at maximum one instance. If the instance you need supported is a named instance, the default registration uses lightweight mode, but you can upgrade to full mode.

- Today we don't support registering the extension for SQL Server Linux containers running in an Azure Virtual Machine.

I asked Aditya Badramraju, Senior Program Manager for SQL Server on Azure Virtual Machines, about the importance of the SQL Server IaaS Agent Extension. He told me, *"Running SQL Server on Azure IaaS is different to other clouds as we provide IaaS++ offerings* such as Automated Backup, SQL VM Best Practices assessment etc. by default, when customers choose to run SQL Server on Azure VMs/IaaS. These offerings are made possible by SQL IaaS Agent extension. This extension helps bringing greatness of both SQL Server and Azure infrastructure together such that customers can confidently run their mission critical workloads."

Deploying SQL Server on an Azure Virtual Machine

Using your knowledge about planning for a deployment, let's go through an exercise with the Azure portal and a marketplace image to see how to deploy SQL Server on an Azure Virtual Machine. This exercise is designed to show you how to deploy a *standalone* instance of SQL Server running Windows Server on an Azure Virtual Machine. You can read more about deploying SQL Server on Linux on an Azure Virtual Machine at `https://docs.microsoft.com/azure/azure-sql/virtual-machines/linux/sql-vm-create-portal-quickstart`. You can read more about deploying a Failover Cluster Instance (FCI) or Always On Availability Group in the section titled "**High Availability**" later in this chapter.

This exercise is based on a quick-start guide in the documentation at `https://docs.microsoft.com/azure/azure-sql/virtual-machines/windows/sql-vm-create-portal-quickstart`.

Prerequisites

- You have reviewed the section in this chapter called "**Planning for Deployment**."

- You will need an Azure subscription with permissions to create an Azure Virtual Machine (typically a member of the Contributor role will do). Verify you also have permissions to create an Azure virtual machine within your subscription quota and the region you want to use is supported within your subscription.

Steps to Deploy

1. Launch the Azure portal at `https://portal.azure.com` and log in in using your Azure subscription.

2. On your home page, select + **Create Resource.** In the search box, type in **Azure SQL**. In the drop-down, select Azure SQL. Select **Create**. You should now see a screen like Figure 10-1.

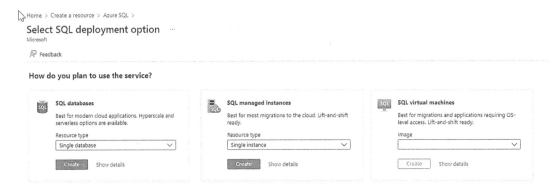

Figure 10-1. *Creating an Azure SQL resource*

SQL Server on Azure Virtual Machines is part of the Azure SQL family, and this screen is a convenient method to choose several SQL virtual machine options.

3. For SQL virtual machines, select the "down arrow" to see marketplace image options. You can scroll through these choices to see the various combinations of OS and SQL versions. For now, choose the option for SQL Server 2022 for a Free License. When SQL Server 2022 becomes generally available, this choice should be **Free SQL Server License: SQL Server 2022 Developer on Windows Server 2022**. (At GA there will also be choices for Standard and Enterprise editions). Click **Create**.

4. Now you will be able to fill out information based on your planning on a series of screens called *blades*. The first blade is **Basics**. Figure 10-2 shows how I filled out the Basics blade for my new VM to create.

Home > Create a resource > Azure SQL > Select SQL deployment option >

Create a virtual machine

Basics   Disks   Networking   Management   Monitoring   Advanced   SQL Server settings   Tags   Review – create

Create a virtual machine that runs Linux or Windows. Select an image from Azure marketplace or use your own customized image. Complete the Basics tab then Review + create to provision a virtual machine with default parameters or review each tab for full customization. Learn more ◻

Project details

Select the subscription to manage deployed resources and costs. Use resource groups like folders to organize and manage all your resources.

Subscription * ○	AzureSQL_bobward ∨
└── Resource group * ○	bwsql2022vms ∨
	Create new

Instance details

Virtual machine name * ○	sql2022vm
Region * ○	(US) East US 2 ∨
Availability options ○	No infrastructure redundancy required ∨
Security type ○	Standard ∨
Image * ○	☑ Free SQL Server License: SQL Server 2022 RC0 Developer on Windows Serv ∨
	See all images | Configure VM generation
VM architecture ○	○ Arm64
	● x64
	❶ Arm64 is not supported with the selected image.
Run with Azure Spot discount ○	☐
Size * ○	Standard_E4ds_v5 – 4 vcpus, 32 GiB memory ($210.24/month) ∨
	See all sizes

Administrator account

Username * ○	sqladmin
Password * ○	••••••••••••••• ⊕
Confirm password * ○	••••••••••••••• ⊕

Inbound port rules

Select which virtual machine network ports are accessible from the public internet. You can specify more limited or granular network access on the Networking tab.

Public inbound ports * ○	○ None
	● Allow selected ports
Select inbound ports *	RDP (3389) ∨

⚠ **This will allow all IP addresses to access your virtual machine.** This is only recommended for testing. Use the Advanced controls in the Networking tab to create rules to limit inbound traffic to known IP addresses.

Licensing

Save up to 49% with a license you already own using Azure Hybrid Benefit. Learn more ◻
Would you like to use an existing ☑
Windows Server license? * ○

☑ I confirm I have an eligible Windows Server license with Software Assurance *
or Windows Server subscription to apply this Azure Hybrid Benefit.

Review Azure hybrid benefit compliance ◻

[Review + create]   [< Previous]   [Next : Disks >]

Figure 10-2. *The Basics blade for Azure virtual machine deployment*

Let's take a closer look at these options:

- Your **Azure subscription** will be filled in based on the default subscription for your account, but you can change this if you have multiple subscriptions.

- I chose an existing **resource group** I've created for multiple virtual machines. You can also create a new one here.

Tip   When you create a virtual machine in a new resource group, a virtual network is created. If you add other virtual machines to the same resource group, the Azure portal will add your new virtual machines to the same Azure network. Therefore, your VMs are now in their own private network easily able to discover each other.

- Choose a **virtual machine name**, which must be unique in your resource group. This becomes the computer name of the VM.

- Choose the **Azure region** to deploy your VM.

- For **Availability options** I don't need anything extra for availability than what Azure already provides. You will need to choose an option here when you build a Failover Cluster Instance (FCI) or Always On Availability Group.

- For **Security type** I chose Standard. You do have some new security options for your VM including options that support features like secure boot and new TPM encryption. SQL Server marketplace images may not be available for all of these options.

- For **Image** I just left the option I chose when using the Azure SQL screen. You could use this to change to a different edition or OS option.

- For **VM architecture** x64 is the only option for SQL Server marketplace images.

- I left **Run with Azure Spot discount** unchecked because that option would not be appropriate for a SQL Server–based virtual machine. (This option means you pay less but may have less built-in availability.)

- **Size** is where it gets interesting. There is where your planning comes into play. If you click **See all sizes**, you can change your size. The Ev5 series is one of the recommend ones for SQL Server, so I chose this one. For my testing purposes, four vCPUs and 32Gb RAM are plenty. There are other limits that come into play based on size mostly around storage performance. So even though you can change this later, it is best to stop and get this as right up front. Consult our site at `https://aka.ms/ SQLIaaSSizing` for more information. Pay close attention to the overall storage performance cap for the virtual machine based on the size choice vs specific storage choices you need for data, log, and tempdb.

Note   There could be scenarios where you want to pay less but don't mind less resources or storage performance such as development scenarios. Consider sizes like the D series or B series for burstable.

- Fill in a username and password for the **administrator account**. Even though you can change the password later (even in the portal if you forget it), you can also create new admin accounts in the virtual machine through standard OS options.

- I will leave the standard rdp port open as public inbound port for testing purposes. For production you may not want to do this and use other options. I'll cover these options in the next section of the chapter, "**Connecting to SQL Server on an Azure Virtual Machine.**"

- For **licensing** I definitely want to save money. Let's say I have existing licenses for Windows Server that are not currently being used. I can check this box and declare I want to use my Windows license to pay for the Windows cost of the virtual machine.

Select **Next: Disks**.

5. For the **Disks** blade, there may be some options for you to explore, but this is only for the OS disk. You will get options later for other data disks to store SQL Server data, log, and tempdb files. Click **Next: Networking**.

6. For the **Networking** blade, I'll leave all the defaults. This is because I'll by default join the Azure virtual network for the resource group. If you selected a new resource group, you would have options to automatically create a new network. There could be specific scenarios where an Azure network is already set up and you can join that network here. There is an option called Accelerated Networking, which I recommend you select to get maximum network performance. It is by default selected if you have a virtual machine size that supports this feature. Click **Next: Management**.

7. For the **Management** blade, I'll use the defaults, but I recommend you explore a few options here including enabling Microsoft Defender for Cloud (I have this auto-enabled with my subscription), auto-shutdown for testing or developer-oriented virtual machines, and Enable hotpatch (but only available with specific OS choices). Click **Next: Monitoring**.

8. On the **Monitoring** blade, I left the defaults, but you should explore some of the other options here for diagnostics. These are independent of SQL and are for the OS and VM. Click **Next: Advanced**.

9. For the **Advanced** blade, I left the defaults, but there could be some customization per your organization needs such as installing different extensions. (This is not where the SQL Server IaaS Agent Extension is chosen. You made that selection by choosing a SQL Server marketplace image.) Click **Next: SQL Server settings**.

10. The **SQL Server settings** blade only appears if you choose a SQL Server marketplace image. It provides several options to configure SQL Server settings and also important options like storage. Figure 10-3 shows the default options when this blade first appeared for me.

Basics   Disks   Networking   Management   Monitoring   Advanced   **SQL Server settings**   Tags   Review + create

Security & Networking

SQL connectivity *   Private (within Virtual Network)   ⌄

Port *   1433

SQL Authentication

SQL Authentication ⓘ   (Disable) Enable

Azure Key Vault integration ⓘ (Disable) Enable

Storage configuration

Customize performance, size, and workload type to optimize storage for this virtual machine. For optimal performance, separate drives will be created for data and log storage by default. Learn more about SQL Server best performance practices.

Storage   SQL Data: 1024 GiB, 5000 IOPS, 200 MB/s
                              SQL Log: 1024 GiB, 5000 IOPS, 200 MB/s
                              SQL TempDb: Use local SSD drive
                              Change configuration

SQL instance settings

Customize additional SQL instance settings including collation, MAXDOP, server memory limit and optimize for ad-hoc workload.

Instance settings   **Default configuration**
                              MAXDOP: 0
                              SQL Server memory limits: 0 - 2147483647 MB
                              Collation: SQL_Latin1_General_CP1_CI_AS
                              Change SQL instance settings

SQL Server License

Save up to 43% with licenses you already own. Already have a SQL Server license? Learn more

SQL Server License ⓘ   ◉ No   ○ Yes

Automated patching

Set a patching window during which all Windows and SQL patches will be applied.

Automated patching ⓘ   **Enabled**
                              Sunday at 2:00
                              Change configuration

Automated backup

Automated backup ⓘ   (Disable) Enable

R Services(Advanced Analytics)

SQL Server Machine Learning Services (Disable) Enable
(In-Database) ⓘ

[Review + create]   [< Previous]   [Next : Tags >]

Figure 10-3. *SQL Server settings during Azure deployment*

Let's learn more about these settings:

- For **Security & Networking**, I recommend you leave the Private option for port 1433. This means any SQL connectivity to SQL Server in the VM will need to come from a computer that is connected in the Azure virtual network (or a network connected to this virtual network). If you choose Public, I highly recommend you change the port number to avoid exposing port 1433 on the public Internet. There are options like creating a Network Security Group (NSG) firewall rule after the fact if you have to use a public endpoint and port 1433.

- For **SQL Authentication** you can choose Enable, and it will allow "mixed-mode" authentication and prompt you for a SQL sysadmin account and password (sa will still be disabled).

- For **Azure Key Vault integration**, you can leave the default disabled and later enable this if you want to store user-managed keys (such as for TDE) in Azure Key Vault.

- Now comes **Storage configuration**, which could be the single most important choice you make for performance for SQL Server on an Azure virtual machine. We have recommend settings for you on the type of managed disk for data, log, and tempdb. I highly recommend you click Change configuration and review these settings. You will be provided with options for how to configure various disks for data, log, and tempdb. Here are a few pointers:

  - I mentioned earlier in the chapter on planning to read over our best practices, which include storage choices, at `https://docs.microsoft.com/azure/azure-sql/virtual-machines/windows/performance-guidelines-best-practices-checklist`.

  - Place tempdb on the temporary drive as recommended. There is no reason not to choose this option. You must have a VM size that supports the temporary disk to use this. Also this screen gives you choices for number of tempdb files and options like autogrow.

  - Look carefully on this screen for a warning like Figure 10-4.

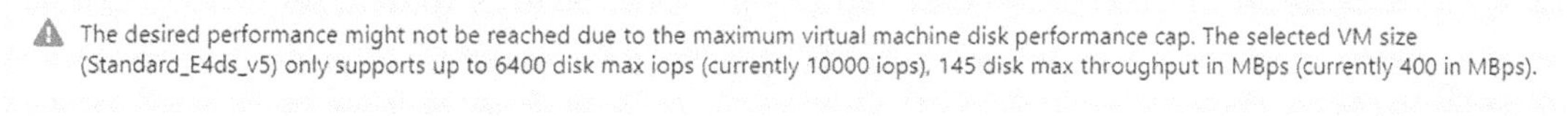

⚠ The desired performance might not be reached due to the maximum virtual machine disk performance cap. The selected VM size (Standard_E4ds_v5) only supports up to 6400 disk max iops (currently 10000 iops), 145 disk max throughput in MBps (currently 400 in MBps).

Figure 10-4. *Virtual machine I/O cap warning*

The disk choices you make on this screen dictate things like IOPS and throughput. Larger disks sizes usually have better performance. However, your virtual machine size choice **could cap the overall I/O throughput of the VM**, and that is what this warning is telling you. I highly recommend for any production virtual machine to align your virtual machine size with your storage choices. For me I changed my storage sizes lower to align with the virtual machine size cap. If you need a larger size, you may need to go back and choose a different VM size.

You do have options to extend the storage configuration after you have deployed.

- Next comes **SQL instance settings**. These are settings that you could normally choose during SQL Server setup such as MAXDOP but even more. For example, you can enable Instant File Initialization (IFI) and Locked Pages in Memory. You are always free inside the VM to make any changes to these later.

- For **SQL Server License**, this is where you can choose to apply an existing SQL Server license to your deployment to save costs. This is the Azure Hybrid Benefit (AHUB) option. My option is grayed out because I chose a free version of SQL Server.

- Your last set of options include configuring automatic backups and security updates and enabling SQL Server machine learning services as a feature. You can change these options later except for machine learning services, which you can add as a feature in the virtual machine through SQL Server setup later.

Select **Next: Tags**.

11. The **Tags** blade is completely optional. It is used for you to label an Azure resource. I recommend using Tags for situations like a shared subscription so you can organize and easily find certain types of Azure resources by usage type or department. Select **Next: Review + create**.

12. You are now presented with a screen, which is kind of your "last chance" before deployment. We do a validation here first, and then you can review estimated costs and all of your settings. When you are ready, select **Create**.

You don't have to wait at this point as the deployment is an asynchronous operation. But if you leave the portal as is, you will be presented with a **Deployment in Progress** screen, which is dynamically updated and shows the progress of creating all the resources for the virtual machine and installing SQL Server.

The times to deploy the virtual machine with SQL Server preinstalled can always vary, sometimes by region. But in my experience the deployment should be complete within about 10 minutes.

When the deployment is complete, select **Go to Resource**. Your screen should look like Figure 10-5.

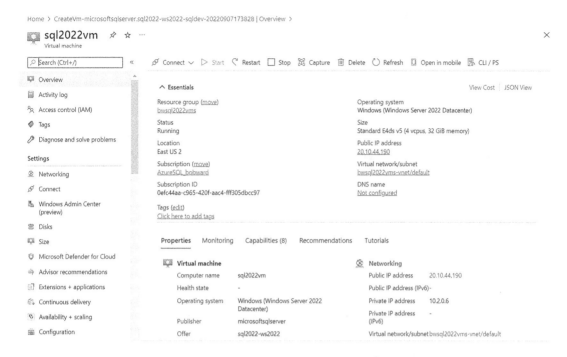

Figure 10-5. *A deployed SQL Server on an Azure Virtual Machine*

Other Deployment Methods

You have other options to deploy an Azure virtual machine than the portal including the az CLI and PowerShell. A very powerful way to deploy Azure virtual machines (and almost all Azure resources) for automation is to use an Azure Resource Manager (ARM) template. Get started with ARM template for virtual machines at `https://docs.` `microsoft.com/azure/virtual-machines/windows/quick-create-template`. Here is also a quick-start guide to deploy SQL Server on an Azure virtual machine with ARM templates at `https://docs.microsoft.com/azure/azure-sql/virtual-machines/` `windows/create-sql-vm-resource-manager-template`.

Now what do you do? Read on to the next section on how to explore your deployment and connect to SQL Server on an Azure Virtual Machine.

Exploring and Connecting to the SQL Server Virtual Machine

Let's learn about how to explore, connect to, and configure your Azure virtual machine and your SQL Server Azure virtual machine.

Exploring Your Azure Virtual Machine in the Portal

Let's explore your Azure virtual machine in the Azure portal wait by examining the deployment as seen in Figure 10-6.

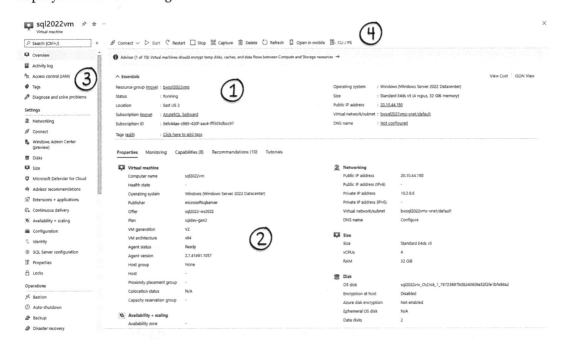

Figure 10-6. *A deployed Azure virtual machine in the portal*

If you want to know how to easily get to a virtual machine deployment, use the Search field on the Azure home page, or on the left-hand menu of the Azure home page, select Virtual machines.

Let's look at the major areas of a deployment and what you can do with each by following the numbers in the figure:

Note   Almost every option you see in the portal to view or configure the virtual machine can also be done via the az command line interface (CLI) or PowerShell. And an easy way to run these is through the Azure Cloud Shell. You will love the cloud shell if you have not seen it. You can read more at `https://docs.microsoft.com/azure/cloud-shell/overview`. In addition there is a mobile application for Azure, and I've been able to manage my virtual machine and other Azure resources from my phone! There is also an API option in the left-hand menu of the portal to allow you to run some az CLI commands. In addition at the top of the screen, you can use the CLI/PS option.

---

1. The top section of the screen is called **Essentials** where you can view basic information about the deployment. One important property is Status so you can see if the virtual machine is Running or Stopped.

2. The main page of the screen includes tabs to see more ***details*** on the properties of the virtual machine, monitoring statistics, other features you can enable, and recommendations. The Monitoring tab is very interesting as seen in Figure 10-7.

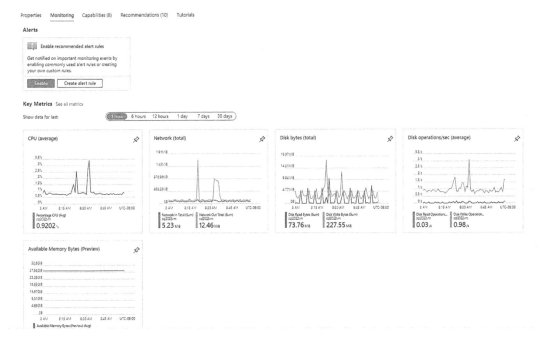

Figure 10-7. *Built-in monitoring with the Azure virtual machine*

It's like having the Windows Task Manager performance information at any time without having to connect inside the VM. Notice the ability to enable alerts. You can configure alerts so you can get notifications if any key metric becomes a problem (e.g., if CPU goes above a threshold).

3. The left-hand side of the screen is called the resource menu (or left-hand menu) and has many options to view and configure the virtual machine. There are so many options it would take another chapter to cover them. Here are few though I regularly use:

    -   **Size** – This is where you would view more details about the virtual machine size or change the size. Read more about resizing a virtual machine at `https://docs.microsoft.com/azure/virtual-machines/resize-vm`.

    -   **Networking** – I may need to go to this option to configure the Network Security Group (NSG), which is like firewall rules.

- **SQL Server configuration** – Here I can go to a SQL Server view of the virtual machine. I'll talk more about this in the section titled "**Exploring a SQL Virtual Machine in the Portal.**"

- **Microsoft Defender for Cloud** – If you enabled this, see Defender recommendations or alerts for security.

- **Bastion** – This option gives you a secure way to have a Remote Desktop experience using a browser.

- **Run command** – An interesting way to run programs inside the virtual machine without connecting to the virtual machine.

- **Metrics** – Get key performance counters without having to connect inside the virtual machine. Some of the performance information such as the virtual machine from a host perspective is only available here.

- **Export template** – You can build an ARM template based on the current deployment. I sometimes deploy through the portal and then use this option to build a template for other virtual machines to deploy.

- **Boot diagnostics** – This is a cool feature to see the "console" screen of the virtual machine to make sure it is not in a hung state.

- **Reset password** – Forgot your admin password? You can reset it here. And if you are concerned with security, only accounts that have permissions to the virtual machine in Azure can do this.

- **Redeploy + reapply** – I've had a few situations come up where using this option allowed my virtual machine to be restarted successfully when it appeared to be in a hung state. You may never need this, but it's nice to know it exists.

- **Serial console** – This is like having the monitor of the computer available to you, and it really pays off when there seems to be an issue starting the virtual machine. Again you may never need this, but it's nice to know it exists.

4. At the top of the screen is a menu of important options:

- **Connect** – This gives you details on how to connect to the virtual machine using Remote Desktop (rdp) or ssh for Linux.

- **Start** – If you shut down the virtual machine inside the OS or stop it using the portal, this is how you would start it again.

- **Restart** – There could be several scenarios where you need to restart the virtual machine without having OS access.

- **Stop** – This option allows you to shut down the virtual machine without OS access. There is a distinct difference between stopping a virtual machine with this option and stopping inside the virtual machine with an OS method. If you shut down the virtual machine with the OS, the virtual machine has a status of **Stopped**, but you are still paying for compute resources. If you use this option, the virtual machine has a status of **Stopped (deallocated)**, and you don't pay for compute resources. Using this option could cause a longer delay to start the virtual machine but is a convenient method to save compute costs.

Now let's review the basics of how to connect to a virtual machine.

Connecting to the Azure Virtual Machine

If you have a virtual machine in your own environment, the two most common methods to connect to the virtual machine for OS access are Remote Desktop (rdp) for Windows and ssh for Linux.

There are basically three methods to connect to the Azure virtual machine. To get started, in the Azure portal select the Connect option in the top menu of the screen. You will see options as shown in Figure 10-8.

⚠ To improve security, enable just-in-time access on this VM. →

RDP   SSH   Bastion

Connect with RDP

⌃ Suggested method for connecting

Azure has checked the status for the most common prerequisites when connecting using this method.

🌐 Checking network security group for inbound access from your client's IP address. Learn more ⬀
✅ The VM's network interface has a Public IP address. Learn more ⬀
✅ The VM is running.

To connect to your virtual machine via RDP, select an IP address, optionally change the port number, and download the RDP file.

IP address *

Public IP address (20.10.44.190)	⌄

Port number *

3389

[**Download RDP File**]

Can't connect?

⚙ Test your connection
🔧 Troubleshoot RDP connectivity issues

How's it going?

🗣 Tell us about your connection experience

Figure 10-8. *Connection options for the Azure virtual machine*

If you are using Windows, you can download a file to use with any program that supports rdp. Note the port number. When you deployed the virtual machine, you enabled the default rdp port to be public. It could be that this is not a secure method for your organization (it is not allowed at Microsoft). One option you have is to change the default rdp port, and then you would need to supply a different port number here. Here is a nice set of steps to change the rdp port in the Azure portal for the virtual machine at `https://docs.microsoft.com/archive/blogs/technet/drew/1195`.

If you are running into issues with rdp to the Azure virtual machine, check out our documentation at `https://docs.microsoft.com/troubleshoot/azure/virtual-machines/troubleshoot-rdp-connection`.

The same options exist for Linux with the ssh tab. Any program or shell that supports ssh can be used.

The third option is the most secure called Bastion. Bastion is a secure Azure service running in your Azure virtual network that allows you to have a rdp or ssh experience in a secure fashion using a web browser. Learn more about Bastion at `https://docs.microsoft.com/azure/bastion/bastion-overview`.

Once you can use rdp or ssh, you can now access the virtual machine like you would any virtual machine in your own machine or data center.

Exploring a SQL Virtual Machine in the Portal

Since we deployed the virtual machine, the SQL Server IaaS Agent Extension was installed, and our SQL Server was registered in full mode. So we can go to the Azure portal and view our virtual machine as a **SQL virtual machine**. There are a few ways to see the SQL virtual machine in the portal. You can use the **SQL Server configuration** option from the Azure virtual machine resource menu or search for SQL virtual machines from the Azure home page. You can also see a SQL virtual machine in a list of Azure SQL resources.

Figure 10-9 shows my SQL virtual machine in the portal.

Figure 10-9. *A deployed SQL Server on an Azure Virtual Machine in the portal*

Notice all the properties, data, and options in the menu are very SQL Server specific. Most of the items that I showed you that were SQL Server specific to deploy the virtual machine are available here to configure as well.

The Storage configuration option is only used to extend the choices you made during deployment, but the same warnings exist if you exceed the storage caps for the virtual machine size.

I will discuss the option SQL best practices assessment in the section titled "**Optimizing Performance**" later in this chapter.

One important point about the options at the top of the screen: The **Delete** option is used to unregister SQL Server with the IaaS Agent Extension. There is also an option on the Delete screen to delete the virtual machine, but that requires you to explicitly choose that option.

Connecting to SQL Server on an Azure Virtual Machine

Now that SQL Server is deployed, how do you connect to SQL Server with tools like SSMS or your application?

That all depends on where you want to connect from. Here are your options:

- Connect inside the virtual machine with tools or applications after you have used rdp or ssh.

- Create another virtual machine or build an application in the same virtual network. Once you have this set up, you are automatically in the same private network, so you can use server names or private IP addresses.

- Connect your on-premises environment or Azure resources to the virtual network using technologies like VPN gateways or Express Route. Learn more at `https://docs.microsoft.com/azure/architecture/reference-architectures/hybrid-networking`.

- Connect to the public IP address or DNS name of the virtual machine. This requires you to enable public connectivity for your virtual machine, but be cautioned. I do not recommend this option if you are going to use port 1433. Even if you change the port, you absolutely want a Network Security Group (NSG) configured. Learn more at `https://docs.microsoft.com/azure/azure-sql/virtual-machines/windows/ways-to-connect-to-sql#connect-to-sql-server-over-the-internet`.

Whatever method you choose, connecting to SQL Server on an Azure Virtual Machine is just like connecting to any SQL Server with the tool or application of your choice that is compatible to connect to SQL Server.

Tip   Our SQL marketplace images include tools like SSMS and Azure Data Studio preinstalled in the virtual machine!

Migrating to SQL Server on an Azure Virtual Machine

You may be deploying SQL Server on an Azure virtual machine with the intention of migrating an existing SQL Server instance from an on-premises environment or other clouds. For an overview of all your options to migrate SQL Server to Azure, check out `https://azure.microsoft.com/migration/sql-server`.

Tip   If you are considering migrating many SQL Server instances to an Azure virtual machine, take a look at the Azure Migrate service at `https://azure.microsoft.com/services/azure-migrate`. This service talks about options for discovery and assessment from on-premises and even other clouds like AWS and GCP.

You have three choices to perform this migration:

1. Deploy SQL Server on an Azure virtual machine. Then perform an **offline migration** using a full backup and restore of your database(s) to Azure. Use Azure storage as the place to host the backup. You will need to manually migrate any other instance-level objects or settings.

2. Deploy SQL Server on an Azure virtual machine. Then perform an offline or online migration using the **Azure SQL migrate extension** with Azure Data Studio. You can learn more about this option at `https://docs.microsoft.com/azure/dms/migration-using-azure-data-studio`. One thing I like about this option

is that the assessment tool can observe your configuration and workload for SQL Server and then provide recommendations for Azure virtual machine sizes and storage. So use this tool first before you deploy. An offline migration is accomplished with backup and restore. An online migration uses log shipping technology to allow for less downtime.

3. You can lift and shift your entire virtual machine from on-premises into Azure using Azure Migrate or Azure Site Recovery. You can learn more about his option at `https://docs.microsoft.com/azure/site-recovery/migrate-tutorial-on-premises-azure`. Be careful with this option because you might have to make some changes to optimize your SQL Server Azure virtual machine settings including storage configuration after you migrate.

Optimizing Performance

If you read previous sections of this chapter, then you have probably done many of the right things to optimize performance of SQL Server on an Azure virtual machine.

But let's review some of the important choices and also introduce you to a new option we have for best practices.

Virtual Machine Size

Your virtual machine size choice determines CPU speed and limits on number of CPUs, memory, local disk, number of disks, maximum storage, storage performance, and more.

So just as it would be an important choice for you to make in other clouds or in your data center, it is important for optimal performance for SQL Server on an Azure virtual machine.

If you look at our guidance at `https://aka.ms/SQLIaaSSizing`, you will notice that our size choices usually point to the E series or M series. But that advice is of the calendar year 2022. I've seen a lot of innovation in Azure virtual machines over the last few years, so stay in touch with this site as we will keep it updated for the latest size advice. And remember as we have shown already in this chapter, even if you have carefully selected the right storage options, your performance may be limited by the virtual machine size. There is a very nice Data Exposed show with David Pless explaining this at `https://docs.microsoft.com/shows/data-exposed/azure-sql-vm-caching-and-storage-capping-ep-1-data-exposed`.

Remember that you can often resize the virtual machine up or down as you can read at `https://docs.microsoft.com/azure/virtual-machines/resize-vm`. This operation can often happen with very little downtime, but I've also seen it take longer in some cases; depending on your subscription and region, some size options are not offered.

Storage Performance

I believe from my experience that storage performance is probably one of the most common issues for customers using SQL Server on an Azure virtual machine.

Pay close attention to your storage choices, use our recommendations during the deployment process, and read our guidance that includes a great checklist at `https://docs.microsoft.com/azure/azure-sql/virtual-machines/windows/performance-guidelines-best-practices-storage`.

Let me summarize a few points from our recommendations:

- Don't store anything related to SQL Server on the OS disk including system databases and the LOG directory.

- Take advantage of storing tempdb on the local SSD.

- Separate data and log into different disks. Use Premium managed disks and size them per our guidance for not just size but IOPS and throughput. Take advantage of our advice for read caching for the data disk and no caching for the log disk.

Note   In the summer of 2022, we announced the preview of Azure Premium disks V2. We are evaluating how to best use these with SQL Server, so stay tuned. Read more about Premium disks V2 at `https://docs.microsoft.com/azure/virtual-machines/disks-types#premium-ssd-v2-preview`.

- If a single disk is not big enough for size, IOPS, or throughput, combine them with technologies like Storage Spaces.

- There is another option called Ultra disks. This is a more expensive option, and you should only consider this option if disk latency is very sensitive to your SQL Server. For example, we have some customers who have used an Ultra disk for the transaction log for In-Memory OLTP.

SQL Best Practices Assessment

One of the nice advantages of registering your SQL Server on an Azure virtual machine is the ability to get best practices from Microsoft in a digital form of recommendations assessing your configuration.

We call this the **SQL best practices assessment.**

To use this feature, you need to enable it after your deployment. In the SQL virtual machine portal, select SQL best practices assessment on the left-hand menu.

Then select **Enable SQL best practices assessment**. You will be asked to check a box to enable the feature and choose a Log Analytics workspace. A Log Analytics workspace is an Azure service where you can host metrics and other "log" information. We have integrated the best practice results into Log Analytics. You have another option to enable scheduling for best practices so that on a regular basis we scan your configuration (not your data) and continually update our recommendations. When you enable this feature, it will take a few minutes as we have to configure the IaaS Agent Extension and configure the Log Analytics.

With this feature enabled, you can wait for a scheduled run or select Run Assessment (or Run at the top menu).

Note   Much of the information we collect for an assessment comes from SQL queries. You can trace with XEvent what the assessment is doing using XEvent Profiler from SSMS. Look for client_app_name of Microsoft SQL Server IaaS Agent and Microsoft SQL Server IaaS Agent Query Service.

An assessment can take a while as it is a very robust check of your virtual machine and SQL Server. When the assessment is done, you can select latest successful assessment. When mine was complete, the results looked like Figure 10-10.

Figure 10-10. *SQL best practices assessment for SQL Server on an Azure virtual machine*

You can see results based on severity and type. You will find a wide range of recommendations including ones related to the virtual machine configuration and others specific to SQL Server. Some of our recommendations are *tried-and-true* recommendations that Microsoft and the community have been using for years.

One of the things I love about the best practices assessment is that when at least one assessment has been run, the top results are right in front of me on the Azure portal home page for the SQL virtual machine like in Figure 10-11.

Figure 10-11. *SQL best practices assessment notifications*

Get all the latest updates for SQL best practices assessment at `https://docs.`
`microsoft.com/azure/azure-sql/virtual-machines/windows/sql-assessment-`
`for-sql-vm.`

High Availability

As part of planning for deployment, you may want to make sure you build a highly
available solution for SQL Server on an Azure virtual machine. Or you just want to make
sure you know the options to extend HA later.

Built-In Fault Tolerance with Azure

Did you know that just by installing SQL Server on an Azure virtual machine, you have
built-in HA and fault tolerance at the VM level? We use the concept of **live migration**
should we need to move your virtual machine due to a problem in the data center
or maintenance. But we go further than just react to a problem. We have machine
learning models helping us take proactive actions to keep you running longer and
more predictably. Read this excellent blog post on how it works behind the scenes in

Azure at `https://azure.microsoft.com/blog/improving-azure-virtual-machine-resiliency-with-predictive-ml-and-live-migration`.

We also have a very robust system for maintenance of hosts and infrastructure to keep you highly available. You can read more at `https://docs.microsoft.com/azure/virtual-machines/maintenance-and-updates`.

Failover Cluster Instance (FCI)

A Failover Cluster Instance (FCI) is a very popular option for SQL Server customers for high availability. Azure virtual machines support building this type of system with Windows Server Failover Cluster (WSFC) and Pacemaker for Linux.

In order to support an FCI, you will need multiple virtual machines at minimum for the SQL Server nodes. This is where you would consider using Availability options when deploying the virtual machine such as **Availability Sets**, which ensure that the VMs you deploy on Azure are distributed across multiple isolated hardware clusters. Or you can choose an **Availability Zone**, which is physically separate locations within each Azure region that are tolerant to local failures. Zones bring you the best redundancy.

Since an FCI requires **shared storage** across nodes, you need to use one of the following choices in Azure:

- **Azure shared disks**

  Effectively this is the same managed disk you set up for an Azure virtual machine for the exercises in this chapter, but you have the ability to make it shared.

- **Storage Spaces Direct (SSD)** – Windows only

  This is a popular option on Windows Server on-premises. SSD uses a virtual Storage Area Network (SAN) approach with local disks.

- **Premium file shares**

  Premium file shares are a feature in Azure for Azure files that are effectively a shared file system.

Out of the three options, Premium file shares support the largest sizes and have the lowest set of limitations.

One last important concept is **quorum**, which is required in FCI to support decisions on failover. Just like on-premises, an Azure virtual machine will support a disk-based *witness* for quorum using Azure disks and file shares. But a unique option I recommend is a **cloud witness**. A cloud witness is easy to set up and uses Azure storage.

To get started with an FCI for SQL Server on an Azure virtual machine, go to `https://docs.microsoft.com/azure/azure-sql/virtual-machines/windows/hadr-windows-server-failover-cluster-overview`.

Always On Availability Groups

While FCI is a popular option for high availability for SQL Server, Always On Availability Groups (AGs) represent a more robust solution using local storage and replicas. And the biggest advantage is that the secondary server is usable (read-only, backups, etc.).

An Azure virtual machine supports Always On Availability Groups in all forms. Remember in Chapter 6 I showed you how to set up a clusterless AG. I did this using Azure virtual machines.

But let's say you wanted automatic failover capabilities. Then you will need the same type of setup for an FCI in Azure but without shared storage. And one of the nice new features for both an FCI and AG setup with WSFC is the ability to use subnets instead of having to configure a load balancer.

Figure 10-12 shows a possible configuration for an AG with multiple subnets in Azure.

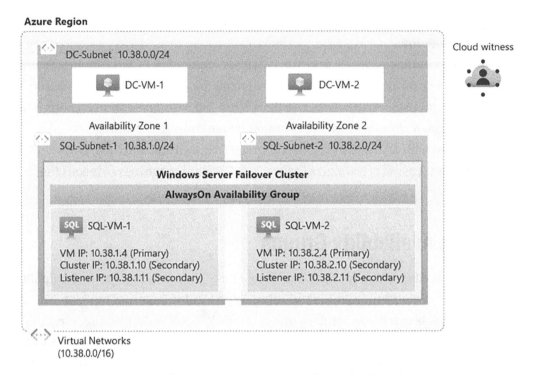

Figure 10-12. An AG configuration in Azure with multiple subnets

To learn more about configuring an AG with subnets, check out `https://docs.microsoft.com/azure/azure-sql/virtual-machines/windows/availability-group-manually-configure-prerequisites-tutorial-multi-subnet`.

The nice thing about configuring an AG with an Azure virtual machine is that the SQL pieces are the same as if you were doing this on-premises once everything is set up for your cluster, network, and domains.

If you are looking for an experience to set up an AG on Linux, we have a great quick-start guide built with our partner Red Hat you can see at `https://docs.microsoft.com/azure/azure-sql/virtual-machines/linux/rhel-high-availability-stonith-tutorial`.

I've always wanted an easy quick way to set up the entire system so I can test and see a complete auto-failover AG in action. My colleague Taryn Pratt, Senior Program Manager who owns HA/DR for SQL Server in Azure VM, showed me this ARM template: `https://github.com/microsoft/tigertoolbox/tree/master/AzureSQLVM/e2e-ag-setup`. So give it a try and use the GitHub issues site to give Taryn feedback. I wanted to know from Taryn our future plans for the HA experience for SQL Server on Azure Virtual Machines. Taryn said, *"The SQL Server on Azure IaaS team is w*orking to improve the

HA/DR experience for customers running on Azure VMs. One of our goals is to enhance the portal to provide a better overall experience from start to finish when using Always On availability groups. This includes adding the ability to deploy a multi-subnet Always On availability group on SQL Server creation, to expanding the existing troubleshooting tools to include more details about the health of an AG. We want to provide *customers with an easy way to create and support SQL Server HA/DR solutions on Azure VMs.*"

Disaster Recovery

While setting up an Always On Availability Group (AG) can also provide a disaster recovery option since your data is replicated to another node using local storage, there are other considerations for disaster recovery with SQL Server on Azure virtual machines.

Storage Fault Tolerance

I've talked earlier in this chapter about storage choices for your databases and log files on Azure storage. Turns out Azure has built-in redundancy options for Azure storage accounts. These options include locally redundant storage (LRS), zone-redundant storage (ZRS), and geo-redundant storage (GRS). Due to the nature of how SQL Server does I/O, we only support LRS for data and log file storage. But even with LRS, your data already has built-in multiple copies automatically kept up to date within the data center.

Backup Database Options

Because we only support LRS for data and log file storage, you will want to create a backup strategy that separates storage for backups from data and log but also choose more redundant options like ZRS or GRS.

And since SQL Server has built-in capabilities to back up to **Azure storage** in the engine, it is not hard to implement a robust backup strategy with Azure. In addition, if you register the IaaS Agent Extension in full mode, you can take advantage of automatic backups, which use the Azure storage account of your choice. One disadvantage of this approach is a 12TB limit for the backup (compression may help you here).

You do have the option of configuring a new **Azure managed disk** to simply back up within the virtual machine to another drive or mounted file system. While using this approach allows for larger backup sizes since you are using BACKUP TO DISK, the disadvantage of this approach is that the virtual machine must be available to get to the backups, whereas with Azure storage you can access your backups at any time.

A third option for a direct Azure backup using T-SQL is **Premium file shares**. When you configure a Premium file share, you will back up your database using BACKUP TO DISK, but storage is independent of the virtual machine, so you can easily attach the Premium file share to another virtual machine. In addition Premium file shares support up to 100TB.

Also remember that in Chapter 6 of the book, we talked about the new **T-SQL snapshot backup** approach for SQL Server 2022, which could be very useful for large databases and greatly reduce the time it takes to back up or restore.

Remember that since you are using the SQL Server engine, you can always set up a log shipping scheme across two SQL Servers on Azure virtual machines. Log shipping is still a popular option for basic HA/DR for SQL Server.

Using Azure Backup

One other option for backups is the **Azure Backup** service. Azure Backup for SQL VMs is an integrated service to schedule automatic backups to a separate Azure storage location called a Recovery Service vault. Azure Backup is a good solution for those wanting to use a central service to manage their backups especially across multiple virtual machines. Get started with Azure Backup with a quick-start guide at `https://docs.microsoft.com/azure/backup/tutorial-sql-backup`.

Monitoring

If you have used SQL Server before, you probably have your own set of processes to use built-in OS and SQL Server capabilities to monitor SQL Server including Performance Monitor for Windows, Grafana for Linux, Dynamic Management Views (DMVs), Query Store, and Extended Events.

Since you don't have direct access to host computers for Azure virtual machines, it would be interesting to know how to monitor SQL Server on an Azure virtual machine outside of Azure.

Azure Monitor

In comes **Azure Monitor**, a monitoring infrastructure for all Azure services. By default for an Azure virtual machine, metrics mostly around performance are stored and available for you to see in the Azure portal. You can see this on the home page of the virtual machine. As well you can dive in further using the **Metrics** option in the left-hand menu. These metrics by default are about the virtual machine from the *host perspective*. It could be very helpful to use these especially to see more about storage performance. Remember virtual machine size cap issues I have mentioned earlier in this chapter? Azure metrics for the host are one way to see if this is happening for your workload.

Virtual Machine Metrics and Logs

What about metrics for the guest virtual machine itself? If you use the Azure virtual machine portal page and select **Diagnostic Settings** on the left-hand menu, you can enable guest machine metrics and logging.

Here you can enable guest machine and SQL Server metrics and log information. When this is enabled, you use the Metrics option with the Azure virtual machine to view key performance metrics for the OS and SQL Server as seen in Figure 10-13.

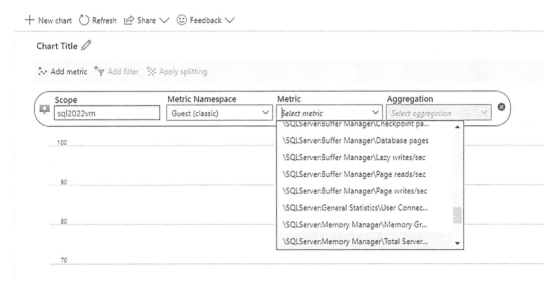

Figure 10-13. *SQL Server metrics from Azure Monitor*

Azure Insights

One of the features I love about Azure virtual machines and monitoring you may not know about is **Insights**. Insights is available from the left-hand menu of the virtual machine portal page. You have to enable Insights, but when you do, look at the rich metrics about the virtual machine you can get as seen in Figure 10-14.

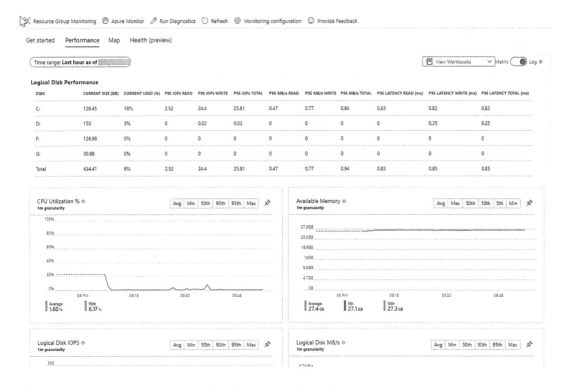

Figure 10-14. *Azure Insights for the virtual machine*

It is like having a multi-window view of Performance Monitor, and it works automatically with history, so you can look for trends over time with alerting.

Azure Is the Best Cloud for SQL Server

I believe Azure is the best cloud for SQL Server especially when used on Azure virtual machines. Consider the following:

- The only way to get the latest versions of SQL Server fastest to market in a cloud service is through Azure.

- Azure has the largest number of options for regions and data centers globally than any other provider.

- Microsoft has the most innovative integration of virtual machines with SQL Server than any cloud provider through our SQL Server IaaS Agent Extension and the features it enables.

- We build the SQL Server product, so we know more than anyone else how to optimize performance, security, and availability for SQL Server on a virtual machine.

- Use your existing SQL Server licenses on Azure with Azure Hybrid Benefit to reduce costs.

- I believe in actual proof to say Azure is the best cloud for SQL Server. GigaOm recently did a benchmark study to compare price and performance of SQL Server on Azure virtual machines vs. AWS EC2. The results speak for themselves at `https://research.gigaom.com/report/sql-transaction-processing-and-analytic-performance-price-performance-testing`.

We are constantly improving the SQL Server on Azure Virtual Machines experience. Keep up to date with all the latest information at `https://aka.ms/azuresqlvm`.

Pam Lahoud manages our team for SQL Server on Azure virtual machines. Pam is a well-known expert on SQL Server in the community and at Microsoft. She summed up for me the value of running SQL Server on Azure:

No one knows SQL Server like Microsoft, so naturally we know how to run it best. On top of ensuring that our customers have the infrastructure options they need to deploy even their most demanding SQL Server workloads on Azure VMs, we also provide a suite of free tools that help you configure your SQL Servers correctly and keep them healthy. Combine this with industry-leading price-performance and Microsoft-only features like Azure Hybrid Benefit and you can easily see why SQL Server runs better on Azure.

CHAPTER 11

SQL Edge to Cloud

When I joined Microsoft in 1993, we had just released SQL Server 4.2 on Windows NT (the predecessor to Windows Server). We had previously only offered SQL Server on OS/2 systems, and our code was still based on the original Sybase server. These are the days of small to medium servers, and we as a product were trying to find our place in the industry.

Fast forward to the last 5 years, and SQL Server has innovated in so many ways it may be hard to keep up with "all the flavors." So I thought a great way to conclude this book is a chapter on all the ways SQL can be deployed from *edge to cloud*. I'll talk about all the options and why you may consider each one for your workload.

Develop Once, Deploy Anywhere

A great way to see all the SQL options is with Figure 11-1.

SQL from edge to cloud

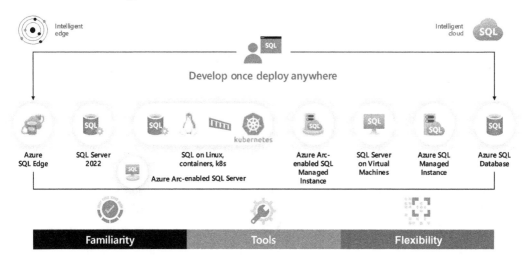

Figure 11-1. *SQL from edge to cloud*

© Bob Ward 2022
B. Ward, *SQL Server 2022 Revealed*, https://doi.org/10.1007/978-1-4842-8894-8_11

I'm not sure I would ever think in my career and lifetime that SQL as a technology could exist in so many different ways. SQL can now be deployed on everything from a small IoT device to the largest servers in the world to public clouds. I use the term *develop once, deploy anywhere* because it is very possible to build an application targeted to SQL and deploy it across all these options without changing the code.

For many customers I talk to today, these options are not an *and* decision but an *or* decision. In other words, many customers may need to deploy SQL in many of these destinations per their business needs. But do all these choices pose a big question? How is it possible to learn all these options?

The good news is not just the *flexibility* that SQL edge to cloud provides. But it is also the common *familiarity* across them. Consider this:

- The same languages and providers such as .Net and Java work across all of these options.

- The same T-SQL language is supported across all of these options. There can be some differences per the needs of a given option, but the same fundamental T-SQL just works.

- The same core database engine code is used across all of these. This is a statement that many customers find hard to believe. We have a common code base for the SQL Server engine edge to cloud. We may turn on some features in only some options. We may build new features and only release them first in some of these options. But the core code is the same.

- Our common tools such as SQL Server Management Studio (SSMS), Azure Data Studio (ADS), sqlcmd, and others work across all of these options. One of the keys is the Tabular Data Stream (TDS) protocol. TDS is supported across all of these because it has the same core engine edge to cloud.

So flexibility with familiarity. A great combination for you to choose which options are best for you. Let's spend the rest of the chapter learning more about each option. For each option I've included a summary of *When to Use...*, so you will understand my recommendation when one of these options may match your requirements. I listed Azure Arc–enable SQL Managed Instance last in this chapter because it is easier to understand this option after comparing it with all the other options for SQL.

> **Note**   I've seen different people use the term *edge* in many ways. For purposes of this chapter, the *edge* refers to SQL running in any option that is not the Azure cloud. What you will find interesting is all the options now connect SQL running on the edge to the cloud. These worlds are coming together.

Azure SQL Edge

IoT devices are part of our world everywhere you look or probably in ways you didn't know. We embarked on a project several years ago to bring database processing *down* to the IoT device itself. We found a clever way to reduce the footprint of the SQL Server engine to only a few hundred megabytes so it could fit on even the smallest IoT device. So the core engine could process data on the device using a SQL Linux container.

Fundamental core engine functionality like columnstore indexes can even run on such a small device. There are some engine features that are not supported, such as In-Memory OLTP, but most of the core engine features that a developer would need work. You can read all the supported features at `https://docs.microsoft.com/azure/azure-sql-edge/features`.

We knew that processing of telemetry data would be important. Therefore, we included specific features to help stream data, process time series data, and analyze data with machine learning.

For streaming we included the popular Kafka stream engine and T-SQL support for streaming based on the same concepts as Azure Stream Analytics. You can read more about streaming with Azure SQL Edge at `https://docs.microsoft.com/azure/azure-sql-edge/stream-data`.

For time series, we included T-SQL functions including DATE_BUCKET(), FIRST_VALUE(), and LAST_VALUE(). One of the reasons to use these functions is to help fill in time gaps in the data. You saw in Chapter 8 how these T-SQL functions now exist in SQL Server 2022.

One of the scenarios that customers and developers seem most excited about Azure SQL Edge is that you can train machine learning models and then execute them directly on the IoT device with SQL Server. Azure SQL Edge supports the T-SQL PREDICT function, which allows a developer to execute a native ONYX model.

So the scenario is complete for Azure SQL Edge. Instead of requiring a device to stream raw telemetry to Azure or even an edge hub, you can *push data processing* down to the device.

Azure SQL Edge also comes with data retention capabilities and the ability to synchronize data with Azure Data Factory or SQL Data Sync.

Even though Azure SQL Edge is comprised of containers including a SQL Server Linux engine, the product is priced with Azure on a per-device basis. You can stay in touch with all the latest information about Azure SQL Edge at `https://aka.ms/azuresqledge`.

When to Use Azure SQL Edge

Azure SQL Edge has a very specific use case for IoT device deployments. Its small footprint and unique features are built specifically for IoT device scenarios.

SQL Server

The entire book has been about SQL Server, but the focus has been on what is new for SQL Server 2022. SQL Server is a licensed product that runs on Windows and Linux operating systems. SQL Server is also known as the "box product" because back in the day that is how we shipped the product, in a box with documentation (yes, hard-bound books) and the software.

SQL Server includes the database engine and features *surrounding* the engine like replication, Polybase, SQL Server Agent, and machine learning services. The SQL Server licensed product also includes services such SQL Server Integration Services (SSIS), SQL Server Analysis Services (SSAS), and SQL Server Reporting Services (SSRS).

SQL Server is purchased using a licensing agreement or directly per instance using a per-core licensing model. A user will choose editions to decide the capabilities of SQL Server for the price you pay. You can choose free editions of SQL Server including Evaluation, Developer, or Express. The best price per value is Standard Edition, which has the surface area of the complete product but has resource limits and doesn't support all features. And finally Enterprise Edition has the highest price of any edition but with all the features and unlimited resource usage.

SQL Server is produced by Microsoft and released through a major version such as SQL Server 2022. There is no specific guarantee from Microsoft when major versions are released, but the pattern since 2016 is every few years. Each major version is updated on a regular cadence through a concept called a cumulative update or security update called General Distribution Release (GDR).

SQL Server is a complete data platform and is now one of the most popular database products in the world. You can deploy SQL Server on laptops, desktops, servers, and virtual machines both private and in public clouds. Customers deploy databases with SQL Server from a few megabytes to several petabytes.

Even though SQL Server solves so many data problems, the burden is on you to deploy and manage it. For example, SQL Server comes with a robust high-availability solution called Always On Availability Groups (you read about the new Contained AGs in this book). But the burden is on you to set it up, configure it, and keep it healthy. SQL Server comes with an intelligent engine helping you do your best, but the full SQL Server product is managed by you.

Our main page to get started to learn everything about SQL Server is `https://aka.ms/sqlserver`.

When to Use SQL Server

SQL Server is your best choice if you need complete control over all aspects of deploying and managing SQL Server. You want every feature that comes with the product, and you want the flexibility to deploy it on any type of machine or virtual machine. You would also want to choose SQL Server if you wanted complete control over configuration aspects such as physical placement of files.

Another reason to choose SQL Server is application version requirements. Let's say your company uses an application that is only supported on specific version(s) of SQL Server. SQL Server is going to be your only choice since options such as Azure SQL Managed Instance, Azure SQL Database, and Azure Arc–enabled SQL Managed Instance are *versionless*.

Note   We have worked over the last few years to convince developers and customers to base support on a database compatibility level (dbcompat) vs. a major version. You can read more at `https://aka.ms/dbcompat`.

Another reason to choose SQL Server is the supported set of services outside the engine such as SSIS, SSAS, and SSRS. Note that only SQL Server on Windows supports SSAS and SSRS.

Azure Arc–Enabled SQL Server

One of the options you can use *in addition* to deploying SQL Server is to connect your instance to Azure through Azure Arc. You saw the process for doing this with SQL Server 2022 in Chapter 3 of the book. Using this capability allows you to see SQL Server information in the Azure portal, secure your SQL Server with Microsoft Defender, and perform a SQL assessment. You saw in Chapter 3 that for SQL Server 2022, you can also configure Azure Active Directory (AAD), which enables you to use Microsoft Purview for policy management.

You can set up SQL Server 2012 and later on Azure Arc-enabled servers on Windows and Linux. Get started with Azure Arc-enabled SQL Server at `https://docs.microsoft.com/sql/sql-server/azure-arc/overview`.

Linux, Containers, and Kubernetes

You have read in Chapter 9 details about how to deploy and use SQL Server on Linux, on containers, and in a Kubernetes cluster.

Here is a summary of when these options may be best for your needs.

When to Use SQL Server on Linux

SQL Server on Linux is the complete "box product" supported for Linux distributions such as Red Hat Enterprise Linux (RHEL), Ubuntu, and SUSE Linux Enterprise Server. SQL Server on Linux supports all editions and is deployed through a set of downloadable packages native to the Linux distribution.

There are some features from SQL Server that are not supported on Linux including services such as SSAS and SSRS. A list of unsupported features for SQL Server 2022 on Linux can be found at `https://docs.microsoft.com/sql/linux/sql-server-linux-editions-and-components-2022#unsupported-features-and-services`.

One of the myths about SQL Server on Linux is that it doesn't support high-availability features like Always On Availability Groups. Far from it. You saw in Chapter 6 of the book the use of a clusterless AG, which was built back in 2017 to support Linux. But SQL Server on Linux can also support automatic failover capabilities using software like Pacemaker.

You should choose SQL Server on Linux when you have the same situation as SQL Server including version support or need for complete control but you want to run SQL Server on Linux operating systems instead of Windows. Don't forget that databases are completely compatible between SQL on Windows and Linux (just back up and restore between them).

When to Use SQL Server Containers

As you learned in Chapter 9, a SQL Server container is a pre-packaged image of a preinstalled SQL Server Linux package(s). So your first decision on using SQL containers is that the SQL Server Linux feature set meets your requirements.

Your second decision to use SQL Server containers is you have reason to use a container. Remember that containers don't replace virtual machines; they complement them. For example, the only way to run multiple instances of SQL Server on Linux is to use multiple containers in a virtual machine. One myth about containers is that they don't perform as fast as a SQL Server on Linux instance installed directly in the virtual machine or on a bare-metal server. This is simply not true. Containers are just processes run in an isolated fashion so they have complete direct access to the Linux operating system. Containers do require a container runtime such as Docker. One consideration for you is that Docker has announced some changes to their pricing and licensing, which you can read at `www.docker.com/pricing`.

Note   SQL Server container images are OCI compliant, so other container runtimes like podman are supported. You can find out more about podman at `https://docs.podman.io/en/latest`.

Another consideration for containers is patching. Containers are never updated. To apply a cumulative update (CU) for SQL Server, you simply "switch" to a new container running the new cumulative update version. You can even safely roll back a CU with this type of switch operation.

One final scenario that is very compelling for containers is developer and DevOps. Since containers are supported anywhere container runtimes like Docker run, SQL Server containers can be used on Windows, Linux, and MacOS systems. Furthermore, the default edition for SQL Server containers is Developer Edition. So as a developer you can build applications for SQL Server for free on any OS and assured it is the same SQL Server engine. How is this possible? That is because container runtimes like Docker are compatible on non-Linux systems. For Windows, Docker can use a virtual machine with Linux or Windows Subsystem for Linux. For MacOS, Docker uses a lightweight virtualization solution. In all cases, it just looks like Linux, so SQL Server containers run the same.

Note Even though SQL Server containers run the same on all of these platforms, it is not fair to do a performance comparison for a SQL Server container running natively on "bare-metal" Linux and the container running in virtualization solutions.

The message here is that for developers on platforms like MacOS, you have a solution to build applications for SQL Server without installing any Windows software. Check out my blog post at `https://aka.ms/sqlmacchallenge` for more details.

SQL Server containers are also used to power the new local developer experience for Azure SQL Database (read more at `https://docs.microsoft.com/azure/azure-sql/database/local-dev-experience-set-up-dev-environment?view=azuresql&tabs=vscode`). In addition, SQL Server containers can be a great solution for DevOps scenarios. Check out my demo for this capability from Microsoft Build 2020 at `https://docs.microsoft.com/en-us/events/build-2020/int128`.

When to Use SQL Server on Kubernetes

Kubernetes (k8s) is a software platform to execute and orchestrate containerized applications. The concept is that if you want to run a complete software system at scale with containers, you should consider running Kubernetes (`https://kubernetes.io`). Kubernetes provides rich networking and storage capabilities built on the Linux OS. It includes built-in high availability and abstraction connection capabilities like load balancers.

Note   If you want a quick fun way to learn k8s, you will love this video: `https://youtu.be/4ht22ReBjno`.

So if you want to run SQL Server containers on Linux in a VM or bare metal, that is perfectly fine for a production solution. But if you want to run many SQL Server containers and other containerized applications at scale, you should consider Kubernetes.

Kubernetes has now been around for over a decade, and there are plenty of case studies on how companies, big and small, have used Kubernetes (`https://kubernetes.io/case-studies`). Kubernetes can be run for free from open source, but you have to manage the entire solution. Kubernetes is also offered with managed solutions like Azure Kubernetes Service (AKS) on Azure Stack HCI, RedHat OpenShift, and Rancher. Kubernetes is also very popular in public clouds like Azure Kubernetes Service (AKS), Google Kubernetes Engine (GKE), and Amazon Elastic Kubernetes Service (EKS).

Because SQL Server supports containers, it automatically supports running in a Kubernetes platform. If you need built-in high availability (think HA without needing a Windows Failover Cluster), load balancing (think listener), and a system to deploy many SQL Server containers at scale, Kubernetes could be the solution for you. The object of execution in Kubernetes is a *pod*, which can be one or more groupings of containers.

I would say for many customers I meet the learning curve for Kubernetes is usually the impedance to moving right to this type of solution. Even though many k8s providers provide a "managed Kubernetes" product or service, there are still concepts you must understand to properly use SQL Server on Kubernetes.

You can get started with SQL Server on Kubernetes at `https://aka.ms/sqlk8s`.

SQL Server on Azure Virtual Machines

SQL Server on Azure Virtual Machines is one of the services in Azure as part of the *Azure SQL* family. Azure Virtual Machines are also known as Infrastructure as a Service (IaaS). You learned all the details of SQL Server 2022 on Azure Virtual Machines in Chapter 10 of the book. You saw in this chapter how to deploy, use, and manage SQL Server 2022 in the Azure Virtual Machine ecosystem. You learned one of the most valuable pieces of information about this option. **It is just SQL Server**. It is the complete SQL Server "box product" running on Windows or Linux operating systems where you manage everything *inside* the virtual machine. Microsoft manages everything outside the virtual machine but also provides the necessary resources (size choices, networking, storage, built-in VM HA, etc.) for a complete managed virtual machine experience.

Because Microsoft manages the infrastructure, we give you options called virtual machine sizes. Think of this like a big dinner menu for what kind of CPU speed you need along with how many CPUs, memory, and storage for your SQL Server. You can find out all the size choices at `https://aka.ms/azurevmsizes`.

Get started with SQL Server on Azure Virtual Machines at `https://aka.ms/azuresqlvm`.

When to Use SQL Server on Azure Virtual Machines

If you need to choose the complete SQL Server product because you need all the features and services like SSAS or SSRS or your application requires a specific version of SQL Server but you don't want to manage the hardware and hosts for a virtual machine, then SQL Server on Azure Virtual Machines could be for you.

As you saw in Chapter 10, we do provide some services to help you with the Azure Virtual Machine experience including easy deployment with the marketplace and the SQL Server IaaS Agent extension to help with backups, security updates, best practices assessment, Microsoft Defender, and a "SQL" Azure portal experience.

Also if you are concerned you cannot build a complete HA solution with failover clusters or Always On Availability Groups, that is all possible in the Azure Virtual Machine environment.

One big difference from SQL Server is that you pay for SQL Server on Azure Virtual Machines using *cloud billing*. This means that you use an Azure subscription to pay for using SQL Server and the virtual machine on a monthly basis. This will seem very different for you at first if you are used to SQL Server licensing and pricing. But we have some options to help. First, you can apply your existing SQL Server licenses using a concept called Azure Hybrid Benefit (`https://aka.ms/azurehybridbenefit`). Furthermore, you can sign up for a contract to use Virtual Machines for a longer period of time and get discounts called Azure Reserved Virtual Machine Instances. Also if an Azure Virtual Machine is stopped (deallocated), then you don't pay for any compute costs until it is started. This could be a very nice option for development and testing purposes.

Many customers are choosing this option to migrate SQL Server on-premises deployments because it can provide the fastest and easiest *lift-and-shift* migration experience. Given it is the complete SQL Server product, there shouldn't be any application compatibility issues because you are just shifting where your existing SQL Server is hosted.

One other point to consider: Once you deploy SQL Server on an Azure Virtual Machine, we have options for you to migrate online in the future to Azure SQL Managed Instance. So an Azure Virtual Machine could be a steppingstone for you to the complete managed experience.

Get started with migration to Azure Virtual Machines at `https://docs.microsoft.com/azure/azure-sql/virtual-machines/windows/migrate-to-vm-from-sql-server`.

Azure SQL Managed Instance

Let's say that you need the complete SQL Server engine with databases and instance capabilities like SQL Server Agent, replication, resource governor, and DTC. However, you are not tied down to a version of SQL Server. In fact, you would love to not have to worry about patching like applying cumulative updates anymore. It is more than patching. You would like a SQL option that is *versionless* so we can provide you with new features on a much more frequent basis than SQL Server. And you really don't care what the virtual machine or OS hosting SQL Server looks like. You want choices on number of cores, memory, storage, and even I/O latency and throughput, but don't want to have to manage the virtual machine or even worry about physical placement of files.

This all sounds very interesting. Let's make it even better. Let's say you would love to have a system that automatically executes backups and even keeps them around at any time you need them for a point-in-time restore. And then it would be nice if the system could provide built-in high availability including Always On Availability Groups. Oh, and I would love the "auto-HA" to come with a money back guarantee.

Welcome to Azure SQL Managed Instance. Azure SQL Managed Instance is an example of *Platform as a Service* (PaaS) and the second option in the Azure SQL family. I remember telling Anna Hoffman one time about how I would summarize Azure SQL Managed Instance: "It is the best of SQL Server and the cloud together." It truly is a *managed SQL Server*. Azure SQL Managed Instance was a large part of my last book, *Azure SQL Revealed*. In the book I compared SQL Server with Azure SQL Managed Instance at a very detailed level. Think of just about any core SQL Server feature you need with a managed SQL Server.

When you connect to Azure SQL Managed instance from SSMS, it looks like a complete SQL Server! One big difference you will notice is that the option for Always On Availability Groups is missing. That is because if you choose the Business Critical service tier for Azure SQL Managed Instance, we create an Always On Availability Group behind the scenes including a free read replica. And then we maintain it for you. Azure SQL Managed Instance is built in the Azure ecosystem and uses a service fabric to support HA decisions. The General Purpose service tier behaves like a Failover Cluster Instance without having to set up a Windows Failover Cluster. You can even connect two instances together across regions with Auto Failover Groups. Furthermore, when you deploy Azure SQL Managed Instance, we provide a Service-Level Agreement (SLA) for availability, which you can read at `https://azure.microsoft.com/support/legal/sla/azure-sql-sql-managed-instance/v1_0`.

Our migration tools support migration from SQL Server to Azure SQL Managed Instance. You can read the migration guide at `https://docs.microsoft.com/azure/azure-sql/migration-guides/managed-instance/sql-server-to-managed-instance-guide`.

Get started with Azure SQL Managed Instance today at `https://aka.ms/azuresqlmi`.

When to Use Azure SQL Managed Instance

Like Azure Virtual Machines, Azure SQL Managed Instance is for users of SQL Server who want Microsoft to manage the infrastructure and hosts behind the computing for SQL Server. Azure SQL Managed Instance goes a step further by managing the virtual machine environment supporting SQL Server.

Combined with a versionless engine, automatic high availability, automated backups, and a Microsoft-backed SLA, Azure SQL Managed Instance as a managed SQL Server can be a very nice option for many customers who use SQL Server today. And remember that in Chapter 3 we introduced the concept of using Azure SQL Managed Instance as part of your disaster recovery system. That may be the way for your start to use Azure SQL Managed Instance.

Like Azure Virtual Machines, you are billed using an Azure subscription but also have the options for Azure Hybrid Benefit and reserved capacity to save costs.

Are there differences from SQL Server that might prevent me from choosing Azure SQL Managed Instance? The answer is yes but not as much as you would think:

- Azure SQL Managed Instance includes the database engine with other features like replication, Polybase, and DTC. If you need services like SSAS or SSRS, Azure SQL Managed Instance would not be your choice. Note that SSIS packages are compatible to work with Azure SQL Managed Instance.

- While most core database engine features are available in Azure SQL Managed Instance, there are a few differences, listed here `https://aka.ms/azuretsqldiff`.

- There are some resource limits to consider. The largest storage for an Azure SQL Managed Instance today is 16TB (this is for all databases for the instance). 80 vCores is the max number of CPUs we support today, and based on our most advanced option today, you have a maximum amount of memory at ~870Gb. We keep growing this limit, so stay in touch with our updates at `https://docs.microsoft.com/azure/azure-sql/managed-instance/resource-limits`.

Azure SQL Database

The final service in the Azure SQL family is Azure SQL Database. Azure SQL Database is where it all started for SQL in the cloud. From the beginning we wanted to create a concept where a developer could just focus on a database and not worry about infrastructure, virtual machines, OS, or even the SQL Server instance. We actually implemented early work on this inside SQL Server as contained databases. I also covered Azure SQL Database in detail in the book *Azure SQL Revealed*.

I believe Azure SQL Database today has achieved all of its initial goals, but there is room to go farther. Azure SQL Database represents the most *managed service* of the Azure SQL family. It is the highest level of PaaS for Azure SQL. It has all the managed capabilities of Azure SQL Managed Instance like versionless, automatic backups, built-in HA, and more. It takes the managed concept further because you don't have to care about the SQL Server instance.

Note   We do confuse people because Azure SQL Database has a concept of a *logical server*, which is really a set of metadata supporting multiple databases and connection/security information about databases. But it is not a physical SQL Server instance.

Unlike Azure SQL Managed Instance, there are two interesting choices when deploying an Azure SQL Database called **Serverless** and **Hyperscale**.

When you deploy an Azure SQL Database, you typically choose the number of vCores for your database like a Managed Instance. Serverless allows you to choose a *range* of vCores so we can auto-scale your workload up or down. This also lights up the ability to pay for Serverless for only the vCores you use. In addition, Serverless has a pause/resume feature. So if you are not using the database, we will pause the compute, and you don't pay for any vCore usage during that time. When you connect again, we "resume" your database, and normal billing continues. For any new developer using Azure SQL Database, this could be a very compelling option.

Hyperscale is built for exactly its name – a way for you to get unlimited database resources, compute, memory, and storage. In fact, Hyperscale today can support a 100TB database in Azure. It is the largest database option we have in the cloud. Hyperscale also offers *automatic* storage. You don't choose a maximum storage option. You just create a database, and we keep scaling your growth as much as you need. You do choose vCores for Hyperscale, which dictates your memory limits. But Hyperscale uses a distributed, tiered architecture with paging systems (which is one of the reasons we can give you speed at 100TB), so those limits do not matter as much when it comes to performance. In addition, one of the ways your application can scale with Hyperscale is replicas including up to 30 read-scale named replicas. This architecture doesn't use Always On Availability Groups but uses log-based change methodology to achieve the same concept at scale with built-in high availability.

Think of these database options. What about a world where we combine Serverless and Hyperscale together! (Stay tuned; it may happen sooner than you think.)

While Azure SQL Database provides you core engine capabilities, it does limit you because you don't have access to instance-level features. So SQL Server Agent jobs, replication (although an Azure SQL Database can be a subscriber), resource governor, and DTC to name a few are not supported with Azure SQL Database. These features are reserved for scenarios where you need a complete SQL Server instance.

The good news is that Azure SQL Database includes most of the innovations you have read in this book for SQL Server 2022 including Synapse Link, Microsoft Purview policies, Azure Active Directory (AAD), Microsoft Defender, built-in query intelligence, Ledger, and more.

Recently we have been investing in developers for Azure SQL Database including a local developer experience (using containers), Azure SQL function bindings, new and improved JSON support, and REST API integration built into the engine. You can learn more about these exciting new features for developers at `https://docs.microsoft.com/events/build-2022/brk20-modernize-your-applications-with-new-innovations-across-sql-server-2022-azure-sql`.

Get started today with Azure SQL Database at `https://aka.ms/azuresqldb`.

When to Use Azure SQL Database

Given that Azure SQL Database is focused on the concept of "just a database," I believe this option is best for developers building new applications, especially applications that are designed to run in Azure. In fact, the focus of the team behind Azure SQL Database is to make it the best developer experience we can for applications that need data.

Don't be fooled by the term "developers." While we want the developer experience to be great, Azure SQL Database has a proven history of supporting enterprise-grade workloads. I remember delivering a keynote address at an event called Visual Studio Live! in the summer of 2022. As part of the keynote, I delivered some stunning numbers on Azure SQL Database:

- On average we support around 160,000+ active customers a month.

- Azure SQL Database applications execute around 35 *trillion* queries a month.

- Azure SQL Database hosts around 8 million active databases a month.

- We manage around 40 petabytes of data across all of Azure SQL Database customers.

- We actively have a customer with a 97TB production database application using Hyperscale.

Even though Azure SQL Database is targeted for these types of modern applications, we have seen customers migrate SQL Server databases to Azure SQL Database namely because they didn't need instance-level features and loved the concepts of options like Hyperscale.

Azure Arc–Enabled SQL Managed Instance

I know many in the community were disappointed to see us retire the SQL Server Big Data Clusters (BDC) option of SQL Server 2019 in early 2022. BDC was all built on container images running on Kubernetes. One benefit of this work was that we learned how to run SQL Server containers in Kubernetes as a managed SQL service. We found we could bring the power of Azure SQL Managed Instance to the infrastructure of your choice using Kubernetes. That is the simplest way to define Azure Arc–enabled SQL Managed Instance (Arc SQL MI). In fact I remember Dinakar Nethi, Principal Program Manager for Azure Arc, once saying to me, *"Azure Arc–enabled Managed Instance is the mirror of Azure SQL Managed Instance outside of Azure."*

Like Azure SQL Managed Instance, Arc SQL MI is versionless and includes built-in HA with replicas, automatic backups, and failover groups. Arc SQL MI even has service tiers like Azure SQL Managed Instance and supports a cloud billing model (including Azure Hybrid Benefit). One advantage Arc SQL MI has over Azure SQL Managed Instance is a free developer edition option for developing applications.

All this is achieved through a series of container images running in pods including the main SQL Server container image and a set of Kubernetes pods called the data controller. Figure 11-2 is an architecture diagram I often use to describe Arc SQL MI.

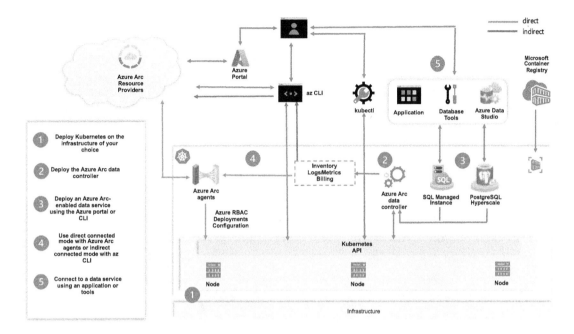

Figure 11-2. *Azure Arc–enabled SQL Managed Instance architecture*

You can learn more about the components of this architecture in a Microsoft Learn module Buck Woody and I developed at `https://aka.ms/learnazurearcdata`.

One of the keys to Arc SQL MI is Kubernetes. Kubernetes provides the software platform to help us achieved a managed service. We provide a list of supported Kubernetes distributions at `https://docs.microsoft.com/azure/azure-arc/data/plan-azure-arc-data-services#deployment-requirements`. We have also built a validation program with our partners so you can see hardware and Kubernetes solutions that are proven and trusted at `https://docs.microsoft.com/azure/azure-arc/data/validation-program`.

Notice in Figure 11-2 the connectivity to Azure. The entire Azure Arc story is built on bringing the power of Azure to your infrastructure or cloud but connecting services to Azure (hence the term Arc or *arcing* together two worlds, Azure and yours). Azure Arc–enabled SQL Managed Instance is considered a full hybrid solution because you can run your managed SQL instance in your data center and yet be connected to Azure for added value (inventory, metrics, logs, cloud billing, and more).

Because Arc SQL MI is based on SQL Server Linux containers, it has the same feature set as SQL Server on Linux and containers. The big difference is that Arc SQL MI doesn't follow a major version. In fact it is our goal to align the feature set and enhancements with Azure SQL Managed Instance.

Get started with Azure Arc-enabled SQL Managed Instance at `https://aka.ms/azurearcsqlmi`.

When to Use Azure Arc–Enabled SQL Managed Instance

If you want the features of Azure SQL Managed Instance but you cannot move to the Azure cloud, then Azure Arc-enabled SQL Managed Instance could be the solution for you. Anywhere you can run a supported Kubernetes distribution, your infrastructure or multi-cloud, we can support your Azure Arc-enabled SQL Managed Instance. Furthermore, you get the added value of connecting your deployment to Azure, either indirect or direct.

In my experience the learning curve is usually Kubernetes. I have found some companies have experience with Kubernetes so are very comfortable with this platform. Others come from a complete Windows Server world so have to figure out if they can make this shift. I've found Azure Stack HCI to be a compelling solution because it includes a Kubernetes distribution Microsoft supports (Azure Kubernetes Service) but also allows you to run virtual machines with SQL Server on Windows or Linux. Learn more at `https://aka.ms/azurestackhci`.

One nice story of Arc SQL MI is database compatibility since this solution is built on the SQL Server on Linux engine. Just back up a database from SQL Server on Windows and restore it to Azure Arc-enabled SQL Managed Instance.

SQL Is Everywhere You Need It

The SQL edge to cloud story is deep, wide, and powerful. SQL is everywhere you need it: familiar, compatible, and flexible. SQL supports the newest startups that aspire to be Fortune 500 companies. We grow and scale with your business using the same application languages, engine, and tools.

Each time I talk to a customer about SQL edge to cloud, they are trying to see how they can choose multiple options. That is because not every workload or business fits into just one slot. The great story about SQL is that you can use your existing skills and knowledge with SQL Server across all options. And you can see that in almost every option SQL connects to each other, bringing hybrid capabilities.

The SQL edge to cloud story is bringing worlds together in new and innovative ways allowing you to maximize and protect your investments. SQL allows you to grow your business and your skills scaling with your future. SQL is no longer just an RDBMS engine. SQL is a truly hybrid data platform, the world's database, edge to cloud.

Index

A

Accelerated Database Recovery (ADR), 247, 304–305, 315

Adutil, 396

Always Encrypted, 15, 265–266

Always On Availability Groups (AGs), 113, 154, 289, 302, 303, 398, 411–412, 447, 459, 465

Ansible, 394

Append-Only Ledger, 250, 251, 260, 261, 265

App login, 261, 262

Auto-drop Statistics, 313

Automatic digest storage, 264

Automatic Plan Correction (APRC), 241

Automatic storage, 468

Automation, 27, 115, 394, 431

Availability Group 1 (AG1), 51

Availability Group 2 (AG2), 51

Availability Groups (AGs), 19, 53, 298, 303, 393

Azure Active Directory (AAD), 17, 36, 113, 118, 124, 126, 246, 419, 469

Azure Active Directory (AAD) account, 48, 116, 118, 121–123, 126, 140–143

Azure Active Directory (AAD) authentication, 49, 128

accounts, 121, 122, 132

applications and services, 113

Azure Key Vault, 118

Azure service, 117

communicates, 114

configure, 115

PaaS services, 114

protocols, 114

SQL Server, 113, 115, 118, 142

sqlusers, 124

subscription, 115, 116

syntax, 114

T-SQL statements, 121

Azure Arc Agent, 38, 48, 49, 396, 418

Azure Arc–enabled SQL Managed Instance, 290, 406, 411, 412, 470–472

Azure Arc–enabled SQL Server, 27, 32, 40, 125, 127, 131, 460

Azure Backup service, 450

Azure Blob Storage (abs), 319, 321

Azure Data Studio (ADS), 276, 310, 325, 346, 395, 403, 456

Azure-enabled capabilities, 47

Azure extension, 27, 32–33, 36, 40, 41, 49, 114–116, 130, 131, 396, 418

Azure Hybrid Benefit (AHUB), 417, 419, 429, 453, 464, 466, 470

Azure Kubernetes Service (AKS), 41, 408, 409, 463, 472

Azure Monitor, 451

Azure PaaS service, 51

Azure Resource Group, 34, 36, 37

Azure Role-Based Access Control (RBAC), 34

Azure SQL Conference, 6, 8, 13

language, 19
statements, 152, 188, 195, 196
TrustServerCertificate, 268
T-SQL Surface Area
DATETRUNC, 360
GREATEST, 363
IS [NOT] DISTINCT FROM, 366–368
LEAST, 363–365
prerequisites, 359
STRING_SPLIT, 369, 370
TRIM, 370, 371
WINDOW, 361, 362

U

Umachandar Jayachandran (UC), 352
Updateable Ledger Table, 248, 249, 253, 264, 265
Use Azure Login, 36

V

Vector-based hardware capabilities, 273
Vector hardware technology, 274
Virtual Device Interface (VDI), 306, 307, 391
Virtual machine (VM), 413
Azure portal, 432, 433, 435
blades, 423
connecting, 436–438

create resource, 422
deployment, 414–417, 421, 424–427
I/O cap warning, 429, 430
migrating, 440, 441
portal, 438, 439
practices assessment, 443–445
prerequisites, 421
size, 441, 442
SSMS, 439, 440
storage performance, 442, 443
Visual Studio Live, 469
Volatility problem, 172
Volume Snapshot Service (VSS), 307, 391, 399

W

WideWorldImporters database, 59, 83, 104, 196, 340
Windows Server Failover Cluster (WSFC), 50, 398, 446, 447
Workload_index_seek.cmd, 199, 201–203

X, Y

XML data types, 312

Z

Zone-redundant storage (ZRS), 449

CPSIA information can be obtained
at www.ICGtesting.com
Printed in the USA
LVHW010051021122
732092LV00001B/1